Readers
as
writers

AwK = awkward
sentence
structure

WW = wrong word

word choice - Diction

Readers as writers

A basic rhetoric

Kate Kiefer

Holt, Rinehart and Winston

NEW YORK CHICAGO SAN FRANCISCO PHILADELPHIA
MONTREAL TORONTO LONDON SYDNEY
TOKYO MEXICO CITY RIO DE JANEIRO MADRID

Publisher:	Susan Katz
Acquisitions Editor:	Charlyce Jones Owen
Developmental Editor:	Heidi Anderson
Senior Production Manager:	Pat Sarcuni
Art Director:	Bob Kopelman
Senior Project Editor:	Gordon Powell
Designer:	William Gray

Library of Congress Cataloging-in-Publication Data
Kiefer, Kate.
    Readers as writers.

    Bibliography: p.
    1. English language—Rhetoric. 2. College readers.
I. Title.
PE1408.K56 1986   808′.0427   85-24779

ISBN 0-03-070409-X

Copyright © 1986 by CBS College Publishing
Address correspondence to:
383 Madison Avenue
New York, N.Y. 10017
All rights reserved
Printed in the United States of America
Published simultaneously in Canada

6 7 8 9 038 9 8 7 6 5 4 3 2 1

CBS COLLEGE PUBLISHING
Holt, Rinehart and Winston
The Dryden Press
Saunders College Publishing

Copyright Acknowledgments

   The author wishes to thank the following for permission to reprint copyrighted material:

Aleksander Afanas'ev (collected by) and Norbert Guterman (translated by) "The Duck with the Golden Eggs." From *Russian Fairy Tales* collected by Aleksander Afanas'ev, translated by Norbert Guterman. Copyright © 1945 by Pantheon Books, Inc. and renewed © 1973 by Random House, Inc. Reprinted by permission of Pantheon Books, a division of Random House, Inc.

Edgar Berman, "Who'd Trade 'Primp Time' for Overtime?" from *USA TODAY,* May 23, 1984. Copyright © 1984 *USA TODAY.* Reprinted with permission.

(continued on p. 417)

For Tim and Xirc, Bill and Dave:
they'll never know how much they helped.

foreword

Why reading?
Why writing?

After all these years of school, you find yourself picking up an assigned textbook that concentrates on reading and writing. You are probably thinking that your teacher considerably underestimates your skills; after all, you have been reading and writing for years. This text does not dispute that you can read and write. In fact, this book assumes only that you have not practiced the skills as much as you might have in order to sharpen them adequately for college work.

First, why do I assume that reading and writing are skills? Just as almost anyone can learn to ride a bicycle or hit a baseball, so anyone can learn to read and write. Bicycling and baseball include specific physical skills—balance, coordination, strength. Writing and reading incorporate varied skills, too, although more of the skills are mental than physical. The physical skills include eye, hand, and brain coordination. We can't write unless we can move a pen or pencil across a page or find the right letters on a typewriter keyboard. We cannot read unless we orient the page so that we can distinguish letters, words, and lines. So we cannot read and write without certain physical or motor skills, and we cannot read and write without certain mental skills. At a very basic level, we must be able to distinguish "b" from "d," "pain" from "pane." We must be able to understand complex grammatical structures so that the relationships of words in sentences create "meaning." We must be able to understand complex relationships among sentences to create "meaning" from paragraphs and essays. If we do not have these skills, we cannot read. In addition to the reading skills writers must master, if we cannot focus our ideas carefully and develop them fully for readers, then we cannot write.

Because reading and writing are skills, then, that anyone can learn, most children who attend school learn to read and write. After all, reading and writing rank highly among the basic skills teachers concentrate on in elementary school, and children spend hours each day perfecting their basic reading and writing skills. But like any physical skill, reading and writing can get rusty if not practiced. Think of some sport you played only as a youngster. Could you, after years, perform that activity as well as you did ten years ago? I can certainly jump rope, but I doubt that I could still run in and out of the turning rope or double rope. Now think of a sport or activity that you learned as an adolescent. If you have not practiced that activity for a few years, you will probably be pretty bad at it for quite some time when you take up the sport again. Skills, even physical skills, do not improve over time unless we practice them. Moreover, skills we acquire as children are usually easier to pick up again because they are less complicated skills. Looking again at reading and writing skills, we see that the basics we learned in elementary school require less complicated coordination of eye and brain—because ideas are simpler—than college reading and writing demand. So, although almost all children learn basic reading and writing skills early in their school years, they need to keep learning new ways to apply those skills, and they need to keep practicing the basic and more complex skills to keep them sharp.

Just what are these more complex reading and writing skills that students should acquire as they go through junior high and high school? For one, readers should learn to adapt their reading pace for the materials read and for the purpose for reading. Reading best-selling romances or sci-fi thrillers is a great form of relaxation, but typically that reading requires less attention than the dense information packed into a technical article or textbook chapter requires. So, one complex skill to practice is varying reading pace. In writing, we know that children typically express their views of the world with themselves at the center, in much the same way as the ancients thought of earth as the center of the universe. This kind of writing tends to fall into specific categories, most often story form. As writers mature, they need to discover ways to take readers into account, to organize ideas so that readers can remember them. Usually, as writers do this, they learn to write explanations or arguments, and they use different perspectives in their writing. But without instruction and practice, these more complex skills do not evolve naturally after students learn basic skills. Moreover, only with practice can readers and writers adapt skills to the variety of reading and writing situations they will find themselves in. Finally, only with practice can readers and writers begin to understand their individual approaches to reading and writing, for each of us assimilates slightly different processes and each of us adapts to specific situations in slightly different ways.

Thus, teachers continually encourage students to learn more complex reading and writing skills. Some of that encouragement comes in the form of varied reading and writing assignments—in all courses, not just English classes. Other encouragement comes in the form of direct instruction—as in this course.

Remember that our reading and writing mature as we do. I am a better writer now than I was ten years ago, and I will be better still in ten more years. One reason we all improve as readers and writers is the experience we gain just by living, considering new ideas, arguing with people, traveling, and so on. As we experience ideas, places, and people, we store those impressions and ideas in our memories, we learn from our experience, and we are able to relate new impressions and experiences to our stored impressions. Practicing reading gives us ways to incorporate new ideas—to learn. Practicing writing often helps us crystallize associations, work out solutions—in short, learn. Reading and writing are perhaps the most important ways we learn as adults, so these processes merit attention.

In fact, because we learn so much by reading and writing, we must also consider them as more than skills. We stimulate our thinking through reading and writing, enhance our memories through reading and writing, clarify or confirm our understanding through reading and writing. In short, reading and writing are intellectual activities that help us mature in our understanding of the world.

Let me finish explaining the last part of my assumption about students using this text. I claim that most readers of this text will probably not have practiced reading and writing skills adequately for college work. I know that most students do not think of writing as fun, particularly the analytic writing that college courses require. Frankly, it has been my experience that most students coming to college would avoid writing if they could. If we can compare writing to playing video games, you can see that if you do not practice the skills you cannot win the game. Unfortunately, without having practiced writing skills in high school, many students coming to college need to work doubly hard to prepare themselves to succeed on college writing assignments. Reading generally inspires less opposition. Most people do not dislike reading, but it does require more attention than watching television does. Because television has made storytelling—and listening—so easy, many readers have become passive viewers. Furthermore, unless readers cover more than just the daily newspaper or a weekly newsmagazine or a favorite special-interest magazine, they probably are not reading varied enough material to prepare them for college reading. In college, students must read hundreds of pages of textbooks, journals, and reports weekly. If students have not practiced the full range of reading skills, they can find themselves falling behind when they take college courses that flood them with new concepts and facts. The demands of college reading and writing can surprise students whose skills are rusty, and this text hopes to polish those skills early in your college career.

Survival is a worthy motive for practicing reading and writing skills, but it is only one of many. As I mentioned before, reading and writing constitute most adults' typical way of learning new ideas and information. Reading and writing can help you discover new things about yourself and your outlook on the world. Reading and writing can help you clarify major decisions you must make. The list goes on and on. Reading and writing are among the most valuable skills you will take away from college because with these skills you can learn almost anything else.

In the first chapter, we will explore in detail the reading and writing processes and consider in depth why researchers' and teachers' new understanding of thinking, language, reading, and writing should encourage you to practice reading and writing.

acknowledgments

I would like to thank all those who have contributed to the making of this text: my family for their support, my editors for their patience and careful readings, my colleagues—

Roger Bresnahan, Michigan State University
Aleeta Christian, Roane State Community College
Ana Jusino, Norwalk Community College
James Kenkel, Bowling Green State University
Sue Lorch, University of South Carolina at Aiken
Nancy Martinez, University of Albuquerque
Carolyn O'Hearn, The University of Texas at El Paso
Daryl Troyer, El Paso Community College
Carlene Walker, The University of Texas at El Paso
William Woods, Wichita State University

—for their critical comments, and most of all, my students for their questions and enthusiasm.

contents

UNIT ONE

chapter 1

chapter 4

chapter 5

UNIT TWO

chapter 6

UNIT THREE

Analyzing   217

chapter 9
Analyzing processes   218

chapter 10
Comparing and contrasting   238

chapter 11
Classifying   255

chapter 12
Defining   274

UNIT FIVE

chapter 15

chapter 19

Readers
as
writers

UNIT ONE

The writing/reading processes

In the first five chapters, we will explore the writing and reading processes in detail so that you can begin to draw upon both sets of skills you have been practicing throughout your school years. Chapter 1 begins with an overview of both the writing and reading processes, and then Chapters 2 through 5 concentrate on basic writing concepts with emphasis on writers as readers. Chapter 2 focuses on early stages of writing—getting ideas and focusing them. Chapter 3 takes up paragraphs, the building blocks of essays. Chapter 4 explains when to choose a single-paragraph essay and when to write a longer paper; it then covers the basics of essay writing. Finally, Chapter 5 returns to the writing process to give you tips on revising your own work, a part of the writing process many students simply don't practice much.

After practicing the reading and writing processes outlined in these chapters, you can handle any of the later chapters, although your instructor will probably direct you to those chapters he or she feels are most useful for you in this course. Don't hesitate to come back to these chapters and review, though, because the concepts in this first unit govern all good writing.

chapter 1

The reading/writing connection

READING AS PROCESS

As researchers and teachers learn more about reading and writing—and the way the human brain handles information—we are less satisfied with older definitions of reading and writing. For example, we used to think of reading and listening as receptive or passive language skills and speaking and writing as active or productive skills.

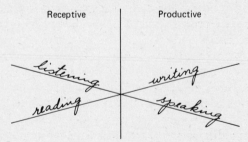

This understanding of readers makes them simple decoders rather than creators of meaning. Teachers of reading now stress that it is active.

Readers create meaning as much as writers do, and to ignore the reader to concentrate only on the writer is to miss half the equation.

Obviously a good writer must also be a good reader. Writers rescan their papers, looking for the main ideas and details, reshaping arguments, adding clarifying details and explanations, reworking unclear sentences, or replacing inappropriate words. Looking back over what's written is essential to remind us just where we were headed two sentences or four paragraphs before.

But how is a reader able to use reading skills to become a better writer? As we'll see, readers predict what they are going to see. And if writers, using those predictive skills, help their readers predict, writing becomes more effective and easier to understand.

Readers Predict Meaning

Let's try a little test to show you how you predict and create meaning when you read:

> The glistening body stood outlined by bright light. Its sleek curves height-ened the sense of power. As Frank observed it critically, he noticed that the last polishing coat was perfect. Not a flaw was visible, he thought, as he circled, slowly checking every detail. Oh what a shame, he thought, to sub-ject this beautiful body to such punishment, but what a waste to keep it hidden from the world.

Can you guess what Frank does for a living? Some readers think Frank is an auto mechanic refinishing a fine sports car or a racing car. Still oth-ers think he's a body builder preparing for competition. Why are such different interpretations possible? As readers, you begin predicting the content of the passage from early clues. If you read "body," "sleek," and "power" and thought of a car, then you kept accumulating clues that fit with your prediction that the paragraph was about an auto mechanic. You probably thought of "punishment" as salt from icy roads or dents in parking lots. If you read "body," "sleek," and "power" and thought of body builders, then you collected clues to strengthen that interpretation. You interpreted "punishment" as the grueling workout sessions to pump up muscles and saw "finishing coat" as the oil body builders apply for competition. When researchers have given hundreds of people passages like this one and asked them to tell what the paragraph is about, most cannot see a second interpretation. Some cannot even admit the second (or third) possibility when it's outlined in detail.

Reading, then, is *not* simply identifying letters that make up words and then stringing together words to make sense of sentences. It's a complex process involving several levels of information processing and hypothesis testing.

Practice—Reading

In the following paragraphs, identify the main ideas that the paragraphs are about. Does the placement of that main idea help you predict what the paragraphs will cover?

During the early negotiations between the Soviet Union and the United States on the control of strategic weapons, the American negotiators made a curious discovery. When they initiated a discussion of the Soviet Union's missiles and weapons, the Americans found that they knew more about them than some of the Russians. The civilians in the Soviet delegation, including a Deputy Foreign Minister, did not know the details of their own country's strategic weaponry. The military men, however, were well informed. One day the senior military officer on the Soviet delegation, Colonel General Nikolai V. Ogarkov, took an American delegate aside and reproached him: there was no reason, the General said, for the Americans to reveal their knowledge of Soviet military matters to the civilian members of his delegation. That sort of information, the General said, was strictly the military's business.
—Robert G. Kaiser, *Russia—The People and the Power*

A pointed Americanism is seeping into the cultural stream too. Right after the Los Angeles Games, ABC broadcast the premier episode of "Call to Glory," a new series, set in the early 1960s, about Air Force fighter pilots. Says a network insider: "The campaign to promote this program was all based on connecting the patriotism the network felt would be generated during the Olympics with that of the new series." The show was the highest rated program the week it aired. *Red Dawn,* a crude fantasy about armed resistance to a Soviet takeover of the U.S., is an enormous box office success. MGM began filming it three months after the downing of the Korean Air Lines Flight 007.
—Kurt Andersen, *Time,* September 24, 1984

Practice—Analyzing

1. Exactly how does an early sentence stating the main idea help you

   predict the point of the paragraph? _____

   _____

2. Is the main point followed by equally general statements or proof of

   the first idea? _____

   _____

3. Outline each of the paragraphs as you would organize material while you are reading.

for Kaiser

I. _____

_____

_____

_____

for Andersen

I. _____

_____

_____

_____

Practice—Reading

Now read paragraphs that may not be as easy to predict because the main idea is not stated early on.

The focus of the living room is the huge brick fireplace that takes up one entire wall. I love to watch the flames dance—casting shadows on the dark, lustrous wood of the mantle—and hear the wood crackle and pop each time we have a fire in there. The thick, wooden mantle holds our stockings stuffed with goodies every Christmas morning. The big, fluffy floor pillows in the corner are where our beagle used to sleep. In another corner sits an antique, wicker rocking chair that creaks. I loved to rock back and forth when I was little, and I remember my feet barely hanging over the edge of the seat. Big plaster crocks and old, green glass bottles dot the shelves and the tables, and they all hold beautiful plants—African violets, philodendra, jades. The big, overstuffed chair with the flowered print material is where my grandfather would always sit. I can still smell his pipe smoke floating through the air. The big wooden trunk against one wall is where my mother would hide our Christmas and birthday presents. The tall, twelve-pane windows rattle every time it thunders very loud in a storm but also bathe the room in early-morning sunlight. The tiny-printed wallpaper and antique furniture match the rest of the colonial decor of the house. In that room, we have shared with friends as well as relatives many holidays and regular days, countless memories that will never fade away.

—Jenna H.

The summer before last, a friend maneuvered his Chevy truck alongside our backyard gate. He unloaded four five-foot boards and several little triangular shaped pieces of wood. With his hammer and a pocketful of tenpenny nails, he built a box that hugged the grass it was placed on. In order to keep the east and west sides of the north fence balanced to the scan of the eye, he measured the distances and situated the box on the appropriate location. By attaching one of the triangular boards to each of the corners, compact seats were created that could accommodate up to four little fannies. Then using a cement-spattered wheelbarrow and shovel, he ferried a half-dozen loads of fine clean sand from his truck to the box.

—*Leslie C.*

Wide, cream-colored noodles that look like the ruffle down the front of a man's tuxedo. Thick, rich, red tomato sauce packed with fat chunks of sausage and ground beef. Melted mozzarella cheese, oozing like melted wax over the different layers of the concoction, colored with green flecks of basil, oregano, and thyme. The pungent odor of garlic, mixed with the stinging smell of onions and other seasonings. The mixture of sensations as you chew: soft, slippery pasta; tangy, spicy Italian sausage filling your mouth with flavorful juices as you bite down; stringy, smooth, rubbery mozzarella; thick, squishy ricotta. Is it normal to bear such a fond affection for a plate of lasagna?

—*Laurie K.*

Practice—Analyzing

1. Can you *predict* what these paragraphs are about? Why? _____

_____

2. Even if you cannot predict, do the paragraphs confuse you? Why?

_____

_____

_____

Practice—Reading

Now try one more paragraph that could have more than one interpretation:

In the last days of August, we were all suffering from the unbearable heat. In a few short weeks, our daily job had turned from a game into hard labor. "All we need now," said the manager in one of his discouraged moods, "is a strike." I listened to him silently but I could not help him. I hit a fly. "I suppose things could get even worse," he continued. "Our most valuable pitchers may crack in this heat. If only we had more fans, we would all feel better I'm sure. I wish our best man could come home. That certainly would improve everyone's morale, especially mine. Oh, well, I know a walk would cheer me up a little."

Practice—Analyzing

1. What two interpretations do you see for this paragraph? _____

_____

2. Which words contribute to each interpretation? _____

_____

3. Once you had created the first meaning, how long did you take to

   find the second interpretation? _____

Practice—Writing

Construct a paragraph of your own that classmates could interpret at least two different ways. (A clue—notice that both preceding samples used words that have two distinct meanings in different contexts; you might start by brainstorming for words that you use differently under different circumstances.)

_____

_____

_____

_____

_____

_____

Readers Use Patterns

Let's examine our definition of reading in more detail.

First, reading isn't linear. Young children spend a good deal of energy decoding letters and words, but more experienced readers pay less attention to letters and words unless they are completely unfamiliar, as with typographical errors and new words. Rather, experienced readers, because they know patterns in the language, expect to see those patterns even at the lowest level—letter clusters. We know, for instance, that in English very few words begin with *ts*. Lots of words (like lots) can end with *ts,* but only a few words like *tsar* and *tse-tse* begin with *ts*. What happens when readers see *ts* at the beginning of a word? Because of their experience as readers, they expect a word borrowed from another language or a mistake. If they see a word like *tsigarrete,* they suspect the writer is playing games, and they begin to relax the usual "rules" (or expectations of conventional usage) they apply in reading. Or readers may simply decide the writer is incompetent, particularly if the misuse of a pattern doesn't create a new, meaningful pattern.

So as we read, we recognize clusters of letters and words that create meaningful units. Once we recognize the clusters, we sometimes don't bother to "read" the entire word or phrase because we expect it to fit the pattern.

Other expected patterns include syntactic patterns, like phrases and sentences. Churchill got laughs from listeners when he complained about newspaper writers who changed his speeches. He especially disliked writers who changed prepositions from the ends of sentences, and he said, "it's changes like these up with which I will not put." Listeners and readers expect the pattern "put up with," even at the end of a sentence. Changing the pattern strikes an audience as silly.

At the sentence level, we expect sentences to have subjects and verbs that express complete ideas. Because of this expectation, incomplete or badly formed sentences attract extra attention, usually unwanted attention. Only if the writer wants to attract attention should sentences not conform to readers' expectations. Readers who must pause to puzzle out unclear sentences can lose track of the main point of the passage, after all.

Readers Form Hypotheses

Meanwhile, even though the brain is processing data about letters, words, and sentences, it is also creating a hypothesis about the content and direction of the prose. The brain tries to predict what's coming next. As more data come in that confirm the hypothesis, the reader becomes surer of the guess. When conflicting data come in, the reader reevaluates the hypothesis, sometimes changing it a little and sometimes starting anew.

What allows the brain to predict? Patterns in language alone cannot account for good predictions. Instead, you might think of the brain tapping into networks of related images, memories, facts, experiences, and so on. In essence, your life experience helps make you a better reader because you evaluate your reading in terms of what you already know.

Think about the last time you read an article or textbook on a subject you knew nothing about. You probably found the reading harder, more tiring, and more time consuming. Why? You probably couldn't depend on expected patterns of words because some of the words were unfamiliar. You had to figure out what the words themselves meant in some cases. Moreover, if you had no experience relating to the topic, you weren't able to tap into the network of ideas already in your head. You may have struggled to see how this new topic was somewhat like something you were familiar with. We all try to find similarities of this sort. If the writer had helped you by giving you a visual image or analogy to another more common experience, then you might have found the reading easier to get through.

Reading Strategies

We call our approaches to reading top-down and bottom-up processing. When we work from the bottom up, we look carefully at letters forming a word to see if we understand the word, its root, or perhaps prefixes or suffixes. Then we look at nearby text to see if we can discover the meaning of the word from its context. Bottom-up processing means working from smaller to larger language features. Top-down processing, on the other hand, means that we ignore those words we don't know in favor of formulating an hypothesis or tapping into the network of experiences. We all use both strategies for different kinds of reading, although some readers favor one strategy over the other. If you were a reader struggling through an article on a new topic, you might pause over each new word until you understood it, and then perhaps start paragraphs and sections over when you forgot what the point of the paragraph was. Or you might just plunge through the article hoping to fill in the conceptual base the first time through and plan to reread for detail and new terminology later.

To summarize, then, reading is an active process of creating meaning by taking in information at all levels of language (letter, word, syntax, discourse) and checking hypotheses about what the writer might mean.

Practice—Reading

Read the following paragraphs on unfamiliar topics. Try both top-down and bottom-up approaches; that is, read one passage for the general concepts the writer is conveying and read the next to understand each sentence as you read along.

In the orderly lexicon of the sport of diving, it was a 307C that finally did it.

Greg Louganis picked a reverse three-and-a-half somersault-tuck from the more than 120 dives approved for platform diving, and on the last dive of the Olympics Sunday won the gold medal and became the first man ever to score more than 700 points in any competition.

Every sport has its crowning moment—Hank Aaron's 715th home run; Bob Beamon's 29-foot, 2.5-inch long jump; Eric Heiden's fifth speed skating gold medal. In diving, it is now Louganis' 710.91 points.

—Mike Madigan, *Rocky Mountain News,* August 13, 1984

Strategic Inc. surveyed 70 large companies that currently use both the IBM PC and at least one mainframe and 100 smaller companies that use the IBM PC and some other mini- or microcomputer.

Strategic's findings confirmed several theories on IBM strategies. According to Strategic, IBM has maintained control of its mainframe customers, dissuading most from adding non-IBM equipment. Further, the December 1983 study found that most mainframe customers are using their PCs in conjunction with their mainframes; ultimately, this habit will increase IBM's mainframe revenues.

Specifically, the study found that the large organizations interviewed had an average of 21 IBM PC's installed; the smaller companies had an average of six. According to the survey results, most of the larger companies consider the standard to be IBM products rather than micro-computers from Apple.

—*Byte,* Fall 1984

A superb masterpiece among the exhibited pictures was still to come, "Rain, Steam and Speed," hung in the Academy of 1844. It was as little conventional and as purely expressive as any of the works Turner did not choose to show publicly. At this late period he was indifferent to the bewilderment of indignation caused by what the *Spectator* termed a "laxity of form and license of effect . . . greater than people will allow." Like the "Snowstorm," the picture was the vivid translation of a personal experience. Leaning out of his railway carriage window Turner was once again absorbed by the action of elemental forces, the enjoyable excitement of driving rain, the rush of movement accompanied by showers of soot and sparks from the engine, the momentary glimpse of wooded slopes and misty distance. He conveys all this, through transferring himself to another viewpoint, the speed of the advancing locomotive being accelerated in effect by the widening perspective of the bridge it is to cross, as well as by the flying strokes of the brush.

—William Gaunt, *Turner*

Practice—Analyzing

1. Which approach seemed most comfortable for you for each passage?

   _____

2. Do you recall when you have used both approaches in reading text-

   books or other new material? _____

   _____

3. Find a sample passage for your classmates to read so that they can practice top-down and bottom-up processing on still more varied topics.

WRITING AS PROCESS

And now we come to the second main component of the reading/ writing connection—the writer. If the reader creates meaning, then why write clearly? Any writer has a point to make, a message to convey, and all writers want readers to get just that point. Because readers are creating meaning for themselves, writers must be especially careful to give them the right clues to set up and confirm one hypothesis for the passage. Being clear and unambiguous takes practice because writing, like reading, is a process that does *not* proceed in a linear sequence and involves different strategies from writer to writer and from one piece of writing to the next.

When most people hear that writing is a process, they think of a time sequence of activities. First, I do step A, then step B, and then C. Writing, however, is not sequential, and so we cannot label a series of steps to follow. Rather, from the moment writers get ideas to write about, they refine the ideas by picking and choosing from among topics. Even when they start writing notes to themselves, they may immediately cross out an idea that doesn't seem to fit or goes in a different direction. Or maybe they pursue the new direction and cross out earlier thoughts. In effect, even while *prewriting,* writers *revise.*

In the same way, as soon as most writers begin to draft a paper, they may be said to *write* the paper, but more often than not they stop to rescan what they've written. Sometimes they cross out words or draw arrows to remind themselves to rearrange sentences. In short, they *revise.* Even more often, they use the ideas they've already written to help them think of new ideas or of ways to strengthen their arguments. In short, as they write they *prewrite.*

These phases of writing—*prewriting, writing,* and *revising*—are the three major chunks of the writing process that most writing textbooks and teachers talk about. They are also the components most writers can recognize in their work because most writers spend some time thinking about what they want to write, writing, and then rewriting. But, in fact, all three phases go on throughout the writing process. In effect, the writing process doubles back on itself. Try making a symbol of this concept for yourself: take a narrow strip of paper at least eight inches long; label the front, left side of the paper A; label the back, right side B; tape A to B. Now run a pencil along the paper, and notice that you can draw a single line that covers the entire paper. You can start drawing a line anywhere on the paper, and if you keep the pencil on the paper, you will always get back to your starting point. The mobius strip reflects a simplified view of the writing process that is far more complex as it twists and turns back upon itself.

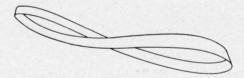

Although we talk about the writing "process," remember that each writer has unique habits and approaches to the various writing he or she must do. Moreover, most writers find that they use different approaches for different kinds of writing. So the writing process has limitless variations.

Practice—Writing

Think about *your* writing habits. What do you do when you have an important paper to write? Many people have well established delaying tactics—cleaning the room, finding exactly the right candle to burn, doing any other chore first. Sometimes these tactics mask "thinking" about the topic. Other writers just plunge right in and write everything that comes

to mind. Find the best way—a list, a string of sentences, a flow chart—
to describe your most common writing strategies by explaining what you
did the last time you wrote an important paper.

For example:

List
   read assignment
   put topic away for a week
   list possible ideas
and so son

String of sentences
   After I read the topic, I put it away for a week.
   Then I jot down possible ideas in several unrelated lists.
   I took another week off, and then. . . .

Flow chart
   read assignment
   put topic away
   list possible topics
   took a week off

READING AND WRITING

Now we know that reading is a complex process going on at several
levels with the reader predicting and confirming hypotheses. And we
know that writing is a recursive process with several mental and physical
activities going on at the same time. How can the two processes comple-
ment each other?

First, we tend to recognize language patterns before we use them. Think
of the infant learning to talk. The child understands commands long
before speaking them. In the same way, reading can help writers recognize patterns and then model them. Throughout this text, we will consider how writers use various strategies for organizing and presenting ideas
by reading papers using those strategies. Then as writers you will model
the pattern from the reading.

Much more importantly, we will consider strategies writers use to help
readers tap into their networks of experiences and thoughts, memories
and images. We will consider structures that guide readers and then practice incorporating those structures. And we'll look at readings as idea-
starters, as passages that can help you get ideas and write about your own
experience on the same topic.

Also, reading helps writers become aware of their audience. Just as we wouldn't tell a six-year-old about quantum mechanics, we must always remember whom we're talking or writing to. By considering the different audiences other writers focus on, we can discover how best to accommodate the knowledgeable reader or the novice, the reader who agrees with us or the one who would never agree unless lightning struck.

Finally, we'll practice reading as writers—looking for weaknesses in organization and development, flaws in wording, ineffective sentences. Throughout the text, student samples in process will show you what choices other writers have made as they have revised their writing.

Reading makes better writers and writing makes better readers. By writing about what we read, we commit ourselves to thinking through the ideas presented in a paper, we summarize (sometimes) the main points the author makes, and we clarify our own response to the paper. If we read as writers, we read more carefully and mentally organize main points and supporting ideas more logically. We take note of ideas that occur to us as potential writers. We let the reading material stir ideas that we think are important to write about or experiences that support or refute the author's point. Often by writing what we think a writer means in a paper, we discover gaps in logic or bad examples that we might have glossed over on a quick reading. So writing about readings makes better readers, too.

Practice—Reading

Let's try out these principles by reading and writing. Read a lengthy story about a student and his teacher. Although you might read the story for other purposes, think about why this teacher is so important to the student, the author. Why is this teacher so special to Samuel Scudder?

Take This Fish and Look at It
by Samuel H. Scudder

It was more than fifteen years ago that I entered the laboratory of Professor Agassiz and told him I had enrolled my name in the Scientific School as a student of natural history. He asked me a few questions about my object in coming, my antecedents generally, the mode in which I afterwards proposed to use the knowledge I might acquire, and, finally, whether I wished to study any special branch. To the latter I replied that, while I wished to be well grounded in all departments of zoology, I purposed to devote myself specially to insects.

"When do you wish to begin?" he asked.

"Now," I replied.

This seemed to please him, and with an energetic, "Very well!" he reached from a shelf a huge jar of specimens in yellow alcohol. "Take this fish," he said, "and look at it; we call it a haemulon; by and by I will ask you what you have seen."

With that he left me, but in a moment returned with explicit instructions as to the care of the object entrusted to me. "No man is fit to be a naturalist," said he, "who does not know how to take care of specimens."

I was to keep the fish before me in a tin tray and occasionally moisten the surface with alcohol from the jar, always taking care to replace the stopper tightly. Those were not the days of ground-glass stoppers and elegantly shaped exhibition jars; all the old students will recall the huge neckless glass bottles with their leaky, wax-besmeared corks, half eaten by insects, and begrimed with cellar dust. Entomology was a cleaner science than ichthyology, but the example of the Professor, who had unhesitatingly plunged to the bottom of the jar to produce the fish, was infectious; and though this alcohol had a "very ancient and fishlike smell," I really dared not show any aversion within these sacred precincts, and treated the alcohol as though it were pure water. Still I was conscious of a passing feeling of disappointment, for gazing at a fish did not commend itself to an ardent entomologist. My friends at home, too, were annoyed when they discovered that no amount of eau-de-Cologne would drown the perfume which haunted me like a shadow.

In ten minutes I had seen all that could be seen in that fish, and started in search of the Professor—who had, however, left the Museum; and when I returned, after lingering over some of the odd animals stored in the upper apartment, my specimen was dry all over. I dashed the fluid over the fish as if to resuscitate the beast from a fainting fit and looked with anxiety for a return of the normal sloppy appearance. This little excitement over, nothing was to be done but to return to a steadfast gaze at my mute companion. Half an hour passed—an hour—another hour; the fish began to look loathsome. I turned it over and around; looked it in the face—ghastly; from behind, beneath, above, sideways, at a three-quarters view—just as ghastly. I was in despair; at an early hour I concluded that lunch was necessary; so, with infinite relief, the fish was carefully replaced in the jar, and for an hour I was free.

On my return, I learned that Professor Agassiz had been at the Museum, but had gone, and would not return for several hours. My fellow-students were too busy to be disturbed by continued conversation. Slowly I drew forth that hideous fish, and with a feeling of desperation again looked at it. I might not use a magnifying-glass; instruments of all kinds were interdicted. My two hands, my two eyes, and the fish: it seemed a most limited field. I pushed my finger down its throat to feel how sharp the teeth were. I began to count the scales in the different rows, until I was convinced that that was nonsense. At last a happy thought struck me—I would draw the fish; and now with surprise I began to discover new features in the creature. Just then the Professor returned.

"That is right," said he; "a pencil is one of your best eyes. I am glad to notice, too, that you keep your specimen wet, and your bottle corked."

With these encouraging words, he added: "Well, what is it like?" He listened attentively to my brief rehearsal of the structure of parts whose names were still unknown to me: the fringed gill-arches and movable operculum; the pores of the head, fleshy lips and lidless eyes; the lateral line, the spinous fins and forked tail; the compressed and arched body. When I finished, he waited as if expecting more, and then, with an air of disappointment: "You have not looked very carefully; why," he continued more earnestly, "you haven't even seen one of the most conspicuous features of the animal, which is as plainly before your eyes as the fish itself; look again, look again!" and he left me to my misery.

I was piqued; I was mortified. Still more of that wretched fish! But now I set myself to the task with a will, and discovered one new thing after another, until I saw how just the Professor's criticism had been. The afternoon passed quickly; and when, towards its close, the Professor inquired: "Do you see it yet?" "No," I replied, "I am certain I do not, but I see how little I saw before."

"That is next best," said he, earnestly, "but I won't hear you now; put away your fish and go home; perhaps you will be ready with a better answer in the morning. I will examine you before you look at the fish."

This was disconcerting. Not only must I think of my fish all night, studying, without the object before me, what this unknown but most visible feature might be; but also, without reviewing my discoveries, I must give an exact account of them the next day. I had a bad memory; so I walked home by Charles River in a distracted state, with my two perplexities.

The cordial greeting from the Professor the next morning was reassuring; here was a man who seemed to be quite as anxious as I that I should see for myself what he saw.

"Do you perhaps mean," I asked, "that the fish has symmetrical sides with paired organs?"

His thoroughly pleased "Of course! of course!" repaid the wakeful hours of the previous night. After he had discoursed most happily and enthusiastically—as he always did—upon the importance of this point, I ventured to ask what I should do next. "Oh, look at your fish!" he said and left me again to my own devices. In a little more than an hour he returned and heard my new catalogue.

"That is good, that is good!" he repeated; "but that is not all; go on; and so for three long days he placed that fish before my eyes, forbidding me to look at anything else, or to use any artificial aid. "Look, look, look," was his repeated injunction. This was the best entomological lesson I ever had—a lesson whose influence has extended to the details of every subsequent study; a legacy the Professor had left to me, as he has left it to many others, of inestimable value, which we could not buy, with which we cannot part.

A year afterward, some of us were amusing ourselves with chalking outlandish beasts on the Museum blackboard. We drew prancing starfishes; frogs in mortal combat; hydra-headed worms; stately crawfishes, standing on their tails, bearing aloft umbrellas; and grotesque fishes with gaping mouths and staring eyes. The Professor came in shortly after and was as amused as any at our experiments. He looked at the fishes.

"Haemulons, every one of them," he said; "Mr. —— drew them."

True; and to this day, if I attempt a fish, I can draw nothing but haemulons.

The fourth day, a second fish of the same group was placed beside the first, and I was bidden to point out the resemblances and differences between the two; another and another followed, until the entire family lay before me, and a whole legion of jars covered the table and surrounding shelves; the odor had become a pleasant perfume; and even now, the sight of an old, six-inch worm-eaten cork brings fragrant memories.

The whole group of haemulons was thus brought in review; and, whether engaged upon the dissection of the internal organs, the preparation and examination of the bony framework, or the description of the various parts, Agassiz's training in the method of observing facts and their orderly arrangement was ever accompanied by the urgent exhortation not to be content with them.

"Facts are stupid things," he would say, "until brought into connection with some general law."

At the end of eight months, it was almost with reluctance that I left these friends and turned to insects; but what I had gained by this outside experience has been of greater value than years of later investigation in my favorite groups.

Practice—Analyzing

1. What did Scudder learn? _____

   _____

2. Does the writer feel positively or negatively about Professor Agassiz?

   _____

3. Where is his clearest statement of the teacher's value to him as a student? Jot down the main point Scudder makes about Agassiz. _____

   _____

   _____

4. Now look again at how you determined the effect of Agassiz on Scudder. Does Scudder *show* Agassiz in action? _____

5. What details does Scudder use?

   _____   _____

   _____   _____

   _____   _____

6. What other technique does Scudder use to show the effect of Agassiz?

   _____

7. List some details of the effects Agassiz has on Scudder.

_____   _____

_____   _____

_____   _____

Although as you continue to read about writing you might want to consider this passage for its structure (narrative) or detail, what does it make you think about teachers? Have you had a teacher who challenged you to learn from your experience? Have you had a teacher who has had such an impact on your learning? Who was your best teacher? Why?

Practice—Writing

Without stopping to think about how to arrange your ideas, just write for ten minutes about your most effective teacher. Don't worry about making sense of your writing now. Just write down everything that comes into your mind about an effective teacher. If you get stuck for ideas, repeat the last word you wrote down. Don't worry about spelling or punctuation, either. Just *write.*

Now put away your writing for a while, and when you come back to it, see if you can't find one reason more important than any other for the effectiveness of that teacher. If you find that reason in what you've written, pick up that idea and any details you may have jotted down. If you don't find a single reason, don't panic. Instead, spend a few more minutes sorting out the ideas. Can you think of a reason for your teacher's effectiveness? Can you show, as Scudder did, why the teacher taught you? Try to think of a specific story that shows how your teacher was effective. Plan what details you must include to convince readers that your teacher was effective. Go ahead and draft a paragraph about your most effective teacher.

SAMPLES

Here's a student's preliminary writing to get ideas flowing:

Back about four years ago, I had a biology teacher whose thoughts and ideas inspired me. This teacher made class so impressive that today my main interest lies in biology. She taught this class as everything was something new and exciting. Which made a lot of people take a special look into it. Therefore with her influence on learning and her enthusiasm in us enjoying it, made it a favorable class.

—*Leslie M.*

And here's that same student's draft once she had considered more at length just what she wanted to concentrate on:

Mr. Hardy, who was my 12th grade film studies teacher, was most effective because he taught me a lot about different film shots that emphasized meaning in different scenes of a film. Mr. Hardy really enjoyed showing how film directors and cameramen work together to develop different types of camera angles to make a film more powerful. An example of this is from the movie "The Graduate" starring Dustin Hoffman. One particular shot was a close-up of Dustin Hoffman staring into a fish tank. The camera focused on Dustin from the other side to make him look like he was inside that tank. Then the camera quickly swung around to an upward angle shot to show Dustin wading in his family's pool. Once again he looks like part of the water because of this shot. After a few quick flash shots from one scene to the other, it started to make the audience understand what he was feeling, that he was going crazy from being kept in view of his parents and his parents' friends and that his freedom was being violated. He was feeling like a fish always being watched and having no way to escape it all. Another example from the same movie is of a downward close-up shot of Dustin when he was being seduced by his mother's girlfriend. The downward shot made him look small and defenseless against this woman. The close up showed the fear and excitement that went through Dustin. Because he taught the different meaning of angle shots, Mr. Hardy's class was a most interesting and rewarding experience.

Practice—Analyzing

The most noticeable difference between the freewriting Leslie did and the draft she produced is that she changed teachers. In her prewriting, Leslie talks about a biology teacher, but in the draft she focuses on her film studies teacher. Why would she have changed directions? Look again at the freewriting sample. Do you see any concrete details or examples like those Scudder uses? Now look for examples in the paragraph about Mr. Hardy. If Leslie had written about her biology teacher, what would have been the main point of the paragraph? What is the main point of the paragraph on Mr. Hardy? Is "teaching angle shots" easier to write about than "inspiring? Why?

As you drafted your paragraph, did you find yourself stating the main reason for your teacher's effectiveness toward the beginning of your paragraph? Or did you wait, like Scudder, to build up some suspense? Did you give details to *show* your teacher in action? Does Leslie show her teacher? What does she do instead of showing the teacher? Is this technique as effective as your approach or the one Scudder uses?

As we go on, we'll talk about arranging your materials to communicate clearly with readers. But always remember, you are a reader and a writer, and you're writing for real readers who are interested in your experience, just as you were interested in Scudder's experience with Professor Agassiz. You have much to write about, and we'll practice repeatedly in the coming chapters.

Practice—Writing

1. Revise your paragraph about an effective teacher. Give examples and details or tell a story that will convince your classmates that this teacher is the most effective you've had.
2. Think of a time when a teacher gave you an assignment that seemed easy at first but became much more difficult as you worked on it. Think about details that will show readers the apparent ease and real difficulty. Jot down a list of details. Now tell the story so that readers in your class will understand how difficult the assignment really was.
3. Assume that you are writing not for students but for teachers, say through a teachers' magazine. Tell about the most memorable assignment you've ever been given. Your purpose will be to convince your readers to give similar assignments to their classes.
4. Imagine that the Parents-Teachers Association has asked you to prepare a short speech for your best teacher's retirement party. Tell a story that shows the teacher in action. Remember, the teacher, your parents, school officials, and friends will be in the audience.

chapter 2
Finding and focusing ideas

WHERE DO WRITING IDEAS COME FROM?

When most of us think about writing, we may groan because we know that getting an idea to write about is one of the hardest tasks associated with writing. Drafting and revising a paper often seem worse at the time, but getting ideas in the first place is usually what most writers dislike about writing. Obviously, if writers don't know what to write about, they cannot go on with any other work in preparing papers. Not having ideas can stop writers in their tracks. So where can writers look for inspiration? They can just look around. Using personal experience, even immediate perceptions, is a valid approach to writing. But this kind of evidence is not always sufficient to make a point. And our surroundings may not always suggest a topic for a paper. Talking to friends is another good source of information, but not necessarily inspiration. So where else can writing ideas come from?

The Idea File

One approach many writers use is to keep a log or list of ideas that occur to them. We've all had the experience of getting a great idea while we're in the shower or out playing center field. Many writers will try to keep those ideas in mind until they can get to a piece of paper to jot down those thoughts. Eventually they collect the pieces of paper or transfer the idea to a notebook. Then, when they need ideas for papers, they simply check through the notes they've made in the notebook. Sometimes they won't find a topic, but at least looking at good ideas for writing often helps them think of a topic appropriate for a particular paper.

Practice—Writing

1. Start an idea file like the one just described. First, list ten topics you would never want to write on. Why? Can you find some way to make these topics personal or humorous for your classmates? For instance, a student once told me he hated pipe smoke but after talking to a smoker discovered that pipes help relax smokers. He later wrote a paper about how pipe smokers "fuss" with their pipes—cleaning, filling, and rubbing the pipe bowl—as outlets for tension.
2. Now jot down ten ideas you think you would like to write about. Why would you like to write about them?

A Journal

In a more disciplined fashion, keeping a journal can serve as an idea file. By writing every day, writers often capture impressions or ideas that they can use later when they need to find inspiration for a paper. Unlike a diary, a journal doesn't limit itself to the personal accomplishments or failures of the day. Some journal entries may capture personal emotions, but more often the entries pose a problem or flesh out an insight, sometimes even an insight about writing and personal writing habits. Some writers have a list of common questions they consider every week or so. Some writers make themselves react to a newspaper editorial or article, to a book, or to a television program every week. A journal can be as structured or as unstructured as the writer wishes. Its main values are that it gives a writer time set aside just for writing every day and that it can remind the writer of a good idea or set the brain in motion making connections between an entry and other experiences with the potential to be good writing material.

Sample Journal Entries on Assignments in Progress

> When writing my objective and subjective paragraphs about my dog's picture I had a lot of feelings running through me. I don't think I've ever written an easier paper; it all came so naturally. I wanted to keep writing even though I had nothing to write about (that's why I'm writing this). I was so excited to write, which is really rare for me but kind of neat. I'll have to remember all these feelings for my future writings.
>
> happy
> excited
> only concentrating on the topic (no distractions)
> determined to finish the paper and make it good!!!
>
> —*Berit M.*

> I've begun work on my descriptive paragraph and I have already learned some very valuable information. I didn't realize how significant my sensory perceptions of objects could be in my writing. The ability to use descriptive words to create a picture of what I see is not only challenging, but exciting as well. Already, I've noticed a change in how I view things because I'm much more perceptive of details. I only hope now I am able to get my thoughts down on paper so that they flow. Creativity is the key. To me that is what I admire the most in writers. Their ability to write in a way that the reader can almost feel themselves in the same situations as the writer.
>
> —*Beth T.*

Freewriting

Still another approach is simply to start writing. Such an exercise, called *freewriting,* serves first to clear the head of cluttering ideas that clog useful thinking. Perhaps even more importantly, freewriting is one of the best ways to tap into the internal conversation of the brain. We often have ideas that we just can't quite capture, and freewriting lets some of those surface. For some writers, ideas can remain trapped forever if the writer doesn't simply start writing. Freewriting is painless, too. Simply set an alarm or put a clock nearby. Tell yourself just to write whatever comes to mind for 10, 15, or 20 minutes. Once you start writing, you can't stop until the set time is up. You needn't use complete sentences or spell words correctly or even keep your mind on a single idea. In fact, the main point is to cover all the ideas in your mind at the time. Let loose and write all the jumbled words as fast as you can.

Looping

After your time is up, you'll sometimes find you have hints of good ideas amid the rubbish. If so, you might want to follow up on one of the ideas. Take the main idea from the first freewriting sheet and write it at the top of a new sheet. Give yourself the same amount of time and write with this idea in mind. If you find yourself wandering away from the idea, don't worry. But try to center the writing around this point. After your time is up again, you can repeat the same step—picking up a main point and freewriting with that point in mind—as many times as seems helpful.

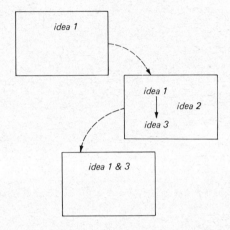

Just as often, you'll find that freewriting hasn't generated any great ideas you want to pursue. Nonetheless, you no longer have a blank page in front of you (a real boon to writers who just can't get started), the writing juices are flowing, and you may have cleared your mind of the worries that were keeping you from concentrating on your writing. Freewriting stimulates ideas, even when the first attempt seems to result in little workable material.

Reading for Topics

If you still haven't got an idea to write about, flip through your school newspaper, city paper, or a handy magazine. Consider the articles and items, paying attention not only to the topic of the piece but also to related issues and problems. Try to connect these issues and problems to your experience. Ask yourself, "Why should I care" about new teaching techniques, rioting in South Africa, or federal deficits? Now you've discovered one of the first ways to use reading to stimulate your ideas. By looking at what others write about, you might discover that you, too, have ideas to contribute on the same topic. When you come across an article or editorial that interests you or that you can imagine writing about, read the article with the "Why should I care" question in mind. Keep trying to bring the substance of the article back to your own experience or concern. Or analyze the argument you're reading to see if it's sensible and logical. If you find a way to make the topic interest you, make a note of the article and your response to "Why should I care?" Even if you can't use the idea for a particular paper, you should keep the article and your reaction in your idea file for later use.

Where else might you look for ideas? Always be sure to check the assignment itself. Even if the teacher doesn't assign a topic, the assignment might have clues about what to write or it might give you some insight into a possible topic. And never hesitate to talk with the teacher. The instructor can generally list a dozen or more topics students have written on in the past. Finally, new computer programs are helping writers find ideas to write about. Check with your writing center to see if they have such programs available.

Practice—Reading and Writing

1. Read this popular article.

The Modern Mount Rushmore

Ralph Shoenstein

My daughter Lori, who is eight, told me last night that she wants to grow up to sing like either Judy Garland or Michael Jackson.

"Try for Judy Garland," I said. "A girl needs a great soprano to be Michael Jackson."

These two singers have become Lori's first hero and heroine. They are hardly figures for commemorative stamps, but many children have NO heroes or heroines anymore, no noble achievers they yearn to emulate. They emulate their parents, most of whom look up to no one but trapeze acts. Recently, when asked to name the women who were her mentors, Jane Fonda replied that she had none. In love with her leotard, Jane is at the center of the Age of Self-Involvement, where heroines like Marie Curie, Joan of Arc and Victoria Regina have been replaced by Marie Osmond, Joan Collins, and Victoria Principal.

When my sister and I were children, our heroes and heroines did no endorsements for vaginal sprays, and no one ever cartwheeled out of the Olympics and into a women's hygiene ad. My sister loved medicine, so she idolized Clara Barton, who had founded the American Red Cross, and Florence Nightingale, the great British nurse in the Crimean War, and Sister Elizabeth Kenny, the Australian nurse who developed a treatment for polio. I, who dreamed of glory in sports, idolized the two classiest champions America has ever known, Joe Louis and Joe DiMaggio, and my third god was Franklin D. Roosevelt, who needed no media consultant to make millions of Americans want to be brave just for him.

A few years later, Joe DiMaggio was promoting a coffee maker and President Roosevelt's affair with Lucy Mercer was being dramatized on television. America—especially its children—had clearly lost something precious. The glory had given way to gossip and the idolatry to "Eyewitness News." Most of our heroes and heroines now had not only feet of clay but heads of Silly Putty too. People lowered their eyes from Mount Rushmore to see if the scandal sheets could tell:

> Was Betsy Ross a lesbian?
> Did Abraham Lincoln cross-dress?
> Was Florence Nightingale's bedside manner better *inside* the bed?

By the 1970s Americans were so busy splattering their heroes with mud that two other giants of my youth, Mohandas Gandhi and Albert Einstein, were revealed as having been cool to their wives. Not Thomas Jefferson, however, who was portrayed by the Broadway Musical "1776" as a man less concerned with acts of Congress than with acts of sex.

A few months ago I started rooting for the San Diego Padres because they gave sanctuary to escapees from that bedlam in the Bronx; but then the daily sports scandal section revealed that three of the Padres belong to the John Birch Society and feel that democracy is overrated. Now that I know that the Padres have fielders who can go to their right like no others in baseball, rooting for this team has become like rooting for Italy in the '36 Olympics.

Watching my three daughters grow up in this land of rampant detraction, where Indiana Jones is not a hero but a satire of one, I nervously waited for the revelation that Mister Rogers owned slums in his neighborhood. Even John F. Kennedy, who had inspired my generation, was pulled off his pedestal and dropped into bed. When my eldest daughter was 10, she came to me one day and said, "Dad, do presidents always have their girlfriends in the White House?"

"Of course not," I replied. "Some of them meet outside."

It is now nearly impossible for a public official to be a hero to anyone. Heroism, in fact, may actually have been a burden to presidential candidate John Glenn, for Americans today find less appeal in the right stuff than in the right fluff. Moreover, in a book that became the top best seller, the mayor of New York presents most of the public officials he has known as weaklings, frauds or fools, and seems to enjoy making them squirm. Like most of us, he is looking down, which is not the view I had when I made heroes of Winston Churchill, Teddy Roosevelt and Oliver Wendell Holmes after reading the stories of their lives. Could Edward Koch be the hero of ANY child today? Only one in a rotten mood.

Where has all his exposing and debunking left our kids? One day last spring I stood before 20 children of eight and nine in Lori's third-grade class to see if any heroes or heroines were inspiring them. I asked each child to give me the names of the three greatest people he had ever heard about.

"Michael Jackson, Brooke Shields and Boy George," said a small blond girl, giving me one from all three sexes.

"Michael Jackson, Spider-Man and God," a boy then said, naming a new holy trinity.

When the other children recited, Michael Jackson's name was spoken again and again, but *Andrew* Jackson, never, nor Washington, Lincoln or any other presidential immortal. Just Ronald Reagan, who made it twice, once behind Batman and once behind Mr. T, a hero who likes to move people by saying, "Sucker, I'll break your face." When my wife was eight, Eleanor Roosevelt was the greatest woman in the world to her, but no child gave a modern equivalent of Eleanor Roosevelt. And I heard no modern equivalent of Charles A. Lindbergh, America's beloved "Lone Eagle," even though with Armstrong and Aldrin, the Eagle had landed on the moon.

What were Lori's classmates' dreams? To make the "Who's Hot" edition of *US* magazine. What were they yearning to be? To be wildly famous, androgynous and good at climbing walls.

In answer to my request for heroes, I had expected to hear such names as Michael Jackson, Mr. T, Brooke Shields, and Spider-Man from the kids, but I had not expected the replies of the eight who answered "Me." Their heroes were themselves. The children of Jane Fonda had spoken.

It is sad enough to see the faces on Mount Rushmore replaced by rock stars, brawlers and cartoons, but it is sadder still to see Mount Rushmore replaced by a mirror.

Summarize the article's main points.

_____

_____

_____

_____

Now list five topics you might write about based on this article.

_____   _____

_____   _____

_____

    2. Find at least two newspaper or magazine articles you can summarize and then write about.

LEARN YOUR WRITING HABITS

    Let's assume now that you have an idea, but you have only a fuzzy notion of what you want to do with it in your paper. Now your own writing habits will make some difference in your approach. Some writers like to put that idea on the back burner, so to speak. They think about the idea for days, rarely writing anything down. Then suddenly, they have the paper focused and ready to write with details. You might think of these writers as having a gestation period for their ideas. And like babies, the ideas come out well formed. Sometimes these writers meditate—formally—by making themselves comfortable and focusing all their energy on the topic. They may use a key term to remind themselves to focus their thoughts. Or they may simply meditate by clearing the mind, hoping to tap into an internal monologue on the topic. (One interesting variation is to engage in vigorous exercise—running, swimming, bicycling—to loosen up ideas.)

    Other writers jot down every fact, impression, sensory detail, example, and related idea they can. Sometimes these jottings are in lists or just randomly scattered across pieces of paper. These writers may doodle, write complete sentences, go back to lists, and so on, but they often write down every idea that occurs to them over several hours or even days.

    Though few writers always fall into these extreme patterns, you may recognize your own writing habits as leaning more toward "write every idea down" or "think it all out in my head before touching a pen." Learn your own habits and get comfortable with the way you write. Experiment with approaches you see other people try, though, and with techniques in this book, because most writers cannot survive with only one approach.

AUDIENCE—PURPOSE

Before getting started with a paper, good writers always ask:

Who am I writing to?
Why? What's the point I want to make to these readers?
How much time/space do I have?

Sooner or later, every writer must answer these questions because they shape the paper. If writers don't consider the readers of the paper, they might write only to themselves, although such writing may not communicate with the real readers. If writers don't consider the purpose of the paper, they may miss an opportunity to use a more effective strategy than the one that first comes to mind. Finally, if writers don't consider the length of the paper, they may try to include too much or too little information, both serious roadblocks to communication.

Why determine the audience?

What difference does the audience make? Think about this situation. You've just returned to your apartment after a long day's work, and you discover that a burglar broke in and stole your stereo. But while breaking in, the burglar broke a valuable stained glass hanging by the window. After you call the police and your insurance agent, you still have two tasks. First, the insurance company wants a complete written explanation of where you were, how you discovered the burglary, and what is missing or damaged. You have to write this report in a letter to the company. You also have to write a letter to your best friend who gave you the stained glass because this friend is visiting you next week and will notice that you don't have the panel hanging where it used to be. How will you write these letters?

As you can imagine, the insurance company wants a factual report. They don't want to know how upset you were to find the shattered stained-glass panel; they simply want to know how it was broken and how much it will cost to replace. Your friend, on the other hand, isn't concerned about the time of day when you returned home. Instead, your friend needs to understand your reaction. A coldly factual report would probably hurt your friend's feelings.

Although we may not often choose between such obvious audiences, we always need to determine who will read the papers we write. The age, sex, educational experience, and political leaning (among other factors) of a reader can change what the writer must say to be convincing. Always take the time to outline the characteristics of your readers. You might use the following chart to help you describe your readers:

Age	Income
Sex	Moral or political stance
Education	Urban or rural
Occupation	

Is your reader interested in your topic?

What does your reader know about your topic?

Has your reader taken a position on your topic?

Why determine purpose?

In the same way, be sure to understand what your readers expect and need from your writing. If they need simple information, don't draw conclusions inappropriately. If they need to *see* an incident to understand it, give them plenty of sensory detail. If they need to understand causes and effects, don't simply give examples but also analyze how the examples *show* causes and effects. Also, if you understand your audience but want to give them more information or analysis than they expect, be sure to have your own goals clearly in mind so that you serve their primary needs as well as add the other elements you want to give readers. In other words, know why you're writing, know your audience's needs, and know your own goals.

Why determine length?

Finally, ask yourself just how much time and space you have for this paper. If the assignment or attention span of the audience can accommodate only three pages, limit the topic appropriately. If you have only a paragraph, limit yourself even more. Even a twenty-page paper, as long as that may sound, is too short for a detailed treatment of a large topic.

Practice—Writing

1. Choose one of the ten topics you'd like to write on and think of at least two different audiences you might write for. Specify why you'll write and how long the paper can be. Using any techniques to generate ideas, distinguish the detail that would appear in each paper.

Teaching in Colorado, I have many students who suggest skiing topics. One they enjoyed working on was a paper describing a ski condo after a wild weekend. They chose friends, the condo owner, the insurance agent, and the police as audiences. How do you suppose they stated their purposes? What details did they change in each paragraph?

2. Read the following short passages on drug abusers. What differences can you detect in audience and purpose for the two pieces?

> The snapshot is frightening: a grinning skeleton of a man wearing a LaCoste shirt. "Look at that," says Paul, 37, a lawyer and owner of a trucking firm. "Matchsticks for arms and slits for eyes. Eighty-seven pounds and coked out of my gourd." In the five years before the photo was taken, Paul explains, he "snorted away" his wife, his suburban home and $500,000. After the drug ate away the cartilage inside his nose, he bought liquid cocaine and droppered it into his eyes. Then a year and a half ago, shortly after posing for the cadaverous photo, Paul pointed a .38 pistol at his head; luckily, his girlfriend managed to wrestle it away. "That night I saw an ad on TV for a cocaine hot line," recalls Paul, who now weighs 200 pounds. "If I hadn't called, you would have read an obituary last year about an 87-pound man who blew his brains out."
>
> —from "Getting Straight," *Newsweek,* June 4, 1984.

> It is so long since I first took opium that if it had been a trifling incident in my life I might have forgotten its date. But cardinal events are not to be forgotten, and from circumstances connected with it I remember that it must be referred to the autumn of 1804. . . . Arrived at my lodgings, it may be supposed that I lost not a moment in taking the quantity prescribed. I was necessarily ignorant of the whole art and mystery of opium-taking, and, what I took, I took under every disadvantage. But I took it, and in an hour, oh! heavens! what a revulsion! what an upheaving from its lowest depths, of the inner spirit! what an apocalypse of the world within me! That my pains had vanished was now a trifle in my eyes: this negative effect was swallowed up in the immensity of those positive effects which had opened before me—in the abyss of divine enjoyment thus suddenly revealed. Here was a panacea for all human woes; here was the secret of happiness, about which philosophers had disputed for so many ages, at once discovered; happiness might now be bought for a penny and carried in the pocket; portable ecstasies might be had corked up in a pint bottle; and peace of mind could be sent down in gallons by the mail-coach. But if I talk in this way, the reader will think I am laughing, and I can assure him, that nobody will laugh long who deals much with opium; its pleasures even are of a grave and solemn complexion.
>
> —from *The Pleasures of Opium* by Thomas De Quincey

1. Are both passages on similar topics? _____

2. What distinguishes the two? _____

_____

3. Who is the *Newsweek* article directed to? _____

4. Who is the De Quincey article directed to? _____

5. Do both pieces have the same purpose or can you specify different

purposes for each? _____

GENERATING IDEAS AND DETAILS

At some time or another, every writer needs help finding ideas and fleshing them out with examples or details. Some writers jot ideas down in ordered or random lists, often called brainstorming or listing.

Clustering

Writers might also use a visual scheme to help them generate details. One such visual aid is called *clustering*. In this prewriting technique, the writer chooses a central idea, emotion, or image and simply free associates all related emotions, experiences, and so on. The writer draws lines to connect associated ideas to the main idea, but the "list" is not logical or ordered in any way. For instance, writers in one class clustered reasons that people tell white lies:

They then chose to explore one of the reasons—spare friend's feelings—to cluster related personal experiences:

Notice that the second cluster around "spare friend's feelings" lists possible "mishaps" that might make us want to be gentle with a friend's feelings but that nothing specific yet appears in the diagrams. Another clustering might generate specific examples from your experience.

Practice—Clustering

Choose one of the ideas you want to write about listed in your idea file. Practice clustering related emotions, sensations, or experiences. Do a second cluster focusing on one of the first emotions or experiences as shown in the following dentist example:

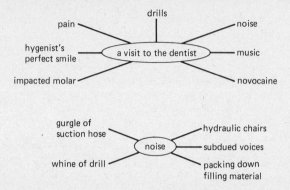

Asking questions—*wh*

Some writers may use one of several brainstorming methods to help them generate details for the idea. They might, for instance, answer the questions familiar to journalists:

Who?
What?
When?
Where?
Why?
How?

Asking questions—*topoi*

Still another formal set of questions comes from an ancient Greek rhetoric by Aristotle. In his discussions of how men spoke in the forum, he divided all the arguments they used into categories he called *topoi*. He first divided all arguments into four broad categories:

Definition
Comparison
Relationship
Testimony

Then he subdivided categories. If we ask questions based on each subdivision, our list would include defining, comparing, analyzing, and researching an idea:

A. Definition
   1. Synonym—Can you use other terms to define the topic?
   2. Formal definition—What is the topic's dictionary meaning or accepted meaning?
   3. Extended definition—Can you define with an analogy or comparison?
   4. Stipulative definition—What does the topic mean to you?
   5. Classification—Can you divide this topic into categories?
   6. Example—Can you give examples from your experience to illustrate the topic?
B. Comparison
   1. Similarity—What is the topic like? How?
   2. Difference—How does the topic differ from similar things?
   3. Degree—How much is the topic alike or different from comparable things?
C. Relationship
   1. Cause and effect—What causes produce your topic? What results occur because of your topic?
   2. Antecedence and consequence—Do other things lead up (though they don't cause) your topic? What generally follows your topic?
D. Testimony—What have experts said about your topic? What sources can you quote?

If you have trouble finding enough to write about your topic, you can answer as many of these questions as possible to generate more ideas.

Other approaches

Less structured approaches include freewriting, looping, and others. We'll try out several of these brainstorming techniques throughout the book, but you should use those most comfortable for you.

NARROWING THE IDEA

Why must writers limit the topic when they write? Think about taking pictures. If you want to take a picture of a mountain range, you need to be far enough away to show mountains contrasted with flat land. But by being so far away, you lose the detail of rock features. If you zero in on just one peak, you get more detail, but you lose the comparison between mountain and lowland. If you zero in still more, you get a good picture of, say, a specific rock formation, but now that rock formation isn't necessarily on a mountain. Or, you might snap only the moss growing on a section of the rock, but now even the rock itself doesn't appear in the picture.

Writing is similar, though of course we have more freedom in moving from the big picture to a more limited one. Still, although we can sketch in the background or setting of the moss description if we want to write about the moss, we cannot spend pages describing the mountain range, the peak, the rock formation at 12,000 feet, and then the rare lichen growing on the south side of the rock. Rather, if we intend to concentrate on the moss, readers expect that we will sketch the background skimpily. Just as photographers do, writers must narrow the main idea of a paper.

The problem is that having worked so hard to get an idea, many writers don't want to spend even more time limiting the idea (in effect, throwing parts of the idea away). Instead, many writers just want to sketch general or broad ideas. While sometimes readers need only general statements, most readers need more; they need detail. But by beginning with such a big "picture," writers can't move easily to detail. Thus, writers must first narrow subjects.

One good technique for narrowing a subject is branching, whereby the writer begins with a broad idea and first narrows and then focuses by specifying possible aspects of the topic:

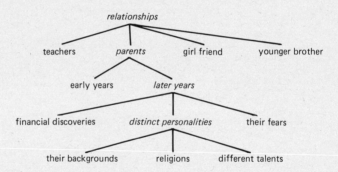

If several branches are still possible, the topic is probably too broad. But once the branches get specific, then writers can tell that the topic is ready to work with.

Practice—Narrowing Subjects

1. Narrow the following broad subjects to topics suitable for paragraphs:

Drugs   Holidays   Exercise
Airplanes   Pollution

2. Practice branching for several broad subjects. Identify several possible topics from each branching.

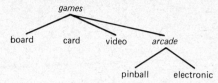

POSSIBLE TOPICS: _____

_____

_____

movies
silent films   musicals   artistic films

POSSIBLE TOPICS: _____

_____

_____

SPORTS

POSSIBLE TOPICS: _____

_____

_____

FRIENDSHIP

POSSIBLE TOPICS: _____

_____

_____

FOCUS

At the same time that writers move from broad, general subjects to more narrow topics, they also *focus* their thoughts on a precise point they want to make. Let's return to the camera analogy. As a good photographer, you've now selected a narrow slice of a picture you want to show to someone. If you simply point the camera and shoot, you may have caught the subject in your photo, but the person or object may be out of focus. Instead of a sharp image, viewers see a blurred object. Maybe they can tell what the picture is, but maybe not. The photographer's responsibility before shooting the picture is to be sure the camera is focused so that the picture has sharp, clear details.

In the same way, writers *focus* a main idea. They narrow the subject for the word picture and then adjust the topic sentence or thesis statement to state a precise point for the paragraph or essay. The paper then gives sharp, clear details to fill in the picture.

Why are details so important?

First, most readers have lived in the world long enough to know general information on most common subjects you might write about. How long do you suppose readers stay interested in reading if writers don't give them new information or insight? General statements don't interest readers; details do.

Moreover, if writers don't guide readers, writers have no control over what details readers connect to the main points writers bring up. Remember when we discussed how readers tap into networks of memories? If writers aren't specific in showing or telling readers what images and information to remember, readers may plug into wrong networks. Readers might then end up with conclusions or images different from what the writer intended. And if the writer wants readers to *act* as a result of reading, then the actions may not be at all what the unfocused writer expects.

Good writers, then, not only get ideas to write about, but they also narrow and focus on a workable bit of that single idea. Whether a paper is one page or forty pages long, good writers leave readers with one main point—and for longer papers, one main point and several less important points.

Ways to focus

As I noted before, some writers like to focus mentally while their ideas simmer on the back burner. But most writers find that jotting down the idea and trying to determine the audience and purpose of the paper help bring the main point into focus. Still other writers now use the W questions (who, what, when, where, why) to help them specify exactly what they'll write about. Any combination of these approaches will work too. The main point is to limit the topic so that what appears in the paper supports the point convincingly.

TOPIC SENTENCES

Because the topic sentence in each paragraph (the thesis in an essay) is so important in setting up expectations for readers, as well as in helping writers stay on track, let's discuss topic sentences in more detail. (We'll look at thesis statements in Chapter 4.) Remember, not every paragraph has a topic sentence—and not every essay has an explicit thesis statement—but until you feel more comfortable practicing advanced techniques to communicate a precise point to your readers, you should include topic sentences in your writing. These focal sentences help writers *and* readers.

What does a topic sentence do?

First, as the name implies, the topic sentence states the topic of the paragraph. To make accurate predictions while reading, readers need to know what the paragraph is about, and the topic sentence announces the point of the paragraph. Look again at a sample from Chapter 1:

> During the early negotiations between the Soviet Union and the United States on the control of strategic weapons, the American negotiators made a curious discovery. When they initiated a discussion of the Soviet Union's missiles and weapons, the Americans found that they knew more about them than some of the Russians. The civilians in the Soviet delegation, including a Deputy Foreign Minister, did not know the details of their own country's strategic weaponry. The military men, however, were well informed. One day the senior military officer on the Soviet delegation, Colonel General Nikolai V. Ogarkov, took an American delegate aside and reproached him: there was no reason, the General said, for the Americans to reveal their knowledge of Soviet military matters to the civilian members of his delegation. That sort of information, the General said, was strictly the military's business.
> —Robert G. Kaiser, *Russia—The People and the Power*

This paragraph was easy to predict. Why? Find its topic sentence and decide if that states the main point of the paragraph.

But most topic sentences do more than just state the main idea: most also indicate the writer's specific intentions for the paragraph. If the topic is relatively broad, the topic sentence not only states that general topic but also shows how the writer will *limit* or focus attention on certain aspects of the topic. Moreover, the topic sentence also defines the writer's position. As I have noted, most writing takes on a persuasive edge as the writer projects a specific viewpoint that the reader should—at least temporarily—adopt. The topic sentence reflects the writer's attitude or point of view.

Briefly, then, the topic sentence states the main point of the paragraph and the writer's stance or attitude about the topic.

Put so bluntly, topic sentences sound easy to write. In fact, they are among the most difficult sentences to write and refine because they require absolute precision from writers. A writer who wants to write about health might be tempted to begin with a topic sentence such as:

Students should be aware of health.

As a reader, my first reaction is "Why?" or "So?" Not only am I not sure what the sentence means, but I'm not enticed to read on at all. And yet, this sentence does state a topic—health—and a writer's attitude implied in "should be aware." The problems begin with the lack of precision. Will this writer talk about students' health problems? If so, the paper could go on to discuss dental, physical, and mental health even before addressing the number of infectious diseases students can contract. Many other limited topics are possibilities from this topic sentence as well. For instance, what age students will the writer treat? If the paper will be about kindergarteners, then health issues differ from those covered in a paper about college students. As a reader, I have just too little to go on to predict accurately what the paper will be about. Unless readers can predict, they lose interest quickly. This topic sentence, though it states a point, does not state a precise, *limited* point.

And so good topic sentences set limits—both for writers and readers. If this writer wanted to discuss a specific health problem, he or she might ask

Who?
What?
When?
Where?
Why?

to limit the topic. Without some limitation, the paper simply has no focus and readers cannot be drawn to read on.

Let's assume that we can answer the questions. We can write about college students who study too much during finals week. Now we have answered "who?" and "when?" Where can we go from here? As you can see, we are practicing again the process of focusing our ideas. As we answer more of the W questions, we will limit the topic more and more. But as we limit the topic, we must keep in mind that we have real readers who will want to learn or be entertained or be persuaded.

Who?	college students
What?	study too hard
When?	finals' week
Where?	in the library
Why?	

As we answer questions, we must keep in mind why we are writing. We want to write about the health of college students. But "what" do we really want to write about? Many students study too hard. What effects does studying overtime have on their health? Now we're beginning to explore the part of the heuristic that will help us focus most effectively:

What?	Stress causes excessive fatigue and decreases memory.
What?	With no time to eat properly, many students eat junk food.
What?	Studying in isolation emphasizes loneliness, causing depression.

Now we're beginning to explore other possibilities for the limited *topic* of this paragraph. Let's assume that we like the idea of writing about junk food and health. Let's answer the questions with just that particular topic in mind:

Who?	college students
What?	study too hard and ignore meals, therefore jeopardizing health and memory
When?	finals week
Where?	XXX
Why?	mistaken assumption that more time is better than quality time

Now we're getting somewhere with this topic, although we must be careful to focus on just *one* point in the topic sentence. When we draft the topic sentence, we cannot include both health and memory. With this point in mind, perhaps we can now develop a more successful topic sentence:

> Being aware of unhealthy foods can help students study more effectively during finals week.

What does the topic sentence now announce as the topic and purpose of this paragraph? The paragraph will focus on the relationship of foods and learning. Moreover, the purpose of the paragraph is becoming clear with the words chosen to convey attitude: "can help students study effectively." This topic sentence suggests that the paragraph can *inform* students so that they can *perform* better. Although it will inform as its primary goal, this paragraph will also persuade readers to change their eating habits.

Is this an acceptable topic sentence? It's a good start, good enough to continue brainstorming for ideas or even to begin drafting a paragraph. But this topic sentence is not yet refined and polished enough to convey a precise point. We cannot fully evaluate topic sentences separately from the paragraphs they control, but this topic sentence is clearly not yet efficient in conveying its main point. Just what does "being aware of" imply for students? Should readers expect that simply knowing the effects of munchies and soft drinks on their abilities to study would improve their studying? That's what the sentence now implies. So the sentence must be explicit and precise. "Being aware" isn't adequate; students must *avoid* certain foods. Let's try more formulations of this topic sentence:

> Eating healthy foods can help students study more effectively during intensive study sessions such as those during finals week.

Do we still have ambiguity about when students eat healthy foods? Can they eat junk food except during intensive study sessions? Let's try again:

> Eating healthy foods during finals week can help students study more effectively during those intensive study sessions.

A more serious problem this version brings up is the amount of territory the paragraph must cover to fulfill the promise of this topic sentence. Can a single paragraph cover all the good foods students might eat? This topic sentence sets up a huge task for the writer—to condense so much information into a paragraph. Perhaps the writer could cover this material in a long essay, but this topic sentence stakes out too big a claim for a single paragraph. A thesis that controls an essay must, of course, be broader than a topic sentence—and we'll discuss the thesis in more detail in Chapter 4—but it too must be limited to cover only the points the writer can develop in the time and space he or she has.

Practice—Topics and Topic Sentences

1. Take any five topics you discovered in the narrowing exercise on pp. 36 and 37 and write topic sentences for possible paragraphs.

2. Discuss problems of focus in the following topic sentences. How could you revise these topic sentences?

A. The day had begun beautifully and had all the makings to turn out perfectly—if only it could have stayed that way.

_____

_____

B. To enhance my ego, I tell little white lies to my friends.

_____

_____

C. Craig can sometimes be so self-centered and so insensitive that he ignores the feelings of others.

_____

_____

D. My grandmother gets along poorly with some members of her family and most other people because she is inconsiderate of other people's feelings.

_____

_____

The topic sentence or thesis statement helps readers predict

A good way to think of the topic sentence or thesis, then, is as a promise to readers. The writer states the main point and promises to detail it fully. Because of this promise from the writer, readers can confidently base their predictions about the passage on the topic sentence—or thesis—and confident predictions allow readers to spend their energy enjoying their reading or retaining information writers want to share.

Let's consider a paragraph in which the topic sentence lets readers predict precisely what the paragraph will communicate:

Most of us, if asked to name the tyrants in history, would immediately think of Hitler and his SS men. But after watching a massacre scene in the movie, *Ghandi,* I realized that even the British—our WWII allies—killed innocent people to control the nation. While watching the movie, the audience sees the tension build between the Indian people, who wanted Indians to control India, and the British, who wanted to continue ruling the country. At one point in the movie, Gandhi (who had been leading the Indian movement) had been arrested, and a group of over one thousand Indians gathered in a fenced-in commons discussing what action they should take. Unknown to them, a British general—followed by a squad of gunmen—was marching towards the crowd. When he arrived at the area, he lined up his gunmen, blocking the only exit. For a moment the unarmed civilians stood in hushed fear, seeing—but not comprehending—the British gunmen who stood with rifles aimed at them. The general gave the order to fire. During the first round of shots, several people fell to the ground, and those who were able to move clasped their children to them in hopeless terror, trying to protect themselves from the bullets by jumping into a blood-spattered pit in the center of the grounds. Others tried to escape by climbing the two-story fences. The general, noticing the climbers' intentions, directed his men to shoot down the figures clutching the fences. The gunmen fired again and again—so many rounds that each had a pile of shell casings at his feet. The last image the audience sees in this scene is a two-year-old girl quietly crying amidst the stacatto of gunfire, surrounded by bleeding men, women, and children. The history books I have read had "forgotten" this ruthless massacre committed—not by our enemies—but by our allies. After watching this brutal scene in the movie, I realized that tyrants are not always in a distant country or in the pages of a history book: they may be our neighbors and our allies.

Notice that the topic sentence answers all the W questions and sets up a specific point for readers. Then the paragraph, with the detailed example, fulfills the promise of the topic sentence by *showing* the incident that proves the writer's point. This topic sentence meets both readers' and writer's needs.

Practice—Topic Sentences

1. In each of the following paragraphs, the topic sentence is not as narrowly focused as it could be, given the details in the paragraph. Read each paragraph and then revise the topic sentence.

A. On a few occasions, telling white lies keeps me from hurting someone's feelings. For instance, at times when my sister from Denver calls and says she's coming to visit, I must struggle to sound pleased. Because we do not have much in common and sometimes she gets on my nerves, I do not enjoy her company too much. However, I try to sound glad that she's coming to see me even if I'm not. Another example of a white lie I use to spare someone's feelings happens with my daughter. Because she's arrived at an age where she loves to try to help do things, I encourage her. I don't want her to grow up lacking in self-confidence so sometimes when I know she's tried extremely hard at something and done her best, I tell her what a great job she did even if it wasn't so wonderful. Another occasion when a white lie comes in handy is when I tell my mother about a night out on the town with a friend. Since she worries, even about her grown children, I sometimes tell her I had one or two beers when I three or four. I tell these white lies to family members in the spirit of love because I don't want to see them hurt.

—Alicia P.

B. Once I wrote a letter to a photographer, asking for a refund and complaining about how bad our senior picture turned out. When school got out the last day, the seniors all crowded into the school's gymnasium. After practicing for the graduation ceremonies, my class lined up on the hard, wooden bleachers to get our senior class picture taken. It would look like the number '84. The boys had on black robes and the girls had red robes on. After the photographer got us in the right places, he snapped the camera 3 times and then said, "This is going to look terrific." We all were so excited and could hardly wait 3 more weeks to get our class picture back. Every week I would go out to the mail box and look for a big, brown envelope. When the envelope did come, I opened it up and pulled the picture out expecting to see a "terrific" picture. To my disappointment, I could barely make out anyone's face. I thought to myself, "I'm not going to keep this if I can't even see where I was standing." I then wrote a letter to the photographer saying how disappointed I was and that I wanted a full refund of $5. Several days later, the photographer sent me a letter apologizing for the picture and gave me the refund. Some people would have just ignored this and would have kept the picture, though disappointed. This proves that sometimes writing a letter of complaint does have good results.

—Kim M.

2. Now consider two paragraphs lacking topic sentences. Add appropriately focused topic sentences to each.

A. When I walked through the door the first time I was invited to one of her popular parties, Sabrena came rushing from the kitchen in an absurd clown costume and asked me if I didn't think she looked cute. A polka-dot leotard stuck to her thick body like Saran Wrap, she had pasted sparkles of every color on her face, her head donned a bright orange Bozo wig, and a bouquet of balloons flew out from her lower back like a tail. I overcame my temptation to gag, swallowed deeply, and murmured in my sweetest voice, "You look perfect." Had I told Sabrena that I really thought she should be wearing sackcloth and a paper bag, she never would have invited me to the Christmas party she threw later that year. This time she invited everyone to a formal dinner party, and she was appropriately dressed in a slinky red gown with a modest string of pearls and low heels. I felt relieved when I assumed I would not have to lie to Sabrena this time. Then she asked me what I thought of her tree decorations. She had cut giant stars out of shiny wrapping paper and hung them on her tree in every available spot. The stars looked ridiculously out of proportion to the tree that was shorter than I was. "How divine," I remarked. "You have such good taste in design." Sabrena beamed with delight at this lie, and I knew I would be invited to her Valentine's Day party, reputed to be the most festive and bachelor-filled of any she put on throughout the year.

—*Susan R.*

B. For example, Heidi and I would be sitting at the table having dinner with Dad when, just as Heidi lifted a glass of tomato juice to her mouth and Dad was intent upon his salad, I would cross my eyes, stretch my lips to their limit, and stick my thumbs in my ears, wiggling my fingers wildly. Heidi would burst out laughing at my ridiculous face, tomato juice squirting everywhere, and since we were forbidden to disrupt the dinner table, Heidi would be sent to her room. When she protested that her accident was my fault because I had made her laugh, I denied every word so that I would not get in trouble and be sent away, too. Another time, Dad had just finished raking the front yard, and a large pile of golden leaves waited on the lawn as Dad went to the garage to find a sack for them. The temptation to jump into those leaves was irresistible, and I sprinted from the house and landed in the middle of the pile as the leaves flew off in every direction. When I noticed that the yard needed raking again, I ran into the house to await Dad's yell. "Who made this mess?" he screamed from the front in a few minutes. I looked timidly out the screen door and mumbled that I had seen Heidi out there recently. Then Dad strode into the house and sent Heidi to her room without a question. When I was a kid, it was much easier to place the blame of my actions on my younger sister so that I would not get in trouble myself.

—*Susan R.*

Practice—Focusing Ideas

Are you ever surprised that people expect you to act in a certain way just because you are, say, a student or a worker at a certain facility? Think about the roles you play as you read about two other writers who have strained against roles people expected them to play:

Practice—Reading

Man's role—how has it affected my life? At thirty-five, I chose to emphasize family togetherness and income and neglect my profession if necessary. At fifty-seven, I see no reward for the time spent with and for the family, in terms of love and appreciation. I see a thousand punishments for neglecting my profession. I'm just tired and have come close to just walking away from it and starting over; just research, publish, teach, administer, play tennis, and travel. Why haven't I? Guilt. And love. And fear of loneliness. How should the man's role in my family change? I really don't know how it can, but I'd like a lot more time to do my thing.

—from H. Goldberg, "In Harness: The Male Condition

Most remarkably, the Motherhood Myth persists in the face of the most overwhelming maternal unhappiness and incompetence. If reproduction were merely superfluous and expensive, if the experience were as rich and rewarding as the cliché would have us believe, if it were a predominantly joyous trip for everyone riding—mother, father, child—then the going everybody-should-have-two-children plan would suffice. Certainly, there are a lot of joyous mothers, and the children and (sometimes, not necessarily) their husbands reflect their joy. But a lot of evidence suggests that for more women than anyone wants to admit, motherhood can be miserable.

—from B. Rollin, "Motherhood: Who Needs It?"

Practice—Focusing

What roles do you play? Do any of them impose limits on your behavior?

Let's retrace a sample brainstorming and focusing session from a composition class. Students were going to write about why a certain role they played made them act as they did. First, they said they couldn't think of roles, so we listed these on the board as they thought of them:

daughter	brother	son
mother	youngest child	waitress
dumb blonde	macho man	boyfriend
babysitter	young professional	college student
engineer	friend	tutor
football star	athlete	cheerleader
brain	movie buff	frat leader
minority student		

The easy categories came out first, and then the more subtle roles we play started occurring to students. Clearly, these are just some of the possibilities that might occur to any given group.

But then we needed to go on to determine what point the assignment was asking for. We discussed the topic and decided that other people's expectations cause us to behave in certain ways when we adopt one of these roles. To write about the effects of role playing, then, we needed to flesh out expectations and resulting actions.

Next, we had to specify the audience. A few students chose to write to their parents to explain why after leaving home for school they couldn't easily adopt the "child" role any longer. But most of the students chose to write to their peers in the class to explain one aspect of the social or educational roles they found themselves in as college students.

Just to get them started, we picked a role most of them knew something about and listed general expectations of someone playing that role. Students decided to brainstorm together about "football star":

We expect a football star to be:

studying game plans more than class notes

concerned about physique

always hanging around with other jocks

talking only about his last winning touchdown

dating the cheerleaders

watching game films rather than "artsy" films

In short, we defined many aspects of a stereotype of a football player. Next, we needed to see just what consequences follow for the "star" everybody expects to act in these ways. We decided just to look at the social pressures that hindered friendships. One student volunteered this explanation:

If the football star gets into a group of people who know who he is, the non-players expect him to talk about his last game. They start the conversation on football and expect him to be comfortable talking about football. They may even want the star to tell them inside stories about the coach and other players. When this limited conversation happens over and over again, the football star decides to hang around with other football players so he can talk about all those things the non-players don't think he can discuss. Besides, the other football players are just as tired of talking about football as he is, and so the conversation always turns to classes, tests, dates, and so on.

Now we have an analysis of how the expectations make the football player act. What else might writers want to include in a paper on this topic? The students in this class felt that their papers would be more convincing if they wrote about their experiences so that they could give real examples of instances when other people's expectations made them act in a certain way. Since we didn't have a football star in the class, each student began brainstorming for the specific focus of his or her own paper. Most students first listed expectations of the role they chose and then listed examples when the person's expectations affected their behavior. The examples included *detail,* specific actions and reactions, that showed the role affecting the writer.

After listing detailed examples, students reviewed the examples and picked two or three that had a common thread. Then they tried to state in one sentence the one main point they wanted readers to remember. With this narrowing of the topic and focus on a main point, students felt ready to begin a draft of the paper.

SAMPLES

Following is an early version of the paper one student wrote:

Being an older brother always seems to mean that I have to hang around watching my two younger sisters. One of the bad aspects of this is that when I am home I usually get stuck keeping an eye on them. Once, not too long ago, I had planned with some friends to go camping the following day, but my parents suddenly planned to go to a party the next evening and asked me to stay home. Realizing that arguing would get nowhere, I unhappily consented and stayed home playing and keeping my sisters happy. Another pain I get from having to be around my sisters is when I am forced to take them somewhere. During Christmas vacation I was asked by my parents if I would take them to see E.T. Not wanting to see E.T. myself I tried to look for an out. Between my sisters begging and my parents threatening, I didn't feel I had much of a choice. Cleaning up after them is another chore that gets tacked on when I happen to be around. They can never put anything away where it goes, and if things are messy I'm usually the one to get blamed. So I've learned to pick up whenever I see toys out or dirty dishes or what not. I just can't wait til they are old enough to handle life on their own, I know mine would be a lot easier.

—*Bill T.*

1. What is Bill's focus now? _____

2. Has he narrowed what he'll discuss sufficiently to show you, the

   reader, what role affects his behavior? _____

After discussing the paragraph with another student in the class and considering again what point he wanted to make, Bill revised his paragraph:

Being an older brother around my house seems to mean that I am responsible, however unwillingly, for keeping track of my two younger sisters. For example, not long ago, I had planned a camping trip one weekend with some friends, when out of the blue, my parents decided to take a trip into southern Colorado. That didn't seem too troublesome until they mentioned that my sisters were not going, which meant that I would have to postpone my own vacation. After a short argument on whether my sisters could or could not take care of themselves, I realized that I would definitely be spending my weekend at home playing games and generally entertaining them (so much for camping). Another annoyance is having to play chauffeur for my sisters whenever they want to go somewhere. This Christmas, for example, my sisters decided that they needed to see the movie E.T., and my parents decided that I should take them. I, on the other hand, had planned on a quiet evening at home reading, but again, nobody seemed to care what I had planned, and between my sisters begging and my parents threatening, I didn't feel I had much of a choice and ended up seeing E.T. for the second time. Cleaning up after my sisters is also one of the assigned duties that I am expected to take care of when home. Though they usually keep things fairly clean, they almost always leave our Atari game scattered about the downstairs after using it, and because I live downstairs, I usually end up picking it up. Sometimes, though, my parents will discover the mess before I do, and then the s———hits the fan. My mom will usually start in about how I try to blame too much on my sisters when I try to speak up for myself, and my dad just mumbles something about being irresponsible and then walks back upstairs. It seems that because the mess is nearest my room, I get blamed for it! My sisters probably love having me do their work for them, but I just can't wait until they are old enough to handle life on their own; I know living mine would be a lot easier.

—*Bill T.*

1. How has Bill narrowed his focus? Why? _____

_____

2. Could you suggest still more revisions? _____

_____

During that class students had taken a broad topic and found a personal perspective they could write from. They had determined just what angle they would each pursue. If we can use the camera analogy again, they had centered the one element they wanted in their picture, with enough detail to let the viewer/reader know exactly what the picture should mean. Each student found a way to communicate a personal insight.

Why is focus so crucial?

Focusing on a specific slice of experience allows writers to communicate effectively. Readers need details because they have enough general experience to know most of the general conclusions writers might draw. So writers need to be specific to be convincing. If we were to diagram the differences between general and specific terms, we might end up with a visual image like this:

a. living creatures
b. mammals
c. bears
d. polar bears
e. polar bears in Manitoba
f. polar bears in Manitoba that raid the Churchill trash dump

We could make the general end more general, and we could extend the specific end as well. And, of course, we could narrow the general idea to many different specific ideas. But that is the point of writing. Writers bring their individual and specific perspectives on narrow ideas to their writing. Such specific perspectives make writing engaging because readers learn something about writers.

To determine the appropriate level of generality for your writing, consider the audience, length, and scope of the assignment. When students write single paragraphs, the "general" idea in the topic sentence must be narrow enough to be developed fully in that one paragraph. For a single paragraph, writers need *specific* topic sentences, perhaps with specific terms much like those on level e here. Details in the paragraph are even more specific than the topic sentence (levels f, g, and h) and present readers with concrete observations and sense perceptions or precisely limited analysis.

Just to see how general and specific terms show up in writing, look again at the samples of the role-playing paragraph. How has Bill used examples of his experience to show how he is expected to take responsibility for his sisters? Find the examples he uses. Now look for details. What details *show* his experience? What details did he add in the revision that help make his point clearer?

Now look at an article that appeared in *USA Today*. Although it doesn't relate to the same topic, role-playing, we could consider the lies we tell as one way of safeguarding certain roles.

Practice—Reading

The Truth about Our Little White Lies

Karen S. Peterson

Gail Safeer, a graduate student in suburban Washington, D.C., doesn't let on to people that two of her three children were born during a previous marriage. "I don't correct people when they assume all three are my husband's," she says. "It's nobody's business. It's a little white lie of omission, like not telling somebody her husband is running around. . . . White lies are not daily currency in my life," adds Safeer. "But we all do it."

Indeed we do. Each of us fibs at least 50 times a day, says psychologist Jerald Jellison of the University of Southern California in Los Angeles, who has spent a decade musing on the truth about our lies. He says we lie most often about the Big Three—age, income and sex—areas where our egos and self-images are most vulnerable. To protect them we even lie non-verbally with gestures, silences, inactions and body language. "You can even lie with your emotions," says Jellison. "The smile you don't mean, or the classic nervous laugh. A man asks a woman, 'Your place or mine?' and then chuckles. If she's offended, he can always elaborate on that laugh by saying, 'Can't you take a joke? I was only kidding.'"

These types of lies are what Jellison calls "little white lies," the kind we throw around as casually as old sneakers but which he claims are our "social justifications." "We lie because it pays," he says. "We use (lies) to escape punishment for our small errors. . . . Also, our social justifications help us avoid disapproval. 'I gave at the office,' or 'I'm sorry.'"

Our most common reason for lying is to spare someone else's feelings, says Jellison. "We often tell ourselves that, but usually we're trying to protect our own best interests. I'll feel that if I tell you the truth, you'll get mad." Adds B.L. Kintz, a psychology professor at Western Washington University in Bellingham: "We lie so often, with such regularity and fluency, so automatically and glibly that we're not even aware we're doing it. The little self-serving deceptions, the compliments we don't mean, stretching the point in a social situation—they are part of reality. Lying is simply something that is."

Jellison couldn't agree more. He believes that white lies are the oil for the machinery of daily life. "Society actually functions fairly well on many small deceptions. They contribute the little, civilized rituals that comfort us. . . . The idea that we must always tell the truth is too simplistic," he says. "Is lying 'right' or 'wrong'? is an impossible question to answer."

Be it right or wrong, we have become so accustomed to lying and being lied to that we only see it as harmful in daily life when we don't realize that it's happening to us. "We take for granted some degree of lying from politicians, government, business, advertising," says psychiatrist Dr. Irving Baran of the USC San Diego Medical School. "We don't get excited about an ad that hypes some product in a way we know isn't true. But the rub comes when we go to someone we need and trust and are deceived. A banker for a loan who says he's got the best interest rate going. A real estate agent who convinces us his is the best package available. An insurance agent pushing an unsound policy. An auto dealer who doesn't tell you the product's safety record. Then our backs go up, and what isn't true—hurts."

Practice—Analyzing

1. What roles do you see people discussing in the article?

_____

_____

2. The first example shows a woman protecting her role as wife and mother, but are the roles in later examples as explicit?

_____

3. Now look for general and specific statements. Would you say the article is more or less general than Bill's paragraph or the paragraphs from Goldberg and Rollin? Why?

_____

_____

4. Find some specific details in the article and label them. Now label more general statements. Could you support any of the more general statements with specific details or examples?

_____

_____

Why is Peterson's article less specific than Bill's paragraph? Is Peterson's topic broader? Not really, because "role playing" and "white lies" are about equally general ideas. Rather, Bill has focused his comments more narrowly because of the specific point of the assignment and because of his audience. Bill knows his audience well because they are his classmates. Although Karen Peterson knows something about the readership of *USA Today,* she must write for a general audience, a much harder group of readers to visualize. Moreover, she has to try to keep everyone's attention, a difficult task, while Bill wants to explain one narrow point to one reader, the fellow who sits next to him. Bill knows clearly what his reader understands about roles and older brothers, but Karen Peterson doesn't know how much her readers know about white lies and the reasons for telling them. If some of her readers know a great deal about white lies, they won't read the article because she doesn't cover much detail that would give them new information. Rather, she assumes that her readers know little about white lies and will be interested in a superficial explanation of the reasons for telling them.

So as you can see, the audience and goals of writing affect how narrowly we focus ideas and how much detail we present.

Practice—Writing

Practice focusing ideas so that you could write about your personal experience to various audiences. Try specifying a main point you would make and the supporting details to convince at least two different audiences:

1. the importance of baking bread—for classmates and class of nutritionists
2. why most college students aren't responsible pet owners—for city council and landlord
3. why teenage marriages seldom succeed—for friend thinking of marrying and class of high school juniors
4. why "lying is simply something that is"—for parents and psychology class
5. why we accept roles that are sometimes uncomfortable for us—for classmates and boyfriend/girlfriend

Use one of your focused ideas to draft a paragraph on the topic.

chapter 3
Paragraphs

Before beginning to read the following selection from *Working Woman,* look carefully at the title and "header" that appear in bold face.

What can the introductory information tell you about what you will read in the excerpt? Does the magazine title give you useful information about the excerpt? How about the section and title itself? Does the header set up any expectations? Does the definition help you understand what you'll read?

Practice—Reading

Now read the excerpt, keeping in mind the audience and purpose:

Health: Saving Your Bones

Rochelle Distelheim

Working Woman, April 1983, pp. 141–43.

Osteoporosis—the thinning of the bones through loss of calcium that makes old people break their hips and lose stature—doesn't show up until you're old, but it starts when you're young. Women are more susceptible than men, it seems, but eating enough calcium now and getting plenty of exercise can help preserve your bones.

Osteoporosis. You've seen its effects, even if you haven't known its name. It's the condition that made Aunt Martha fall and break her hip at age 72, that gave Cousin Louise "dowager's hump" in her 60s, that made Grandmother Lewis seem to shrink more and more as she entered her 80s. It happens to women almost three times as often as men and has been widely regarded as an almost inevitable penalty of aging.

Not so. The encouraging news is that, while osteoporosis cannot be "cured," it can be headed off by a calcium-rich diet plus steady exercise; and the earlier we begin the better. The condition (a progressive decline of bone mass) takes place slowly over a long period of time, leaving bones narrower, less dense, more fragile and more vulnerable to fractures. The condition is seen most often in older women, but it starts—silently, and without symptoms—as early as the 30s. "Probably the most important factor in determining if an older woman will break her hip is the amount of bone she has, and there is reason to believe this might be influenced by the amount of calcium in her diet, especially up to age 35," says Robert P. Heaney, MD, vice-president for the health sciences at Creighton University and a member of the American Society for Bone and Mineral Research.

How much calcium is enough? There is some controversy about the accepted RDA (recommended daily allowance, set by the Food and Nutrition Board of the National Academy of Sciences in Washington, DC) of 800 milligrams daily for adults. This is the amount provided by three glasses of milk. Some nutrition experts now believe that is not enough. "The position taken by Dr. Heaney, myself, and others is that 800 milligrams is too low," says G. Donald Whedon, formerly director of the National Institute of Arthritis, Diabetes, Digestive and Kidney diseases. "A more realistic RDA is at least 1,000 to 1,200 milligrams, and possibly more," he says. Heaney cites studies showing that 1,500 milligrams of calcium a day are appropriate for postmenopausal women. "My basic feeling is that if a woman has a good, if not abundant, intake of calcium over the years, beginning in early life, she can slow down osteoporosis. We don't know yet if that will stop it cold, but the evidence suggests that," Whedon says. "As research continues, there is some hope of bone replacement, but at present it is experimental, and our best recommendations are still with regard to retarding bone loss through diet and exercise." What if you are older? According to Spencer, taking calcium still helps to retard osteoporosis, although not as much as it would have if you started taking it earlier.

The second most important measure for preventing the disorder is proper exercise. Robert Rosenzweig, MD, an orthopedic surgeon, points out that women who are generally active and who adhere to a steady schedule of "keeping fit" have much less chance of developing symptoms of osteoporosis than those who are sedentary. He suggests exercises done in an upright position, such as jogging, weight lifting, uphill cycling and even walking, because they place stress on the skeleton and thus stimulate the formation of bone mass. One hour three times a week is an adequate regime. But an hour every day is even better. Rosenzweig, who treats a number of professional athletes, notably the Chicago Stings (a soccer team), cites studies of athletes that have shown that exercise and muscle development lead to denser bones. "Women who place no stress on their skeletons can suffer loss of bone tissue," he says, "as if the body were ridding itself of what it wasn't using."

Practice—Analyzing

1. Who is the main audience for this article? Although you might guess "women" from the title of the magazine, can you be more specific?

   _____

2. What is the main point of the article?

   _____

3. Is the writer equally concerned with informing and persuading? Which effort seems more important? Why?

   _____

4. If you didn't know anything about bones, would you still be able to understand these paragraphs? Why?

_____

5. What do the title and header contribute to your predictions about the

   passage? _____

   What does the header do? _____

   Why would the writer "give away" so much of the article before read-

   ers even begin to read it? _____

6. Do the definition in the header and the examples in paragraph 1 give

   you a vivid image of osteoporosis? _____

READING PARAGRAPHS

Even though we have just seen an example of an article that sets up readers' expectations through its title and introductory section, its paragraphs convey the bulk of the information and make the main effort to persuade readers. Why do we organize our writing so that we have distinct paragraphs rather than one long block of text? Let's look at just what paragraphs do for readers and writers.

Why readers need paragraphs

Just what is a paragraph—for a reader? It's the material between indentations or between blank lines. Both indentations and blank lines signal typographical breaks between chunks of text. Paragraphs can be any length, although we have seen a tendency toward shorter paragraphs in the last 25 years. For readers, specifically, a paragraph represents the information that functions as a logical unit of thought separate from the unit before and after; it represents related ideas put together for some reason.

Why do readers need paragraphs? If you think about all the information you read every day, you must agree that you couldn't possibly remember every tiny detail. But if you relate ideas to one another, if you remember details as they connect to a larger idea, chances are you'll remember more from what you read. Paragraphs help readers organize ideas so that they can remember them and remember more details. Enhancing memory is especially true of paragraphs that have a hierarchical arrangement; that is, the first sentence is the most general and the later sentences are more specific. The general statement gives readers a framework for filing the specific information in memory.

Paragraph indentations signal to readers that related ideas follow. At least some research indicates that readers store information from a single paragraph in short-term memory until the end of the paragraph. Then the most important, reordered ideas get transferred into long-term memory. So readers rely on paragraphs to help them see the logical progression of writers' ideas and to organize what they remember. Without paragraph breaks, readers would struggle to remember what they read at the beginning of the piece: the information would overflow their short-term memory.

How readers use paragraphs

Look again at the paragraphs in the excerpt on "Osteoporosis." What do you notice about the first line in each paragraph? In each case, the first sentence sets up readers for what will appear in the paragraph. The first two paragraphs begin with less fully defined "controlling ideas," but when we read "Osteoporosis" at the beginning of paragraph 1, we predict we'll see a more detailed definition of the term. And that's what appears in the paragraph. Then paragraph 2 builds on the close of paragraph 1, setting up readers to expect counterevidence to an explanation of the claim in paragraph 1 that osteoporosis is the unavoidable penalty of aging.

1. Osteoporosis. You've seen its effects even if you don't know its name.

2. The encouraging news is that, while osteoporosis cannot be "cured," it can be headed off by a calcium-rich diet plus steady exercise; and the earlier we begin the better.

The question at the beginning of paragraph 3 leads readers to expect a paragraph on the controversy of adequate calcium, and paragraph 4 opens with a sentence that leads readers clearly into the discussion of exercise. Although not all essays follow this pattern—with a clear controlling idea stated

3. How much calcium is enough?

4 The second most important measure for preventing the disorder is proper exercise.

at the beginning of each paragraph—many
do because readers need an orientation to the
material. As we said in Chapter 1, readers
need data with which to begin predicting the
course of the reading. An early statement of
the main point of the paragraph is readers'
best aid for early prediction.

The paragraphs from *Working Woman* come from different sections of a four-page article. Nonetheless, because of the direction set up by the topic sentences, readers have no difficulty following the flow of ideas. Not all paragraphs in all essays or documents have controlling ideas stated clearly at the beginning of the paragraph, however. Depending on the subject of the piece, the intended audience, and the goals of the writing, writers may dispense with overt topic sentences. It is probably safe to say, though, that most informative materials—magazine articles, textbook chapters, and so on—have consistent statements of the main points of paragraphs. You'll notice that in many of my paragraphs the main point comes not in the first sentence but in the second or even third sentence. Sometimes the main point is at the end of the paragraph. But most informative material includes an explicit controlling idea for each paragraph. Readers who don't see that idea as the first sentence still expect to see it somewhere in the paragraph.

Why is a topic sentence or controlling idea so important? As I said, with the topic sentence, readers begin predicting the course of the paragraphs, and they begin to relate this material to other knowledge they have on the subject. Moreover, with a controlling idea, readers can organize details into a logical pattern, as I noted in the preceding section.

Readers also use paragraphs to see the logical patterns of the entire essay or article. One handy prereading tip illustrates how much we count on paragraphs for structure. Reading teachers suggest that readers begin by reading headings and first and last sentences of each paragraph before they begin reading a textbook chapter. Not only will they probably pick up most of the main points to help them predict what support will appear in the paragraphs themselves (and remember the main points), but readers will see the chapter's overall design or structure. Readers use paragraphs to cluster related details that fit into the whole picture.

If we concentrate on just one paragraph at a time, readers also bring certain expectations to this kind of writing. Like any other essay, a single-paragraph essay focuses on one main point, usually stated in a topic sentence, and includes detail that coherently and fully develops only that single main point. Readers expect writers to abide by this convention because that is what they count on in reading paragraphs.

Practice—Reading

Read the following paragraphs to determine just how the topic sentences help you as reader:

> Ever since childhood, when I lived within earshot of the Boston and Maine, I have seldom heard a train go by and not wished I was on it. Those whistles sing bewitchment: railways are irresistible bazaars, snaking along perfectly level no matter what the landscape, improving your mood with speed, and never upsetting your drink. The train can reassure you in awful places—a far cry from the anxious sweats of doom airplanes inspire, or the nauseating gas-sickness of the long-distance bus, or the paralysis that afflicts the car passenger. If a train is large and comfortable you don't even need a destination; a corner seat is enough, and you can be one of those travelers who stay in motion, straddling the tracks, and never arrive or feel they ought to—like the lucky man who lives on Italian Railways because he is retired and has a free pass. Better to go first class than to arrive, or, as the English novelist Michael Trayn once rephrased McLuhan: "the journey is the goal."
>
> —Paul Theroux, *The Great Railway Bazaar,* p. 1.

1. Which sentence is the topic sentence? _____

2. Does the topic sentence help you predict the content of the passage?

   _____

3. Does the topic sentence help you organize the information the writer

   includes in the paragraph? _____

4. Does the topic sentence help you tap into your memories and expe-

   riences of trains? _____

5. Do you see any material unrelated to the main point of the

   paragraph? _____

> The signature building of the Harvard Yard was the Widener Library, its gray facade and pillars dominating all the open inner space. Widener was the crownpiece of the largest university library in the world and its architecture made a flat statement: that books and learning were what a school was all about. But the rest of the Yard spoke history. Across the green was the chapel built to commemorate Harvard men fallen in the First World

War, which would, in time, have carved on its tablets the names of thirty-two of my classmates who were to fall in World War II. Across the street from the Yard, on the edge of Cambridge Common, stood the Washington Elm, where, legend claims, George Washington took command of the Continental Army in 1775. Beyond rose the gorgeous Romanesque bulk of "Mem" Hall—the memorial for the veterans of the Civil War. To the north were acres and acres of a university no one person has ever fully explored— law school, graduate schools, museums, laboratories. To the south the residential houses rose along the Charles and there, beneath their turrets of red and blue and yellow, one could lie on the grass beside the slow-flowing Charles River with a friend and gaze at the Harvard Business School across the river. The business school, though few knew it, had its roots in history, too. It had sprung out of the Spanish-American War, when a few public-spirited alumni decided that America, for its new empire, needed a colonial school of administration to match Britain's imperial and colonial civil services. The school they envisioned became, in the course of time, the Harvard Graduate School of Business Administration, eventually fulfilling the imperial dreams of its sponsors by staffing the multinational corporations of the twentieth century.

—Theodore H. White, *In Search of History,* p. 40–41.

1. Which sentence is the topic sentence? _____

   _____

2. Does the topic sentence help you predict the content of the passage?

   _____

3. Does the topic sentence help you organize the information the writer

   includes in the paragraph? _____

4. Do you see any material unrelated to the main point of the

   paragraph? _____

To me my father represents my personal ideal of a hero because of his strong moral character. In raising his children, he exposed us early in life to religious activities. This, he believed, would form the basis by which we could develop our own standards of right and wrong. Thus, in this area, he fulfilled his own moral obligation of giving to his children a philosophical direction in life. To this day, though we are adults, he pointedly tells us when we act in a manner which seems wrong to him. His moral character is further illustrated in his approach to dealing with other people. He believes in treating all people with the dignity and respect they deserve. He is sometimes brutally honest but is, at the same time, sympathetic and caring towards their personal needs. Through his sense of morality, he is incapable of cheating anyone whether they are personal friends or his customers. My father is very predictable and immovable in his moral ideas, and thus my admiration for him endures.

—*Mike M.*

1. Which sentence is the topic sentence? _____

    _____

2. Does the topic sentence help you predict the content of the passage?

    _____

3. Does the topic sentence help you organize the information the writer

    includes in the paragraph? _____

4. Do you see any material unrelated to the main point of the

    paragraph? _____

WRITING PARAGRAPHS

Because we know what readers expect in reading paragraphs, we can use those expectations to write better, more effective paragraphs. First, though, we should examine why writers need paragraphs and how they use them.

Why writers need paragraphs

Writers have somewhat different needs when organizing their ideas, and paragraphs help them impose structure on their thoughts. What is a paragraph for a writer? It's a set of logically related sentences supporting a main idea. It can be of any length, but it must fully develop the main point or topic sentence without overtaxing readers. Writers needs paragraphs to help focus their ideas, develop them fully, and arrange them logically or coherently.

These principles of paragraphs account for the good match between readers' expectations and writers' work. Readers expect one idea per paragraph, and writers observe paragraph *unity*. Readers expect that idea to be narrow, and writers *focus*. Readers expect that single, focused idea to be supported convincingly, and writers *develop* concrete, detailed support. Finally, readers expect orderly arrangement of ideas, and writers observe *coherence* between sentences and from the beginning to the end of the paragraph. The paragraph provides the smallest unit of writing that draws upon all these principles of good writing. Writers must use paragraph principles to communicate clearly with readers.

Practice—Writing

Newspaper articles usually ignore the paragraph principles just outlined. Why? Writers in this context understand that readers will probably not read the entire article and want the most important ideas at the beginning of the article, less important ideas later. Newswriters also assume readers scan rather than carefully read. The more frequent paragraph breaks help readers digest scanned information quickly. But when we retype a news article so that the paragraphs appear not in narrow columns but on standard paper, the short paragraphs can be distracting. Revise the following article to conform to more developed, coherent paragraphs. As you combine ideas, you might consider reducing the number of repetitions.

Toxic Seepage Threatens California Drinking Water

Rocky Mountain News, August 8, 1984, p. 4

Toxic chemicals—including acids, heavy metals and pesticides—are seeping rapidly underground toward drinking water supplies that serve 500,000 people in Southern California, according to a study released Tuesday.

The contamination is headed toward the main flow of the Chino Basin aquifer near Ontario, Calif., and would affect other underground reservoirs in the region that are connected with Chino Basin.

A conservative estimate is that the pollution will enter the main flow within 12 to 18 months, the study says—and it already may be too late to stop it completely.

The study was prepared by G.J. Trezek of the University of California-Berkeley under contract for the congressional Office of Technology Assessment. It paints the bleakest picture to date of the threat posed to drinking water supplies that serve the eastern portion of the Los Angeles basin.

The study was released by three congressmen involved in the debate over what to do about the Stringfellow acid pits near Riverside, Calif., the source of the toxic pollution and California's top priority site under the $1.6 billion "superfund" toxic waste cleanup program.

The congressmen—Reps. John Dingell, D-Mich., chairman of the House Energy and Commerce Committee; James J. Florio, D-N.J., author of the "superfund" law; and George E. Brown Jr., D-Calif., who represents the area—also sent a copy to Environmental Protection Agency chief William Ruckelshaus, along with a letter saying contamination from the site "has reached emergency proportions."

The study said wastes are moving underground toward the aquifer's main flow at a rate of 0.5 to 3.5 feet per day. The latter figure is based on better and more recent data and thus probably is more accurate and may indicate the toxic plume is picking up speed, the study said.

The toxic wastes in the plume include the heavy metals chromium and cadmium, both suspected of causing cancer; acids, which increase the ability of heavy metals to dissolve in water; and pesticides, including DDT.

Some monitoring wells also have shown radioactivity in excess of drinking water standards, even though no radioactive material was supposed to have been dumped at Stringfellow, the study said.

"The contaminant plume has now migrated to the edge of the Chino Basin (aquifer)," the study said. "When its rate of travel is conservatively estimated, it appears the plume will enter the main flow of the basin within the next 12 to 18 months. . . .

"While it may no longer be possible to prevent all pollution of the basin from Stringfellow, attention can be given to limiting the extent of contamination," the study said. But, it added, costly action must be undertaken quickly to remove the wastes at their source.

"Rapid excavation and on-site storage in temporary, above-ground tanks together with more effective pumping downgradient might prevent major contamination of the Chino Basin, if it has not already occurred by some route not yet observed," the study said.

The study said Stringfellow—where between 32 million and 34 million gallons of hazardous liquid wastes were dumped between 1956 and 1972—has been an environmental time bomb virtually since it began operation.

How writers use paragraphs

Obviously, writers use paragraphs to communicate, but the infinite variety of writers and the infinite variety of messages mean that all writers communicate in unique ways. Nonetheless, without certain agreed-upon conventions readers and writers couldn't get past the barriers of their individual differences. So writers use paragraphs to move from a general statement to specific support showing the accuracy of the general observation. Or they move from specific to general. Or they state a topic and give their personal perspective with illustrations. Or they use other approaches. Sometimes they tell stories, describe scenes, give examples, compare and contrast, analyze causes, define, and so on. Depending on the audience and purpose of the writing, writers use paragraphs to organize ideas so that readers extract the meaning writers intend. The difficulty with writing is knowing the best approach for the message being conveyed to a given audience.

In later chapters, we will look at strategies for developing ideas so that you can practice using specific frameworks for your ideas. Having practiced each strategy, you will have some experience to draw on about which strategy works well for certain kinds of messages.

But no matter what the approach, focus, unity, coherence, and development are principles we apply to all good writing. We've already looked at how to focus ideas. Keep techniques for focusing in mind as we discuss the other concepts in more detail.

Practice—Reading

To get some concrete instances of paragraphs in front of us, read the beginning of this lengthy article that appeared in *Health* magazine (if you're interested in finishing the article, the remainder appears at the end of the chapter). In it, readers are introduced to the idea that not only teenagers suffer from drug addiction that can distort behavior.

Grandma Junkies
by Andrew D. Gilman

One cold February morning last year a woman we will call Anna Spencer was found dead in her nightgown on the sidewalk under her 10th-floor apartment window. Anna Spencer was 80 years old and had lived alone for years, but in no sense was she one of the impoverished and neglected elderly whose loneliness and despair might be supposed to make them candidates for suicide. Anna Spencer's married children called her daily, visited her frequently, and if she wanted luxuries her own comfortable income could not provide, they were pleased to supply them. The large co-op complex in which Anna Spencer lived was a haven for older people who could safely visit each other's apartments, join in planned communal activities or sit together in good weather on comfortable benches placed on the park-like grounds. Anna Spencer had many park-bench acquaintances and even some relatives of her own generation there.

Unable to find any other explanation for Anna Spencer's fatal fall from her apartment window, the police listed her death as accidental, but Anna Spencer's son disagrees. "It's not as simple as that," says Max Spencer, who still cannot speak of his mother without coming close to tears. "It wasn't suicide—my mother was a neat and *proper* woman who would never choose to be seen outside in her nightgown under any circumstances. And it wasn't quite crime because what was done to my mother was probably mostly legal. But I think that what happened was that she was so disoriented and confused on legal drugs—medicines—that she just *went* out that window when she didn't know what she was doing. What's the word for that kind of death?"

There are many words for it. One that comes to mind is *tragic.* Another is *unnecessary.* And don't forget *common.* Anna Spencer, mother, grandmother, sister, friend, is unique to her family, but not to doctors, social workers, police and politicians. To them, she is one among many, a member of a growing segment of the American population we may call geriatric junkies. Our own parents, grandparents, relatives, friends—we ourselves in a number of years—are likely candidates for this unexclusive club of older men and women whose perceptions are distorted and whose bodies are malfunctioning thanks to the interactions, effects and side effects of the astonishing number of drugs they consume, with or without doctor's orders. In fact, a 1976 study reported that 30,000 elderly Americans die each year from "drug misadventures." Anna Spencer was one of them.

Anna's "misadventure" was more like an odyssey through a pharmacopoeia. In the last months before her death, Anna Spencer had visited more than 20 doctors, most of them in her immediate neighborhood. Tracing her steps, her family found that she had accumulated several dozen prescription drugs from these physicians. She also had a large supply of over-the-counter medications. Some of the drugs were for relief of angina and other physical problems common to older people considered to be in reasonably good health. Others were potent tranquilizers, laxatives, cold suppressants, sleeping aids. Some of the medications found all over Anna Spencer's apartment by the police and her family could not be identified because they consisted of various capsules, pills and tablets jumbled together in unmarked bottles.

"I know where they came from," says Max Spencer. "Many times when I sat with my mother on the benches outside I would see the other old people swapping pills. I would hear one say, 'This is a good one—try this one,' and give a pill to someone else. It went on all the time. They were just trying to help each other, especially because medicine is so expensive. My mother never traded drugs with anyone in front of me, but she must have been doing it. She was taking crazy amounts of medication, but when I asked her, she'd deny it. What should we have done—had our mother put away as a junkie? Put her into a nursing home when she wanted to live out her life in her own apartment? I don't know how our family could have prevented this—but I do know that something has to be wrong in a society where my mother falls out of a window because her system is full of drugs. . . .

Practice—Analyzing

1. What is the main point or controlling idea of the whole article?

   _____

2. Where do you find a clear statement of that idea?

   _____

Usually we call the controlling idea for a paragraph its *topic sentence* and for an essay its *thesis*. Just as topic sentences help readers organize ideas in paragraphs, thesis statements help readers organize all the ideas in a longer paper.

3. But now we're mainly interested in paragraphs. What is the focus of

   paragraph 1? _____

Remember, we noted that not all paragraphs have an explicit topic sentence at the beginning of the paragraph. Topic sentences can appear anywhere in the paragraph—beginning, middle, or end. And some paragraphs have no topic sentences; frequently, narratives and descriptions don't have topic sentences. So read for what the paragraph is about. What is it concentrating on? If you were taking a picture and had to label all the parts contained by all the sentences in the paragraph, what sentence would you pick as the caption?

Paragraph 1?

_____

Paragraph 2?

_____

Paragraph 3?

_____

Paragraph 4?

_____

Paragraph 5?

_____

Paragraph 1 focuses on Anna's background and living conditions, but the main point is that she was not unhappy or lonely. The knowledge—that the rest of the paragraph will give details to show that she was loved and surrounded by friends—lets readers organize the information. What kind of details does the paragraph include? We see details about her family, friends, neighbors, and "park-bench" acquaintances. What if sentence one had been the topic sentence? Would the details in the rest of the paragraph add up to a logical unit? No, because the rest of the paragraph does not focus on Anna's death. It begins to explore why her death was not suicide, but it does not tie details to the discovery of her body. The *focus* for the paragraph determines what links emerge between sentences in a paragraph. The controlling idea *unifies* all other sentences in the paragraph. At the same time, other sentences that support the focus *develop* the paragraph.

Moving on the paragraph 2, we find a topic sentence at the beginning of the paragraph.

> Unable to find any other explanation for Anna Spencer's fatal fall from her apartment window, the police listed her death as accidental, but Anna Spencer's son disagrees.

Is this focus as precise as the one in paragraph 1? Can you predict from "but her son disagrees" exactly what the rest of the paragraph will be about? Because of the title, readers can make good guesses, but even so, this topic sentence doesn't give precise guidance. Usually readers expect a clearer statement of the main point in the topic sentence. Here, we know only that the son feels his mother's death was not "accidental." Does the rest of the paragraph relate to the focus? Is the paragraph unified around this one main idea? Paragraph unity means that all sentences con-

TRANSITIONAL WORDS AND PHRASES

Logical connection	*Transitions*
Adding ideas	and, also, in addition to, moreover, furthermore, again, another, plus, as well as
Cause/effect	because, due to, as a result of, for, resulting from, so that
Comparing	similarly, in like manner, likewise
Conceding	although, though, even though, granted that, admittedly, obviously
Concluding	so, in conclusion, finally, in summary, to sum up, in short
Contrasting	but, yet, on the other hand, in contrast, nevertheless, however, notwithstanding, nonetheless, instead, rather than, unlike
Giving examples	for example, for instance, in particular, in other words, as an illustration of, a case in point
Emphasizing	indeed, in fact, certainly, clearly, of course, more important, most important, frankly, oddly enough
Hypothesizing	if, as if, whether,
Sequencing	first, second, third, next, then, after, later, meanwhile
Showing results	thus, therefore, hence, then, consequently
Showing time	before, after, until, while, since, when, whenever, till

tribute to the single main point without introducing unnecessary or unrelated material.

How is paragraph 2 put together? Does it give several examples or describe or tell a story? No, it really looks at possible categories or labels for the cause of death and then rejects them. First, Max dismisses suicide and then criminal activity because the drugs were apparently legally prescribed and dispensed. He concludes by asking just what category his mother's death fits into. We might call this a brief classification of types with Max discovering that his mother's death fits into no standard class. But notice how the writer moves from one category to the next. This paragraph exemplifies good *coherence* because readers move smoothly from "it wasn't suicide" to "it wasn't crime" to "it was" an overdose. Gilman could have achieved coherence by using transitional words and phrases—"first" and "second" or "on the one hand" and "on the other hand." Writers create coherence by connecting sentences clearly, either with specific words and phrases (see box on page 71) or with repeated words, synonyms, pronouns, or parallel structure. We'll look again at these devices later.

What kind of development do you see in paragraph 3? After you identify the controlling idea in this paragraph, do you see how the writer is setting readers up for the "pitch" of the rest of the essay? Gilman doesn't drop Anna Spencer from the article, but now he wants readers to understand the problem he's discussing. Especially with his introduction to this paragraph (and transition from the preceding paragraph), he gets readers thinking about "tragic," "unnecessary," and "common," and then he goes on to cite statistics that bring the problem right into readers' homes.

There are many words for it. One that comes to mind is *tragic.* Another is *unnecessary.* And don't forget *common.* Anna Spencer, mother, grandmother, sister, friend, is unique to her family, but not to doctors, social workers, police and politicians. To them, she is one among many, a member of a growing segment of the American population we call geriatric junkies. Our own parents, grandparents, relatives, friends—we ourselves in a number of years—are likely candidates for the unexclusive club of older men and women whose perceptions are distorted and whose bodies are malfunctioning thanks to the interactions, effects and side effects of the astonishing number of drugs they consume, with or without doctor's orders. In fact, a 1976 study reported that 30,000 elderly Americans die each year from "drug misadventures."

Paragraph 4 has interesting details to support the topic sentence. Do you know what a pharmacopoeia is? It's a collection or stock of drugs. Someone taking an odyssey or journey through a stockroom of drugs should have plenty of drugs around. The paragraph goes on to show that. It doesn't list brand names but suggests drugs for heart pains, sleeplessness, tension, constipation, and even the common cold. Could Gilman have used still more details? Would you have liked to know more about the drugs Anna Spencer used or does Gilman make his point with this list? One of the greatest challenges of writing is knowing when you've included enough detail to let readers see why you believe what you do about an issue or why you look at something from a certain perspective. As you read other texts and articles, pay attention to the kind and number of details writers include.

... Tracing her steps, her family found that she had accumulated several dozen prescription drugs. She also had a large supply of over-the-counter medications. Some of the drugs were for the relief of angina and other physical problems common to older people considered to be in reasonably good health. Others were potent tranquilizers, laxatives, cold suppressants, sleeping aids. Some of the medications found all over Anna Spencer's apartment could not be identified because they consisted of various capsules, pills and tablets jumbled together in unmarked bottles.

This article interests me because it begins with a specific case, someone I can see in my mind. It includes quotations from family members, objective facts and statistics, description, and, later, analysis of the problem. I don't have any elderly relatives abusing drugs in this way, but I can imagine the way the problem starts in a culture that advertises drugs of all sorts on television about twice as often as any other kind of product. But this issue is not one I know much about, so I need the *general* background as well as some specific instances to show me that the problem exists.

This, then, is how determining audience and purpose, focusing, and then using paragraph principles structures writing. There's no easy recipe for success in writing, but reading like a writer will give you examples of writers incorporating these principles to get and keep your attention and to help you understand and remember the message.

To give you more practice in identifying paragraph concepts in action, we'll work through revisions of several student paragraphs written about various kinds of addiction.

SAMPLES

Alcohol affects different people in different ways. For example, a good friend of mine, Jim, is usually good-natured and quiet, but after he has had a few beers he becomes very aggressive and mean. Another friend of mine named Randy seems to never be able to tell when he's had enough alcohol. He can be so drunk that he doesn't even know what he's talking about, and yet he still would not consider himself as being under the influence. The only girl I know that drinks alcoholic beverages frequently is Cris. Cris becomes depressed every time she drinks and sometimes even cries. Alcohol affects all my friends in different ways. I think it is impossible to say how alcohol will affect any one person.

Practice—Analyzing

1. What is the stated point of the paragraph? _____

_____

2. Why doesn't "alcohol affects different people in different ways" *focus*

this paragraph? _____

_____

This sentence is the controlling idea now, but it doesn't focus on a narrow point that the writer can develop in detail. A clear, precise topic sentence tells readers exactly what the paragraph contains. Vague words like "nice," "interesting," "fun," and "different" don't give readers a precise focus. And because the paragraph doesn't go on for pages, readers need a tight focus like the picture of lichen mentioned before. The topic sentence should tell precisely who, what, and why.

If you were to begin revising this paragraph, what might you do first? If I had to begin with this material, I would think of it as freewriting that could spark still more brainstorming. So far, this writer has not generated material that addresses the topic of addiction, except that getting drunk reflects an addiction to alcohol. And, with the current controlling idea, this paragraph could go on to describe every person the writer knows. This writer hasn't yet found a focus.

Practice—Writing

Think about alcohol as an addictive drug, and freewrite for at least ten minutes. You needn't focus on any point yet, but, like the preceding writer, you might begin by listing the effects of alcohol on friends. After your first ten minutes, find the main point you have uncovered through freewriting. Use that point to start a second freewriting loop.

Practice—Reading

Alcoholism sneaks up on many people today because media advertising portrays drinking as the natural thing to do. The way alcohol is advertised on TV promotes the idea that alcohol is cool and sexy. Many different athletes are shown drinking beer after some physical activity. One commercial even shows a woman getting sexually aroused after drinking some wine. Radio is constantly airing songs dealing with drinking and how fun it is. Looking in a magazine and finding a picture of someone drinking is quite common. Advertising dealing with alcohol makes up a large part of all advertising. Realizing your own alcoholism is difficult for the most part because of the way that the media make drinking acceptable.

—Bill B.

Practice—Analyzing

Bill has a much better start on his paragraph than the preceding writer. He has focused on alcoholism, not just occasional drinking, to show an addiction. More importantly, he draws a connection between alcoholism and advertising, specifically that the media make drinking acceptable, thus masking alcoholism.

1. Do you think this paragraph is adequately focused to be developed

   in one paragraph? _____

2. Would the paragraph be more effective if it focused on one age- group particularly susceptible to the kinds of advertising Bill mentions?

   _____

3. Are teenagers more likely to listen to top–40 songs about drinking? Are young adult males more likely to be influenced by TV beer ads

   during sporting events? _____

4. How else could you focus this paragraph more precisely? (You might try asking the W questions here.)

   Who?
   What?
   When?
   Where?
   Why?

5. Even if the paragraph were not more narrowly focused, what revi-

sions would you make in the paragraph? _____

_____

Does one other paragraph concept seem to be lacking here? If you answered *development,* you're right. The paragraph isn't effective because readers have to guess about which beer and wine commercials and which songs influence people to think positively about drinking. Moreover, Bill's argument is that the ads show drinking as natural. Unless readers see some details from the ads, we cannot judge if they portray drinking as acceptable or not. We might agree with Bill to begin with, but his paragraph won't convince any reader who doesn't yet agree.

Practice—Writing

List some TV commercials for beer and wine that show drinking in a positive light. Now fill in details for at least three of the commercials. Do the same with billboard or magazine ads. If you can think of songs that promote drinking, jot down lyrics.

Revise Bill's paragraph with specific examples you can detail. You will need to revise the topic sentence to match the specific point your detailed examples make.

Alcoholism sneaks up on many people today because media advertising portrays drinking as the natural thing to do. The way alcohol is advertised on TV promotes the idea that alcohol is cool and sexy. Many different athletes are shown drinking beer after some physical activity. One commercial even shows a woman getting sexually aroused after drinking some wine. Radio is constantly airing songs dealing with drinking and how fun it is. Looking in a magazine and finding a picture of someone drinking is quite common. Advertising dealing with alcohol makes up a large part of all advertising. Realizing your own alcoholism is difficult for the most part because of the way that the media make drinking acceptable.

—*Bill B.*

Practice—Reading

My addiction to acting on my strange whims makes me lose friends as fast as I find them. The summer of '81 I vacationed on the Spanish island, Ibiza. Most of the time I went out with the same group of people, and a Scottish guy in that group, named Bill, became a good friend of mine. All was going well until one day he stood by the pool talking to a girl and had the bag with his photographic equipment over his shoulder and his portable radio in one hand, when I walked by. This looked so tempting that I could not resist. I pushed him into the pool. Even though his friends beat me up and I had to pay him double for his equipment, I could hardly eat the next few days because the memory of seeing my former good friend crawling up from the pool, soaking wet, with his burnt-out radio and his expensive camera already starting to rust, made me continually shake with laughter. A year ago I met a fellow in Grand Junction, Colorado. We had drinks together and found out that we were both headed for the Grand Canyon the next day. We decided to drive together, and about noon the next day we were parked near the edge of a cliff, enjoying the magnificent view. When we had looked all we wanted, we lay down and dozed in the hot sun, but a few minutes later I stood up and said I was just going to stretch my legs. I walked up to his beautiful, shining, red Mustang, put it in neutral, and gave it a little push so it slid down to the edge and zoomed off. Oh, what a sight it was; the car dove down into the canyon like an eagle diving for a rabbit, only it didn't land as softly as an eagle would have. It landed so hard it blew up into a million pieces. I lost my newfound friend there and then as well as my silver Corvette and all my luggage but even though he left me there empty-handed and I had to walk fifty miles to the nearest phone, it was worth every cent and footstep. I laughed all the way at the memory of the surprised and furious look on his face when he saw what had happened.

—*Hordur O.*

Practice—Analyzing

Hordur has found an unusual addiction for his humorous paragraph, but does his topic sentence state exactly the point that his examples make? His examples are nicely detailed and develop a common point clearly. Development is certainly not a problem in this paragraph. But if the point he wants to make is that the strange whim costs him friends, then the two sentences that show his laughter seem out of place. We can call this a problem with *unity* because the topic sentence does not state the idea that each sentence in the paragraph supports. Revising either the topic sentence or the paragraph should be easy, though, because the examples are so strong.

A second problem in the paragraph involves *coherence*. Notice that Hordur jumps from his topic sentence into the first example and jumps from example one to example two without any transitional devices. What

transitional words or phrases might you add to smooth out these connections? Can you think of a way to use repeated words or phrases as transitional elements in this paragraph? Also notice that he does not conclude
the paragraph. He concludes the second example, but he doesn't close the
circle and draw the reader back to the main point of the topic sentence.
Readers generally expect closure, even of so short a piece of writing as a
paragraph. Conclusions tie together the beginning and end of a paragraph.
If writers wouldn't "stop" an essay, they should not make that mistake
with paragraphs. Add a conclusion to Hordur's paragraph.

Do you see any other sentences where Hordur could revise to improve
coherence? Could you cut out any information in sentences 2 and 3 to
improve connections between the topic sentence and the first example?
What can you do to revise the sentence describing Bill's tempting pose
by the pool? Remember, coherence applies not only to connections
between larger units (between paragraphs or sections) but also between
parts of the paragraph and even parts of sentences.

My addiction to acting on my strange
whims makes me lose friends as fast as I find
them. The summer of '81 I vacationed on
the Spanish island, Ibiza. Most of the time I
went out with the same group of people, and
a Scottish guy in that group, named Bill,
became a good friend of mine. All was going
well until one day he stood by the pool
talking to a girl and had the bag with his
photographic equipment over his shoulder
and his portable radio in one hand, when I
walked by. This looked so tempting that I
could not resist. I pushed him into the pool.
Even though his friends beat me up and I
had to pay him double for his equipment, I
could hardly eat the next few days because
the memory of seeing my former good friend
crawling up from the pool, soaking wet, with
his burnt-out radio and his expensive camera
already starting to rust, made me continually
shake with laughter. A year ago I met a
fellow in Grand Junction, Colorado. We had
drinks together and found out that we were
both headed for the Grand Canyon the next
day. We decided to drive together, and about
noon the next day we were parked near the
edge of a cliff, enjoying the magnificent view.

When we had looked all we wanted, we lay
down and dozed in the hot sun, but a few
minutes later I stood up and said I was just
going to stretch my legs. I walked up to his
beautiful, shining, red Mustang, put it in
neutral, and gave it a little push so it slid
down to the edge and zoomed off. Oh, what
a sight it was; the car dove down into the
canyon like an eagle diving for a rabbit, only
it didn't land as softly as an eagle would
have. It landed so hard it blew up into a
million pieces. I lost my newfound friend
there and then as well as my silver Corvette
and all my luggage but even though he left
me there empty-handed and I had to walk
fifty miles to the nearest phone, it was worth
every cent and footstep. I laughed all the way
at the memory of the surprised and furious
look on his face when he saw what had
happened.

—Hordur O.

Practice—Writing

Use the following questions derived from classical topics to generate
more ideas on addiction. You might want to begin with the point on categories so that you have several kinds of addiction you can choose from.
(You might also use the questions as they appear on p. 34.)

What is it?
  give synonyms
  give a dictionary definition
  give an illustrative definition
  make up your own definition
  outline its categories
  give examples of it
What is it like?
  show similarities to other behaviors
  show differences from other behaviors
  show how much it is like or unlike other behaviors

What happens because of it?

   show its causes

   show its effects

   show how it begins

   show how it grows

What do other people have to say about it?

Finally, let's look at an early draft and revised version of a paragraph on still another kind of addiction. Notice how Lisa limits her focus not just to workaholics but to those who are putting in overtime for education. Be aware of words that reflect Lisa's attitude toward this kind of addiction:

Practice—Reading

Some professional people sacrifice themselves in single-minded efforts to attain more education. Luke's determination for furthering his education in preparation for job advancement in his career can be shown in several ways. While most people are still snoring, the jarring jangle of Luke's alarm clock bounces off the walls of his bedroom. The brightly lit den of his house contrasts sharply with the blackness just outside the window, as Luke studies intensely for two to three hours before dawn. When he leaves his study cell, he climbs aboard his red Schwinn and pedals the three miles to Hewlett-Packard where he works as a reputable electrical engineer. After a harrowing day of fielding phone calls, Luke heads homeward to be greeted by the usual and the unusual: the irksome routine of domestic duties, the challenge of facing a still-undone remodeling project on his Victorian home, and the scholastic work associated with a Master's of Business Administration program calling out to him to be done. His friends know not to call, for the phone is off the hook and his engagement calendar allows very little time for social fun until the end of final exam week. Judy, a former graduate student and now a high school English teacher, is suddenly awakened by the early morning wake-up cries of Megan, who is fussing in her crib downstairs. After the baby is quieted, Judy captures a few fleeting but enjoyable moments at the chaotic breakfast table with her student husband, Gary, before he rushes off to attend his university classes. After she leaves Megan at the sitter's, Judy feels the usual pang of selfish guilt and wonders if she's doing the right thing by pursuing her career and her doctorate degree instead of becoming a "domestic engineer" and a full-time mother for Megan. In the evening, amidst papers to be graded, baby toys, and chapters to be read, she tells Gary about an organized escape weekend being made up by a large group of teachers from the high school. Looking up from his book, Gary says, "Sorry, hon, but I have a rough test on Monday and our monstrous tuition bill is due on Wednesday." She thinks of all the fun, the laughter, and the memories she'll miss, but she dreams of the day when the glorious word "Doctor" is placed in front of her name forever, enabling her to get on to bigger and better teaching arenas.

—Lisa K.

Practice—Analyzing

1. Does Lisa feel positively or negatively about this kind of addiction?

   _____

2. Where do you get the strongest impression of her attitude?

   _____

3. One function of the topic sentence or controlling idea of writing based on personal experience is to let readers know exactly what attitude the writer has toward the topic. Has Lisa conveyed her attitude

   clearly in her topic sentence? _____

4. How could you improve her stance? _____

5. Would you improve the focus of the paragraph in any other way?

   _____

6. Assuming that you've discovered what changes you would make in the topic sentence, what else in the paragraph needs attention?

   _____

7. Is development adequate? _____

8. Does Lisa use enough details to show Luke and Judy in action?

   _____

9. What about paragraph unity? Do all sentences relate to the stated

   topic? _____

10. If Lisa has included irrelevant detail, we would call that a unity problem. What connection do you see between the topic sentence and

Luke's remodeling project? _____

11. Is Gary or Judy the focus of the second example? _____

Finally, look at coherence. Like Hordur, Lisa needs transitions between examples. She, too, needs a conclusion to tie the end of the paragraph back to the main point stated in the topic sentence. Draft a conclusion for the paragraph before you read Lisa's revision.

_____

_____

_____

Many ambitious professional people sacrifice themselves in single-minded efforts to attain more education. Luke's determination for furthering his education in preparation for job advancement in his career can be shown in several ways. While most people are still snoring, the jarring jangle of Luke's alarm clock bounces off the walls of his bedroom. The brightly lit den of his house contrasts sharply with the blackness just outside the window, as Luke studies intensely for two to three hours before dawn. When he leaves his study cell, he climbs aboard his red Schwinn and pedals the three miles to Hewlett-Packard where he works as a reputable electrical engineer. After a harrowing day of fielding phone calls, Luke heads homeward to be greeted by the usual and the unusual: the irksome routine of domestic duties, a mailbox full of notes from friends asking whether he is still alive, and the scholastic work associated with a Master's of Business Administration program calling out to him to be done. His friends know not to call, for the phone is off the hook and his engagement calendar allows very little time for social fun until the end of final exam week. Another example of a workaholic professional seeking educational goals is Judy. A former graduate student and now a high school English teacher, she is suddenly awakened by the early morning wake-up cries of Megan, who is fussing in her crib downstairs. After the baby is quieted, Judy captures a few fleeting but enjoyable moments at the chaotic breakfast table with her student husband, Gary, before he rushes off to attend his university classes. After she leaves Megan at the sitter's, Judy feels the usual pang of selfish guilt and wonders if she's doing the right thing by pursuing her career and her doctorate degree instead of becoming a "domestic engineer" and a full-time mother for Megan. In the evening, amidst papers to be graded, baby toys, and chapters to be read, she tells Gary about an organized escape weekend being made up by a large group of teachers from the high school.

Looking up from his book, Gary says, "Sorry, hon, but our monstrous tuition bill is due on Wednesday." She thinks of all the fun, the laughter, and the memories she'll miss, but she dreams of the day when the glorious word "Doctor" is placed in front of her name forever, enabling her to get on to bigger and better teaching arenas. The sacrifices that Luke and Judy are making now may seem unreasonable, but they are determined to reach goals of further knowledge and career advancement.

—*Lisa K.*

Practice—Writing

Now draft your own paragraph on some form of addiction. Remember, this is a first draft; you can revise considerably over several drafts. So concentrate now on getting ideas down and then look carefully at *focus, unity, coherence,* and *development.* Revise to improve these areas with help from your peers and teacher.

Alternative topics

1. Tell the story of how you last broke a bad habit. Be sure to have a point to your story and to include only the details that support this point.
2. When does a preference become an addiction? Write about examples that show the boundary between wanting to do something and being addicted to it.
3. Some psychologists claim that certain people have "addictive personalities." Think of someone you know who is a smoker, a health-food fanatic, a workaholic, or an addict in some other way. Describe the characteristics that make up that person's "addictive personality."
4. How can someone hooked on cigarettes, work, video games, or some other unhealthy behavior get over the addiction? Outline in a humorous paragraph how you would help someone "kick a habit."

Practice—Revising Paragraphs for Focus, Unity, Coherence, and Development

Each of the following paragraphs has weaknesses in different paragraph skills. Identify the weaknesses and suggest possible revisions for each. Note that many students find focus and development are the most difficult paragraph skills to master. Consider especially how you might more carefully focus topic sentences and add appropriate detail to the body of the paragraph.

My younger brother Steven should look for a part-time job because his afternoons are free, therefore giving him a great deal of time to accomplish a skill. An incident of this was when my father was racing stock cars. Dad needed an engine hoist, and Steven had a little background in welding. It took Steven two months to complete, but the job he did was magnificent. The welds at every corner looked like a professional had done the work. Welding is something Steven loves to do. There is a smile from ear to ear on his face when he completes a project. Another incident was when Steven decided to weld and build a tool box for Dad and give it to him on Father's Day. Steven worked two to three hours every day for two weeks. When he was finished, the red tool box shone and so did the expression on Steven's face. Steven receives a great deal of self-worth when he has accomplished a project. He enjoys welding and has discovered a valuable skill. Steven would accomplish a skill and be paid for it.

—*Diane I.*

Many skills we are taught in life are explained first but can only be mastered by actually doing the process. For example, in my drawing class we are told to draw with a conte crayon. At first our drawings are choppy and unskilled, but through practice with the crayon we learn to use the medium well. Another example is driving. One must sit behind the wheel and actually drive a car in order to learn how to handle it with confidence. Still another illustration can be shown with gymnastics. A cartwheel can only be learned by actually doing it because one needs to know how to manipulate the body. In conclusion, the explanation of a skill is necessary for learning, but the real teacher is working through the skill by doing it yourself.

—*Jennifer H.*

I find that the method "rehearsal buffer," which means to continue to review the material, and the method of chunking work best for me because I am able to learn more efficiently and effectively. For example, let's say I'm studying for a history test which involves an endless list of names and dates. If I were to continue to rehearse the list and put it into chunks, meaning to learn six names and dates at a time, I would be able to memorize the list and automatically respond to any given question on the test. I have proven these methods of learning in almost every class I've taken and they've always been helpful, especially when these are self-taught skills of my own. Rehearsal buffer and chunking are two skills of learning that have worked to my advantage in studying, and because of these two methods I am able to learn any material efficiently and very effectively.

—*Susie P.*

Grandma Junkies

Andrew D. Gilman

One cold February morning last year a woman we will call Anna Spencer was found dead in her nightgown on the sidewalk under her 10th-floor apartment window. Anna Spencer was 80 years old and had lived alone for years, but in no sense was she one of the impoverished and neglected elderly whose loneliness and despair might be supposed to make them candidates for suicide. Anna Spencer's married children called her daily, visited her frequently, and if she wanted luxuries her own comfortable income could not provide, they were pleased to supply them.

Anna Spencer lived in the Bronx, a section of New York City that has a bad name for crime, but the police investigation of her death showed no evidence of robbery or violence; indeed, the large co-op complex in which Anna Spencer lived was a haven for older people who could safely visit each other's apartments, join in planned communal activities or sit together in good weather on comfortable benches placed on the park-like grounds. Anna Spencer had many park-bench acquaintances and even some relatives of her own generation there.

Unable to find any other explanation for Anna Spencer's fatal fall from her apartment window, the police listed her death as accidental. But Anna Spencer's son disagrees. "It's not as simple as that," says Max Spencer, who still cannot speak of his mother without coming close to tears. "I'm not saying it was suicide—my mother was a neat and *proper* woman who would never choose to be seen outside in her nightgown under any circumstances. And it wasn't quite crime because what was done to my mother was probably mostly legal. But I think that what happened was that she was so disoriented and confused on legal drugs—medicines— that she just *went* out that window when she didn't know what she was doing. What's the word for that kind of death?"

There are many words for it. One that comes to mind is *tragic.* Another is *unnecessary.* And don't forget *common.* Anna Spencer, mother, grand-mother, sister, friend, is unique to her family, but not to doctors, social workers, police and politicians. To them, she is one among many, a mem-ber of a growing segment of the American population we may call geria-tric junkies. Our own parents, grandparents, relatives, friends—we our-selves in a number of years—are likely candidates for this unexclusive club of older men and women whose perceptions are distorted and whose bodies are malfunctioning thanks to the interactions, effects and side effects of the astonishing number of drugs they consume, with or without doctor's orders. In fact, a 1976 study reported that 30,000 elderly Amer-icans die each year from "drug misadventures." Anna Spencer was one of them.

In the last months before her death, Anna Spencer had visited more than 20 doctors, most of them in her immediate neighborhood. Tracing her steps, her family found that she had accumulated several dozen pre-scription drugs from these physicians. She also had a large supply of over-the-counter medications. Some of the drugs were for relief of angina and other physical problems common to older people considered to be in rea-sonably good health. Others were potent tranquilizers, laxatives, cold suppressants, sleeping aids. Some of the medications found all over Anna Spencer's apartment by the police and her family could not be identified because they consisted of various capsules, pills and tablets jumbled together in unmarked bottles.

"I know where they came from," says Max Spencer. "Many times when I sat with my mother on the benches outside I would see the other old people swapping pills. I would hear one say, 'This is a good one—try this one,' and give a pill to someone else. It went on all the time. They were just trying to help each other, especially because medicine is so expensive. My mother never traded drugs with anyone in front of me, but she must have been doing it. She was taking crazy amounts of medication, but when I asked her, she'd deny it. What should we have done—had our mother put away as a junkie? Put her into a nursing home when she wanted to live out her life in her own apartment? I don't know how our family could have prevented this—but I do know that something has to be wrong in a society where my mother falls out of a window because her system is full of drugs."

Max Spencer has good reason for bewilderment and frustration. His emotions are shared by many experts who are also struggling to find a solution to a vast and growing problem. At present there are more than 7,000 prescription drugs and over 100,000 over-the-counter (OTC) medications available in this country—and the U.S. Food and Drug Administration (FDA), which authorizes them, has never insisted that they be specially tested to determine proper dosages for the elderly, even though it is recognized that for various metabolic reasons older people need lower doses of most drugs, larger doses of some, and can be seriously mismedicated on standard prescriptions.

This is most dismaying in light of the fact that although Americans over the age of 65 make up only 11 percent of our current population, they take more than 25 percent of all prescription drugs. The average *healthy* senior citizen takes at least 11 different prescription medicines in the course of a year. To compound the problem still further, we know that medications can have such potent side effects that the cost of drug-induced hospital visits for Americans of ALL ages is $21 billion a year—and a person over age 60 is two to seven times more likely than a younger patient to suffer adverse side effects.

Nor is this all. At a recent joint House/Senate hearing on drug use and abuse, Rep. Claude Pepper (D-Florida) said, "Studies show that up to half of those patients over the age of sixty-five do not take their prescriptions as instructed; about ten percent never get them filled. Thirty-five percent leave the doctor's office with no information on the drugs; seventy-four percent are not told about possible side effects and only six percent get written information on the drug."

"The problem is so complicated," says Jonathan Leiff, MD, a psychiatrist and geriatrics specialist at Hahnemann Hospital, Boston. "The elderly have a lot more illnesses than the general population. Because of that, they take more drugs. When you're taking six to seven medications, each three or four times a day, who remembers how to take this antibiotic or that diuretic?"

Finally, according to Robert Butler, MD, chairman of the department of geriatrics and adult development at Mt. Sinai Hospital and Medical School in New York City and author of the Pulitzer Prize-winning book, *Why Survive: Being Old in America,* most physicians do not receive adequate training to enable them to deal effectively with elderly patients. Only 15 out of 127 medical schools in this country require courses in geriatric medicine, and Mt. Sinai is one of only three or four that have formal departments in that interdisciplinary field.

Clearly, there is no single villain in the tragedy of Anna Spencer. The doctors her family traced claimed that Anna Spencer never told them she was seeing other physicians or taking medications besides the ones they prescribed—and that may be true. On the other hand, few of them claimed to have exerted themselves to get such information from her. Some may have prescribed medications she didn't really need in the hope of calming her flow of complaints about a variety of vague symptoms. Few probably made sure she knew how the drugs they prescribed acted or what side effects they might cause—alone or together.

Similarly, only one of the pharmacists Anna Spencer used kept a patient profile on his elderly customers to warn them of dangerous drug interactions—and of course, Anna Spencer did not get all her medications in one place. The FDA, which has not insisted on tested dosages for older patients, may bear part of the blame, as do Anna Spencer's well-meaning friends who contributed to the stock of medications that fuddled her mind and interfered with her balance. And so, of course, does Anna Spencer herself, stubbornly going from doctor to doctor, pill to pill, perhaps in the hope of finding the impossible: the cure for growing old.

"But it's of no real value to point fingers," says Peter Lamy, PhD, professor and director of the Center for the Study of Pharmacy and Therapeutics for the Elderly at the University of Maryland School of Pharmacy in Baltimore. Lamy believes that a great deal of information that can help the elderly has already been accumulated. "We have to disseminate what we know," he says. "The information has yet to trickle down to the people who need it. There's no one way to address the problem. It requires concerted, consistent effort by all involved."

Some efforts are already underway. One is Up Front, a drug information center in Miami, Florida, where many older people live. According to Jim Hall, the director of Up Front, more than 33 percent of all calls coming into its drug hotline are not from youngsters involved in drug abuse but from older citizens who simply want basic information about their medicines. "What are seniors asking for?" Hall says. "They want to know what their prescription medications are for, what side effects they may have, and if they can safely combine various medicines. Nearly half the callers are taking two or more medications at the time of the call.

"One recent caller, a very confused and worried Mrs. J., asked us about *thirteen* medications prescribed by four different doctors, plus two more prescriptions she had not yet filled. She told us that she takes pills from Dr. A. on Tuesday, Dr. B. on Monday and Thursday, and from Dr. C. whenever she feels the need. After checking her list, we advised Mrs. J. that she was in real danger of falling into a depressant overdose, and we suggested that she take all her medications to her pharmacist to straighten out the situation," Hall says. "Since we are an anonymous assistance agency I don't know what happened to Mrs. J. However, many of our callers do let us know that they are doing better."

In addition to direct-contact groups like Up Front, various public and private organizations are attempting to disseminate information and prevent disasters. Among them:

- The newly formed National Council on Patient Information and Education has released public service television ads encouraging consumers to ask their pharmacists for information about prescription drugs they buy.
- The American Association of Retired Persons (AARP) Pharmacy Service has produced a series of Medication Information Leaflets (MILS) distributed through pharmacies. Forty-five are already available, offering information on 150 drugs. MILS report the various names under which the medication is sold, the conditions for which it is prescribed and the side effects and interactions with food and alcohol that may occur, and tell patients what information to give their doctors to prevent problems.
- For $.50 per pad, the American Medical Association will provide doctors with special prescription pads that list the side effects and risks of many frequently prescribed medications.
- A program called ElderCare, designed to inform pharmacists about the specific problems of geriatric customers, has been initiated by the Parke-Davis Division of the Warner Lambert Company. Another pharmaceutical house, Hoffmann-LaRoche, has a Medication Education program in operation, and a number of other drug companies are developing programs.
- At the University of Maryland School of Pharmacy, Lamy heads an Elder-Health program that sends students to visit senior citizens in community centers and nursing homes. Other pharmacy schools are following suit.
- Many pharmacies now employ computers to maintain patient profiles and give warnings of drug interactions.

- Last summer, at the request of the FDA, warning messages and advice about drug use were inserted into 36 million Social Security check envelopes, 60 percent of which went to elderly Americans. Then-FDA Commissioner Arthur Hull Hayes Jr. also sent out a letter on the topic to 110,000 physicians.

- Perhaps most important, individual doctors and pharmacists are becoming more aware of the problem and taking increased pains to see that their patients and clients do not become geriatric junkies.

One patient whose life was saved by timely medical intervention is 67-year-old Rose Zimny of Everett, Massachusetts. "At the peak of my illness," Rose Zimny told a Congressional inquiry, "I could not walk. I had lost control of most of my bodily functions. I felt like I had the mind of a three-year-old." What caused these disabilities? Dramatically, Rose Zimny spread out on a table the contents of three shopping bags filled with medications. "I was taking more than forty pills in twenty-four hours," she said. The doctors who prescribed the medications, she went on, did not encourage her to ask about them; in fact, they made it plain they did not want questions. The pharmacists who filled the prescriptions did not consider it proper to question the doctors' judgment. Nonetheless, Rose Zimny was more fortunate than Anna Spencer. Her case was brought to the attention of physicians who took prompt action, withdrawing Rose Zimny from virtually all her medications. Today she takes only three or four necessary drugs for asthma and a nervous disorder. Her health has been restored.

chapter 4
From the paragraph to the essay

WHY CONCENTRATE ON PARAGRAPHS?

Since essays and longer papers are more common forms of writing, you might wonder why writers should concentrate on learning to write paragraphs. As you've seen already, paragraphs are like the building blocks of longer papers. Though readers expect to read an entire paper, letter, or document, they do so one paragraph at a time. Readers expect paragraphs to cluster ideas meaningfully to make the paper easier to understand. And so practicing how to write paragraphs makes writing essays easier. As you work your way through this text, you may occasionally want to write single paragraphs, but you may also want to write essays. This chapter will help you to see how you can explore ideas differently in shorter and longer papers.

WHEN DO WE USE THE SINGLE
PARAGRAPH IN COLLEGE WRITING?

As you have probably noticed by now, when professors in any discipline give an "essay" test, they often include several questions that students respond to. More often than not, students can write successful answers in just one paragraph. Some teachers call these "short-answer essays," but we can call them single-paragraph essays. Because writers answering test questions in an hour just don't have much time to develop ideas at great length, the single paragraph is a convenient form to use for such tests.

But tests are not the only places where single paragraphs are useful and appropriate forms for writing. Think of lab reports: the sections introducing the experiment, describing the lab setup, and reporting simple conclusions might all be single paragraphs. Similarly, in any classes, summaries of assigned articles can often occur in single paragraphs. Update notes for case studies, descriptions of extracurricular activities on applications, and many other writing situations demand the focused, crisp *paragraph* rather than a longer response.

WHEN SHOULD A WRITER CHOOSE TO
WRITE AN ESSAY INSTEAD OF A SINGLE
PARAGRAPH?

Think back to our discussions of audience, purpose, and focus. If your readers expect exhaustive treatment of a narrow subject for some specific purpose, you can probably write a single paragraph. But if you are writing to explain a more complex or broader topic, then you will have to write a longer paper. Though readers can comprehend extremely long paragraphs, our common practice nowadays is to write shorter paragraphs, partly because newspapers have adopted the practice of including just one or two sentences in each short paragraph. Two hundred years ago, paragraphs might go on for several pages, and readers were accustomed to keeping those ideas in mind for that long. But readers now expect shorter paragraphs, generally about 100 to 300 words at most. If you have a topic that will require more than about 300 words, you should think about writing an essay rather than a single paragraph.

The attention span of readers is not your only concern either. Think about why you are writing. If you have two or three points to make, readers will see those points more clearly if you separate each into its own paragraph. Paragraphs are signals to readers that ideas clustered into the paragraph belong together logically. As a writer, then, you decide how to cluster ideas by how you mark paragraphs. If you want to include three points in a paragraph, you certainly can, but those points usually get less detailed development if they are included in a single paragraph. If each of the points needs more development than you can provide in one or two sentences, then you should probably consider putting each point in its own paragraph. You signal the importance of points by the level of detail you use to support them.

For example, read this long paragraph that would be easier to organize mentally if it were broken into shorter paragraphs.

Practice—Reading

My Solution for Stress

Handling stress and minimizing its harmful effects on the body may take a little more effort than a quiet walk through the park or meditating in an empty room. My release valve for stress is an aggressive hour of shooting baskets. I first discovered basketball was an effective combatant for stress one day at the park. I wasn't taking my shots very seriously, more or less just passing the time away, carelessly lobbing the ball through the hoop. When I was through, I went back to my car where I found a note lying on the seat. It was from a lovely lady whom I had been seeing for some time. The letter was brief and to the point. She had "fallen in love" with another, and our relationship was "history." My frustration grew with each shocking word. It hurt to think that she could be so insensitive as to just drop a note on the seat of my car without even giving me the chance to respond. I crumpled the note and tossed it onto the floor of my car and then angrily picked up the basketball and hurtled it across the court against a tree. As I walked to retrieve the ball, I kicked at the small rocks at my feet. A rage was growing inside my stomach. I picked up the ball and hooked it toward the basket—swish, into the hoop. I raced for the rebound, scooped the ball up and laid it in for another two points. The next thing I knew, the evening lights were coming on and I was soaking wet with sweat. I had gotten so consumed in my play that I had burned out all the stress. Although I was still angry and hurt, the aggressive workout enabled me to see things more rationally. At the time, I wasn't really sure that playing basketball was the medicine I suspected it to be. I wanted to test my theory, but those stressful situations don't always conveniently pop up. Summer employment isn't normally too stressful, but the summer that I landed a job on a private golf course proved to be the test that I was looking for. I was the youngest maintenance man hired—16—and the other seven members of the crew had been seasonal for several years. At first, I didn't mind pulling weeds in the sand traps or whistling down the overgrowth around the lakes, but after a while, I became frustrated that I always got stuck doing jobs no one else wanted to do. Still, I waited to complain until I had rooted myself in the company. Then one day, the duty schedules were handed out and mine read like a prison sentence. I had been assigned the pleasant job of raking the sand traps and digging a drainage ditch from one of the greens. I knew that it was almost time. I went out and neatly raked all 62 sand traps. By the time I was at the last trap I was so tense that I could have raked it with my fingers. I could feel the tension grow with each stroke of the rake. On my way back down to the shop to trade my rake for a shovel, I decided I would plead my case. My boss was understanding, but not compromising. Our discussing turned to arguing, and I ended up quite angry, with shovel in hand. I arrived at the number 6 green where the digging was to occur. I leaped from my cart and violently plunged the shovel blade into the soil. Shovelful after shovelful I grumbled about my situation. The stress grew enormously. I felt like a steam kettle ready to explode, and I was one more shovelful from quitting my job. But I saw by the hands on my watch that it was lunchtime, and almost at the same instant I remembered that I had my basketball in my car and there was a net at the clubhouse. For the entire hour I pounded myself against the hot sun. I extended my throws, netting shots like I never had before. After my vigorous workout, I headed back to my dismal task, but when I got there, to my surprise, there were four other guys to help me. Once again, basketball had gotten me over that irrational hump caused by stress. I now carry a basketball in my car nearly all the time—for medicinal purposes only—and while I know that it doesn't solve my problems, shooting hoops aggressively does help me overcome the stress associated with them.

—*Roy S.*

Practice—Analyzing

1. Where would you break this single paragraph essay into more

   paragraphs? _____

   _____

   _____

2. Why would more paragraphs help readers get through Roy's essay?

   _____

   _____

   _____

3. What is the focus of Roy's paper? _____

   _____

4. Would dividing the paragraph into several paragraphs change the focus? Why? _____

_____

5. Would dividing the paragraph into several paragraphs improve coherence in the essay ? Why? _____

_____

_____

6. If you divided the essay into several paragraphs, where would you delete details now included? Where would you add details? _____

_____

_____

_____

7. If you divided the essay into several paragraphs, would you need to expand the introduction to the essay? Why? _____

_____

_____

A Reminder: Paragraphs Help Readers

As you can see from Roy's paper, paragraphs help readers cluster ideas meaningfully. Although readers can understand and remember extremely long paragraphs (Roy's paper even included another long example in its earlier drafts), writers should help readers by breaking up longer paragraphs if an essay will make the point clearer for readers. Moreover, Roy includes plenty of detail in his paragraph, but because the reader gets no break to separate background information from the actual situations of stress, some of Roy's well-detailed points get lost in this long paragraph. So remember, help your readers by giving them a clear structure for ideas through your paragraph breaks.

Practice—Breaking up long paragraphs

Indicate with a paragraph symbol (¶) where you would break each of the following single-paragraph essays into shorter paragraphs. Then answer the questions following each sample.

Professional Determination

Many ambitious professional people sacrifice themselves because of their determination to reach a goal in higher education. Luke shows his single-minded determination to further his education as a means to advance his career. While most people are still snoring, the jangle of Luke's alarm clock bounces off the walls of his bedroom. The brightly lit den of his house contrasts sharply with the blackness just outside the window, as Luke studies intensely for two to three hours before dawn. When he leaves his study cell, he climbs aboard his red Schwinn and pedals the three miles to Hewlett-Packard Company where he works as a reputable electrical engineer. After a harrowing day of fielding phone calls and debugging computer programs, Luke heads homeward to be greeted by the usual and the unusual: the irksome routine of domestic duties, a mailbox full of notes from friends asking whether he is still alive, and the scholastic work associated with a Master's of Business Administration program calling out to him to be done. His friends know not to call, for the phone is off the hook and his engagement calendar allows very little time for social fun until the end of finals' week. Another example of a determined professional is Judy. A former graduate teaching assistant and now a Berthoud High School English teacher, she is suddenly awakened by the early morning wake-up cries of Megan, who is fussing in her crib downstairs. After the baby is quieted, Judy captures a few fleeting but enjoyable moments at the chaotic breakfast table with her student husband, Gary, before he rushes off to attend his classes. After she leaves Megan at the sitter's, Judy feels the usual pang of selfish guilt and wonders if she's doing the right thing by pursuing her career and her doctoral degree instead of becoming a "domestic engineer" and a full-time mother for Megan. In the evening, amidst papers to be graded, baby toys, and chapters to be read, she tells Gary about an organized "escape weekend" to Jackson Hole being made by a large group of teachers from BHS. Looking up from his *Fish Biology* text, Gary says, "Sorry, hon, but I have a rough test on Monday and our monstrous tuition bill is due on Wednesday." She thinks of all the fun, laughter, and memories she'll miss, but she dreams of the day when the glorious word "Doctor" is placed in front of her name forever, enabling her to get on to bigger and better teaching arenas. The sacrifices that Luke and Judy are making now may seem unreasonable, but they are determined to reach a goal of further knowledge; I think they're both well on their way toward this and other related goals.

—Lisa K.

1. Having marked paragraphs, do you need to add details to any body paragraphs? What might you suggest to Lisa?

_____

_____

2. Having marked paragraphs, do you need to suggest revisions of connectors between and within body paragraphs?

_____

_____

3. Do you think Lisa needs a fuller introduction to her essay? Jot down some ideas that might fit into the intro.

_____

_____

_____

_____

4. Does Lisa also need a fuller conclusion? Again, jot down a possible conclusion.

_____

_____

_____

_____

New-Found Friends

For me a short-term relationship with new-found friends can be exciting and a way to let my imagination go without the worry of condemnation. For example, when I was about ten, my father brought home his boss' red-haired, freckle-faced daughter to play with me. I took her outside to play on my swingset, and while flying through the sky I told her my uncle was a millionaire and he had taken me to Hollywood to meet my idol, Elvis Presley. I watched her expressionless face change into an expression of exquisite delight because she had actually met someone who personally knew Elvis. I decided to stretch the truth a bit more, so I told her I had given Elvis a kiss right on the lips! She was overwhelmed with this thought and she kept saying, "I don't believe it; it couldn't be true," when I knew she had taken every word I had said to heart. I knew my freckle-faced friend would spread this enchanting tale to every friend she had, but I didn't care because I would never see her again. Another time when I let my imagination get the best of me was when I was twelve. My mother, two sisters, and I were traveling to California for a vacation when we stopped for the night at a Motel 6 in Santa Fe, New Mexico. Since the motel had a pool, my younger sister and I decided to go for a swim. While in the pool, we met two girls, also sisters, on vacation with their parents to visit an aunt in Denver. After we introduced ourselves, we began to tell something about ourselves. My sister and I created an exciting story about our father. We told them that he was a trapper in South Africa and was tracking down elephants to get their tusks for ivory. The girls' eyes grew bigger as our story grew longer. By the time the story ended, we had our imaginary safari father trapping cougars, lions, and panthers for personal pleasure. The girls couldn't believe what they had heard, and we couldn't believe what we had said, but we didn't care because we knew we would never see these girls again; besides, who was going to say our story wasn't legitimate? One other occasion when I got a chance to use my clever imagination was on a girl standing next to me at the Denver airport. My mother and I had gone to pick up my cousin who was coming to stay with us for a while. When we finally found the right gate, my mother sat down and began reading the newspaper, but I decided to stand by the big bay windows and watch the planes land and take off. I was soon joined by a girl with blonde, curly hair who resembled Shirley Temple. She was about two years my junior, my being an adult, mature fifteen at the time. We began to talk of unimportant subjects—the weather, school, celebrity gossip—when my imagination got in the way. Since I knew we would never meet again, I told Miss Temple about my boyfriend I was waiting for. I told her that he was an older man of eighteen and had been in Hollywood making a screen test for an upcoming movie. I built my cousin up bigger than John Wayne. Just by the mystified look in her eyes, I could tell she envied me, and I ate up every bit of it. I began to drag the story on when the doors of the terminal swung open and out stepped my cousin. I ran up and gave him a great big kiss on the cheek. With my arms still around his neck, I waved to the blonde girl who simply smiled in admiration. Once again I had let my imagination go to get a little bit of excitement in return. Short-term relationships can have a rewarding effect on your ego, let alone your imagination, to create such tales. I knew in each one of these situations that I would not be questioned about whether the story I was telling was true or not; after all, why would these people doubt me when they didn't even know me.

—*Julie L.*

1. Having marked paragraphs, do you need to add details to any body paragraphs? What might you suggest to Julie?

_____

_____

2. Having marked paragraphs, do you need to suggest revisions of connectors between and within body paragraphs?

   _____

   _____

3. Do you think Julie needs a fuller introduction to her essay? Jot down some ideas that might fit into the intro.

   _____

   _____

   _____

   _____

4. Does Julie also need a fuller conclusion? Again, jot down a possible conclusion.

   _____

   _____

   _____

   _____

HOW ARE ESSAYS LIKE PARAGRAPHS?

Let's compare essays and paragraphs by referring to one sample of each form. Read these two samples carefully, and think to yourself how they are alike and different.

On Your Own

Moving away from home and going to college is an experience that teaches a person how to become independent and do particular tasks on his own. When I lived at home with my parents, everything was easy under their guidance. My mother would put warm, delicious food on the table for me three times a day. I could thoroughly enjoy my meals in the comfort of my own home. Now that I am at college, I have to walk across the courtyard at three specific times each day to eat reheated casseroles and starchy potatoes. Handling your own money can be a difficult task too. When I was at home I always had my parents to help me with my banking and money problems. Now that I am on my own, I have to learn how to do this by myself. I am now teaching myself how to manage my money and make it go as far as I can. I am also learning how to use a checkbook and balance it diligently. A great luxury of home that I had to give up when I went away to school was having my mother do my laundry. Every week at home I had no problem at all finding a clean shirt or an unused pair of underwear. At college I realized that this was now my job. After making a white shirt pink and creating new sizes for some t-shirts, I soon became an expert at this task by learning from my mistakes. In the last two months I have learned how to do many different tasks and handle different circumstances on my own. I have become used to living away from home, and that has made me more independent than I have ever been.

—*Jeff P.*

Formula for Success?

Imagine your goal as the target, and the path you take to reach your goal as the flight pattern. Think of yourself as a self-guided missile, charging forward toward your goal, using your radar to range the target, making small adjustments in the flight plan as you encounter unexpected obstacles, until finally you have reached your goal. You have succeeded.

One analogy I have frequently heard, especially when I was in high school, concerns the pursuit of a specific goal for a person's life. Dr. Maxwell Maltz said that we all have a "built-in goal-striving device with which to achieve our goals." Dr. Maltz further said, "I call this creative psycho-cybernetics, or steering your mind to a productive goal." The analogy that Dr. Maltz uses in his book *Psycho-Cybernetics,* and which has been played up by the popular self-help book industry, is that attaining one of your life goals is simple, (just as easy as fantastic weight loss); reaching your goal is just like a guided missile seeking its target. A missile is given a "look" at its target, then is fired. As the missile moves toward the target, it uses radar to see how close it is and corrects its course several times before it reaches its goal, the target. Using this analogy to show how a person should set goals for his or her life is not a bad idea, until one looks more closely at the implications of this analogy, especially when it is all that is taught (or learned) about reaching goals.

By implying that this self-motivation system is present in all of us and only needs activation and practice, we demean the accomplishments of mankind. The people who most need to make and pursue goals are tempted to be lazy about them because these people have heard that achieving goals is all built-in (like an autopilot) and achieving goals will just happen.

The analogy also emphasizes that the course the person takes to reach the goals will constantly change, and the person will change with it. It implies nothing about changing the goal to fit a changing person. When the missile is fired, it will spend its entire "life" seeking that one goal and will either succeed or fail. I have friends who have evidently heard this theory for success. One has no real talent for engineering and is hanging on by a thread, if even that, but he is willing to hang on by that thread because he perceives that to do anything else is to be a failure. He has his autopilot set on a career in engineering, and he will not waver from that target whatsoever, no matter how impractical the target is. Whenever grades are going bad, engineering students joke about transferring out of the engineering school into forestry, saying in effect, "if I can't make it here, I know I can make it there." This attitude implies that forestry is an easy major, and probably is easier than engineering for most people, but the real meaning here is that for those who strictly adhere to this analogy—who now have incorporated the analogy into their philosophy—success does not happen in degrees, but rather is absolute. You've either succeeded or failed; there are no gray areas. Isn't this a simplistic view of life?

If followed blindly, this analogy can inhibit the goal-seeker from achieving his or her goal by leaving the impression that to be a success, one must fanatically follow the detailed guidelines that were mapped out and then must re-evaluate those guidelines periodically. (The onboard computer frequently sends out radar signals and corrects its course, based on the most recent information it has.) This doesn't give much room for intuition, spontaneity, and creativity in pursuing a goal that moves off the primary target. As I look around, I see people whose goals have been taken so seriously that they have no (or few) other interests and specifically have "no time" to pursue anything else. John Lennon said, "Life is what happens to you while you're busy making other plans." These goal-seekers have become egocentric and narrow-minded, and their attitude is best expressed in their standard question, "What's in it for me?" Every time they have the chance to get involved in worthwhile, developmental activities that stray off the outlined path, they decide against growth and stick to their established doctrine.

Yes, I understand that we need specialization in today's complex society, and I respect those who have dedicated themselves to their specialized fields and are truly successful in them. But some of these people, though "occupationally" successful, are not getting their money's worth from life, because they were led to believe they could only pursue a limited set of goals, perhaps only one at a time, and if they wanted to be successful they couldn't stray off that plan. Is this one of the causes of so many abrupt career changes in our society? Why do people suddenly start a new, unrelated career after decades in the old one? Do people set goals so early that they grow out of their enthusiasm and interest before they reach the goal and yet refuse to change the goal? Why is it that some achievers get to the top of the "mountain" just to quit and "go back to basics?" Why do some self-destruct just when they appear to be great successes (just like the "successful" missile does when it reaches its target)?

If the analogy were different, how would the attitudes and perceptions of goal-setters and goal-setting be different? Here's an alternative analogy. How about the analogy that goal-setting is like a shotgun fired at a group of targets? If your aim is on, you can expect to hit several goals (targets) at once. The goals are closer, too, and you can see them and correct your aim if needed. You have the chance to reload and try again, as well. An analogy should be a tool used to attain goals, not a philosophical cure-all for living.

—*Chuck D.*

Beginning, middle, and end

Like the paragraph, the essay has a beginning, middle, and end. In a paragraph, the beginning may be one or two introductory sentences or even the topic sentence; the middle includes supporting details; the end wraps up the paragraph by pointing back to the topic sentence. In an essay, the beginning is generally a brief introductory paragraph with the thesis as the final sentence; the middle of an essay consists of one or more paragraphs of details; the end, generally a short paragraph of about the same length as the introductory paragraph, wraps up the essay by pointing back to the thesis. In both the paragraph and essay, the end usually does not summarize because unless the essay is very long readers do not need a summary. (See the section following on introductory and concluding paragraphs.)

BEGINNING

Jeff	Chuck
Moving away from home and going to college is an experience that teaches a person how to become independent and do particular tasks on his own.	Imagine your goal as the target and the path you take to reach as the flight pattern. Think of yourself as a self-guided missile, charging forward toward your goal, using your radar to range the target, making small adjustments in the flight plan as you encounter unexpected obstacles, until finally you have reached your goal. You have succeeded.

MIDDLE

All between beginning and end

END

Jeff	Chuck
In the last two months I have learned to do many different tasks and handle different circumstances on my own. I have become used to living away from home, and that has made me more independent than I have ever been.	If the analogy were different, how would the attitudes and perceptions of goalsetters and goalsetting be different? Here's an alternative analogy. How about the analogy that goalsetting is like a shotgun fired at a group of targets? If your aim is on, you can

expect to hit several goals (targets) at once. The goals are closer, too, and you can see them and correct your aim if needed. You have the chance to reload and try again, as well. An analogy should be a tool used to attain goals, not a philosophical cure-all for living.

Focus

Similarly, paragraphs and essays focus on narrow ideas that they can develop sufficiently to convince readers of the stance taken in the topic sentence or thesis statement. Essays, like paragraphs, must be *focused*.

Topic Sentence—Jeff	Thesis statement—Chuck
Moving away from home and going to college is an experience that teaches a person how to become independent and do particular tasks on his own.	Using this analogy to show how a person should set goals for his or her life is not a bad idea, until one looks more closely at the implications of this analogy, especially when it is all that is taught (or learned) about reaching goals.

Jeff could be more precise about his focus because "experience" includes so much area for development, but he does concentrate on independence and specific tasks, both in the topic sentence and throughout the paragraph. Chuck, similarly, sets readers up to expect an analysis of the implications of the analogy of the guided missile to goal setting. And like Jeff, Chuck follows through on this single idea through his essay.

Unity

Another important similarity between the paragraph and the essay is that each focuses on *one* main idea. Just as paragraphs observe the principle of *unity*, so also do essays. Like the topic sentence, a thesis statement tells readers what one idea the writer will address.

Development

Paragraphs and essays can be developed by using the same kinds of materials. Just as paragraphs may use examples, so may essays. Likewise, both forms may use comparison/contrast, description, narration, causal analysis, and so on. Because essays are longer, they often combine more varieties of development, but combinations are possible in either form. You probably noticed as you read Jeff's and Chuck's papers that both used comparison, although Jeff both compares and contrasts while Chuck develops an analogy or extended comparison and examines its implications.

List below some of the details that Jeff and Chuck use in developing their comparison/contrast papers:

Jeff	Chuck
_____	_____
_____	_____
_____	_____
_____	_____

Coherence

Like paragraphs, essays must observe principles of coherence. The transitional words and phrases paragraph writers use show up in full essays. Essay writers, too, use parallelism, pronoun substitution, synonym substitution, and repetition of key words to create coherence in the entire essay just as paragraph writers do in the single paragraph.

Jeff	Chuck
Transitional words and phrases:	
Now that I am at college, now that I am on my own, when I lived at home	finally, also, one, yes
Pronouns:	
I, my, myself, they, this	you, your, yourself, one, this, which, it, its
Synonyms:	
task, problem, job, circumstance	self-guided missile, self-motivation system, autopilot; goal, target, plan, mountain; analogy, theory, philosophy

Repetition of key words:
at home, at college, tasks,   analogy, missile, target, goal,
   independence   success, failure

In short, because both forms aim at clear communication with readers, the principles of good writing apply, no matter how long or short the piece of writing. Essays, then, build on the skills that writers can practice in shorter, single-paragraph essays. And essay writers often improve their skills by practicing on shorter, single-paragraph pieces.

HOW ARE ESSAYS UNLIKE PARAGRAPHS?

Length

Obviously, length is the most noticeable difference between a single paragraph and a full essay. Paragraphs nowadays average between 100 and 300 words at most. But essays can range from 300 to several thousand words, although most college writers find that the 700 to 1000 word essay is a common length.

Breadth of focus

When writers confine themselves to a single paragraph, they are careful to focus their main idea so narrowly that it clearly includes only one main point. An essay similarly announces one main idea for the essay, but the essay may include more information on a slightly broader topic. By broadening the thesis statement somewhat, writers can include more detail in the body of the essay. Good writers are still careful in focusing their thesis statements, though, so that they can adequately develop their essay topics just as they thoroughly develop their topic sentences. (See also the section on focusing.)

Essay map

In addition to a carefully focused thesis statement, though, many writers find that an "essay map" outlining the major points to be covered in an essay helps them to organize the subpoints they will include in each body paragraph. Because a paragraph covers as much as readers can hold in short-term memory at one time, topic sentences needn't be supplemented with "maps." But thesis statements sometimes have accompanying essay maps to outline the body paragraphs of the essay. Notice the major subpoints that Greg suggests with his essay map:

In necessary attempts to combat alcohol and drug use, poor grades, and poor attendance school boards have begun to use suspension from athletics as a deterrent.

Just from this single sentence, a reader can safely predict that the essay will focus on suspension from athletic competition as a cure for disciplinary problems of high-school athletes. Moreover, the first body paragraph will deal with the first cause of disciplinary problems—alcohol and drug use; the second body paragraph with the second problem—poor grades; and the third body paragraph with the third problem—poor attendance. Now see how the essay map accurately predicts the structure of Greg's essay.

The Privilege of Sports

Each year in the nation's high schools, thousands of students participate in some type of sport. In necessary attempts to combat alcohol and drug use, poor grades, and poor attendance school boards have begun to use suspension from athletics as a deterrent. Previously lenient school boards now find that suspension of what many consider a right—athletics—will result in controlling hard-to-control students.

My high school requires the signing of a contract before participation in a sport. The contract explicitly states that any use of alcohol or drugs during the season will result in immediate suspension from the team. Some chose not to take this contract seriously and did drink on occasion. After a Friday night football game, seven pompoms (cheerleaders) decided to celebrate by breaking out a few bottles of champagne and in doing so broke the rules of their contract. This resulted in suspension for them for the rest of the fall and from all future competitions. Many students considered this too strict but the fact remains—they did sign a contract and in drinking alcohol broke a state law. Teaching teenagers in a lenient society requires more than laws; an effective system would require that the student will lose a privilege if he breaks a rule. The star wide-receiver for the football team, a chronic pot smoker, received a suspension for four games when caught at the beginning of the season using drugs. After that he gave up marijuana, at least for the football season, and abided by the rules of his contract. This example clearly illustrates that the loss of the privilege of playing on the football team can straighten up a drug user, at least temporarily. With the growing use of drugs and alcohol in high schools this form of punishment can begin to control the problem.

The high occurrence of failures in classes also requires the school board's attention. Many administrators deal with this problem by prompt removal of the student-athlete from his team. Bruce Greiner, a sophomore tennis player at Columbine, had just made the team and while waiting for the season to begin found out from his coach that he was not passing economics. After sitting out the season he made a much better effort the next year to receive passing grades. Unlike drugs, grades do not affect an athlete's performance, so some might think that suspension will not improve grades.

Thinking of sports as a privilege with certain duties makes the student-athlete abide by the rules. In college as well as in high school, grades come before athletics, and if the duty of grades isn't kept up, then the privilege of sports will end.

Poor class attendance, related to grades, continues to grow as a problem in the nation's high schools. Here, too, school boards use athletic suspension as a method to keep students in class. For example, the Jefferson county school board has made attendance mandatory the day before and the day of a sporting event. The center for the Columbine basketball team decided to test this rule by missing his first class the day of an important game. Once the attendance office recorded his absence he could not play in the game, and thereafter he managed to make it to all his classes on game day. Three unexcused absences in Arapahoe county high schools will result in a three-week suspension from all sports while one unexcused absence in Douglas county during the week of a game will end in suspension. All these examples clearly illustrate that school boards will not tolerate "ditchers." The sole example of a Columbine athlete receiving suspension from a sporting event because of an absence shows that suspension has worked. School boards in the eighties find that strict, effective athletic suspension will keep the students in class.

In the so-called tightening of reins on the high school generation of the eighties, school boards have tried many methods—from suspension from classes to reporting undisciplined students to parents—to control students. But in my mind none has shown better results than suspension from athletics. While going through their education students will learn that they must earn the privilege of playing sports. Adults set the rules and if the kids don't obey them then they will lose the privilege of playing sports. If trends continue towards a less permissive society, then school boards should become even stricter in their policy about sports, a needed change in many school systems.

—*Greg H.*

An essay map lets readers know exactly what to expect in each body paragraph, and so can help readers predict the direction of the essay. But essay maps can also help writers control what they include in essays and how they organize materials. You should practice using essay maps when they help you focus your thesis and organize your ideas.

Practice—Identifying essay maps

Identify the thesis statements and essay maps in the following introductory paragraphs. Remember that an essay map need not be contained in the same sentence as the thesis, nor need it fit into one sentence, although that is the most common kind of map.

1. On December 20, 1982, I was going home for Christmas on highway 350 westbound. The traffic was exceptionally thick due to the holiday season, so it was moving along rather slowly. Further down the highway in front of me I could see a car approaching in my lane. He was unable to reenter his lane of traffic, so I was forced to the side of the road. Encounters with careless drivers cause me to become red with rage; consequently, they cause me to express my anger daringly through the use of my own vehicle as a tool. The drivers who upset me most are those who pass cars on two-lane highways when the oncoming traffic is closely approaching, those who don't use their signals when changing lanes, and those who drive down the middle of the road at forty miles per hour.

2. Another "F," another hangover, another rude remark: this describes my sister Betsy's senior year of high school. Betsy remained in Texas to finish school when my parents moved to Oklahoma. Having Betsy go with them would have been a better idea because teenagers need guidance and discipline during their formative high-school years. Although my college-aged brother, with whom Betsy lived, disciplined her, lack of parental discipline resulted in poor grades, immature social decisions, and lack of consideration for other people.

3. Some parents assume that a hands-off approach to dealing with teen-agers will help minimize any conflict that may arise during these years. In fact these are the same parents who are buying one-way tickets home for their sons and daughters who cannot survive their freshman year of college. Consequently, parental supervision of teenagers' academic progress should be increased, because through supervision young people can avoid the problem of too much free time, they can develop a process of self discipline, and they will be better able to acquire the skills necessary for academic success.

Paragraph Hooks

As we will discuss in more detail shortly (see "linking paragraphs"), essays, unlike paragraphs, require more obvious links between paragraphs. Because the paragraph is one unit, it holds together with straightforward coherence devices. But the essay needs more elaborate hooks to connect paragraphs into a coherent larger unit. Paragraph hooks are not difficult to learn to use, but you will practice using them only in essays, not single paragraphs.

HOW CAN I FOCUS A THESIS?

Having reviewed similarities and differences between paragraphs and essays, let's now consider certain elements of essay writing in more detail. In Chapter 2 we looked at the process whereby writers focus their main ideas, mainly concentrating on topic sentences. But even essay writers generally follow similar processes. Writers of all papers determine for whom they are writing, what the purpose of writing is, and then they try to come up with one main point they would like to make. Sometimes that idea comes through brainstorming, freewriting, looping, mapping, answering questions, or just thinking about an assigned topic. Sometimes writers begin to write hoping that the main point will become clear to them as they compose a discovery draft.

Once writers have some main point—no matter how they arrive at it— then they begin narrowing and focusing. Remember that we used the camera analogy—focusing on a narrow slice of experience or picture of reality—to explain focusing for a writing assignment. Because essay writers have more time to develop their ideas, they need not focus quite so narrowly as paragraph writers, but the best writers still limit their ideas so that they can develop them adequately in the paper.

Let's consider a thesis statement. Why wouldn't this thesis focus a 1000-word essay (about 5 pages)?

Pollution is a problem everyone can help with.

1. What is the subject of the "thesis? _____

2. What does the writer assert about the subject? _____

_____

3. What does the writer predict about the paper? _____

_____

4. Can you detect the writer's attitude toward the subject from this

thesis? _____

5. List here as many possible topics as you can imagine falling under this thesis statement:

_____   _____

_____   _____

_____   _____

_____   _____

_____   _____

As you can tell from my questions, thesis statements announce the subject of the paper, but they announce a subject that can be exhausted in the length of the paper. Furthermore, good thesis statements generally reveal the writer's attitude toward the subject. Finally, good thesis statements help readers *predict* what will appear in the essay. A broad or unfocused thesis statement like this one cannot help readers predict because it simply allows too many different options for the writer to develop. Readers, then, cannot know from the thesis what direction the essay will take.

How might this writer go about focusing this thesis? First, the writer should probably specify who is the audience for the paper and whether the paper is to be informative or persuasive. If this writer intends to inform students about reducing pollution on campus, the approach will be very different from persuading city leaders to spend money on cleaning up pollution. What are some possibilities for each audience and purpose?

CAMPUS POLLUTION	CITY POLLUTION
Audience: fellow students	Audience: city council
Possible subjects: noise pollution, litter, air pollution	Possible subjects: noise pollution, litter, air pollution, chemical spills on the railway, water pollution from the city dump

Can you see already that the difference in audience creates differences in the possible subjects? Students may not be concerned about chemical spills on campus, since that is an unlikely occurrence on most campuses, but they will be concerned about noise pollution, especially in dorms. If the campus is urban, students might be exposed to high levels of air pollution from automobile traffic near and on campus. Because they are more immediate for students living on campus, both of these concerns are more focused subjects appropriate for the audience.

The city council, on the other hand, needs to concern itself with several kinds of pollution, including noise pollution, but probably not noise from stereos. Instead, construction crews, road-repair crews, traffic, and other noises create unhealthy decibel levels on many city streets. Even if we wrote both papers about noise pollution, we'd probably focus even more carefully on different varieties of that pollution. And so the audience makes a clear difference in what we write about. What about the other half of our first thesis statement:

Pollution is a problem everyone can help with.

As you can see, we need to revise this part of the thesis to be more specific too. Let's consider just noise pollution—of the kinds that each audience must care about—as we explore a more precise thesis.

CAMPUS POLLUTION	CITY POLLUTION
Audience: fellow students	Audience: city council
Purpose: inform	Purpose: persuade to spend money
Possible narrowed subject: Noise pollution from dorm stereos	Possible narrowed subject: Noise pollution from street-repair crews
Assertion: can inhibit neighbor's efficiency in studying Assertion: can intrude on neighbor's privacy	Assertion: should be kept to a minimum during working hours
Assertion: can result in escalating "stereo wars"	Assertion: can be reduced by paying street crews overtime to work at night
Assertion: can give close city residents a bad opinion of college students	Assertion: should be reduced to give visitors a more positive image of our beautiful, peaceful city

Do you see any major differences between the assertions in the two columns? The ones directed toward the college audience reflect concerns that college students probably have, while the ones directed at the city council address its concerns. Another difference between the two columns is that the ones on the left are mainly informative while those on the right suggest what the council "should" or "could" do, a more persuasive position. In keeping with the difference in purposes, the thesis statements that result from each set of assertions will reflect either the goal of informing or persuading.

Do you see attitudes reflected in the assertions? Remember that most thesis statements take a position—even the informative ones—so that readers know the perspective of the writer. Choose precise words in a thesis to suggest how you feel about the issue you're writing on.

Practice—Writing

You should try writing focused thesis statements on this subject for each audience. Be sure to choose precise words—you might try answering the W questions—so that your thesis will predict the direction of the essay for your readers. Also try to include your attitude toward the subject.

1. College students: _____

_____

2. College students: _____

_____

3. College students: _____

_____

4. City council: _____

_____

5. City council: _____

_____

6. City council: _____

_____

More practice on thesis statements

Most writers discover that focusing a thesis statement as precisely as possible takes much more practice than they think. Of course, thesis statements separated from essays are like fish out of water. But readers might just stop reading when they reach your thesis—if it doesn't encourage them to keep reading by suggesting exactly what your essay will cover. And so readers often consider thesis statements separately from the entire essay.

Let's review the principles of focusing a thesis by thinking critically about another thesis that seems focused:

> Victims of medical malpractice should not be allowed to sue for punitive damages.

On the positive side, this thesis statement makes its position clear, and the writer's attitude is certainly apparent. But what else might we do to improve the thesis? This statement came from the American Medical Association. Can you tell who the audience might be? It's safe to say that the audience is *not* victims of medical malpractice. Do you suppose the general population is the audience? I don't think so because many members of the general public will be put off by such a blanket statement. If the spokesperson for the AMA wanted to persuade the general public, I think she might have used a more tempered approach to explain the AMA side of the issue.

So to whom is the spokesperson appealing? The insurance industry? Congress? The legal system? The spokesperson went on to say that most people assume that modern medical technology can work miracles and that they are disappointed with the modest results most doctors can provide. She argued that fewer than 10 percent of the current malpractice cases have any merit, and that punitive damages simply encourage disgruntled patients to hope for large settlements of unreasonable claims. Does this information make her audience clearer to you? If the spokesperson wanted to appeal to a broader audience, how might she change her thesis?

Assuming that she is appealing to some legislative body with the authority to change current malpractice law and settlements, what else strikes you as particularly flawed in the thesis? If you are bothered by the blanket assertion that *all* victims should be denied punitive claims, then you are reacting as a good reader. Whenever we use an unqualified word like "victims" in a thesis, we imply "all victims." For this thesis, I would argue that even if 90 percent of the cases have no merit, the 10 percent shouldn't be denied their rights. Moreover, doctors can make mistakes, and some doctors are badly trained. Some even have fake degrees. Why should victims of these doctors be denied protection under the law for actions that might leave them crippled or even dead? By not restricting the thesis, this spokesperson undercuts her case with thinking listeners and readers. Be sure not to do the same in your thesis statements. If you mean to discuss only freshmen at your school, say so; if you mean to discuss only school children between the ages of 10 and 12, say so; if you mean only Vietnam veterans, say so. And always protect your position by further qualifying with "some," "most," "many," or the appropriate limiting word. Otherwise, your opponent need only find one counterexample to destroy your argument.

In short, think about the logic of your thesis and the position you take. Don't turn readers off with fuzzy logic.

Some other tips for thesis statements

Be sure to choose a subject you care about. If you don't care, you cannot write a thesis statement that will interest readers. If you analyze your audience carefully, you should be able to discover some shared interest that will help you write papers—and thesis statements—that will interest both you and your readers.

Choose precise words. As we discussed with topic sentences, vague words simply don't convey precise ideas about your essays. Avoid "problem," "situation," "experience," and other vague words that can mean almost anything. Give your readers as much help in predicting as you possibly can.

Be concise as well. You needn't include "I believe" or "in my opinion" in your thesis. Your readers will know this is your opinion and so you don't have to include phrases of that sort. When you do, you only weaken your thesis.

Don't simply state a fact. A thesis takes a position, and yours should always be clear in your thesis.

Practice—Revising thesis statement

Analyze the following thesis statements to determine strengths and weaknesses. You will probably need to specify an audience and purpose for each thesis. Then rewrite the statements to make them more precise, more focused, and more predictive for readers.

1. I think college students read fewer magazines than they did ten years

   ago. _____

   _____

2. The experience was one I'll never forget. _____

   _____

3. If we could only stamp out child abuse now, we could raise healthy

   children forever. _____

   _____

4. Because the evidence is so overwhelming, pregnant women shouldn't

   smoke cigarettes. _____

   _____

5. Whenever I think of human beings torturing animals in laboratories,

I get sick to my stomach. _____

_____

6. I am sure that once I explain my position to you, you will agree that

we must change this policy. _____

_____

    You should now narrow these subjects and write focused thesis statements for a specified audience. Be sure to choose precise words—you might try answering the W questions—so that your thesis will predict the direction of the essay for your readers. Also try to include your attitude toward the subject.

1. Roommates (written for incoming freshmen at your school)

Narrowed subject: _____

Narrowed subject: _____

Narrowed subject: _____

Thesis statement: _____

_____

_____

2. Pets (written for distribution through the local humane society)

Narrowed subject: _____

Narrowed subject: _____

Narrowed subject: _____

Thesis statement: _____

_____

_____

3. Furnishing a new apartment (for your off-campus housing office)

Narrowed subject: _____

Narrowed subject: _____

Narrowed subject: _____

Thesis statement: _____

_____

_____

4. Friendships (for high school buddies)

Narrowed subject: _____

Narrowed subject: _____

Narrowed subject: _____

Thesis statement: _____

_____

_____

5. Family ties (for your parents)

Narrowed subject: _____

Narrowed subject: _____

Narrowed subject: _____

Thesis statement: _____

_____

_____

_____

HOW CAN I LINK PARAGRAPHS
IN MY ESSAY?

Of course you can use transitional words and phrases, such as those listed in Chapter 3, to connect paragraphs in an essay. But most writers discover that more sophisticated hooks help readers move smoothly through a longer paper.

In essence, a paragraph hook is a device of repetition. When you conclude one paragraph, you round out the paragraph with some idea repetition from the topic sentence or thesis statement. At the beginning of the next paragraph, you repeat a key word from the concluding sentence (or perhaps the second last sentence) of the preceding paragraph. Or you might repeat a phrase. Or you might substitute a synonym at the beginning of the next paragraph. Generally, though, we can visualize paragraph hooks as verbal connections between two paragraphs, usually with direct repetition but occasionally with synonyms.

Moreover, because the reader should always be aware of the main point of the essay, most paragraph hooks also tie back to the thesis. So a particularly good technique for linking paragraphs is to repeat key words from the thesis—or synonyms of some sort—near the end of a paragraph and to use that repetition as your hook to the next paragraph. Let's see how Capon links his paragraphs.

Practice—Reading

Food for Thought: A Philosophy of Eating

Robert Farrar Capon

[1]   The subject of food, like all topics in which the human race has a large and inescapable interest, is anything but a simple piece of business. Cooking and eating, no less than sex, birth, and death, give rise to a perennial

bumper crop of horror tales and assorted lunacies—frequently fed and watered by such sciences, respectable or otherwise, as can be dragooned into service. There is probably not an edible substance in the world that has not somewhere, sometime and for some ostensibly "scientific" reason been declared inedible or even deadly.

2   Each age and culture, of course, makes its unique contribution to the general insanity. Tomatoes, when they were first introduced, were considered either magical or lethal, depending on which school of thought you listened to. Even within living memory, there was a time when, in accordance with old-wifely culinary science, vegetables were deemed harmful unless cooked to mush, eggplant unacceptable unless soaked in brine, cucumbers poisonous unless rubbed to a froth at the cut end and mussels unemployable except as bait. But it is our own age that has come up with the largest list yet of food phobias.

3   What has not been proscribed in recent years? We have been told not to eat white flour because nutrients have been taken out, prepared foods because chemicals have been put in, natural foods (animal fats, salt) because nature has designed them with malign components, and snack foods because man has violated nature by designing them. More bizarre still, we are told to fear most something that is not even a substance, let alone a comestible: the calorie. In fact, of course, calories are measurements, not things. One could as soon fry an inch or boil a foot-pound as cook a calorie.

4   This modern orgy of witch-hunting inevitably drags in not only physical sciences such as chemistry and biology but humanistic ones such as psychology, ethics, aesthetics and even religion. Not content simply to alarm the public with empirically proven truths ("Science Establishes Link Between Saturated Fats and Heart Disease"), the media terrorize us with the dicta of any other discipline they can make headlines of ("The Dinner Hour: Communal Blessing or Psychological Trauma?"; "Junk Food Held Threat to National Values").

5   But the grand master of goodness or badness in food lies not in the province of a particular science or art (even food chemistry or culinary technique) but in the province of the science of all the sciences, philosophy. It is not enough to allow each several science to have its say; nor is it enough for all of them to offer their respective criticism of one another. That way lies only a continuation of the chaos. What is needed is a referee who, while honoring each, holds all of them responsible to nothing less than the whole interest of human nature.

6   Indeed, it is the absence of just such a referee that is the cause of the present chaos. Take, for example, the cry so often raised about "chemical" additives in the food supply. To a chemist, the complaint has an air of near illiteracy about it: Every foodstuff, by its very nature, has some determinate chemical composition. The chemist has done nothing more

than add yet another chemical substance to something already loaded with them.

7   Note, however, that in making that last assertion he has wandered out the back door of the house of chemistry into the common courtyard (namely, philosophy) onto which the back doors of all other disciplines open as well. His good and sufficient reason, in that open air, cannot be established by chemical criteria alone. Ethics, for instance, will want to ask him if he has investigated all possible side effects of his additive; psychology will want to know, perhaps, whether it will enhance or detract from the quality of life; and aesthetics will ask if it makes the food taste better or worse. But the last word on the whole question can be given only by a mind that can work its way through the particular sciences to the wisdom that lies beyond.

8   If that seems a bit high-flown in an essay about something the general public mindlessly tucks into three times a day, it nevertheless remains true that food is a perfect paradigm of what happens when the philosophical referee is, as it were, out to lunch. To demonstrate the point, let me pose three apparently down-to-earth food questions.

9   The first is, "Why put nondairy instant creamer, and not heavy cream, in coffee?" Notice how none of the particular sciences or arts can possibly give a satisfactory answer to that question. Chemistry can tell you that nondairy creamer is theoretically possible; technology, that it is commercially feasible; and economics, that it may be cost-effectively produced. Medicine may applaud the whole development as a boon to the cardiovascular system. On the other hand, aesthetics may lament the loss of cream; ethics, the displacement of the good by the indifferent; and metaphysics, the iniquity of equating an inadequate imitation of what cream *does* with the entire marvel of what cream *is*. In any case, although the dialogue is now definitely warmer, the participants are further than ever from coming up with a single answer. My point, therefore, is quite simple. All of us use either cream, noncream or neither; whichever it is, though, our decision is arrived at out in the common courtyard of philosophy, where the love of wisdom, and not simply correct information, is the touchstone of judgment. The rightness of our decision can be neither conclusively proved nor effectively challenged by an appeal to any particular science.

10   The second question is, "Why frozen, butter-sauced vegetables in a boilable plastic pouch?" I leave you to work out for yourself the permutations and combinations of the answers given to this poser by the various arts and sciences; in any case, the result will be the same brouhaha of conflicting voices, all arguing quite plausibly from their several back porches. And in the end, each one of us will decide—more or less satisfactorily but nonetheless philosophically—whether to drop somebody else's handiwork into a pot or to do the job ourselves.

[11]   But if I have so far refrained from urging my own philosophico-culinary conclusions upon you, that restraint vanishes with my third question: "Why, oh why, in the name of all the glorious materialities of the world, should there be such a monomaniacally restrictive thing as the macrobiotic diet?" Oh, I know. You feel, perhaps, that you can justify it on medical or physiological grounds—or possibly, that you can demolish it on the very same basis. But as I have been at pains to point out, no specific discipline can answer what is fundamentally a philosophical question. On the other hand, you may be itching to tell me that it is precisely on grand and philosophical grounds that you have so attached yourself to brown rice—that you find it fraught with cosmic significances.

[12]   Well, for all I know, you do. But a small flag goes up in my mind when people talk like that; it sounds rather more like religion (which, speaking intellectually as we are, is just another discipline that needs a referee) than it does like philosophy. There is a very old name for our penchant for expecting certain rearrangements of matter to be capable of vast and immaterial effects: it is called idolatry.

[13]   I do not mean to single out the macrobiotic diet. Our whole approach to food is riddled with idolatrous notions. We confidently expect that this diet will be our salvation or that indulgence will give us status. We eat not so much for geniune material and spiritual reasons (delight, nourishment, sociability) as for spurious and immaterial ones (cachet, purification, enlistment on the side of the angels). Food has become more a talisman than a good in its own right; eating is more often incantatory than enjoyable. All of which, I think, is simply a shame. When any material subject is exalted for what it can be made to *mean* rather than for what it *is*, the door is opened to rampant fakery. The next step after idolatry is always bad art; drown food in significance and all you are sure to get is dreadful cookery.

[14]   And yet, food is such a vast, wonderful, homey thing. Quite on its own—and for most of the history of the race, at least when philosophy wasn't asleep at the switch—it has kept the cooks and eaters of the world completely happy to be just that. It is time, I think, to blow the whistle on the idolatry and get the subject back on track.

Practice—Analyzing paragraph links

What repetition or substitution links paragraph 1 and 2?

_____

2 and 3? _____

3 and 4? _____

4 and 5? _____

5 and 6? _____

6 and 7? _____

7 and 8? _____

8 and 9? _____

9 and 10? _____

10 and 11? _____

11 and 12? _____

12 and 13? _____

13 and 14? _____

Where you do not find paragraph hooks, do other transitional devices connect paragraphs?

HOW CAN I INTRODUCE AND CONCLUDE MY ESSAY?

Introductions and conclusions are often parts of essays that writers find most difficult to complete. After all, the title and introduction set the tone and attitude of the paper for readers. If the introduction doesn't get readers' attention, they may simply quit reading. And yet many writers fear giving away too much in the introduction. Just remember that readers are looking for guidelines about what will appear in the essay. You should capture their attention, but don't hesitate to fill in background and lead up to your thesis.

One image I have found successful in the past is the swimming pool. Few swimmers just dive right into the pool without testing the waters. Fewer readers will be willing to jump into your essay with you. Rather, your introduction should first invite readers to the pool's edge and then encourage them to get their toes wet. In another sentence or two, you attract readers into sitting on the edge of the pool. Then you pull them into the waist-deep water. Finally, with your thesis statement at the end of the intro paragraph, you invite readers to swim with you.

Some techniques for introductions

If you look through the professional and student essays in this text, you'll find that they often use the following devices to introduce essays:

1. A vivid, brief story—A crisp narrative can attract readers' attention quickly, set the tone of your paper, and create a sense of personal involvement.
2. A vivid description—Similarly, setting the scene for readers often draws them into the topic of the paper.
3. A startling fact or statistic—This technique attracts attention because readers may be surprised to see unknown information or information presented in a way they hadn't thought of before.
4. A question—Although you won't want to overuse this technique, it can draw readers on to see the answer. Be sure not to ask obvious questions.
5. A definition—Especially if your paper tackles a specialized topic, you may want to begin with a definition of a key term. Or you may want to define your common terms in a unique way, another use of definition that draws readers into your paper. Dictionary definitions are rarely successful in capturing readers' attention, so write your own definition. See Chapter 12 for suggestions.
6. A quotation—Like the statistic, a quotation can pique readers' interest.
7. Dialogue—Like the narrative, a brief dialogue can set a scene and create personal involvement in the essay.

One other tip you might find helpful: If you can't start at the beginning, start in the middle. Many writers find the introduction easier to write after they finish a draft of the entire essay. Then, as they say, they know what they're introducing.

Conclusions

Because conclusions evolve out of the essay itself, they are probably even more difficult for writers. One sure rule-of-thumb: don't use a summary for a short essay. Give readers credit for remembering a three-page essay. Save the summary for essays of ten pages or more. Rather, try for a final statement of your main point or the final impression you want to leave in readers' minds. Sometimes you can restate your thesis and its implications. Sometimes you will want to explore a slightly more general idea—but be sure it's covered in your thesis. You can't introduce a new idea at the end of an essay.

Again, look at sample essays in this text. Writers sometimes use quotations, stories, and puns, but more often they recapture the main idea in slightly different terms than appear in the thesis.

Practice—Writing

Write introductory paragraphs for at least three of the thesis statements you generated for the preceding exercise on pp. 114–116. Try different techniques for the different audiences. Then compare notes with classmates about which techniques will be most effective with which readers.

Writing Assignments

1. Write the complete essay for any of the introductions you generated in the preceding exercise.
2. Write an essay to a specified audience on any of the topics in the exercise on pp. 111–112.
3. Write an essay on pollution in your environment. Be sure to specify an audience and purpose for your essay. Then carefully focus on one type of pollution appropriate to write about for your audience and purpose in the essay.
4. Write an essay on your philosophy of food. You might direct it toward the readers of *Science Digest* or toward your writing class. Be sure to focus carefully.
5. Write an essay on how you handle stress.
6. Write an essay on anger.

chapter 5

Revising and editing your work

WHAT IS REVISION?

As we mentioned in Chapter 1, revision is an important component of the writing process. As you also recall, revising does not come only toward the end of the process but occurs throughout the thinking, planning, drafting, and editing of a paper. Remember that we called writing *recursive,* that is, the parts of the process intertwine so that they are not easily separated.

And yet to talk about revising, we must separate it from prewriting and writing because no teacher can address the revising you do mentally or the revising that works itself into prewriting and writing. So, just for this discussion, let's concentrate on the revision that occurs mainly after a paper is drafted. When we do this, revising means literally *re-seeing.* In revising, we look again at the audience and purpose of our papers and judge whether the paper matches the audience's needs. We reconsider whether we have presented ourselves in the right persona—friend, colleague, expert, and so on. We look again at focus of ideas, organization and arrangement of support, and logical coherence throughout the paper.

We decide if we need to add, delete, substitute, or rearrange material. In short, we step back and look again at the piece as a whole, evaluating what is successful and what is not.

WHAT IS EDITING?

Some teachers use revising and editing interchangeably, but I think of editing as a process quite different from revising. For me, editing means replacing a weak word with a stronger one, a vague word with a more specific one, an abstract or general word with a more concrete or precise one. Editing also means checking for correct *usage,* that is, spelling, punctuation, subject-verb agreement, pronoun use, and so on. It may also include combining ideas differently in sentences or rearranging sentence parts. But editing rarely includes any work beyond a sentence or two at a time. In this text, we will consider editing in Unit 5 and concentrate on revising in this chapter.

WHEN DO WE REVISE?

Far too many writers—and I among them—don't always revise enough. Most of us can't change the amount of revising we do mentally or as we write a paper because the flow of ideas is not usually under conscious control. But many writers, once they have a version of the paper down, decide that "it's good enough." For these writers, revising probably doesn't get enough attention. As a result, their papers may sometimes help readers, but usually they do not. These papers may sometimes communicate a point clearly, but usually they are blurred or ineffective. Revising is difficult because it requires distance from one's writing, especially when the writer feels pressed for time. But revising is always worthwhile because it strengthens papers.

One of the best tips I can suggest to help you revise effectively is to leave your paper alone for at least a day, longer if possible. When writers try to revise immediately after finishing a first draft, they usually see only what they wanted to do with the paper, not what actually appears on the page. If writers give themselves 24 hours away from a paper, they can see more objectively what is on the page and thus *re-see* what the paper should do that it now doesn't.

Of course, this advice requires you to start writing well in advance of a paper's deadline. If you wait till the day before a paper is due to start writing, you clearly won't have time to put the paper aside to let it—and your mind—cool down. The sooner you can start an assignment, the more time you will have to revise thoroughly before a paper is due.

WHEN DO WE EDIT?

Unfortunately, many writers edit as they draft a paper, and this bad habit can create more writers' blocks than good papers. Like revising, editing should be left until after a draft is finished. If while writing you can't find the precise word you want, don't race to a dictionary or thesaurus. Instead, put in some word close to your meaning and circle it; check later for a more precise word. Similarly, if you are unsure of how to use a semicolon, don't keep rewriting a sentence to avoid the semicolon or check its use in a handbook. Instead, get the sentence down and keep on writing. If you stop yourself to edit while you are drafting, you'll more likely interfere with the prewriting and revising that your mind is trying to do while you force yourself to recall the "rules" of good writing.

The best reason for not editing while you draft, however, is that if you truly revise your work, you may delete or reorder or add to the material already in your paper. As you do so, you may eliminate that word, phrase, or sentence you labored over. Why waste your energy editing if the edited sentence won't appear in the final version?

HOW CAN YOU REVISE MORE EFFECTIVELY?

Time

As I mentioned before, allowing time between your drafting and revising helps your revision. All writers need distance between themselves and their papers. Putting a paper aside works better than any other approach for most writers. If you can't take a day between drafting and revising, then at least provide a real break. Work on other assignments, go to a movie, get some exercise, take a nap, or somehow provide a real transition between your drafting and revising. If you can reread your paper with a fresh perspective, you'll find revising easier and more rewarding.

Audience

Before you look at your paper, redefine your primary audience. Try to visualize the representative person who best illustrates your readers. If possible, jot down those characteristics you think are most important for readers of your paper. Then compare this audience analysis with your prewriting analysis to see how your notion of your readers has changed. If it hasn't, then be sure your paper meets the needs of these readers. If it has changed, you'll probably need to check that your paper hasn't taken shortcuts that will confuse your readers.

Purpose

Just as you should reconsider audience, reconsider purpose. Again, don't look at your paper but consider just what is the most important function of your paper for your readers. Compare that purpose with your prewriting purpose.

Focus

Now that you have drafted the paper, you should be able to recall the main point you made in the draft. Without rereading your paper, jot down on a separate sheet what you think is your main point. If you have written a discovery draft, the thesis or topic sentence you jot down now will reflect what you learned by writing the paper. You'll probably want to revise your original thesis or topic sentence to show this new understanding of what your paper focuses on. To help readers, this step is probably among the most crucial of any revision practices.

If you have not written a discovery draft, your main point and your original thesis or topic sentence should be relatively similar. Often, though, students find that they can capture that main idea better at this stage, and so they refine the thesis or topic sentence based on this step.

Remember, readers predict what your paper will include by using your topic sentence or thesis statement. Make that sentence as precise and clear as possible.

One other useful way to help you refine focus is to find a friend who will read your paper and then tell you what he or she thinks is the main idea. If that main idea doesn't match your topic sentence or thesis, you need to revise your focus in the paper. (Don't hesitate to use real readers as guinea pigs in helping you revise your papers. But be sure to ask specific questions and not to let them simply say, "It sounds fine to me.")

Development, coherence, unity

To be sure that you have included all the material your readers might need to relate to your main idea, ask yourself about development and unity. Also check for transitions, paragraph hooks, repeated words, pronouns, and other coherence devices. You should not detect any breaks in the logical flow of ideas.

Create your own revision checklist

Because you are most familiar with strengths and weaknesses in your writing, you should create a list of questions you plan to use every time you revise papers. Your checklist should include the elements I've just noted, but you might want to list four questions for coherence or three different ways of checking focus if you have problems revising in those areas. You might also use comments teachers have written on papers to help you decide what questions to include on your checklist. I've included general checklists at the end of each of the next nine chapters, but your personal checklist will probably help you better exploit your strengths in writing and improve your weaknesses.

CHOOSING APPROPRIATE STRATEGIES

In the next nine chapters, you will practice reading and writing each of the most common organizational strategies, but we must consider the more typical reading and writing you will do. Very seldom will your reading ask only that you deal with comparison or classification. Typically, definitions appear mixed with examples combined with analysis of causes or effects. Any combination of strategies is possible, and writers must choose which patterns meet their goals for their readers. Thus, choosing the best strategies to convey information or to persuade your readers is an important part of writing, and checking those strategies will be an important part of revising.

Let's read a few samples and try to notice what changes occur in your reading process as you shift from one strategy to the next and why writers choose specific methods of organizing their ideas.

The Tire Trap

Stephen Hall, *Science 84*

Living in a society that discards almost as much as it consumes, Americans take a lot of rubbish for granted—including used tires. Each year they discard about 200 million tires, and there is virtually no way to get rid of them. Burning them produces noxious fumes. Buried in landfills, they eerily rise to the surface. In some cases, they can be frozen with liquid nitrogen, smashed into little pieces, and used to make asphalt. "But that isn't too practical for steel-belted radials," notes researcher Barry Beaty.

Unfortunately for Americans, mosquitoes do not take tires for granted. They take them for homes. Scientists would be hard pressed to design a better breeding chamber for mosquitoes—and disease.

The larvae of *Aedes triseriatus,* the mosquito that infects young children with La Crosse encephalitis virus, thrive in old tires. The tires retain water nicely and fill up with the kind of nutrient-rich debris that larvae voraciously devour. By some estimates, the mosquitoes that hatch in tires are larger, live longer, and emerge as much as four weeks earlier than adults that hatch in tree holes. Some 4,867 larvae—and 12 separate isolates—were harvested from a single tire found outside Chardon, Ohio, near Cleveland.

The danger of such situations is borne out by fieldwork by the Vector-Borne Disease Unit of Ohio's department of health; in Ohio there have been 558 cases of La Crosse encephalitis—and five fatalities—since 1963. Follow-up studies on 69 diagnosed cases in 1981–82 showed that tires were present in 72.5 percent of the cases and were considered the "predominant source" of *A. triseriatus* 54 percent of the time.

Statistics linking old tires to cases of encephalitis are confirmed by haunting personal anecdotes. A 1983 case in Perry County, Ohio, for example, occurred at the rural home of a man who was in the business of recycling tires. Public health investigators found hundreds of tires, and large numbers of *A. triseriatus* mosquitoes, at the site. The victim: the man's two-year-old daughter. A puzzling 1977 case in a suburb of Milwaukee, well outside the endemic area, made sense when it was found that a neighbor of the victim had previously lived in a rural area north of La Cross—and had hauled old tires along to Milwaukee when he relocated.

Researchers are terrified by the implications of that last case and others like it. "The capacity for spread of this disease is enormous," says George B. Craig, Jr., of Notre Dame. "Old tires get shipped all around the country, and the mosquitoes inside the tires get shipped, too." Ohio health officials are concerned that two mosquitoes not normally found in Ohio, *A. aegypti,* vector of both yellow fever and dengue, and *A. atropalpus,* have turned up in the state in the last 10 years—apparently via tires.

In La Crosse, where it all began, an ambitious mosquito control program was initiated in 1978. Health officials systematically eliminated breeding sites—filled in tree holes, removed tires. According to pediatrician Cameron Gundersen of the Gundersen Clinic-La Crosse Lutheran Hospital, no new cases have turned up in La Crosse County in two years.

But as long as surplus tires lie around, the worry remains. "It's been thought that La Crosse [encephalitis] is a sylvan disease, where a young boy would go into a woodlot, play in his treehouse, and get bitten by a mosquito," says Craig. "I think that's probably a minority of the cases. It isn't tree holes. It's the tires!"

Practice—Analyzing

1. What methods of development does Hall use in the article? Be sure to look carefully for the strategies you've practiced. _____

   _____

   _____

   _____

2. Did any details strike you as particularly effective? Which ones?

   _____

   _____

3. Does the opening paragraph get and keep your attention? Why?

   _____

   _____

4. Where does Hall state the main point of his article? Is this an effective placement? _____

   _____

   _____

5. What unfamiliar words slowed you down? Were you able to discover meanings from the context? _____

   _____

   _____

6. Will you *do* anything as a result of reading this article? What?

READING

Because few readers will be familiar with the technicalities of diseases spread by insects, this article presents some difficulties. But all readers are familiar with mosquitoes and old tires, and some readers may have experience with or knowledge of encephalitis. So this article represents material that is not wholly familiar or unfamiliar. As we discussed in Chapter 1, we read this kind of passage working from both the top and the bottom—using that knowledge we have to help structure the new information and make sense of the whole. Most readers, for instance, will understand what *A. triseriatus* does, but few will remember the name very long after reading the article. For most readers, the name is less important than understanding the point of the article. And so we read.

Notice, though, that although the article does not set out to persuade readers to change their behavior, you and your classmates may have decided never to keep old tires around your homes or to transport them with you across the country. Even essays written simply to explain often have a persuasive effect on readers.

WRITING

Similarly, though certain academic assignments may call explicitly for a certain pattern of development—the essay test that asks for comparison of two leaders, for instance—most writing on the job requires that writers understand just what readers need. Then writers must organize material in the most effective way to communicate with readers. If writers want only to explain, they will organize materials in different ways than if they want to persuade. So writers must begin by determining audience and purpose.

After establishing what the reader needs and why, writers can gather, select, arrange, and polish materials. Writers must, of course, match their own interests and knowledge with the goals they set for their writing. If writers do not know enough to explain thoroughly or convince readers, then they must gather more details through reading, research, interviews, and so on. Basically, writers follow the process we will practice repeatedly throughout this text: they prewrite, draft, revise, edit, and proofread, always remembering that the process is not linear.

Let's look at some sample essays developed to meet writers' goals to communicate a message to readers. The first essay was written to explain an American "value" by way of some personal experience and analysis. Notice how Susan gets readers involved and what strategies of development she uses.

SAMPLES

If it's your pleasure to watch spiders weave their silk, then sit back in your easy chair and relax because it's time for another TV commercial break and you are about to be the victim in a giant, illusory, mythical web of promises.

TV commercials used to be a potty break for a late night movie watcher, a quick minute to whisk the kids off to bed or just a time to switch channels to make sure a more dramatic show was not on. Today, however, commercials are as popular as the TV sitcoms and dramas themselves, and advertisers are capitalizing on America's changing values by embodying these values in the commercials. For example, in the past five years this country has seen a complete turn around from the popularity of the slurp and burp fast food restaurant. Today Americans are eating more nutritiously, watching their weight, and embarking on serious exercise regimens. The new importance on appearance has America spending $30 billion a year on running shoes, health club memberships and other sundries. Today there are more than 10,000 fitness clubs nationwide, and by flipping through a Rocky Mountain *News* one can easily find a club with appeal. In a recent Sunday issue there were more than 36 advertisements for different health clubs and diet plans. With this change in values the commercial industry has been stirred up like a giant caesar salad, and catering to this change in tastes, advertisers are promoting certain foods and beverages that promise to make a slim beauty out of both you and me. I myself have been a victim of these promotions, and I can remember one event quite clearly.

As I sat in front of my cheap black-and-white with the volume turned down trying desperately to figure out a physics problem that had something to do with magnetic dipole, I was interrupted by a snappy yogurt commercial jingle. Now, I am not a yogurt fan, but the lively jingle accompanied by what I saw on the screen was enough to make me shove my physics book aside. There were no dancing blueberries on the screen—only 6 or 7 slim and toned males and females working out in a gym. There was no grunting and groaning as the young, vibrant, healthy individuals pushed and pulled the weights, only euphoric smiles and sparkling eyes. The next frame focused on a pair of slim, natural California-blonde twins roller skating down a luscious green parkway. With pink shorts and tee shirts and striped bobby socks perfectly aligned, these two beauties glowed with health and vitality. Finally the last all-absorbing shot centered on a young, healthy energetic couple biking up a mountain lane. The girl's long brown hair whipping in the wind and the boy's taut thigh muscles gleaming of suntan oil only further enhanced this notion of slim, toned, youthful vitality. Behind each frame of gorgeous bodies a pleasant-voiced female sang "Who can? You can; get a Dannon body, wow!!!" as if she were calling out a familiar homecoming cheer. Not being quite clear on the definition of a Dannon body but hoping it had something to do with looking slim and beautiful, I quickly shoveled the snow off my driveway, scraped my car windows and drove to the store for six containers of yogurt. I ate one container and with great anticipation sat back and waited for the miracle to occur. I wasn't sure whether my fat would drip off slowly or whether the transformation would occur all at once. After two minutes nothing happened so I ate another container and another. Still nothing happened. The commercial had not specified how much yogurt you have to eat to get a Dannon body or pinpointed how long it takes. In fact, the commercial had little to do with yogurt at all. Only once was a container of yogurt actually shown and then for only a few seconds. What the commercial focused on was beautiful bodies, and that's what I wanted, a slimmer, trimmer, more toned body.

About ten days later as I was standing in front of the refrigerator looking for some goodie, I spotted the other three unopened containers of yogurt which had now been pushed towards the back. As the memory of my mania flooded back to me, I let out a tiny giggle. I never did get a Dannon body; the only thing I did get from Dannon was nausea. But why had I believed the commercial in the first place? Was I as vain and vulnerable as some of my friends and countless other Americans who believe everything that comes out over the screen. I had definitely fallen into the way of thinking that the advertisers wanted, but it was all a myth. Although ounce for ounce Dannon yogurt has more calories than a chocolate shake, the commercial promises that if we eat Dannon yogurt we'll get a Dannon body. Consequently, supermarket sales are up and the Dannon company is sitting in the black. Because Hollywood and glamour magazines have made stars out of women who are thin and gorgeous and men who are meaty yet well-defined, these stars have come to embody what we would all like to be. Every day we are bombarded by the radio, TV, and the print media that "thin is in; consequently, we come to dislike our bodies and our overall appearance. As Americans we are never satisfied with our looks or appearance because we are comparing ourselves to the small percentage of beauties that we see on the screen and in magazines. However, what we must keep in mind is that our neighbors, relatives, and most of our friends look just like us. They are average in looks and work with what they have. It's a conscious, everyday battle not to get caught up in the mythical webs called commercials that are so intricately weaved for us by product sponsors and advertisers. We become vulnerable when we see the slim, tanned, toned bodies on the screen and want to succumb to the ideas and ideologies they're promoting. However if we as Americans can just remember that beauty comes from within and not from outside appearance, then we can begin to avoid getting caught up in these values and stay clear of any sticky webs that may be just waiting to entangle us.

—*Susan P.*

In this first version, Susan isn't sure what she wants to emphasize, and so her narrative covers more territory than she can reasonably develop in this short essay. Moreover, she hasn't yet determined if she is more interested in discussing the value Americans place on being thin and beautiful or the value placed on being fit. Finally, she recognized that her paragraphs didn't cluster material to make clear connections among ideas. Can you determine what she revised? Did the revisions make her selection of strategies more appropriate given the message she wants to communicate? What else do her revisions do to improve the paper?

If it's to your pleasure to watch spiders weave their silk webs, then sit back in your easy chair and relax because it's time for another TV commercial break and you are about to be the victim in a giant, illusory, mythical web of promises.

TV commercials used to be a potty break for a late night movie watcher, a quick minute to whisk the kids off to bed, or just a time to switch channels to make sure a more dramatic show was not on. Today, however, commercials are as popular as the TV sitcoms and dramas themselves; and advertisers are capitalizing on America's changing values by embodying cultural values in the commercials. For example, in the past three to five years this country has witnessed a fitness craze that has Americans spending $30 billion a year on running shoes, health club memberships and other sundries. In a recent Sunday issue of the *Rocky Mountain News* there were more than 36 advertisements for different health clubs and diet plans alone, and today there are more than 10,000 fitness clubs nationwide. Americans are concerned about fitness, but more importantly they are concerned with beauty and overall good looks. Because proper diet and exercise help maintain more youthful skin and hair as well as firmer muscles, many people have embarked on serious weight control programs and exercise regimens in order to improve their bodies and spruce up their overall appearance. Whatever people's motives may be, this change in values has stirred up the commercial industry like a giant Caesar salad, and advertisers are catering to these new concerns of beauty and good looks by promoting all kinds of products, mainly foods and beverages that promise to change your looks and thus make you prettier.

Dannon yogurt is a prime example of a commercial that makes a vast array of promises about what the product can do for one's looks. The commercial starts out not with dancing blueberries, mind you, but with 5 or 6 slim and toned males and females working out in a gym. There is no grunting and groaning as the young, vibrant, healthy individuals push and pull the weights, only euphoric smiles and sparkling eyes. Further on, the commercial focuses on a pair of pretty, slim, California blonde twins roller skating down a luscious green parkway. With pink shorts and tee shirts and striped bobby socks perfectly aligned, these two beauties glow with health and vitality. Finally, the last all-absorbing shot centers on a young, handsome, energetic couple biking up a mountain lane. The girl's long brown hair whipping in the wind, and the boy's taut thigh muscles gleaming of suntan oil only further enhance this notion of slim, toned, beautiful, youthful vitality. Behind each frame of gorgeous bodies a pleasant-voiced female sings "Who can? You can; get a Dannon body. WOW!!" as if she were calling out a familiar homecoming cheer.

With the snappy jingle and visual impact alone the Dannon company promotes its yogurt as a food that will give you great looks and a better body. Although the commercial doesn't specify how much yogurt one has to eat to get a Dannon body or exactly what a Dannon body is, it's taken for granted that it has something to do with good looks because of the testimonies of the beauties on the screen. These vague but visual commercials have come to embody America's changing values. More than any other country in the world, America is concerned with beauty and aesthetics, especially of the human body. In our society, if people are particularly handsome or pretty, we assume that they are also more successful, wealthy, and powerful. The value of beauty has stemmed largely from Hollywood as well as glamour magazines. Every day we're bombarded with stars and celebrities who've for the most part made it big because they were pretty or handsome. Because of this emphasis on beauty and better looks, everyone from teenagers to grandmothers is taking measures to improve their looks.

The Dannon commercial embodies this cultural importance on appearance. For example, every male and female that Dannon shows in the commercial from the blonde twins to the guys working out in the gym are pretty—and not just average pretty; these people resemble Greek gods with their clear, rosy skin and healthy, bouncy hair. While the commercial pushes that eating Dannon is the key to a better body, it is clear that the commercial is not just focusing on fitness but on great looks also. If the commercial were just stressing a better body, it could have used an average person such as a bald man. Although he may not be beautiful, he could be perfectly fit with a great body to match. After all, I know plenty of people who are perfectly fit and take great care of their bodies but who are about as pretty as a bulldog. However, the people at Dannon know how important beauty is to us and they know that they would sell little yogurt if they employed just the average-looking Joe.

Another cultural value that the commercial implies is that Slim is In! While all people in the Dannon commercial are beautiful, they are also *very slim*. According to Hollywood and the glamour magazines, thinness is a very attractive quality, so consequently the average American who may not be overweight at all feels fat in our thin-conscious society. I know plenty of people who are in great shape but who aren't twiggies like the one we see in the Dannon commercial. Dannon plays on this stereotype of extreme thinness and with marked success as Dannon is one of today's most popular brands.

Some final cultural values that Dannon implies in its yogurt commercial are sex appeal and success in personal relationships. For example, as the two blonde twins rollerskate down the parkway, there are men in the background commenting on and eyeing their gorgeous figures. Furthermore, every person shown exercising on the screen is doing so with a member of the opposite sex. What Dannon is trying to imply is that if you eat Dannon yogurt and get a Dannon body, you'll be more attractive to the opposite sex and have better luck at securing relationships. While commercials of this type imply in subtle overtones, nevertheless the connections are there. If relationships and the institution of marriage were not important in this culture, practically all commercials, except perhaps for toilet bowl cleaner, would be as exciting as vanilla. The commercials, such as Dannon's, embody our cultural values including sex, relationships, and marriage.

It's a conscious everyday battle not to get caught up in the mythical web called commercials that are so intricately woven for us by product sponsors and advertisers. It's easy to become vulnerable when we hear of a product that can do miracles with our looks and see the slim beauties on the television as well as in magazines. However, if Americans can just remember that beauty is in the eyes of the beholder, then everyone must be special in at least one person's eyes. Beauty comes from within and not from outside, and when we can all realize this, then we can begin to avoid getting caught up in these stereotypical values and stay clear of any sticky webs that may be just waiting to entangle us.

Practice—Analyzing

1. Can you define the characteristics of Susan's audience? How could she tailor the essay to appeal more to the readers you describe?

_____

_____

_____

_____

2. What methods of development does Susan now use? _____

_____

_____

_____

3. Did any details strike you as particularly effective? Which ones?

_____

_____

4. Does the opening paragraph get and keep your attention? Why?

_____

_____

5. Where does Susan now state the main point of the article? Is this an

   effective placement? _____

_____

_____

6. What further revisions could you suggest for Susan's next version?

_____

_____

_____

_____

Now consider this primarily descriptive paragraph. Does it make a point beyond the description?

> When Mom and Dad unexpectedly walked into my residence hall room, they saw an unorganized, filthy living area, its disorder resulting from an untimely wild party the night before. The first disgusting sight they saw was the window stained with dried beer, put there by a beer fight between two drunken friends. The windows were stained to the point where it kept sunlight from entering the room, making it dreary and cold. As my parents walked in further, they stepped on a disorderly pile of textbooks strewn carelessly on the floor, left there after I hastily cleared my desk for use as a platform in a game of quarters. Among the pile of books stood a broken lamp, its metal twisted like a pretzel from its use as a substitute football during an in-hallway game of drunks. The carpet, covered with butter-

stained popcorn spilled by unwary floormates, was stained enough to give it the appearance of a mini oil slick; the floor became so slippery my Dad nearly fell. Disappointed with me and my living surroundings, Mom and Dad dejectedly turned around and began to walk out of the room, just in time to fall over the back wheel of my bicycle, which my friend next door carelessly left lying next to the door after taking the bike on a casual ride through the residence hall. Although my parents weren't hurt, they became upset over my disgraceful, dirty room, wondering if they'd raised a slob; I will never hold parties in my room again.

—Joseph W.

Practice—Analyzing

1. Who is Joseph writing to? What details suggest the audience most clearly? _____

_____

_____

2. How does Joseph analyze the reason for the room's condition?

_____

_____

3. Why does the paragraph conclude as it does? Is this an effective close?

_____

_____

_____

4. What further revisions could you suggest for Joseph's next version?

_____

_____

_____

_____

Let's look at what just one more student did in revising and editing his own work:

> Holding down a job in high school can be a valuable experience that teaches responsibility in managing finances that is sure to be called on later in college. Holding down a job in high school allows the student to get the feeling of handling money. It instills a sense of independance for the student and allows them to make decisions on how to distribute funds. The ability to manage your dollars wisely is an absolute necessity when a student reaches college age and is forced to make these decisions for themselves. Without the practical experience that one can get from a part time job in high school it isn't easy for a student to realize the importance of money. Earning your own money also makes one appreciate the value of the dollar and how much it takes to earn it. As a college freshman I felt all the difficulties of adjusting to college and how hard it was to be on your own, but the problem of managing funds was one of those steps that didn't scare me at all, due to my experience of part time work I felt compleatly confident on my knowledge of finance, which made trips to the bookstore easy. For the reasons I've stated here I find that the experience of a part time job is priceless when a student is confronted with the problems with money that can arise if they inexperienced in dealing with it, I hope you agree.
>
> —*Jim M.*

As you can see, Jim has much work to do to revise this paper. He needs a clearer focus to help him stay on a single point in the paragraph. He needs to concentrate on his own experience so that he can provide more details. When he has revised focus, unity, and development, then he can worry about editing for errors. Now see just what Jim did as he reworked his paper:

> Holding down a job in high school was a valuable experience that taught me a sense of responsibility in managing finances that was sure to be called on later in college. Holding down a job allowed me to get the feeling of handling money and gave me a sense of independence by allowing me to make decisions on how to distribute funds. The ability to manage dollars wisely was an absolute necessity when I reached college and was forced to make these decisions alone. Without the practical experience of managing money I was almost certain to face difficulty in budgeting my funds. As a CSU freshman I felt all the difficulties of adjusting to college and how hard it was to be on my own, but because I had a job in high school the problems of manipulating money were easier. Because I had to make car payments, save for college and come up with my own spending money while I was still in high school, knowing how to spend money wisely wasn't a problem I faced during my first year away from home. I feel that my knowledge in this area helped me in being able to manage a checkbook, pay bills and allocate money towards entertainment and recreation. In my opinion, holding down

a job in high school is a priceless opportunity that all secondary students should look into for the valuable knowledge it offers when preparing for college and later life.

As you have no doubt discovered, revision can be hard, time-consuming work. But in each case, the revised paper is more effective than the earlier draft. Like Susan, Joseph, and Jim, you too can revise effectively by re-envisioning what your paper must do for your readers. Add your own questions to this preliminary list to help you revise *your* papers:

1. Have you set your paper aside to give you time to look objectively at it?
2. Have you determined as precisely as possible the audience and purpose of your paper?
3. Have you focused your main idea carefully?
4. Have you maintained that single main idea throughout your paper?
5. Have you supported your main idea with complete details?
6. Have you connected parts of your paper so that readers proceed smoothly, seeing clear logical links?
7. Have you considered different strategies or different arrangement for parts of your paper?

HOW CAN YOU EDIT MORE EFFECTIVELY?

In the last unit of this text, we'll review the major editing problems students commonly struggle with, but my best advice is not to worry about editing until you are ready to prepare a paper to give to a reader. Yes, readers will notice errors or confusing sentences, but worrying about how to avoid errors may distract you from getting your ideas on paper in the first place. Besides, editing is not so difficult if you develop a step-by-step checklist of your own typical errors. Do not try to cover more than one of these points at a time as you go through your papers. When you are more sure of what errors you make or what weaknesses you need to improve, then you can condense the list or personalize it. But always edit your paper for one problem at a time.

I find that beginning with the bigger issues is most helpful in editing.

1. Do I need to combine sentences for clarity, precision, variation?
   To answer this question, most students go through the paper concentrating on one sentence at a time or on two adjacent sentences. If they see wordy repetition, they combine sentences to reduce repeated words and phrases. If they see sentences repeatedly beginning with

the subject, they reorder sentence parts. If they see a phrase that doesn't fit or make sense where it is, they rearrange or rewrite. Reading the paper aloud often helps writers catch those sentences that need work.

2. Do I need to change sentence punctuation?

   Because readers find these errors so distracting, writers should edit separately for sentence punctuation if they have any problem at all in using periods, commas, and semicolons correctly.

3. Do I need to choose more precise, active words?

   In some papers, particularly those that express a personal perspective, you'll want to check for words that create your personal impression. In persuasive papers, you may want to check for neutral words to avoid emotionalism. Let the audience and purpose of your paper determine how much time to spend on this step.

   After dealing with the bigger issues, then I look for nitty-gritty details:

4. Do I see any errors in subject-verb agreement?
5. Do I see any errors in pronoun usage?
6. Do I see any wordy, clichéd, or empty sentences I should rewrite?
7. Do I see any proofreading errors?
   a. Comma usage
   b. Apostrophes
   c. Commonly confused words
   d. Spelling
   e. Other errors I know I make

Practice—Writing

Look through your journal or notebook where you've been keeping ideas to write about. Select a topic and begin defining an audience for an essay that will primarily inform but persuade as well (though persuasion is a secondary concern). Using one or more of the methods we've practiced, brainstorm for ideas and then consider which strategies will best develop your paper.

Writing assignments

1. Illustrate the writing process for someone who has not had a course like this one. You might use as your audience students still in high school or adults who have not attended college. Be specific as you define your readers. Use your reading and experience to explain as

fully as possible what goes into writing a paper. You might compare your process now with your assumptions before you began the course, compare your process with someone else's, or compare the process with some other common process your readers might be more familiar with. You might devise an extended analogy for the writing process, or you might narrate your most frustrating or rewarding experiences as a writer. You might warn or excite younger students about what lies ahead for them in college writing. Define your goals clearly and then determine which writing strategies will best meet your goals.

2. Write again about any of the topics you've covered so far in the text. Take a different perspective or define a different audience for this paper.

3. Explain some personal or cultural values—such as cleanliness or fitness, for instance—so that readers see both the value and why you or your culture cherishes it.

UNIT TWO

Illustrating

Sometimes when we practice a skill, we like to practice on relatively easier pieces until we build a little more confidence to try harder work. This unit collects those patterns of developing ideas that come more easily to most writers. After all, we tell stories, describe pictures, and give examples often in our conversations with friends and family. We also see these patterns of development most frequently in reading because they are such good ways to communicate ideas. And so beginning with these patterns may make writing a little more approachable—and perhaps even fun.

Don't be fooled, though, into thinking that these patterns won't require you to think and work. The topics in these chapters will be fun but challenging, and you will learn more about reading and writing from practicing these kinds of writing.

chapter 6
Narrating

a snatch of experience

WHAT IS NARRATION?

Among the oldest written texts we have are stories or narratives. Narration means simply storytelling, and it's a skill we practice orally from childhood. Readers and writers quickly learn to use stories as entertainment or education. Even the Bible is structured mainly as a story with shorter stories or parables to make specific points.

WHEN DO WE USE NARRATION IN COLLEGE WRITING?

We might use personal experiences as stories to make a point any time that detailed personal experiences would convince readers. For instance, in making out an application to a professional program, say Occupational Therapy, you might tell about a particularly rewarding experience you had helping a handicapped person. Stories or narratives also give a good sense of time and place and so might bring alive a history, geography, or

146

even political science paper. Similarly, you can tell a story to make an argument, as for instance the editorialist who writes about more funding for teenage suicide programs because his own son committed suicide. Narratives put readers in touch with writers while they also appeal to our human drive to tell and listen to stories; thus, they can be effective in almost any writing context.

Fairy tales and fables, especially, are stories that define our culture, our beliefs, some of our strongest values. What does the following fairy tale suggest about the importance of families?

"The Duck with Golden Eggs"
A Russian Fairy Tale

Once upon a time there were two brothers, one rich and the other poor. The poor one had a wife and children, but the rich one lived all alone. The poor brother went to the rich one and begged of him: "Brother, give me some food for myself and my poor children; today I have not even anything for dinner." "Today I have no time for you," said the rich brother. "Today princes and boyars are visiting me; I have no place for a poor man." The poor brother wept bitterly and went to catch fish, hoping to get at least enough fish to make a soup for his children. The moment he cast his net, he brought up an old jug. "Drag me out and break me on the shore, " said a voice inside the jug, "and I will show you the way to fortune." He dragged out the jug, broke it, and a spirit came out of it and said: "On a green meadow stands a birch. Under its root is a duck. Cut the roots of the birch and take the duck home. The duck will lay eggs—on one day a golden egg, the next day a silver one." The poor brother went to the birch, got the duck, and took it home. The duck began to lay eggs—on one day a golden egg, the next day a silver one. The poor man sold the eggs to merchants and boyars and grew rich in a very short time. "My children," he said, "pray to God. The Lord has had mercy upon us."

The rich brother grew envious and spiteful. "Why has my brother grown so rich?" he wondered. "Now I have become poorer, and he wealthier. Surely he has committed some sin." He lodged a complaint in court. The matter reached the tsar, and the brother who had been poor and was now rich was summoned to the tsar's presence. What could he do with the duck? His children were small, and he had to leave the duck with his wife. She began to go to the bazaar, selling the eggs for a high price. Now, she was very pretty, and she fell in love with a barin. "How have you become so rich?" the barin asked her. "It was the will of God," she replied. But he insisted, saying, "No, tell me the truth; if you do not, I won't love you; I won't come to see you any more." He stopped visiting her for a day or two. Then she called him to her house and told him. "We have a duck," she said. "Each day it lays an egg—on one day a golden egg, the next day a silver one." "Show me that duck," said the barin. "I want to see what kind of a bird it is." He examined the duck and saw an inscription in golden letters on its belly; the inscription said that whoever ate the duck's head would be a king, and whoever ate its heart would spit gold.

The prospect of such great fortune made the barin's mouth water, and he began to press the woman to slaughter the duck. For some time she refused, but in the end she slaughtered the duck and put it in the oven to roast. It was a holiday; she went to mass, and during that time her two sons came home. They wanted to eat something, looked into the oven, and pulled out the duck; the elder one ate its head and the younger its heart. The mother returned from church, the barin came, they sat at table; the barin saw that the duck's head and heart were missing. "Who ate them?" he asked, and finally discovered that the boys had done it. He began to press their mother: "Kill your sons and take out the brains of one and the heart of the other; if you do not kill them our friendship is ended." When he had said this he left her; she languished for a whole week, then could not stand it any longer, and sent for the barin. "Come to me," she begged. "So be it! I won't even spare my children for your sake." As she sat whetting a knife, her elder son saw her thus, began to weep bitterly, and implored her: "Dear mother, permit us to take a walk in the garden." "Well, go, but don't go far," she said. But the boys, instead of taking a walk, took to their heels.

They ran and ran, then grew tired and hungry. In an open field they saw a herdsman tending cows. "Herdsman, herdsman, give us some bread," they said. "Here is a little piece," said the herdsman. "That's all I have left. Eat, and may it serve your health." The elder brother gave the bread to the younger, saying: "Eat it; you are weaker than I; I can wait." "No, brother," the younger said, "you have led me by my hand all this time; you are more tired than I; let us divide the bread equally." They divided it equally and ate it, and both were sated.

They went on farther; they walked straight ahead along a wide road, and then the road branched into two forks. At the crossroads stood a post, and the post bore an inscription: "He who goes to the right will be a king; he who goes to the left will be wealthy." The younger brother said to the elder: "Brother, you go to the right. You know more than I do; you can understand more." The elder brother went to the right, and the younger to the left.

The elder brother walked and walked till he came to a foreign kingdom. He asked an old woman to give him shelter for the night, and in the morning he arose, washed himself, got dressed, and said his prayers. The king of that kingdom had just died, and all the people assembled in the church, carrying candles; it was the law that he whose candle lighted first of itself should be the new king. "Do you too go to church, my child," said the old woman. "Perhaps your candle will light first." She gave him a candle. He went to the church and had no sooner entered than his candle lighted of itself. The princes and boyars became envious; they tried to put out the candle and drive the boy out. But the queen from high on her throne said: "Don't touch him! Whether he is good or bad, he is my fate." The boy was taken by the arm and led to the queen; she put her golden seal on his forehead, took him to her palace, led him to the throne, proclaimed him king, and married him.

They lived together for some time; then the new king said to his wife: "Give me leave to go and search for my brother." "Go, and God be with you," the queen said. He traveled for a long time through various lands and found his younger brother living in great wealth. Great piles of gold filled his barns; whenever he spat, he spat out gold. He had nowhere to put all his wealth. "Brother," said the younger to the elder, "let us go to our father and see how he is faring." "I am ready," said the elder brother. They drove to the place where their father and mother lived and asked for shelter in their parents' house without telling who they were. They sat at table, and the older brother began to talk about the duck that laid golden eggs and about the wicked mother. The mother constantly interrupted him and changed the subject. The father guessed the truth. "Are you my children?" he asked. "We are, dear father," they replied. There was kissing and embracing and no end of talk. The elder brother took the father to live with him in his kingdom, the younger went to find a bride for himself, and the mother was left all alone.

Practice—Analyzing

1. As one kind of folklore, fairy tales have served important functions in teaching members of a society the informal rules of that culture. What points does this fairy tale teach?

_____

_____

2. Why would a society place such emphasis on family trust and sharing?

_____

_____

3. Who are the two brothers focused on at the beginning of the story? And the two at the end? How do the two pairs differ? Cite specific evidence about their differences.

_____

_____

_____

4. Keeping in mind that one point of this tale is to emphasize the sacredness of family ties, can you explain why the mother was left alone at the end of the story?

_____

_____

5. Look back at paragraph 1 and the first lines of paragraph 2. What did you expect to happen in the story when you first reached this point in reading? Why were you right or wrong?

_____

_____

6. Does this tale leave out any information readers *might* want to know? Does it omit *essential* information? Where would you add any details?

_____

_____

7. What purpose do paragraphs serve in this tale?

_____

_____

8. Other than because it's a fairy tale, why do you expect a happy ending to this tale? Is it happy?

_____

HOW DO WE READ NARRATION?

From the beginning of recorded ideas, people of all cultures have used stories to record their personal experiences, to teach conventional morality, and to entertain. We still read stories in many different contexts: newspapers contain feature stories highlighting a specific individual's achievements or shortcomings, novels develop detailed stories about characters, and even business reports contain stories of successes and failures of new products or management decisions. And we probably tell or hear stories almost daily—when a friend talks about an amusing incident during registration for classes, when a classmate tells a joke, or when we recount the frustrations of the day to a roommate, spouse, or parent.

Because stories are so familiar, and because we internalize their structures early in life when we hear and later tell stories, narration is one of the most familiar kinds of reading and writing. Given a conventional story, few readers have any difficulty reading with understanding. Readers need to know why they are reading a narrative—to learn a moral point, to entertain themselves, to see an illustration of experience—and then they can enjoy and extract meaningful information from their reading.

Readers look for a "point" to the story

If readers are more concerned about the "point" of a narrative, then they may pay less attention to the details. For example, most of us are familiar with Christ's parables in the New Testament. The parables convey information rather than simply entertain. Although readers thoroughly familiar with the parables can remember great detail about the characters in the parables, most readers remember the moral issue. In short, most readers won't remember the color of the Good Samaritan's cloak but will remember why Christ told the parable.

Typically, readers entertaining themselves with a good story will remember details from the plot, character, and setting descriptions. The details of sight, sound, smell, taste, and touch create a world that readers immerse themselves in. In addition, readers truly caught up in reading narratives supply more detail from their own experience. Reading provides a link between reader and writer through the words on the page and the ideas evoked in the reader's mind.

Readers predict outcomes of stories

Reading narratives or stories is so familiar that we pay little attention to the work it involves. For instance, how many of you realized that when you read "once upon a time" you were already beginning to make judgments about the passage at the beginning of this chapter? Most of you read the title of the fairy tale and "A Russian fairy tale" and began creating a framework that would allow you to make sense of the passage. If you didn't know "boyars" and "barins," you probably guessed that they were Russian nobles and read on. You undoubtedly noticed the repetition and accepted it as a normal feature of fairy tales. You probably did the same with the unrealistic elements—the talking jug, the inscribed duck, the crossroads marker. We all perform such mental actions when we read fairy tales or narratives of other sorts. We try to locate the action in a particular place, at a particular time, and we try to determine why characters act in a certain way. We need to create such a structure so that the details make sense to us. But because narratives are so familiar from childhood and through daily exposure to stories and jokes, we do most of this work without it requiring any conscious effort. Only when we read a narrative that doesn't fit into a common pattern do we realize the effort we expend reading stories as simple as fairy tales.

HOW DO WE WRITE NARRATION?

Writing narratives in expository writing is probably less enjoyable than in creative writing, but because stories come so naturally to us, writing them seems almost effortless at first glance. When we examine the requirements of a good narrative piece, then we realize that polishing a story is not as easy as beginning to write it.

Narratives as evidence

When writers determine that the most persuasive piece of information or evidence they have is a snatch of experience, then they choose narration as the best means to present this evidence. In writing a narrative, any writer keeps in mind just why she wants to tell the story. For example, just this morning I was reading a magazine article about young career women looking to married men in their business world as mentors or special guides in learning the ropes. As the article discussed the pros and cons of such relationships, the writer needed a solid example to substantiate the point she was making. She included a narrative example about Mary Cunningham of Seagram's and her experience with the Bendix Corporation. By *showing* just what she meant about advantages and disadvantages for young women looking for mentors, that writer made her point more clearly than if she had simply stated the point baldly or supported it with general statements. Narrative examples serve the same function in much writing.

Consider, for a moment, that in your psychology course your instructor asks you to comment on sibling rivalry, particularly on the appropriate parental response to "warring" brothers. As you formulate a position you might talk about whether or not parents should intervene to stop brothers from fighting, you recall an incident from your own past. When you and your brother had a chance to work out problems on your own, you felt much closer afterward. By using your personal experience, you will be more convincing when you present your case for parents not interfering because your teacher and classmates will understand that you are relying on an actual event to support your point. Narratives work the same way in writing for any field.

Narratives as explanations

When we get to Chapter 10 on causes and effects, we'll look in detail at another form of evidence plus analysis. The narrative can provide such evidence and suggest explanations of a process or cause/effect relationship. Narratives can also support other kinds of analysis as well. Consider the following narrative and think about its implied explanations of faith.

"Revelation," *The Wooster Anthology*, pp. 5–7.

Jerry Thomas

Reading *A Portrait of the Artist as a Young Man* makes me think of religion and my own religious experience—not capitalized, not an event, but the overall experience of religion in my life. I remember a time when I was considering the ministry—what does a twelve-year-old know? I thought I knew a lot at the time, including the definite existence of God and Jesus Christ his son, my savior, my passport to eternal life and salvation from the sins of this world. I was sure of my life after death and fairly sure of my life before—I wanted to share my profound knowledge from the pulpit.

I had been properly trained in the Christian Church—Disciples of Christ—since the age of five or six (much can be accomplished in a few short years). My parents were regular churchgoers, and therefore so was I. I listened attentively and learned well. Love your neighbor. Believe in Christ. Don't lie, cheat, or steal. Turn the other cheek. Live a "Christian" life and the rewards of Heaven are yours forever after. I never became fanatical about my religion; I just believed unquestioningly and acted accordingly.

But then a certain summer occurred. It was July and I was going to be a freshman in high school. I spent that entire month with my brother in the religious center of the West—Berkeley, California. I was thrown by it all at first; I was just on the brink of adolescence and hadn't left the Midwest but once—for Raleigh, North Carolina, which could hardly be considered a center of modern liberalism and innovative realities. I suppose whether Berkeley is could be debated as well. But to me at that time it was, with people in long white robes and bald heads chanting blessings to a god unheard of, and street people with their wares offering a religion (they would deny that label), and the *Barb,* Berkeley's hometown weekly, sacrificing the female body at their altar (I could have been massaged right through my teens with one issue). On the whole I refused these services (I did partake of a short communion with the street people who offered their bread and wine at a good price—a new belt, a wallet, a string art piece, freshly squeezed lemonade), but I accepted the religion of my brother—the religion of disbelief.

Most people don't enter a period of religious introspection until much later, at least late high school or early college years. But I was lucky. There I was in Berkeley, where everything orthodox is questioned and everything heretical accepted without question. And I had an older brother who was in the depths of the question and shared it with his younger brother. I can still remember sitting in his apartment splitting a beer (I had just discovered Coors) and arguing about what I insisted I knew and he insisted I could not know, only believe.

"How do you *know* there is a god? Or that Jesus was more than a mortal man?"

"I just *do!*"

"You can't possibly *know*. You might *believe*—millions of people do. But you can't know."

We argued for a long time, but I realized fairly quickly (though I wouldn't admit it at the time—sibling rivalry still burned hotly within me) that my brother was right. Any belief I possessed was on faith, not knowledge. Suddenly the foundation was weakened. I thought I knew God, but how could I? How could anyone? Wouldn't it take something tangible, something you could see or hear, experience in some way? I had no proof of God's existence. And could I believe in Him without proof? Something inside of me said no, I couldn't. And I didn't.

Since that Berkeley summer, I have grown progressively further from religion. I'm now more of an atheist than anything else. This fact was emphasized to me when I served as a teaching apprentice in a freshman college course. We read in the course several works in which religion was a major thematic component (*Antigone,* Plato's *Apology, A Man for All Seasons, Inherit the Wind*). It was incredible to listen to some of the freshman comments. So young they seemed—so unquestioning—so naive—so—fresh! I remember the day I revealed my atheistic tendencies. We were discussing the separation of church and state in the context of public education. I proposed the removal of religious-based holidays from school calendars and an end to organized activities which are connected with religious celebrations (my example was Christmas plays). The professor commented that such thinking has led to the suggestion that all religious discussion be extracted from school texts as well, so as to avoid a possible interpretive presentation by the author. My suggestions didn't seem so radical to me, but they did to the students. It was quiet in the room and I received several inquisitive looks, as if they weren't sure what to make of me anymore. They seemed wary of what my comments revealed about my personality. (Is he some kind of subversive? After all, he said before that he was a conscientious objector!) Maybe they assumed a Presbyterian College wouldn't permit an atheist to assistant teach a course. One of them asked me that evening, "Do you *really* feel that way, or did Professor Thomas just have you say that?"

"His suggestion carried it further than I would have, but—"

"Oh good," she interrupted, "I thought you were an atheist or something."

"Well, I am most of the time."

"Oh."

It's strange; I wish I could believe as easily as most of the freshmen believe. I want to believe. But it all seems quite unbelievable, if anything. Yet there's always that nagging doubt in my head. What if it's true? What if I'm damning myself with every word, thought, deed that shows I'm a nonbeliever? I live largely by the Christian philosophy—I say because I like it, but it's probably more out of convenience than anything; I know nothing else—but will my actions void of belief be enough if it all turns out to be a reality? I have difficulty understanding people who don't question, who believe without ever questioning. But if I ever believe again, I'll have no doubt—and my mind won't be changed. I wonder if I'll ever see that time. I doubt it. Why do I want to? Security, the human need to explain what we fear and can't explain. When I believed, it was much easier to think of death. Maybe a part of me somewhere in there still believes. I can't think of death without that nagging doubt occurring— what if they are right? What if there is something after all of this? Something wonderful, something beautiful; something I too could share in if only I believed?

The conversation with my brother took place about eight years ago. He still doesn't believe, and still questions. So do I. Unfortunately, religious reflection is easily placed aside. I hope by the time I die my belief or lack of belief is free of question. If I'm in turmoil I won't be happy. Just to believe—totally—one way or the other, and I could die peacefully. The tendency to question religion, to not believe, is strong; so is the desire to believe. But neither is as strong as belief itself. I find myself in a bit of a bind. I doubt I'll ever *believe* again unless I *know,* and that would take nothing short of a revelation (I think). Yet, can I *not believe* without knowing? Doesn't not believing imply the opposite—that I believe there is no god? Or am I in limbo somewhere? I can't *know* either way, and can't believe without knowing, yet by not believing that there is a god— or not knowing—I am implicitly saying that I believe there isn't. I guess. Oh God! How do I know?

I feel (I hesitate to use the word believe) that if I do ever have faith again, it will be true faith. Perhaps that is unattainable without a period of questioning in one's life. I wonder if I ever will believe again. I'd like to. I want to. But I don't.

Practice—Analyzing

1. Briefly, what story does Thomas tell?

_____

_____

2. How does he focus the story to concentrate on the main points of the narrative that will explain his problem?

_____

_____

3. What narrative details suggest *explanation* rather than simply storytelling?

_____

_____

_____

4. Do you find the story a convincing way for Thomas to explain his dilemma?

_____

_____

Narratives are focused

Depending on the purpose of the writing and the strength of personal experience, writers decide if using a narrative will make a strong case convincing to readers. If so, writers state the point of the narrative as clearly as possible—as a guide to themselves and perhaps as a topic sentence or thesis for readers. Then writers *focus* on the precise segment of the experience that illustrates the main point. Although every experience relates to every other experience we have, we can't go back to birth for the lead-in for a recent incident. Rather, readers want to see the crucial moment in great detail but to read only absolutely necessary introductory or "scene-setting" details. For instance, people often ask why I wear a bicycle helmet whenever I ride my bike around town, even on hot summer days. Instead of simply telling them, "it's safer," I let them draw their own conclusions from my story of a bike-car accident when I was on the bike. I have to get to the point, though, and so I don't tell them what a beautiful, sunny morning it was or how long it took for bruises to disappear. Rather, I tell them about the collision—in as much gory detail as I feel is appropriate for each occasion. My story is much more effective than any injunction to "be safe or sorry."

As you might guess, then, narratives don't always have explicit topic sentences or thesis statements. But if a clearly stated main point will help readers, writers include a topic sentence. If so, then the topic sentence must be as precise as possible in stating the point the story will illustrate. Typically, such topic sentences also indicate the writer's attitude toward the incident or the point of the story.

Practice—Focusing narratives

Which of the following paragraphs have adequately focused topic sentences that tell readers the main point of the narrative? Revise topic sentences that are not focused.

> One August morning as I awoke while camping in the mountains, I noticed the beauty and peacefulness the mountains held. My first sensation was of the air. The air that morning was so clean and fresh that I felt as if I could take a knife and slice myself a piece to let my lungs savor. Then as I opened my eyes, I could see around me trees tall as buildings with brilliant colors of green aged to perfection. While thinking of the glory of camping, I noticed the stream of clear water. In its bed jagged rocks and pebbles were washed by water as calm as the blue sky that lay above it. The most beautiful experience of all that glorious morning was that the peaceful mountains I never noticed before would never go unnoticed again.
>
> —Tim M.

Revised topic sentence:

_____

_____

_____

death of a father figure / Bud / accident

Writing, an important skill which allows people to communicate with one another, often helps in expressing feelings. For example, when my girlfriend Kristy and I got into an argument concerning her mother, Kristy wouldn't talk to me for weeks. I realized how stupid the argument was, and so I sat down to express my feelings on paper. On this piece of notebook paper I jotted down a few ideas as to why the argument happened and ways that we could work things out. Then I compiled all of my ideas together and wrote her this letter to let her know how I felt. She received my letter and was quite impressed. Kristy then called me up, asking if we could talk things over. Writing helped me to gather my thoughts and also to think of what to say to her rather than blurt out something stupid to her face. It gave me a second chance because she was not willing to listen to me before. In conclusion, writing helped me to express my thoughts and let my girlfriend know my feelings.

—Scott L.

Revised topic sentence:

_____

_____

_____

As you revise the topic sentence in this final sample, look also at details you might need to delete to fit the new focus of the paragraph.

It was late Thursday night, and the roads were deserted. On my way home from a friends I would never have expected what lay before me. An accident of all things, certainly the one thing I did not need. I was driving home, casually listening to the radio when without warning it happened. It was a car coming from the other direction. He suddenly turned into my lane. It happened so fast that all I had time to do was hit the brakes. If you have ever been in an accident you know what came next. That unforgettable sound when two cars collide. It is an extremely loud, almost indescribable crash as the metal crumples like a piece of paper. Along with this is the sound of glass as it shatters. But before this comes the warning sound of the brakes as they squeal in an attempt to stop the vehicle. When the car did stop I got out and proceeded to the other car so fast that I did not realize what I was doing. While at the other car I commenced to inform the driver of my opinion of him. Then I felt something warm and sticky trickling down my face. I reached up to my forehead to discover that I was bleeding. At that moment a feeling of fear unlike any I have ever felt before took over my body, and I began to panic. Unconsciously I returned to my car. Standing beside it I managed to stop some people. From here my memory becomes blurry. All I remember is some voices and sirens and lights and a few fuzzy figures. The next thing I recall is sitting down in the car. My jacket that was white was now a deep red. I also remember looking at the windshield. It was not completely broken. There was only one hole about the size of my head; there were also a few pieces of hair stuck to the glass. Around the hole the glass looked like an intricately woven web. From there I only remember the ambulance and the hospital. They both looked sterile and smelled of the usual disinfectant. Now I know whenever I tell this story I am asked two questions: 1) Were you drunk?—the answer is no. 2) Was it your fault?—again, no. The last answer can be proven, because it was the other driver who received a ticket for driving on the wrong side of the road. One of the things that make this situation so hard is that I had no control. It was not due to my driving, and there was nothing I could do to avoid the accident. But then, is that not how it always is?

—Pam D.

Revised topic sentence:

_____

_____

_____

Narratives follow chronological order

Most narratives, like the preceding fairy tale, follow chronological order, that is, order of time. When we tell stories to friends, we are careful to tell actions in the order they occurred. Similarly, most narratives do the same so that readers can follow the flow of action. After we become familiar with this predominant pattern of narration, then we learn about flashback techniques and other nonchronological orderings of narrative details. But such techniques are usually reserved for artistic narratives. When we want to use narration to support a point in expository writing, we follow the chronological pattern easiest for readers to follow so that the point of the narrative rather than the technique is uppermost in readers' minds.

To summarize, then, writing narratives involves determining if a narrative is appropriate evidence for the position you're taking, finding a strong narrative example, focusing on the key elements of the experience, and then developing sensory detail to bring the experience to life.

Practice—Writing

You've been thinking, I hope, about families—sharing in good times and bad, protecting one another, being faithful to the family. Do we still value family relationships today as the Russians must have centuries ago? What can family ties contribute in a world where couples might have jobs in Boston and Los Angeles and see each other only twice a month, but where we can "reach out and touch someone"? A world where few of us think about bread and soup for subsistence, where sharing might mean giving a family member an expensive mail-order Christmas gift but not sharing any time, where 50 percent of marriages end in divorce? What does your family mean to you?

Let's look at possible approaches to a topic on family ties. Assume that your instructor wants you to write about some experience of yours like that of the brothers in the fairy tale. Have you ever relied on a member of your family to get you over some crisis and then shared the rewards together? Just what have been your experiences of the strength—or weakness—of family ties? Think about your experiences as you read through these two paragraphs.

APPLYING NARRATION

A suppertime conversation one fall evening several years ago shows how both my parents can join forces to make me feel worse than I already do. My mother slammed the knives and forks on the table with a startling clatter and stormed back to the sink. A bright yellow tablecloth with red roses did nothing to counteract the tension that hung about our usually cheery kitchen. Quizzically my father glanced at me, but I lowered my eyes quickly and labored at my grapefruit until I squeezed it dry. My brother solemnly leaned over his lamb chops and string beans. The large black, yellow, and blue marks on his arm stood out, the result of a fight with me that afternoon. Again mother stalked to the table, her brown eyes moist, the glass salt shaker clenched in her hand. She let loose her rage in a violent burst of words. "Are you crazy? Do you want to break your brother's arm?" I slouched lower in my chair, taking a piece of broiled meat in my mouth but unable to swallow it. My father looked at me through steel grey eyes. "I told you never to raise your hands in anger in this house," his voice boomed. The words echoed in my head as I felt my face warm. My mother shrieked at the top of her voice, "Why can't you get along with your brother the way your cousins do? They laugh and play together, but not you, not Allen of the jungle; you have to fight and punch your brother." Quietly, sternly, my father said, "I've never hit you, Allen, without first discussing the situation with you like civilized people, have I?" I stirred uncomfortably in my chair and murmured an acknowledgement. My father's words weakened the wall that I built to fight my mother's assault. "I've brought you up to respect your brother and him you. We won't speak about this again, but in the future you'd better think before raising your hands." Feeling ashamed for my childish behavior, I excused myself from the table and tramped off sullenly to my cave.

—Allen

As a child, I can clearly recall a summer afternoon in the Rocky Mountains when my father, brother, and I experienced the closeness of one another by sharing the beauty of a cool rainstorm. As the wondrous event began, drops of clear water fell from the bright blue sky. The three of us looked at each other with quiet reservation and hurriedly ran into the fluorescent orange tent. The air, slowly losing its enfolding warmth, caused us to snuggle up together in our soft, fluffy sleeping bags. Sticking our heads out of the protective tents, we listened quietly to the noisy thunder slowly rolling toward us. Electricity and intensity in the crisp air made us shiver and held us with excitement and wonder. Suddenly, a loud clap of lightning fell from the gray sky and shook the lush nature around the tent. Nervous looks and laughter swiftly darted to and from each person. The mischievous drops of water sneakingly fell on the tent with a sharp "plink." Wet, musical rain fell faster and harder on the thick surrounding forest. The precipitation dropped on the tall pine trees with careless concentration. Soft green grass and colorful pink and yellow wild flowers shook and glittered with the pure crystal drops of rain. Beetles, squirrels, sparrows, and other small wildlife scurried to the protective arms of the forest. The storm lasted twenty minutes, letting us admire the beautiful show together until it slowly and quietly retired. Thunder passed over our heads as we sadly watched the finale of the wet event. Fresh air filled our lungs and we sniffed the sweet smells of wet pine and dewy grass. Time seemed to smile on us for those brief moments that we shared watching the beautiful play of nature. I will forever hold this glorious memory, recalling the loving bond my family shared between nature and ourselves.

—Anita

Obviously, Allen and Anita have different experiences that they feel show their attitudes toward the strength of family ties. For Allen, seeing his parents allied in disciplining him taught him a valuable lesson; for Anita, closeness means not so much the activity of the family as the activity of nature, so that in her paragraph we see details of nature's storm rather than an emotional storm. Yet both paragraphs make a point clearly, a personal point, but one that speaks to readers who can share the writer's perspective.

GETTING IDEAS FOR NARRATION

A moment ago I asked what experiences you have had that suggest the strength or weakness of family ties. Like me, you have probably experienced a range of feelings about your family. I have experienced closeness with each member of my family, and I have experienced anger and resentment. But if I had to choose one story that captured the essence of family relationships, I might want to consider one of the following kinds of activity:

when, as a youngster, my brothers and I collected soft drink bottles so that we could spend the refund money on candy

when we played games during car trips each summer

the emotional reaction to my brother's broken arm

moving day

"leaving home"

Each of these activities captures part of what I feel about family ties. As a writer, I would want to select that precise incident that could bring my feelings to life for my readers. I would be sure to focus on a slice of the experience so that I could develop my experience with precise details. I couldn't, for example, talk about the whole moving day, but I might want to recreate the feeling when I walked down into an empty basement in the house we were leaving. Or I might sketch our reactions to finding my brother asleep on a rug by the door after we moved furniture into the new house. As we will see when we consider description in the next chapter, part of my work as a writer will involve describing the physical location, but I want to emphasize the story, the event that shows my family's closeness.

For many people special occasions bring out the closeness they feel toward family members. Jot down some of the special events you can recall that might help you write about your family ties.

_____

_____

_____

Has a crisis ever made you feel closer to or farther apart from your family? Think of some of those instances.

_____

_____

_____

Just as unusual times can emphasize family relationships, some ordinary, everyday activities might best illustrate ties. Do you commonly share a meal, a prayer, a weekly outing that shows your family in action? List some of those experiences.

_____

_____

_____

_____

You probably now have several different possible incidents that will illustrate your point about family ties. Be sure to focus on a specific occasion so that you can develop precise details to recreate the scene for readers. Try answering the W questions (who, what, when, where, why, how) about each incident you've just listed. You might also try filling in details before you write a topic sentence. You might even decide that the point you want to make is so clear that you don't need a topic sentence to guide your readers. Start jotting down specific details of the incident that illustrates family ties. After you have sketched the incident in more detail, formulate the main point you want your paragraph to show. Eliminate those details that do not support your main point and fill in more details that do. Finally decide whether or not this paper needs a topic sentence or thesis statement.

If you are finding that family ties is not a good topic for you, you might think about other relationships—between friends, between teacher and pupil, between competitors. Start to work on the topic by listing incidents that show these relationships. Then refine your point and your narrative by working on details and the statement of your main point.

WRITING NARRATION

Think of an experience that illustrates the strength of family ties. Prepare a list of details of the incident. Now specify in a precise and focused topic sentence the controlling idea of the paragraph. Write the paragraph using appropriate details to support your main point.

Alternative topics

1. Friends, too, can support and console us when we need help. Think of a time when a friend helped you through a difficult time. Write the story so that a reader understands the importance of this friendship under trying circumstances.
2. Unfortunately, friends can let us down as well as lift us. Can you think of an instance when you counted on a friend only to be disappointed? Tell that story to a group of junior high students who might be pressured by peers into not helping a friend in need.
3. Look again at "Revelation." Can you think of a breakthrough you have had? Don't write about religious experiences, but select any other experience that you recall as a sudden understanding, a revelation.

REVISING FOR COHERENT NARRATIVES

Look again at the fairy tale at the beginning of the chapter. Did you have any difficulty following the flow of action as you read the story? Did you have any trouble reading the stories by Allen and Anita? Why not? Most likely, you will agree that the stories are easy to read because they follow chronological order. As I mentioned before, chronological or time order is the most common pattern for details in a narrative. In fact, readers expect to see details in time order. Think of the last time someone told you a story and kept saying, "Oh yeah, I forgot to tell you that Liz and Marybeth had a fight two days before the argument over Dan's phone call. And I forgot to mention the note Liz forgot to give MB." You probably found that story extremely frustrating to listen to. Similarly, readers expect to follow the action in a narrative as it happens, not as the writer haphazardly remembers details. If you can't remember all the details in chronological order as you first write them down, don't worry. But be sure to check for correct order when you add details, and be sure to rearrange all details in chronological order. Just for practice, try summarizing the plot of the last movie you saw. Would someone reading your plot summary be able to understand exactly how the movie progressed?

Consider this paragraph. Does it represent a coherent flow of action?

The fall morning of October 18, 1975, brought my father and me a lot closer together by sharing each other's company in a beautiful moment while hunting together. The morning was cold and crisp; our cheeks were rosy and noses numb. But being with my dad I didn't feel the cold. He wanted to stop, but he knew we had to keep going to stay warm. Because he was short and plump, my dad gasped for air as we went up a hill. We moved like one through the woods, as I crept behind my dad. We both got really excited. Through the trees we heard animals sounding like crashing cars. When we got to the spot where the animals were, there was steam coming off the ground from the animals' body heat. Their hooves marked up the frost that covered the ground. We decided to sit down and split a candy bar. As we sat, my father broke the silence as he said, "Son, it's not if we get an elk or not. The point of this experience is to enjoy what you are doing and who you are with."

—Brent

Some points in Brent's paragraph do not follow the order of action—notably, the father's gasping and wanting to stop for a breather and the crashing sound and the rising excitement. But other points do not flow smoothly even though they follow the order of events in Brent's story. Why not? Brent has left out details that connect one idea to the next. For example, what is the connection between the frosty ground and the candy bar? Obviously, because the elk had passed on, father and son decided they could not catch those animals so they could take a break. But Brent doesn't say so in his paragraph. Writers must include all relevant details so that readers see connections between sentences in narrative paragraphs. Brent also needs to consider his readers by providing more explicit transitional words and phrases. By using words such as "then," "next," "afterward," "meanwhile," and so on, Brent could supply some of the missing logical connections in his paragraph.

Look also at the following paragraph for coherence. Suggest revisions.

The most recent experience I have had
which illustrates the strength of family ties is
calling my mother last night and telling her
how hard up for money I was and then
receiving a check in the mail. She began to
tell me how she owed $800 on taxes for the
house she takes care of, and how she had to
borrow $500 from my brother, but then she
asked how hard up I was. By the time I
heard how tough things were for all of
them—my sister's tuition hadn't come in
yet, my younger brother had quit his high
paying job for one easier on his body but
harder on his budget—I didn't feel so hard
up, but my mother still could see my plight.
She said she thought my brother wasn't as
hard up as me and she would send me
money. I hung up feeling like no matter how
tough things were for anyone, my family
would always try to help in some way.

—Scott L.

In checking coherence in a narrative paragraph, read the paragraph aloud to listen to the connections between ideas. You may find that you "hear" gaps more easily than you see them.

REVISING FOR DETAILED NARRATIVES

A typical problem writers have is knowing just how much detail to include in their narratives. A writer must *select* detail so that only relevant detail appears in the paragraph or essay; that is, the writer must include only detail that helps make the point the story supports. But at the same time, the writer must include enough detail to be convincing. Consider the following essay and suggest where Dan might include more detail to make his story more effective in developing a single emotional impression. You may have to delete entire paragraphs and generate new details once you decide on the main point Dan wants to illustrate.

Like many other two-year-olds, Amanda's curiosity often got the best of her. This time it created real trouble for her. Motorcycles played as much a part in her life on the ranch as did the horses, ducks, and cows. When told she could go for a ride with her dad or brothers, Amanda would shout with excitement. Unfortunately, this did not happen as often as she wanted. One day she wanted to go but couldn't and wouldn't take "no" for an answer. Little did she know she was in for the ride of her life, an ordeal no youngster needs to experience.

By sitting unguarded, the Kawasaki set the stage. With Mom cooking in the kitchen, Amanda trudged out to what would eventually become an experience she is not likely to forget. Since no one was with her, we can only speculate what happened, although the outcome was apparent. Amanda, while trying to climb on the bike, managed to pull it over on top of her. Like any startled toddler she informed everyone within earshot that she was injured. As we came running, bewilderment and surprise dominated everyone's faces. Mom and Dad decided it best to leave everyone else at the ranch while they drove Amanda to the hospital. The injury appeared obvious; she had crushed her right leg. We soon learned she needed about a month in traction; the fuzzy picture of this problem's results was slowly becoming clear.

Looking at her scared and painful expression caused even the most stonefaced person to shed a tear. She lay there with both legs, tightly wrapped in Ace bandages, pointing straight up in the air. She looked as though she was being tortured for a crime she did not commit. Since she was too young to know what was happening, Mom and Dad decided that they would stay overnight at the hospital with her for the first week or until she adjusted to her new surroundings. The first days caused the most trouble for her so she slept often to escape from her problems. Amanda's emotional state fluctuated: she would laugh one minute and cry the next. The only successful method to stop her tears was to turn on her musical windup toys. After two weeks she had adjusted pretty well and found other activities to keep entertained. Although stuffed animals occupied most of her time, Amanda's favorite pastime was blowing bubbles out of liquid soap. Mom and Dad often brought in special gifts, such as coloring books, during one of their two daily visits.

While Amanda suffered the most, we all bore the burden of her most unfortunate mishap. Throughout the early days we took turns holding her hand and reiterating that her leg would heal. The helplessness and sorrow we endured was bad, but we missed her most during family gatherings. We looked forward to our daily visits as the entire family noticed her empty chair at the dinner table.

She progressed remarkably well and her left leg, which did not break, was removed from traction after the first two weeks. The right leg continued to heal correctly, and after four weeks of daily x-rays she was finally ready to get her body cast and go home. Her final day in the hospital was busy and exciting because all the nurses came by to wish her luck and say goodbye. While lying flat on her back in the back seat of the family car, she returned home. Life around the house was cheery on her return but not quite the same as before. She couldn't walk and needed to be either carried or pulled in her wagon. Under these circumstances, Amanda occupied the center stage for the next month. She had finally concluded the hardest part of an experience that few two-year-olds must undertake.

Revision checklist

1. Have you determined whom you will write your story to?
2. Have you determined the point your story will make? Have you stated that point as precisely as possible to guide your selection of details?
3. Does your topic sentence get your intended reader's attention?
4. Does the paragraph include enough detail to make the point?
5. Does the paragraph include only details that make the point?
6. Does the paragraph follow a clear, chronological order?
7. Have you remembered to conclude your story and your paragraph?

chapter 7
Describing

WHAT IS DESCRIPTION?

Describing a scene, object, or person means letting the reader recreate an image from your words. But unlike painting, which generally appeals only to sight, description appeals to all senses. A thorough description takes account of touch, taste, hearing, and smell as well as sight. Moreover, to guarantee that readers recreate an accurate image, writers use precise words that convey clearly the object but also, often, their feelings about that object.

WHEN DO WE USE DESCRIPTION IN COLLEGE WRITING?

Description is more common in college writing than you might first think. In lab reports, students typically write what they see under microscopes, but they also report other data they perceive—color shifts, odors from chemical mixtures, observed changes on oscilloscopes and other measurement devices, and so on. All these changes require description for clear reporting. In more advanced laboratory courses—anatomy and pathology—students describe the shape, color, texture, and perhaps smell of whatever they examine by dissection or under the microscope.

But description is not limited to lab sciences. Students of art history spend time learning accurate descriptive terms for periods of painting and sculpture and then use those terms to describe works of art. Film buffs, too, describe cinematic techniques and scenes as they evaluate movies. In broadcasting or political science courses, writers might describe the setting of a political debate. In public relations and advertising, writers describe ad campaigns, billboards, magazine covers, and so on. And if students are lucky enough to take cooking or wine tasting courses, then the descriptions can include more pleasant—but not less analytical—perceptions of good food and wine.

In the following passages from *Lords of the Arctic,* explorer and naturalist Richard Davids captures scenes from the arctic. As you read, notice how he uses details from several senses to help you recreate the scene.

"The Land of Arktos"
Richard C. Davids

The arctic is a beautiful, haunting land. The skies are often intensely blue, the snow so white that the horizon is a firm line that separates ice and sky as if a child had drawn it. At sunset, a shaft of brilliant ruby may shoot straight up, piercing the deep blue with unaccountable brilliance. The arctic is dreamlike and supernatural, as one explorer, Elisha Kent Kane, wrote a century ago, "a landscape such as Milton or Dante might imagine—inorganic, desolate, mysterious." Its beauty moved that man of action, Robert Peary, to write of a moonlit arctic night: "The great dark dome of the heavens seems far, far away. The stars twinkle with a clearness that pierces everything. There is a stillness, too—a great, wonderful silence. The aurora with its everchanging shape and color is a constant feast."

Where there are trees, they are often flagged by the wind, their branches on one side only, like pennants flying in a stiff breeze. Very little snow falls, but winds unimpeded by trees or other obstructions keep whipping it up, giving the illusion of frequent blizzards. . . .

There is one other attribute of the arctic that is extraordinary, and that is its silence. One July day, Dan and I set our tents up on a high cliff above an ice-locked bay on Brevoort Island, where hundreds of seals lay sunning. Snowbanks surrounded us on the rocky slopes, and, as the day wore on, tiny streams of water began flowing from them, tinkling across the flat rocks. By late afternoon, the tinkle had changed to a distant roar as thousands of little freshets merged into a cascade down the rocky ravines. Then, as the sun sank below a mountain at midnight, every stream turned silent. And what silence! It was as real an ingredient as rock and ice and sky. A lone snow bunting called; he seemed to shatter the crystalline air. Two glaucous gulls passed over; we could hear the soft beat of their wings. There was no other sound as we lay in our sleeping bags.

Practice—Analyzing

1. Why is it important to Davids that readers "see" his surroundings?

   _____

   _____

2. List some details appealing to each of the senses Davids includes.

   _____

   _____

3. In line 3, he compares the horizon to a child's drawing. How is this

   metaphor or comparison effective? _____

   _____

   _____

4. Why does he refer to Milton and Dante in paragraph 1? Does the reference help you, as a reader, reconstruct the scene of the arctic?

_____

_____

5. We've talked about levels of generality. Identify general description
   and details of description in this passage. _____

   _____

   _____

   _____

6. Can you characterize Davids' attitude toward the arctic? How would
   you define his emotions? _____

   _____

7. Does he try to make readers feel the same emotions? _____

   _____

HOW DO WE READ DESCRIPTION?

Because we rely on our sense perceptions for information about the
world around us, writers incorporate description and descriptive detail to
recreate a scene or to make readers aware of physical reality. Vivid
descriptive detail invites readers to participate fully in the writer's experience. As readers, we build up the details of the scene, in essence creating
a mental picture from the sensory details of physical surroundings. We
create spatial relationships among objects or parts of objects; we set up a
perspective with both background and foreground; we create an atmosphere—both physical and emotional—of warmth or cold, of color and
shadow, of noise or silence. Like viewing a fine oil painting, we, as readers, assemble details and create a sense of wholeness.

When reading description, we must remember that we bring our own
experiences to the reading. The mental picture we draw depends in part
on our ability to combine the writer's details but also in part on our personal perspectives. For instance, the Vietnam war veteran who reads a

description of an intense fire may bring to that image details of experience with napalm bombings. Or, when reading Davids' description of the arctic, readers invoke the shade of sky blue they can remember. Perhaps they brighten the color somewhat, but most readers work from their own experience.

Practice — Reading for sensory details

As you read Scudder's story about Professor Agassiz in Chapter 1, did you notice any descriptive details that helped to bring his story alive? Look again at a paragraph from that narrative.

> I was to keep the fish before me in a tin tray and occasionally moisten the surface with alcohol from the jar, always taking care to replace the stopper tightly. Those were not the days of ground-glass stoppers and elegantly shaped exhibition jars; all the old students will recall the huge neckless glass bottles with their leaky, wax-besmeared corks, half eaten by insects, and begrimed with cellar dust. Entomology was a cleaner science than ichthyology, but the example of the Professor, who had unhesitatingly plunged to the bottom of the jar to produce the fish, was infectious; and though this alcohol had a "very ancient and fishlike smell," I really dared not show any aversion within these sacred precincts, and treated the alcohol as though it were pure water. Still I was conscious of a passing feeling of disappointment, for gazing at a fish did not commend itself to an ardent entomologist. My friends at home, too, were annoyed when they discovered that no amount of eau-de-Cologne would drown the perfume which haunted me like a shadow.

1. What does Scudder describe here? _____

_____

2. What effects do details about the jar and stopper have on you?

_____

_____

3. Can you visualize those jars even though you are not an "old student" who can recall the jars? Why? _____

_____

4. And what does he describe in the second half of the paragraph?

_____

_____

5. What sense of the fish odor do you have from reading his

description? _____

_____

_____

6. What details give you the best sense of the "ancient and fishlike

smell"? _____

_____

_____

Using all senses

In describing, writers are sometimes tempted to use only visual details. Although we rely so heavily on vision, it is only one of the senses a good writer draws upon in description. Scudder and Davids not only both use visual details, but Scudder also appeals effectively to our sense of smell and Davids to our sense of hearing. The good reader, then, must also be prepared to respond to details of sound, touch, taste, and smell. Moreover, although we do not often acknowledge other sources of information about our world, we also take in information about balance, pressure, and innumerable other physical relationships. Readers do not consciously consider these experiences when they recreate a described scene, but since we can hardly exist in the world without the experiences, they undoubtedly color our understanding of an item described in our reading.

The good writer of description, then, creates a little world, and the good reader of description recreates that world in the mind.

Practice—Reading

"Denys L'Auxerrois," *Imaginary Portraits*

Walter Pater

A peculiar usage long perpetuated itself at Auxerre. On Easter Day the canons, in the very centre of the great church, played solemnly at ball. Vespers being sung, instead of conducting the bishop to his palace, they proceeded in order into the nave, the people standing in two long rows to watch. Girding up their skirts a little way, the whole body of clerics awaited their turn in silence, while the captain of the singing-boys cast the ball into the air, as high as he might, along the vaulted roof of the central aisle to be caught by any boy who could, and tossed again with hand or foot till it passed on to the portly chanters, the chaplains, the canons themselves, who finally played out the game with all the decorum of an ecclesiastical ceremony. It was just then, just as the canons took the ball to themselves so gravely, that Denys—Denys l'Auxerrois, as he was afterwards called—appeared for the first time. Leaping in among the timid children, he made the thing really a game. The boys played like boys, the men almost like madmen, and all with a delightful glee which became contagious, first in the clerical body, and then among the spectators. The aged Dean of the Chapter, Protonotary of his Holiness, held up his purple skirt a little higher, and stepping from the ranks with an amazing levity, as if suddenly relieved of his burden of eighty years, tossed the ball with his foot to the venerable capitular Homilist, equal to the occasion. And then, unable to stand inactive any longer, the laity carried on the game among themselves, with shouts of not too boisterous amusement; the sport continuing till the flight of the ball could no longer be traced along the dusky aisles.

Practice—Analyzing

1. What descriptive details are most effective?

   _____

   _____

2. As Pater continues, he begins to tell a story. Does he also continue to describe? If so, what details add to the description of the game?

   _____

   _____

   _____

3. What senses does Pater appeal to? Where?

   _____

   _____

   _____

   _____

4. What is Pater's attitude or stance in this passage? How can you best determine that attitude?

   _____

   _____

   _____

5. Could you imagine a different attitude toward this game? What details would you have to change or add to change the stance and the reader's reaction?

   _____

   _____

   _____

HOW DO WE WRITE DESCRIPTION?

When we talked about reading description, we noted that readers bring their own experiences to the description and build images based on similar experiences. Of course, readers contribute only part of the input for description: writers must provide details as well. Writers must observe and capture not only what they see but also what they sense with other perceptions. Details of odors, tastes, sounds, and tactile perceptions contribute to the fully detailed description.

Writers might describe any number of things—people, places, objects, sensations. Writers might describe objectively so that readers see only the item being described without any interpretation. Or they might describe subjectively so that readers share writers' interpretations. Which of these options a writer chooses depends on the purpose and audience of the description.

APPLYING DESCRIPTION

Consider the following brief description of maps.

Another way of representing the position of a point is by means of the kinds of maps which geographers call Flamsteed or Mollweide projection maps, and mathematicians call curvilinear co-ordinates. The meridians of longitude on the curved surface of the globe are not parallel like the circles of latitude. They converge at the poles. The Mercator projection map in which the meridians of longitude are represented by parallel straight lines distorts the relative sizes of the continents and oceans, making countries like Greenland which lie far north of the equator appear to be much larger then they actually are. Maps like the Flamsteed projection map, in which the meridians are represented by curved lines converging towards the poles, correct this distortion.

—*L. Hogben*

Practice—Analyzing

1. Would you call this an objective or subjective description?

2. Do the details encourage you to take the writer's perspective or do

they encourage you to think of the object without the writer's interpretation? Why?

_____

_____

3. Could you visualize each kind of map? Why or why not?

_____

_____

4. Whom do you suppose this description is written for?

_____

_____

This description is objective because it does not impose the writer's interpretation, even though the writer admits that Mercator maps distort relative sizes. This shortcoming is one geographers agree on, and so it is not only the writer's view. The description comes from a mathematics text called *Mathematics for the Million,* a text aimed at a more general audience than most mathematics books talking about mapping points on planes.

Now let's consider a subjective description, the introductory paragraph from an essay entitled, "Litter":

> A feathery grey cloud disappears into the vibrant red sun as it slowly drifts behind the purple hues defining every crack in Mount Half Moon. Half Moon rises sharply above acres of rocky mountain pine as the spring run-off flowing into Blue Lake sings its song of freedom. Blue Lake, now a deep indigo, eagerly waits for me to snap the perfect photo. At just that precise moment my finger slides into position, and then a tarnished, yellow, foreign object drifts rudely into the lower corner of my field of view. After three hours of waiting, my picture has been ruined; I run down to the edge of the lake, bending over to fish out a styrofoam beer cooler! I scream, stomp over to the tripod, grab it, and hastily set out for the car. On the way out, Smokey the Bear smiles at me, holding his "Keep America Beautiful" sign.
>
> —*Angela A.*

1. Has Angela used words to show her emotional reaction to the scene and event? _____

2. How would you say she feels about Mount Half Moon and Blue Lake? _____

3. How does she feel about the beer cooler? _____

_____

4. What words and details in the paragraph let you build up these impressions of her perspective? _____

_____

_____

_____

5. What do you suppose her position will be in the rest of the essay?

_____

6. Who is she trying to convince about her attitude toward litter?

_____

_____

Angela went on in her essay to discuss ways she and other volunteers tried to enlighten thoughtless hikers and picnickers that littering was actually harmful not only to other persons but also to nature.

Describing with a stance

When writers describe, they frequently try to create an emotional atmosphere as well as a physical description. Do you recall that we considered Davids' attitude or stance in the passages from *Lords of the Arctic?* Subjective description helps writers set a tone or mood for their writing. It economically conveys how they feel about the described item without making them say so explicitly.

Practice—Identifying stance

How does the following paragraph communicate its attitude? Underline specific words and phrases that show the writer's stance.

> As I sit in the kitchen of my parents' home, I look around me and wonder why this room symbolizes home to me. Is it the big picture window? I look, and my mind's eye sees the backyard covered in a soft, white blanket while big, fluffy snowflakes fall in silence, and I, a wide-eyed five-year-old, eat my Cream of Wheat in the warmth and comfort of the kitchen. Perhaps it's the large oval oak table and chairs, polished smooth with the wear of innumerable dinners, the site of sometimes angry, sometimes hilarious family discussions, the symbol of hospitality. My eyes travel around the room to the old stove where homemade bread baked on cold winter afternoons and hot spiced cider simmered on the back burner, its fragrance filling me with warm, cozy feelings; to the big, rough pine cabinet standing in the corner and the smooth wooden floor in front of it where Mom and I would sit with a cup of coffee, chatting and solving all the problems in my little world. That's why this room is "home" to me: it is the room of my growing up, decorated with memories.
>
> *—Beth T.*

Precision and coherence in description

Whether the description is objective or subjective, writers must always observe two points for careful, clear description. First, writers must choose precise language. Davids' description of the arctic would not create such vivid images for readers had he used "red" for "ruby," blown" for "flagged," trickle" for "freshet," or "bird" for "snow bunting." Part of Davids' success comes from being specific, for "snow bunting" is far more specific than "bird." But part also comes from choosing words carefully and precisely. When a more general word appears, readers might let it stand for any number of concepts. But when writers choose precisely the word that captures the meaning they intend, then readers pick up that same meaning. The point is not to use flowery, unfamiliar words, but simply to choose words for their precise meaning, and general words have less precise meanings than specific words.

The other major feature to look for in clear description is coherence. No matter how precise and detailed a description, unless it orients readers they won't understand it. Consider, for instance, an objective description of a shortwave radio. If the writer were to jump from describing the band selector knob to the frequency readout to the antenna to the headphone jack to other miscellaneous dials and readouts, most readers would not be able to construct a mental picture of the object. In describing objects, people, or places, writers observe a coherent movement; they might describe from top to bottom, front to back, right to left, clockwise, or any other consistent way for readers to visualize the item. Sometimes descriptions follow order of climax, but only when the item being described is one readers will recognize. For example, if I were to describe the stripes on my cat, readers would know what a cat looks like to begin with. I could use order of climax to bring out the increasingly complex circles that appear on the cat's legs, head, and sides. Even though I didn't describe the cat from front to back, no reader should have trouble understanding how the cat is put together when the concentric stripes making a bullseye on the cat's side are the last ones mentioned.

No matter what order of coherence, be sure to use clear transitions, including "next to," "to the left," "under," "looking to the right," "moving clockwise," "across," and so on.

GETTING IDEAS FOR DESCRIPTION

Being precise and including enough detail usually take most of the descriptive writer's attention. Let's try a procedure called mapping to help generate and organize details for a description.

First, quickly list all the qualities, uses, and varieties of a common object near you. I'll work on facial tissues:

soft	white	blue	green	yellow
pink	flowers	two-layered	folded	pop-up
paper	perfumed	sneezing	soak up spills	
remove makeup		clean glasses		

With this initial list, I want to organize the attributes into categories. I have color, texture, uses, varieties. I can organize these categories and attributes on a map, a visual aid to let me see how ideas relate to one another:

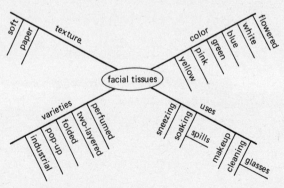

Just by organizing the initial thoughts I had, I can see two problems: first, I don't know if "perfumed" is a variety of tissue, and so maybe the categories don't include all the characteristics of tissues; second, the flowered tissues can have the same colors as tissues with no pattern. Already I can see ways to organize my ideas more logically:

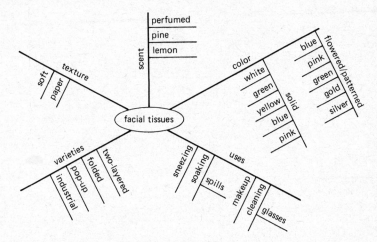

And now I can start adding even more categories or using the existing entries to help me think of more ideas to add to the list:

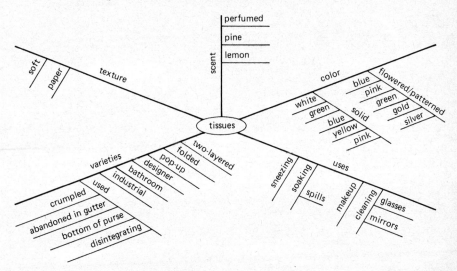

What does this map suggest? If I want to describe a facial tissue, I will have a more difficult time writing about a clean white tissue than about tissues that have more character—dirty wads from the bottom of the purse or gooey blobs left on sidewalks in the rain. A map of this sort helps writers see how they can concentrate their energies on a focus they have more to write about. Or the map might help them discover how much more work they will need to do to generate details for certain points on the map. Now, if I wanted to, I could draw another map with "used tissues" as the central focus and try to map out the varieties I would like to describe. I might pick three or four varieties and list the details that distinguish each type on its "arm" of the map. Depending on the amount of detail I listed, I would then have an idea about how much more I might have to focus my paper, because descriptions are most effective when they focus on a specific point and give adequate detail to create the writer's exact impression.

WRITING DESCRIPTION

1. Work with a partner and generate a list of impressions about another classmate. You might want to describe someone who dresses particularly neatly or sloppily, someone whose notebooks are organized or disorganized, someone whose dress reflects his or her personality. After you list details, map the details around a focusing idea. Use the map to help you add still more details. Rework your map if necessary. Then choose one arm of the map and try to break that into categories so that your details are still more specific. When you finish generating details, write the paragraph, but be sure to revise for adequate detail.
2. Describe a place that makes you feel a certain way. Perhaps your family's kitchen makes you feel secure or a childhood hiding place made you feel older and wiser than your years. Be sure to include the details that describe the place as well as your emotion.
3. What is the first impression guests would have if they walked into your living quarters right now—messiness, filthiness, gloominess, brightness? Use as specific an impression as you can capture in your topic sentence and then describe the room.
4. Describe some common object without naming it. Be sure to choose an object your readers know, but write your paragraph as a riddle.
5. Describe an outfit that would outrage your parents if they saw you dressed to go out for a date.

REVISING TO INCLUDE RELEVANT AND ADEQUATE DETAIL

In the following early draft of his descriptive paragraph, John begins to outline his dorm room. As you read, consider the focus he wants readers to understand and the detail he uses to help readers recreate his room in their minds:

> My dorm room is like living in a trash can. First, the beer stained carpet is barely visible under the piles of dirty clothes and paper. Second, to the right of the door is the sink. Above the sink hangs the mirror smeared with toothpaste. The walls are so porous that when it rains the whole room becomes a cesspool. Furthermore, against the far wall rests a pile of crushed Coors cans which gives the room its own unique odor. Above the pile of Coors cans stands the window. The window is so covered with dirt that you can not see out. To the left of the window sits my beat up desk. It is covered with stacks of books, pens, pencils, and papers. Finally, on the right of the window lies my bed. It never gets made up unless I change the sheets. I have been told that it could be worse, so I consider myself lucky to live in such a nice trash can.
>
> —*John P.*

1. What impression does John want readers to get from his paragraph?

   _____

2. What do you think of when you imagine a trash can? Do you think

   of grime and smells? _____

   _____

3. Do any other senses contribute to your idea of a trash can? _____

   _____

   _____

4. What kind of messiness should a room like a trash can have? Could you add detail to John's paragraph, especially detail that created

   more of the sense of a trash can? _____

   _____

   _____

   _____

Here's what John did in his next draft:

> My dorm room is like living in a trash can. First, the beer-stained carpet is barely visible under the piles of dirty clothes and paper. Second, to the right of the door is the sink, covered with dirty dishes, empty bottles, old eggshells, and sticky glasses. Above the sink hangs the mirror smeared with toothpaste. The walls are so porous that when it rains the whole room becomes a cesspool. Furthermore, against the far wall rests a pile of crushed Coors cans which gives the room its own unique odor. It smells like a mixture of stale beer and mold. Above the pile of Coors cans stands the window. The window is so covered with dirt that you cannot see out. To the left of the window sits my beat up desk. It is covered with stacks of books, pens, pencils, and papers with a peanut-butter-and-jelly sandwich from last month. Finally, to the right of the window lies my bed. It never gets made up unless I change the sheets. I have been told that it could be worse, so I consider myself lucky to live in such a nice trash can.
>
> —*John P.*

John has now added details that show what the sink, window, and desk look like and what the room smells like. When you thought about trash cans, did you come up with any other impressions? I always think of grimy, greasy cans, so I would probably add still more details about how thick the dirt on the window was. How could I show that? I might add a line like this:

> In fact, someone once visiting my room once scratched "clean me" in the dirt, and now the words are almost completely blotted out by still more dirt that has made the windows brown.

Or I might emphasize the greasiness by showing random fuzz sticking to the gooey windows. I would also add to the thoroughly disgusting smell by noting that the odor from the beer cans is mixed with locker room smells from the sweaty sneakers poking out from under the bed. I might also try to emphasize the caked-on dirt in the sink and on the mirror. In short, the paragraph, while it now conveys an impression of trash-can living, could be still more effective in use of descriptive detail.

Add still more details to John's paragraph so that it reflects your notion of a trash can.

Practice—Revising for adequate detail

Practice adding detail to another pair of paragraphs, the first an objective description and the second subjective. You'll have to imagine what you think this room should look like.

After entering the house's library through the giant double doors, your eyes measure the room's grandest feature—the twelve foot cathedral ceilings. The walls in front and to the right of you are lined with rich oak shelves containing dusty volumes of faded leather. In contrast to the colorful books are the two opposite walls of cool green hung with portraits of long-past ancestors. Covering the floor, the Persian rug of deep green is worn from use but still warm and exotic. The fine furniture pieces of brass and leather are few and sparse, yet they do not seem alone amid the many potted ferns.

Yet, for all the dust and age of the library, its faded colors and rich texture make it the warmest room in the house. The grand cathedral ceilings repeat the ancient lines of a Greek colonnade. The walls of book titles tell of science and history, while the Persian rug tells of distant lands and adventures. From the mellowed colors and the portraits on the wall, there come a sense of ancientness, of calm. It is a man's room, and it in are the memories of pipe tobacco, brandy, and a faithful dog. Yet it is not each piece, but a combination of them all that makes this room the best place in the house to curl up with a book and fall asleep.

—*Mary Ellen K.*

Now consider Jon's paragraph. Do any details not support the main impression of the paragraph? Bracket these and add relevant details.

Since I first heard the all-too-familiar click of a dead battery, I've purchased a Sears Diehard, and now my car runs beautifully. Its dual-exhaust system accounts for the smooth rumbling sound, much like an amplified cat's purr, while adding horsepower for quicker acceleration. The Alpine 7151 receiver/cassette deck combined with an Award power booster belts out music

to the tune of 30 watts per channel, while the
engine cranks out 18 miles per gallon in the
city and 23 mpg on the highway. The brand
new tires, power steering, and sturdy shocks
make for a velvety-smooth ride, making my
car much superior to all those rinky-dink
four-cylinder foreign cars on the market
today. The 1969 Mustang—Built Ford
Tough and made to stay that way.

—*Jon S.*

REVISING TO INCLUDE COHERENT, RELEVANT DETAIL

Here's another early draft of a descriptive paragraph that you will want
to consider coherence in.

The design of my dorm room is fairly basic. Upon entering, it's first discovered that an enormous heap of scattered laundry exists in the center of
the room. It is set on the putred-yellow shag carpet which is sparsely covered with prominent bare patches. Ingrained in the carpet are crumbs from
last year's snacks, paper clips, and other particle forms. The combination
of the carpet and laundry creates an arrangement of several foul odors forming a persistent, distasteful aroma. The unmade bed is located directly
against the bland white-bricked wall which is to the right of the doorway.
There is an orderly arrangement of books and study supplies on my desk,
along with an enormously large, exuberant green plant positioned on the
upper-left corner. The desk faces the disenchantingly white-bricked wall,
and is located directly across from the bed. Directly across from the desk
on the opposite brick wall is the algae-coated fish tank, which exudes a perpetually incessant hum which pervades the room. The final touch of class
displayed in the room is added by the bold fluorescent posters which cover
ninety percent of the implicitly bleak white-bricked wall.

—*Kenny P.*

Practice—Analyzing

1. If you were to begin revising Kenny's paragraph, you might want to
   start with the precise focus of his paragraph. Does he talk consistently
   about "design" throughout the paragraph?

   _____

   _____

2. Is "design" the most important point he could make with the details he has here?

_____

_____

3. If "design" is the appropriate focus for the paragraph, do the details about the laundry and crumby carpet belong in the paragraph?

_____

_____

4. Now consider the placement of items in the room. Has Kenny followed a consistent pattern of arrangement in talking about items?

_____

5. Does he follow an order of movement or order of climax?

_____

6. Try drawing a map of Kenny's room. Did you put the fish tank on the bed? In this draft, Kenny has used transitional devices—"directly across from," "to the left"—but he has not used them carefully enough to let readers know that the tank is next to the bed.

Revise Kenny's paragraph, first focusing carefully, then maintaining a clear, coherent pattern of movement in listing details.

The design of my dorm room is fairly
basic. Upon entering, it's first discovered
that an enormous heap of scattered laundry
exists in the center of the room. It is set on
the putred-yellow shag carpet which is
sparsely covered with prominent bare
patches. Ingrained in the carpet are crumbs
from last year's snacks, paper clips, and other
particle forms. The combination of the
carpet and laundry creates an arrangement of
several foul odors forming a persistent,
distasteful aroma. The unmade bed is

located directly against the bland white-
bricked wall which is to the right of the
doorway. There is an orderly arrangement of
books and study supplies on my desk, along
with an enormously large, exuberant green
plant positioned on the upper-left corner.
The desk faces the disenchantingly white-
bricked wall, and is located directly across
from the bed. Directly across from the desk
on the opposite brick wall is the algae-coated
fish tank, which exudes a perpetually
incessant hum which pervades the room.
The final touch of class displayed in the
room is added by the bold fluorescent
posters which cover ninety percent of the
implicitly bleak white-bricked wall.

—Kenny P.

A note on word choice

Choosing clear, precise words creates the specific impression readers
take away from a descriptive passage. Can you improve John's and Kenny's paragraphs by choosing more precise words? Kenny uses some vivid
words—"exudes," for instance—but in other places he selects vague
words or repeats himself. Choosing words carefully is worth the time
invested because writers typically don't want sentences like this one to
show up in their papers: "Many illiterates drop out of school and lead a
spiceless life." Even if poorly educated people lead dull lives, readers
chuckle over this word choice before they get the point the writer is trying
to make. Always check any words you haven't used often in your writing.
If you use a thesaurus to help you find synonyms, check their meanings
in a good dictionary because words listed in the thesaurus are not always
true synonyms.

Revision checklist

1. If you have a topic sentence, does it identify the person, place, or
   object you will describe?
2. Is your attitude toward the person, place, or object clear? Especially
   if you want to describe in order to convey emotion, is the emotion
   clear in the topic sentence?

3. Can readers develop their own picture of the person, place, or object you describe?
4. Have you included details appealing to all senses?
5. Have you ordered the details so readers can create a coherent picture?
6. Have you chosen precise, active, concrete words for your description?

chapter 8
Using examples

WHAT IS AN EXAMPLE?

An example is a concrete incident or specific instance. If we think of examples from a philosophical perspective, they are instances that prove reality. In more concrete terms, if I tell you that the concept "house" is a meaningful idea, and then I show you a house, you have to agree that "house" means something.

We don't often use examples simply to show what words mean. Rather, we use examples to prove that things could happen because they have happened in the past. Or we might use examples to show that our general statements are based on several specific occurrences. We might use examples to show that our analysis of causes and effects best explains events. We might use examples to convince readers that the action we suggest will best solve a current problem.

As we have expanded the list of ways to use examples, you have probably realized that examples are among the most useful kinds of proof writers can draw upon. Because human beings like to *see* writers' proof, examples show events, people, and objects that support the generalizations we make in topic sentences and thesis statements.

WHEN DO WE USE EXAMPLES IN COLLEGE WRITING?

Because examples are so common as proof in writing, we use examples almost every time we write. On a history test, a writer might analyze Napoleon's march into Russia as an example of bad military strategy. In a chemistry lab experiment, the writer might cite a color change as an example of a specific chemical reaction. In sociology, instances of capital punishment might be examples of our criminal justice system dealing with increased crime rates. In a law class, those same instances of capital punishment might be treated as examples of constitutional arguments.

In short, we use examples in every kind of college writing, from business letters to lab reports to research papers to exams. Practicing how to communicate effectively with examples will help you in almost every writing situation you'll face in college.

We're all used to giving examples to show or support our points, and we've already considered narration, a form of extended example. As we look at other ways to use examples in writing, consider Alvin Toffler's use of an example to show how people move through our lives more quickly than ever before.

Short-term Relationships

Alvin Toffler, *Future Shock*

Each spring an immense lemming-like migration begins all over the Eastern United States. Singly and in groups, burdened with sleeping bags, blankets and bathing suits, some 15,000 American college students toss aside their texts and follow a highly accurate homing instinct that leads them to the sun-bleached shoreline of Fort Lauderdale, Florida. There, for approximately a week, this teeming, milling mass of sun and sex worshippers swims, sleeps, flirts, guzzles beer, sprawls and brawls in the sands. At the end of this period the bikini-clad girls and their bronzed admirers pack their kits and join in a mass exodus. Anyone near the booth set up by the resort city to welcome this rambunctious army can now hear the loudspeaker booming: "Car with two can take rider as far as Atlanta. . . Need ride to Washington. . . Leaving at 10:00 for Louisville. . . . " In a few hours nothing is left of the great "beach-and-booze party" except butts and beer cans in the sand and money in the cash registers of local merchants.

What attracts the young people is more than an irrepressible passion for sunshine. Nor is it mere sex, a commodity available in other places as well. Rather it is a sense of freedom without responsibility. In the words of a nineteen-year-old co-ed, "You're not worried about what you do or say here because, frankly, you'll never see these people again."

What the Fort Lauderdale rite supplies is a transient agglomeration of people that makes possible a great diversity of temporary interpersonal relationships. And it is precisely this—temporariness—that increasingly characterizes human relations as we move further toward super-industrialism. For just as things and places flow through our lives at a faster clip, so, too, do people.

Practice—Analyzing

1. What is Toffler's main point in this excerpt? _____

_____

_____

2. Can you find one sentence that best summarizes the main idea he wants you, the reader, to remember after reading this passage?

_____

_____

3. How does Toffler get your attention? _____

_____

_____

_____

4. What major example does Toffler use to highlight his main idea?

_____

_____

5. Point out some details he uses in this example.

_____   _____

_____   _____

_____   _____

_____   _____

6. Why does Toffler use three paragraphs? Does he have three different ideas in this excerpt? What connects the first and second paragraphs? What is the relationship between the second and third

   paragraphs? _____

   _____

   _____

7. What is a lemming? What aspects of lemming behavior do college

   students show? What aspects do they not show? _____

   _____

   _____

8. Are there any words in the passage that you don't know? Do you
   understand what "irrepressible," agglomeration," rambunctious,"
   and "transient" mean in this passage? Why would Toffler use these

   words instead of simpler synonyms? _____

   _____

   _____

   _____

9. Do you know of any other places where young people go to indulge

in short-term interpersonal relationships? _____

_____

HOW DO WE READ EXAMPLES?

Reading illustrations is probably among the easiest analytic reading because illustration or giving examples is among the most common kind of support for ideas. In the passage from *Future Shock,* Toffler begins with the example and lets readers build a sense of the point of the illustration. But only in the second and third paragraphs does he explicitly state his main point. Because we have previously read essays that use examples, we know, as we read this passage, that Toffler will tell us what point the example supports. As we read details of the short-lived beach party, we hold our judgment in suspension because we expect a statement that provides a framework for understanding the example.

What do we do when we read an example? Our understanding of examples depends on the arrangement of the example and the generalization it supports. Typically, when we see the generalization first, we use the example as a test case. We acknowledge the position the writer takes, and then, as the details of a supporting example unfold, we check them against our understanding of the generalization. To use the language of Chapter 1, the generalization gives readers the hypothesis that the details confirm. In short, seeing the generalization first lets us use top-down processing as we read. If the details in the example "add up" to a specific instance of the generalization, then we note the strength of the example. (Could Toffler have stated his point first and then moved into the illustration of the point? Would this arrangement be as effective as his current approach?)

If we see the example before we read the generalization, as we do in Toffler's passage, we apply bottom-up processing, and we usually begin formulating our own hypothesis about what the example supports. We mentally organize details so that they create a meaningful unit. As you read Toffler's example, what mental image were you forming? What words in paragraph 1 lead you to expect the point he makes in paragraph 2? When writers give the example before the generalization, they must take special care to provide enough clues about the point of the example so that readers see the "fit" between the example and the generalization when it's stated. Here, what we suspend is our commitment to a main point. The two approaches—moving from general to specific or from specific to general—correspond to what we do in deductive and inductive reasoning.

Practice—Writing

How can you rewrite Toffler's passage to put the main idea first? Is this organization as effective as Toffler's original structure?

Practice—Reading

Read the following short article and consider the different ways the author uses examples to support her point.

Alcoholism: We All Feel the Pain

Denise Kalette, *USA Today*

More Americans than ever say heavy drinking is a major problem in the USA, a Louis Harris poll has found. Among the study's other findings:

- 68 percent of Americans know someone who drinks too much—up from 60 percent in 1973.
- 56 percent say a heavy drinker is "close to me."
- 38 percent of the nation's households are beset with alcoholism problems, Harris estimates.
- Nearly half the households with teenagers are worried about teen drinking.

Those findings—in a poll conducted by Louis Harris and Associates for *USA Today*—come on the eve of the National Council on Alcoholism's 14th National Alcoholism Forum in Houston, which is expected to draw 1,000 professionals Thursday. Among the presentations will be new evidence that alcoholism may be an inherited disease.

Dr. Henri Begleiter of the Downstate Medical Center in Brooklyn will present research showing that sons of alcoholic fathers have brain-wave patterns different from other youngsters, indicating they may be more likely to become alcoholics themselves.

There are 7 million children under 20 with at least one alcoholic parent, the Council on Alcoholism says. It suggests that about half of these children may develop the disease.

But beyond the risk is the real cost: drinking ranks third as a cause of birth defects; it's involved in 8 of 10 fire deaths, 2 of 3 drownings, 7 of 10 fatal falls and half of violent crimes. It plays a role in 95,000 deaths annually.

But the toll of alcoholism hasn't always been as openly discussed as it is today. A decade ago, the drinking problem of one of the most powerful men in Congress, Wilbur Mills, chairman of the House Ways and Means Committee, was a scandal that made headlines across the USA. "It was an embarrassment to me and my family," Mills says of the episode involving stripper Fanne Foxe, and the drinking that landed him in the National Naval Medical Center in Bethesda, MD. Now 73, a tax attorney in Washington, D.C., and sober for eight years, he says, "You don't ever want to forget you're an alcoholic. You've got to be totally honest. You're never cured."

By the time former first lady Betty Ford admitted her alcoholism in 1978, the public was calling it a disease, not a sin. And now actor Jason Robards announces his alcoholism in prime-time TV ads, then says he found he doesn't need to drink.

Openness is needed by each of the USA's 13 million alcoholics because each alcoholic affects the lives of four others, often tragically. Two poll respondents relate their experiences:

- Lettie Ward, 76, of Chicago, watched her brother Herbert, a minister, struggle with the disease for years—and leave the pulpit because of it.
- John McMullen of Hamden, Conn., has seen "thousands" of alcoholics during his four years as a jail guard and his current work for a guard agency. He says the public cost is enormous. "We had meat cutters, carpenters, plumbers, doctors, lawyers," McMullen says. His own son-in-law was a heavy drinker who finally "dried out" but is now unemployed.

The Harris poll also found:

- More than any other age group, people aged 30–49 know someone who drinks "too much." Nearly as many 18- to 29-year-olds know a heavy drinker. Those over 50 had less contact with heavy drinkers.
- More males than females say they know someone who drinks too much.
- People making more than $35,000 are more likely to know a heavy drinker than those making less money.
- Executives drink more heavily than professionals or skilled laborers.
- More Democrats know a heavy drinker than Republicans or Independents.
- More than two-thirds of Americans favor making 21 the legal age for buying alcoholic beverages. (Fifteen percent of high schoolers are problem drinkers, says the Council on Alcoholism's Joanne Yurman. Nearly 1 of 3 gets drunk at least six times a year, she adds; about 5,000 teenagers die in alcohol-related traffic accidents each year.)

Practice—Analyzing

1. What are the first examples Kalette cites? _____

   _____

2. How do statistics function as a kind of example in this article?

   _____

   _____

3. What personal examples does Kalette include? _____

   _____

   _____

   _____

4. How do personal examples convince you to agree with Kalette?

   _____

   _____

5. How do personal examples differ from statistics in their effect on

   readers? _____

   _____

   _____

6. What other examples does Kalette include? _____

   _____

   _____

   _____

7. Are the examples effectively arranged? _____

   _____

8. Does Kalette state a thesis for the article? If not, can you formulate

   a statement that captures the main point? _____

   _____

   _____

   _____

Reading—Example and detail

In reading illustrations, most readers quickly distinguish between the examples and the details that give life to the example. If we think of a topic sentence as the framework that holds together parts of a paragraph, then we should think of the example as a smaller framework that holds details together. But skilled writers can use examples that have no details, as, for instance, when a writer supports a point about advertising wars among brewers by referring briefly to three beer ads. In this case, the writer assumes that the examples are familiar to readers so that he needs no specific details to explain the relationship between the examples and the generalization.

Practice—Example and detail

Read the first paragraphs of an article on relaxation. What examples and details do you see?

Cooling Out: Keys to the Lost Art of Relaxing

Richard Grossman

Believe it or not, in a certain junior high school in Berkeley, California, it is a detention offense for students in a science class to be found "sitting quietly doing no work."

So much for the daydream of young Isaac Newton, lazing under his apple tree. So much for the curious Albert Einstein, stopping in the woods to stare, wonderingly, at the sky above him. And so much for the wisdom of the great essayist E. B. White, who once said, "Never ask a writer what he's doing staring at the wall; that's when the work gets done."

Example 1 _____

   Detail _____

   Detail _____

Example 2 _____

   Detail _____

   Detail _____

Example 3 _____

Detail _____

Detail _____

Example 4 _____

Detail _____

Detail _____

Now consider how Dr. Oppenheim uses examples in his article on TV violence:

TV Isn't Violent Enough

Mike Oppenheim, M.D., *T.V. Guide*

Caught in an ambush, there's no way our hero (Matt Dillon, Eliot Ness, Kojak, Hoss Cartwright...) can survive. Yet, visibly weakening, he blazes away, and we suspect he'll pull through. Sure enough, he's around for the final clinch wearing the traditional badge of the honorable but harmless wound: a sling.

As a teenager with a budding interest in medicine, I knew this was nonsense and loved to annoy my friends with the facts.

"Aw, the poor guy! He's crippled for life!"

"What do you mean? He's just shot in the shoulder."

"That's the worst place! Vital structures everywhere. There's the blood supply for the arm: axillary artery and vein. One nick and you can bleed to death on the spot."

"So he was lucky."

"OK. If it missed the vessels it hit the brachial plexus: the nerve supply. Paralyzes his arm for life. He's gotta turn in his badge and apply for disability."

"So he's *really* lucky."

"OK. Missed the artery. Missed the vein. Missed the nerves. Just went through the shoulder joint. But joint cartilage doesn't heal so well. A little crease in the bone leaves him with traumatic arthritis. He's in pain the rest of his life—stuffing himself with codeine, spending his money on acupuncture and chiropractors, losing his friends because he complains all the time. . . . Don't ever get shot in the shoulder. It's the end. . . ."

Today, as a physician, I still sneer at TV violence, though not because of any moral objection. I enjoy a well-done scene of gore and slaughter as well as the next viewer, but "well-done" is something I rarely see on a typical evening in spite of the plethora of shootings, stabbings, muggings and brawls. Who can believe the stuff they show? Anyone who remembers high-school biology knows the human body can't possibly respond to violent trauma as it's usually portrayed.

On a recent episode, Matt Houston is at a fancy resort, on the trail of a vicious killer who specializes in knifing beautiful women in their hotel rooms in broad daylight. The only actual murder sequence was in the best of taste: all the action off screen, the flash of a knife, moans on the sound track.

In two scenes, Matt arrives only minutes too late. The hotel is alerted, but the killer's identity remains a mystery. Absurd! It's impossible to kill someone instantly with a knife thrust—or even render him unconscious. Several minutes of strenuous work are required to cut enough blood vessels so the victim bleeds to death. Tony Perkins in "Psycho" gave an accurate, though abbreviated, demonstration. Furthermore, anyone who has watched an inexperienced farmhand slaughter a pig knows that the resulting mess must be seen to be believed.

If consulted by Matt Houston, I'd have suggested a clue: "Keep your eyes peeled for someone panting with exhaustion and covered with blood. That might be your man."

Many Americans were puzzled at the films of the assassination attempt on President Reagan. Shot in the chest, he did not behave as TV had taught us to expect ("clutch chest, stagger backward, collapse"). Only after he complained of a vague chest pain and was taken to the hospital did he discover his wound. Many viewers assumed Mr. Reagan is some sort of superman. In fact, there was nothing extraordinary about his behavior. A pistol is certainly a deadly weapon, but not predictably so. Unlike a knife wound, one bullet can kill instantly—provided it strikes a small area at the base of the brain. Otherwise, it's no different: a matter of ripping and tearing enough tissue to cause death by bleeding. Professional gangland killers understand the problem. They prefer a shotgun at close range.

The trail of quiet corpses left by TV's good guys, bad guys and assorted ill-tempered gun owners is ridiculously unreal. Firearms reliably produce pain, bleeding and permanent, crippling injury (witness Mr. Reagan's press secretary, James Brady: shot directly in the brain but very much alive). For a quick, clean death, they are no match for Luke Skywalker's light saber.

No less unreal is what happens when T. J. Hooker, Magnum, or a Simon brother meets a bad guy in manly combat. Pow! Our hero's fist crashes into the villain's head. Villain reels backward, tipping over chairs and lamps, finally falling to the floor, unconscious. Handshakes all around. . . . Sheer fantasy! After hitting the villain, our hero would shake no one's hand. He'd be too busy waving his own about wildly, screaming with the pain of a shattered fifth metacarpal (the bone behind the fifth knuckle), an injury so predictable it's called the "boxer's fracture." The human fist is far more delicate than the human skull. In any contest between the two, the fist will lose.

The human skull is tougher than TV writers give it credit. Clunked with a blunt object, such as traditional pistol butt, most victims would not fall conveniently unconscious for a few minutes. More likely, they'd suffer a nasty scalp laceration, be stunned for a second or two, then be extremely upset. I've sewn up many. A real-life, no-nonsense criminal with a blackjack (a piece of iron weighing several pounds) has a much better success rate. The result is a large number of deaths and permanent damage from brain hemorrhage.

Critics of TV violence claim it teaches children sadism and cruelty. I honestly don't know whether or not TV violence is harmful, but if so the critics have it backward. Children can't learn to enjoy cruelty from the neat, sanitized mayhem on the average series. There isn't any! What they learn is far more malignant: that guns or fists are clean, efficient, exciting ways to deal with a difficult situation. Bang!—you're dead! Bop!—you're unconscious (temporarily)!

"Truth-in-advertising" laws eliminated many absurd commercial claims. I often daydream about what would happen if we had "truth in violence"—if every show had to pass scrutiny by a board of doctors who had no power to censor but could insist that any action scene have at least a vague resemblance to medical reality ("Stop the projector! . . . You have your hero waylaid by three Mafia thugs who beat him brutally before he struggles free. The next day he shows up with this cute little band-aid over his eyebrow. We can't pass that. You'll have to add one eye swollen shut, three missing front teeth, at least 20 stitches over the lips and eyes, and a wired jaw. Got that? Roll 'em. . . ").

Seriously, real-life violence is dirty, painful, bloody, disgusting. It causes mutilation and misery, and it doesn't solve problems. It makes them worse. If we're genuinely interested in protecting our children, we should stop campaigning to "clean up" TV violence. It's already too antiseptic. Ironically, the problem with TV violence is: it's not violent enough.

---

1. Why does Oppenheim begin his essay with an example?

   _____

   _____

2. What point is Oppenheim making in this essay? Where does he first

   state that point concretely? _____

   _____

3. What is the most effective example in the essay for you as a reader?

   _____

   _____

4. What is the most detailed example? Which details make the example

   more effective? _____

   _____

   _____

5. Does Oppenheim include any examples that he does not flesh out

   with details? _____

   _____

   _____

HOW DO WE WRITE EXAMPLES?

Writing with examples, like reading examples, occurs often so that using examples is one of the easier ways to explain ideas. As always, writers determine what they need to communicate to a specific audience before they choose a method of developing the idea. Look again at the passage from *Future Shock*. With whom was Toffler trying to communicate? Although he probably hoped to appeal to a general audience, he undoubtedly expected more college-educated readers to work through his text on superindustrialism. Given his expected audience, is his example effective? Why? We also read so many examples that Kalette's various uses of examples are easy to understand. The examples support points differently—statistics make one point while personal examples make another. But examples *do* support the writer's position if they are selected and arranged effectively.

The process of finding examples

If writers know that they have strong examples to support a point for a given audience, they often follow a process somewhat like this:

I know I have good personal examples I can use to explain my attitude toward short-term relationships to my high-school friends.

What categories of examples of short-term relationships do I have? Where do I experience short-term relationships?

grocery lines
ski lifts
bus stops
elevators
vacations

What differs in my behavior in each of these places?

I'm outspoken when people cut in front of me in grocery lines
I brag when I'm on ski lifts
I withdraw when I'm at a bus stop
I withdraw when I'm in an elevator
I do outrageous things when I'm on vacation

So far, I've found two places where I act in a similar manner—bus stops and elevators—and perhaps my behavior in lines falls under the general category of "outrageous" for vacations. I seem to have plenty of potential short-term relationships to write about, so I would focus on the one place that most interests me or might interest my readers. I don't think my behavior at bus stops or on elevators is unusual, so perhaps writing about that would result in a boring paper. I am most interested in writing about my outrageous behavior on vacations, so I'll work out a few examples for that topic:

> In New York city, I went to the Central Park zoo and jumped into an animal pen to have my picture taken with gazelles.
>
> In Paris, I started climbing the outside of the Notre Dame cathedral.
>
> In Houston, I jogged around the Astrodome every morning.
>
> In Iowa, at my grandmother's house, I would skinny-dip in a neighboring pond.

Now I might decide which of the examples illustrate "outrageous," but I also need to consider "short-term relationships." Does "outrageous" mean that I didn't care if onlookers thought I was crazy or immoral? Does "outrageous" mean that I was willing to make short-term acquaintances with police? I must find a focus for this paragraph before I can choose which examples will best illustrate my outrageous behavior in short-term relationships on vacations and decide which details create significant examples. Or I might decide to consider people I've known for a few days or a few weeks:

> characters in movies or books
>
> classmates for one semester
>
> people who share hospital rooms
>
> people who work on extracurricular projects

If so, I could find different generalizations I might want to support—how volunteers on community projects show the good side of people, how sharing pain brings families together quickly, and so on.

Once I determine the point I wish to make, I can refine my examples, perhaps thinking of new ones. Then I can carefully focus as I rework my generalization into a strong topic sentence and use that focus to help me select details appropriate for the example. Finally, I can draft the paragraph and begin to look at the examples as they will communicate precisely to readers.

This process—moving from general idea to examples to a more specific main idea to better examples to topic sentence to detailed examples—typifies the narrowing of focus and revising that goes on when brainstorming for and writing an example paper.

Practice—Writing

Work through the process of generating specific examples to support a generalization for several of the following possible short-term relationships:

> characters in movies or books
> classmates for one semester
> people who share hospital rooms
> volunteers

Coherence when using examples

To help readers, writers using illustration try to meet certain expectations. First, if they state the generalization or topic sentence at the beginning of the paragraph, they set up the examples by using clear transitions to alert readers to the method of development. Among the common transitions for using examples:

for example	for instance
in particular	as an illustration
once	in another case

Writers sometimes use full sentences to move from the topic sentence to the first example and from one example to another within the paragraph. Generally, these transitional sentences also provide explicit connections between the example and the generalization so that readers have no doubt about how to relate examples to the main point. Notice how this student uses short paragraphs as transitional devices between examples:

Spare Me the Sponges

I am terrified of something that doesn't hiss, sting, bite, or growl. It doesn't snort or sneer or spit. Ssssshhh! Quick! While no one is looking, I will expose this embarrassing obsession. Closer! I don't reveal this to just anyone. Ready? . . . I shrink away with fear when I see a sponge.

Let me qualify that. Loofah sponges, spongey Nerf footballs, and sponge cake don't affect me. My peculiar fear is only about kitchen sponges! I blame my obsession specifically on my aunt's hairy bathroom, a babysitting job, and several teeny, tiny, revolting white worms.

My first enlightening experience with a kitchen sponge shocked me at the tender age of six. My otherwise flawless aunt took her kitchen sponge and headed for the bathroom, with me seriously trailing behind. She proceeded without guilt to clean gobs of hairy grime and grit from her bathtub. Yuck.

Worse yet, she didn't stop until she'd cleaned the gooey vaseline off the marble countertop, the slimy soap ring from the basin, and the sticky, smeared Aim toothpaste from the bathroom tile. I watched bug-eyed as she casually tossed the infected sponge back into the kitchen and told me to run along.

End of round one. I wasn't emotionally disturbed about kitchen sponges—yet.

The next time a kitchen sponge confronted me, I was babysitting. The two slobbery baby twin girls and their slobbery monster of a brother, Blake, screamed and slobbered for lunch. Feeling like a harried housewife I shushed them up and towed the hungry crew into the kitchen for some PBJ fixings. Blake knocked over a glass of cherry Kool-aid, and I reached instinctively into the sink for a dishcloth. I squelched a scream when I touched something unknown. I peeked into the sink and came face-to-face with a crusty, slimy, square—bound by a stringy piece of egg spaghetti, smeared with peanut butter, with a few trapped blonde hairs and brown raisins smushed revoltingly into some cracks and all topped off with slimy baby slobber; it faintly resembled a sponge. I escaped the kitchen, leaving Kool-aid on the linoleum, slobbery kids to fend for themselves, and feeling extremely suspicious of sponges.

Coincidence or not, I come across a crawly kitchen sponge nearly every time I babysit.

My third wrenching experience left me with a confirmed fear of kitchen sponges. Mom thoughtlessly bought some innocent looking sponges (of the kitchen species) and stored them under the kitchen sink—behind the Arm and Hammer oven cleaner, under the disposal pipe, and directly beside the beef-flavored doggy biscuits. They sat there for months without use, until the fatal day I dropped an egg, smashing it into bits of yolk and shell. I reached for paper toweling but found instead an empty cardboard tube. I searched for a dishcloth, but they were all in the laundry. Finally, suppressing my fear and fighting off my abnormal anxiety, I groped for a sponge near the back of the musty cupboard. As I began wiping the gooey egg off the floor, a little brush of my finger startled me. I continued cleaning, refusing to believe any of the morbid thoughts scrambling about my head. I glanced down when I felt the feather-light brush again. Little white worms oozed out of the holes of the sponge. They squiggled and squirmed as I screamed and jumped about five feet in the air.

That was the last time I ever touched a kitchen sponge.

Some may find my fear irrational, but my revolting experiences make me feel entirely sane to ask others: do you know what can be trapped in a kitchen sponge?

—*Tami R.*

Arranging examples

If writers start with an example rather than a precise statement of the main point, they generally begin with a vividly detailed example that helps readers create a sense of the main idea, as Toffler does. In beginning with an example, writers also remind themselves that conclusions reached by two readers may differ because one reader may have experienced something like the example when the second reader has not. As long as writers keep in mind that readers bring their own experiences to the reading, writers remember to include adequate detail to control the impressions readers organize.

Next, writers order their strongest examples. Arranging examples usually means determining if the examples should follow chronological order or order of importance. If I were using the examples just noted, I might use the swimming example before the Notre Dame example if skinny-dipping happened as a youngster and climbing as a teenager. If I were ordering the examples by importance, the gazelle caper is less dangerous than the Notre Dame climb, but perhaps the penalty in New York was heavier than that in Paris. I could emphasize the penalty—and hence the short-term relationship with the police—by putting the New York example after the Paris one.

Using detailed examples

Perhaps even more importantly, writers check examples for complete and relevant detail. Details convince readers that examples do support the generalizations; details also keep readers' attention and provide a rich fabric of connections between the example and the generalization. Remember, also, that readers construct meaning based on their knowledge of similar experiences or illustrations. Details help readers relate examples to their similar experiences. Consider the following paragraph. Which details create connections adding up to "crazy and unpredictable? Do the detailed examples convince you that Carla has a valid point about temporary relationships?

When I'm at Meadow Mountain Ranch Girl Scout Camp, I feel free to act crazy and unpredictable because the temporary relationships make me feel anonymous. During my first stay at camp, for instance, I acted extremely out of character by joining in a group of streaking girls. The girls dashed naked by my tent, and I instantly ripped off my nightgown, pulled off my socks, and joined in. We ran all the way to the front gate of camp and back again, then collapsed in our cots after an exhausting three miles. I would never have dared to join in at home, but knowing my relationship with the girls would last only one week, I followed suit. The following year on the last night of camp, we built a bonfire the size of a forest fire and each unit performed a comical skit. The girls in my unit talked me into dressing in a suit and tie, putting my hair in ponytails, and behaving like a man who thought he was a dog. I spent the rest of the night panting with my tongue hanging out. I decided because I would probably never see those girls again after that night that I would give it a try. To my astonishment I won an award that night, the "Crazy Award." Two years later off at camp again, I was in the leader position as a counselor. The counselors planned a banquet for the last night of camp and required the girls to be dressed in full girl scout uniform for the dinner. I dressed for the dinner in ragged blue jeans and an old t-shirt with the expression "Fort Morgan Inmate" written across the front. When I arrived at dinner I acted totally out of character by slurping my jello, eating with my fingers, and throwing peas into my mouth. My unit of girls disowned me and promptly moved to the next table. Because each of these situations with the girls formed only temporary relationships, I was able to act crazy and unpredictable and do things I would have otherwise never dared.

—Carla F.

Now consider Brad's paragraph on short-term relationships:

Because I find plane trips extremely dull, I pass the time by telling false stories about myself to the gullible passengers I sit with. For instance, as I nervously flew to college for the first time, I was assigned a seat next to a middle-aged businessman. After we had introduced ourselves, he casually asked me where I was going. As my face took on a sad expression, I began telling him a sob story. I told him of the recent firey automobile accident which took the lives of my parents and left my pregnant little sister in the hospital in a coma. I added further that my poor sister may lose her young fetus. I finished the dreadful tale by commenting that I had to quit medical school so I could return home and take care of my family's estate. He answered sympathetically that he was very sorry; then he remained deathly quiet for the remainder of the flight. Another time, during a flight to Omaha, I managed to quiet a young girl who asked me numerous questions. She rambled off the standard question about where I came from. I slowly responded that I had been in a dirty, old, Mexican prison. She then hesitantly asked me what I had been in prison for. I glared at her with cold eyes and said, "I was there for violently murdering my little sister because she talked on the phone too much." My last tale was told while flying to Hawaii for a vacation. Sitting next to me was a vulnerable appearing woman of about sixty. She politely asked me if I had ever ventured to the islands before. I answered that I traveled there once a year for the national surfing championships. I informed her that I was a professional surfer from California. I then concluded the story by bragging to her that I was the current national surfing champion. She excitedly wished me good luck. Never would I have told such outlandish tales if I had met these people before or would see them again.

—Brad K.

GETTING IDEAS FOR EXAMPLES

Once again, let's consider short-term relationships as you practice brainstorming for an illustration paragraph. What kinds of people do you have short-term relationships with?

_____

_____

_____

On p. 206, I mentioned grocery lines, ski lifts, bus stops, elevators, and vacations as places or situations that created short-term relationships. Carla wrote about Girl Scout camp. What other places or situations can

you think of that include temporary personal relationships?

_____   _____

(If you're stuck, try thinking about different kinds of lines.)

_____

_____

_____

_____

Now jot down some examples of your behavior in different short-term relationships:

_____

_____

_____

_____

_____

Categorize those. Pick the more interesting examples and try to think of related examples.

Do you see any common thread in three or more examples that holds them together? Can you state that idea about short-term relationships in a sentence? Continue working on examples and refining your statement of the generalization until you feel you have a workable topic sentence and examples to support it.

Practice—Writing

1. List several short-term relationships you have—with instructors, classmates, dormmates, high school acquaintances—or places where you find yourself involved in short-term relationships. Now think of several specific examples of events that occurred because you knew that the relationship was short-term. (For example, you wouldn't have written the note to your history professor last semester if you knew you'd ever see the prof again; you wouldn't have kicked your roommate out of your apartment if it weren't two days before the end of the semester.) What do two or three examples have in common? Be as specific as possible in stating a common point for these examples. Then use the examples to support the generalization in your topic sentence.

2. Re-read the excerpt from "Alcoholism: We all feel the pain," from *USA Today*. What examples of the costs or pain of alcoholism does Denise Kalette cite? What examples of changing attitudes toward alcoholism does she cite? List several examples of your own experiences with alcohol abuse—in your own life, in friends' lives, on campus, and so on. Decide if three or more of the examples have something in common. Do they illustrate the cost of alcoholism? Do they show changing attitudes? Do they illustrate the problem of teenage alcohol abuse? You may use examples to develop any point you would like to make about alcohol abuse, but be sure to state that point precisely in the topic sentence you formulate after you have chosen related examples. Then develop the examples with full, specific details that support exactly the point you state in your topic sentence.

3. Of course, you can write paragraphs using examples to illustrate any point you'd like to communicate to a specific audience. Follow the same procedure for a subject of your choice or your teacher's choice. Or you might use one of these subjects:

   dealing with stress
   children should be seen but not heard
   family values in teen sex or sex after sixty
   family ties
   freedom without responsibility
   short-term relationships with things

   After you've worked through the process of determining the audience, narrowing the subject, finding preliminary examples, stating the focus, and refining examples, check to be sure you have an adequately focused topic and a clear topic sentence.

Looking at relevant detail

Consider the following paragraph. Where might Pam use relevant, specific detail to create more convincing examples of her unusual behavior? As you revise this paragraph to include more details and eliminate sentences that contribute little to the development of the examples, you might also try to refine the topic sentence so that it states a more precise point.

When involved in a temporary relationship I feel that I can be less inhibited by other people. This is especially evident when I am out dancing at bars. While at a bar called Thirsties over Christmas break I proved just how different I can be. I was there with a few friends that I had not seen in a long time, and we were all getting drunk and wild. Four of us got up on chairs and started dancing. Later that same evening we all went to another bar called After the Gold Rush because it stays open later and continues to play music. Everyone in my group was out on the dance floor when the song "I'll Tumble for You" by Culture Club came on. Without planning it several of us began to do somersalts on the floor at the same time. Yet another time I grabbed the guy that I was dancing with by the arm and we joined a bunny hop. But since I would never see him again, or at least I hope not, there was nothing embarrassing about the bunny hop in front of strangers. So when I am dancing at bars I feel less inhibited by others around me, and I do many out-of-the-ordinary things.

—*Pam D.*

Now suggest how Denice might similarly revise her paragraph for focus and development:

When I get home late at night, telling white lies is an easy way to get out of being punished. My first experience with telling white lies was after a good party. When I got home, my mother was waiting up for me, so I told her there had been an accident and the officer needed to talk to me because I had been the only witness. Another time white lies were used was when I knew my parents would not believe that time had slipped by and that I did not realize the time. Quickly I decided that my friend, Chriser, had "gotten sick" and needed me to get her home safely. Instead of being grounded, I found myself praised for my good judgment. The best white lie used to avoid punishment explained why I was late and why my eyes were bloodshot from drinking. The story was simple; my boyfriend and I had fought all night. Telling my parents about how much I cried covered up for the eyes. My parents felt sorry for me and said they hoped everything worked out. By using white lies to explain my late nights, I was spared my inevitable punishment for telling the truth.

—Denice D.

Revision checklist

1. Does the topic sentence focus on a narrow point?
2. Can you support that point with examples?
3. Do the examples support the main point of the paragraph?
4. Do you develop the examples with adequate details?
5. Do all the details relate to the topic sentence?
6. Do you provide smooth transitions between examples?
7. Have you arranged the examples in the most effective order?

UNIT THREE

Analyzing

This unit includes the many ways writers can break apart an idea to explain it to readers. In this unit, you can practice writing about processes and causes/effects. You can compare and contrast. You can classify or define. In short, you can work on several ways that we dissect ideas to reconstruct those ideas for readers. What links all these methods is not only analysis but also information sharing. Each of these patterns of organizing ideas helps readers see relationships in slightly different ways. Although you will practice several of these methods of developing ideas, remember that you, the writer, must determine what is the best approach for your readers given what you want to communicate. But also remember that without practicing the various ways to organize ideas, you won't easily be able to choose the most effective pattern or patterns of development.

As I mentioned at the beginning of Unit Two, some patterns of development come more naturally to writers. Process analysis and comparison/contrast are probably the easiest of this group of patterns. For most writers, causal analysis is the most difficult. But as you practice each pattern or the patterns that your teacher selects, you will build experience and skill that will make the later patterns easier for you to conquer.

chapter 9
Analyzing processes

WHAT IS PROCESS ANALYSIS?

Whenever we investigate how we do things—what steps we follow—we are analyzing a process. Process analysis typically includes a list of tools necessary for the process and then a step-by-step description of the actions necessary to complete the task. Giving directions to your dorm or apartment or explaining how to register for a course both qualify as process analysis. If you ask yourself "how do I do this?" and answer with a list of steps, you've analyzed the process of doing the action.

WHEN DO WE USE PROCESS ANALYSIS
IN COLLEGE WRITING?

Although you can think of many instances when you read process analyses, you might think you rarely write them. Indeed, you read process analysis every time you study the directions for making a can of soup or any recipe, for that matter. If you read cereal boxes and see the steps for entering a contest, you are reading process analysis. But what about writing these analyses?

If you've ever enrolled in a laboratory class and recounted the steps you took to complete an experiment, you've written a process analysis. If you've ever answered a question on military strategy gone wrong with a list of steps, you've written a process analysis. If you've ever written down steps for logging on to your college computer or finding a book in the library or loading film into a particular camera, you've written a process analysis. Although we probably don't write such papers every day, they are not particularly uncommon. More importantly, if you can recognize when a process analysis will best help your readers, you can organize your paper most clearly to meet their needs.

Despite its title, "What Happens When Earthworms Eat?" the following article from *Organic Gardening* isn't only about earthworms. Rather, Robert Rodale uses the earthworm as an instance of two larger processes or chains of action. Look for several "process analyses" as you read.

What Happens When Earthworms Eat?

Robert Rodale, *Organic Gardening*

I've been out of school for over 30 years, yet no matter how I manage to arrange my life, I still keep learning. In fact, I seem to learn faster the further in time I get from my school experience. Why should that be? It didn't occur to me to ask myself that question until just now, but in asking it—and also in guessing at an answer—I think I may have learned the biggest lesson of my life. When you are in school, you are asked the questions and are expected to be able to find the answers. Presumably, when you are sufficiently filled up with correct answers, you are educated and are then released.

I now believe, though, that real learning occurs when you become able to ask important questions. Then you are on the doorstep of wisdom, because by asking important questions you project your mind into the exploration of new territory. In my experience, very few people have learned how important is the asking of good questions, and even fewer have made a habit of asking them. Even in my own case, I had to wait until I'd almost totally forgotten the experience of schooling to be able to switch my mind into the asking as well as the answering mode.

Let's demonstrate how important questions are by asking what appears to be a simple one. What happens when earthworms eat? Have you ever wondered about that? Have you asked yourself that question *seriously,* thus opening your mind to the possibility that the eating habits of earthworms could literally change the nature of our world? Think about it for a minute.

Charles Darwin did ask himself that question and actually spent 42 years of his life pondering the result of the appetite of earthworms. And the result of that work appeared in his last book, published just before his death 100 years ago this year. The title of that book was *The Formation of Vegetable Mould through the Action of Earthworms,* and it was received by the scientific press of the time as yet another example of Darwin's scientific genius. But since then, few scientists have asked about the eating habits of earthworms, and our agriculture has lost an important part of its regenerative capacity as a result.

Darwin asked himself about the work of earthworms because he was interested in the slow ways that the natural world changes. He suspected that earthworms, eating unseen beneath the surface, caused momentous happenings. There were several clues that led him to suspect that worms were up to something big. Both he and his famous uncle, Josiah Wedgwood, wondered why objects left on the surface of the earth gradually sank into the soil. And he asked these questions, too: Why is there always a layer of "vegetable mould" on the surface of undisturbed earth? Why are there always several inches of fine soil at the surface of an undisturbed pasture, even if the soil below is full of stones?

And after 42 years of watching the eating habits of earthworms, what conclusions did Charles Darwin reach? Of course, he made many small observations, which he noted carefully. But they all added up to one big conclusion: earthworms persistently bring soil from lower parts of the soil profile to the surface—thereby performing a very significant plowing function. "Worms have played a more important part in the history of the world than most persons would at first suppose," he concluded. Without earthworms, there would not be that protective layer of vegetable mould at the surface. The soil would be less fertile. In fact, the soil itself might not even exist in its present form.

Have you ever looked closely at an earthworm cast? It is a lumpy glob of earth and organic particles brought to the surface by a worm from one of the several species. When an earthworm eats, it is seeking the food value that is in organic materials primarily. But it also can't avoid eating some earth, or does so deliberately in order to create living and moving space for itself. Going on within an earthworm is a constant process of grinding and digesting of the soil, and especially the mixing of its organic food with particles of soil.

That grinding of small soil particles is step one of the important process of soil regeneration carried on by earthworms. It is important to realize that almost every soil has tremendous mineral riches locked up in its particles of silt. Those minerals are in a form unavailable to plants. But when the particles are ground, by the physical action of water or pressure or earthworm digestion, the locked-up minerals are gradually released and made available. The worm does that extremely important work of soil genesis and in addition brings the casts of digested and improved earth to the surface, where it can be used most easily by plants.

Charles Darwin measured the rate at which earthworms moved the earth in that way and reported the observations of others. His conclusion was that, given favorable weather and a good soil, earthworms could deposit a layer .22 inch thick on top of a soil each year. He estimated that 26,886 worms lived on a typical acre of soil, and that each worm ate 20 ounces of soil in a year. And on that single acre, about 15 tons of soil passed through the gizzards of worms each year, Darwin concluded.

In the hundred years since Darwin's death, the earthworm has not been forgotten. But neither has it become on object of serious and beneficially intensive research. Other counts of earthworm numbers and measures of their activity have been made, and of course some vary from the numbers Darwin presented to the world in 1881. But his general conclusions and observations have stood the test of time.

What has largely been overlooked, though, is the general thrust of his lesson, as well as the importance of continuing to ask the question: what happens when earthworms eat? By failing to continue to ask ourselves that question, we have also failed to continue to see the other question hidden within it that I feel sure Darwin pondered but didn't deal with specifically. That is: what would happen to us if the earthworms weren't there and if soil stopped being regenerated by their actions?

Now is an excellent time to ask that additional question because the earthworm, as the saying goes, has largely been factored out of modern agriculture. Worms aren't studied much today by mainline scientists because they aren't found often in modern farm fields. The constant shower of insecticides, weed-killers and fertilizers creates an environment hostile to their existence. Worms like pastures and sod best, where they can get into their circular rhythm of movement and regeneration, without having their whole world turned upside down every year. Indeed, the modern farming world is not friendly to worms. No wonder they are so little thought of or studied.

What else do we need to learn about earthworms? That is another important question. My guess is that we will begin to see the answer to that question more clearly when we learn more about what happens when ordinary farmland is converted to organic agriculture. There is growing evidence that, when land is cultivated organically, fertility somehow springs from the earth itself. Fertilizers, even the natural kind, often don't do much to increase yields of plants.

Could it be that the fertility that earthworms raise from the depths of soil to its surface is much greater and more important than even Charles Darwin realized? While Darwin measured the *amount* of soil worms bring to the surface, he didn't have the tools, or perhaps the time, to try to measure the earthworms' influence on fertility. Some research of that kind has been done in recent years, but far more is needed.

What happens when earthworms eat?

That's a good question, and the full answer is yet to come.

Practice—Analyzing

1. Even though the title of this article focuses on one process, Rodale opens his article with references to two processes before he begins to explore how earthworms eat. What processes are they? Which one is the more important process? Why doesn't Rodale develop both pro-

cesses at the beginning of the essay? _____

_____

_____

2. In addition, Rodale moves from the earthworm process to a larger one. What is it? Does he list steps in this process? How much detail

does he give? _____

_____

_____

3. Who is the audience for this article? *Organic Gardening* appeals to readers who prefer not to use chemical or artificial fertilizers and pesticides but would rather use organic compost to fertilize gardens and

would rather control insects by planting crops that repel each other's pests or introducing natural predators into the garden. Does the audience affect what Rodale includes? How would his approach have changed if he were writing to students in an agricultural college?

Would he have included other information? _____

_____

_____

_____

4. Can you trace what happens when earthworms eat? Where does

    Rodale address this process? _____

    _____

    _____

5. How do references to Charles Darwin contribute to Rodale's argu-

    ment? _____

    _____

    _____

6. Where does Rodale first begin to move beyond the explanation of the process of earthworm digestion to concerns about fertility? Does Rodale convince you that the earthworm process is connected to the

    larger process? _____

    _____

    _____

    _____

    _____

    _____

7. Does the "questioning process" tie the beginning and end of the essay

together? Is this an effective technique? _____

_____

_____

_____

HOW DO WE READ PROCESS ANALYSIS?

When you saw the title of this chapter, you may have thought to yourself, "What's so difficult about reading or explaining a process? I do that all the time." Explaining how to perform the steps in a process is a common activity: look at all the cookbooks and instruction manuals that get printed every day. But think also about the last time you used a recipe that was confusing or tried to follow directions in an instruction manual when steps were missing.

Successfully reading process analysis requires that we recognize the analysis when we begin reading it. If we pick up an instruction manual or cookbook, we know what to expect: we will see a list of necessary tools or utensils, a list of ingredients, and then a step-by-step list of what to do. Although we will often read completely through such a process analysis, typically we pay most attention to each step as we perform it. Only if instructions are unclear do most of us have trouble reading this kind of process analysis.

Process analysis is usually combined with other strategies for explaining. We probably won't stumble across a cookbook recipe in our everyday reading. More likely, we will see analyses of common activities or natural events. Rodale's article is a good example. Even though he announces the topic of the paper as a process analysis—how earthworms digest soil— the process of questioning simple operations around us is his more important topic. Similarly, I just read a *Scientific American* article that explained several different processes for determining the amount of carbon dioxide in the atmosphere or ways to measure the building "greenhouse effect." Even in the morning paper, I read an analysis of thunderstorm formation.

Because such process analyses appear in articles explaining more than the process, readers need to be alert to the beginning of a process analysis. Typically, a process analysis fits into a longer analysis or explanation so that "how something happens or works" is only one way of explaining the phenomenon. Just as Rodale sets up a historical perspective for his question about earthworms, other writers explaining the development of, say, *CAT* scans, might talk about the history of such devices and then quickly explain how they work. Still other writers might find that explaining how quickly the first personal computer became outdated leads naturally into an explanation of how the newest generation of home computers works. As we've noted before, explanations can include a variety of information; process analysis is one kind of information that can help readers—and writers—explain or instruct.

Recognizing process analysis

How can a reader recognize that a process analysis is contained within a longer piece of writing? All process analyses—from the brownie recipe to the discussion of thunderstorm formation—follow the chronological sequence of events. If the writer wants you, the reader, to follow instructions, the writer addresses the reader directly by using "you" and giving imperative directions. Generally, the steps appear with transitions denoting sequence—"first," "next," "then," "meanwhile," "finally." Even if the process is not a sequence of instructions, most descriptions of processes follow the sequence of operations, and most writers are concerned to help readers follow the sequence by using transitions that highlight steps. And process analysis also goes by the description of "how to" do X. Being aware that you are reading "how to" will plug you into careful reading of the process.

How does Rodale fit the process analysis into his essay?

Does Rodale take care to help readers see the steps in earthworm digestion? Does he begin with the first or the last step in the process? If you look again at paragraph 6, you'll notice that he states the conclusion before he details what the earthworm does. Did you find the sequence of actions difficult to follow, though? Probably not, because Rodale brings up earthworm digestion as part of Darwin's study, and he follows a long series of questions Darwin asked with the conclusion he reached. Then in the next two paragraphs, Rodale finally answers his title question, what happens when earthworms eat? The earthworm takes in organic matter

And after 42 years of watching the eating habits of earthworms, what conclusions did Charles Darwin reach? Of course, he made many small observations, which he noted carefully. But they all added up to one big conclusion: earthworms persistently bring soil from lower parts of the soil profile to the surface—thereby performing a very significant plowing function.

and earth, grinds the soil, mixing organic particles into the soil, and deposits casts on the surface of the pasture or garden for plants to use. But you'll notice that Rodale does not label the steps for the reader's convenience. He expects the careful reader to see that he is answering his own question before he poses still more questions. Because Rodale has prepared readers so carefully to look for the earthworm process (with such a title he can't avoid telling us the process), he can dispense with obvious transitions for this process. Nonetheless, the sequence of actions the earthworm goes through does follow in order, even if they are separated in Rodale's paragraphs by other observations and conclusions.

The process analysis, then, usually does not stand completely alone, although a writer might wish to explain how something works by giving so much detail that the reader needs no other information to understand the writer's point. More often, though, readers should look for the process analysis as part of a larger explanation.

Let's consider a second process analysis excerpted from a longer essay:

A New Way to Burn

Walt Peterson, *Science 83* (April 1983, p. 65)

One afternoon more than a decade ago, a British engineer named Douglas Elliott tapped a bit of coal, ground to crumbs in a kitchen blender, into a tin can mounted on the wall. Below the can was an ordinary small open fireplace—ordinary, that is, at a casual glance.

For instead of burning coals, a red-hot bed of sand gently undulated like simmering lava. As the coal trickled out of the can onto the glowing bed below, each crumb exploded into flame with a pop and a blue-white flare. It burned only about two pounds of coal an hour, but the little fireplace glowed fiercely, delivering much more warmth than its size suggested.

The fireplace, at Aston University in Birmingham, England, was no mere conversation piece. It was a simple, striking demonstration of a concept called fluidized bed combustion. Some say that FBC will transform the use of humanity's oldest technology—fire.

Like any combustion system, the end product of FBC is heat, which can generate hot water or steam or run turbines to produce electricity. Unlike other systems, however, FBC boilers can burn low-grade fuels, everything from high-sulfur coal to rice hulls. Suitably designed, an FBC system can use soaking wet coal mixed with rock. It can burn peat, heavy oil, and oil shale; wood and wood waste, including sawdust; urban and industrial trash; even, at one plant in Wales, sewage sludge that is half water. Yet emission of sulfur and nitrogen oxides is kept so low that neither tall stacks to disperse the flue gases nor fussy wet scrubbers to trap them in liquid are needed. If nothing else, FBC means that coal, our most abundant but naggingly pollution-prone energy source, could be exploited in almost any form, helping to stave off future energy crunches.

The basic principle of FBC is simple: blow air up through a box full of fine sand. When the air just lifts the sand grains, they churn and tumble like a boiling fluid. They have become a "fluidized" bed. Stirred with a spoon, it feels like thin oatmeal. A block of wood will float on it. Then the churning particles are heated red-hot, to about 900 degrees Fahrenheit. This can be done by injecting propane or natural gas into the airstream and igniting it in the bed. Once the bed is hot, the start-up gas can be shut off and fuel fed in. The heat released by the burning fuel will keep the bubbling bed of sand incandescent at about 1,500 degrees Fahrenheit. The hot sand stores heat so well that even cold, wet fuel such as wet coal will not appreciably chill the bed. Heat is transferred through direct contact with the hot sand particles, so water tubes or air tubes immersed in the bed will collect heat perhaps five times faster than in an ordinary boiler. That means an FBC unit can be smaller than an ordinary boiler that puts out the same amount of steam and costs less.

Practice—Analyzing

1. In what paragraph does a process analysis occur? Is there only one

   process analysis in this essay? _____

   _____

2. What other methods of explanation does the author use in this passage? _____

_____

3. What kind of readers might be interested in this article? Does Peterson appeal effectively to his audience? _____

_____

4. How might you change what Peterson shows his readers to explain fluidized bed combustion to a second grader? _____

_____

_____

_____

HOW DO WE WRITE PROCESS ANALYSIS?

Although reading process analysis usually presents few problems, writing process analysis can be much more difficult. Think back to the last time you followed an instruction manual that left out steps or explained poorly what you were required to do at each step. That writer failed to follow guidelines for writing a clear process analysis. Just what must a writer do to write a clear explanation of process?

Audience

First, every writer must consider the audience. Although writers must evaluate the audience for each piece of writing, knowing the audience is crucial for process analysis. Writers must know how much to expect of readers. Will readers know the names of common tools or basic parts of machinery? Imagine, for instance, a teenager new to the kitchen. When he reads that he must have a spring form pan to make a cheesecake, he may have no idea what to look for. Similarly, someone new to bicycle repair may not be able to distinguish a free wheel from a wheel. Knowing your audience may save you as a writer from giving too much or too little detail as you describe the process. In extreme cases, you may decide that *you* don't know enough about the process to describe it to someone completely unfamiliar with the field. For example, after having taken one astrophysics course, you might want to describe the birth of a star, but could you write that explanation for your ten-year-old cousin just learning about gases and heat? In some cases, you may decide that to analyze a process thoroughly for an uninformed audience will take too long; you might then decide to change your approach or topic. Careful audience analysis can save time at this stage of writing.

Topic sentence

Although not all process analysis paragraphs have topic sentences, they do focus on a main impression or idea. Rodale, for instance, implies that knowing how earthworms eat will lead us to ask more important questions. Peterson suggests that knowing about FBC will revolutionize our thinking about heat. In your paragraphs, you may want to write more explicit topic sentences to help readers see why reading the process will be useful. Such topic sentences will state the process and a reason for knowing it, as Phil does for his humorous approach to dog attacks. Then the details of the process are related to the reason stated in the topic sentences.

> Dog attacks on joggers are an extremely frequent occurrence that can be avoided by knowing some tips on how to frighten these pesky pooches before they attack.

Practice — Revising topic sentences

Revise the following topic sentences to more precisely focus process analysis paragraphs:

1. In the process of restoring my '66 Mustang, the door panels needed immediate attention and I took it upon myself to do the job; what a

   mistake! _____

   _____

   _____

   _____

2. To meet a new friend, it is important to leave the person with a good impression, and it can be done simply by following the steps below.

_____

_____

3. Failing a big test comes long before the actual date of the test itself.

_____

_____

4. Whoever started the myth that children learn to cook by making fudge has never made real fudge. _____

_____

_____

_____

5. With winter rapidly approaching, romantics and economy-minded people alike may spark the notion of stoking up a fire in the fireplace.

_____

_____

Parts of the process analysis

After determining how much to expect from the audience, writers of an instructional process analysis list tools and necessary parts or ingredients. Then they list steps in the process as carefully as possible. Rarely is the list complete on the first try. Most writers spend a good bit of time outlining the steps before they try to draft the analysis. In a rough outline, a writer can more easily insert missing steps. Whenever possible, the best writers retrace their activities as they perform the process themselves. Or if the process is an explanation rather than a set of instructions, writers test each step to see if it leads to the following stage.

Once writers have completed an outline of the steps, they check to make sure that all steps are in exact order. As I noted before, process analysis follows strict chronological order. Transitional elements help readers follow the order of steps, particularly if two steps happen simultaneously. Good writers provide a smooth, coherent flow of instructions in their process analysis papers.

Most writers are surprised to learn just how difficult a clear process analysis is to write. You might start by trying a limited, straightforward process—computing gas mileage, changing a flat tire, filling out a class registration form—to get a feel for the difficulty of telling someone who knows nothing about mileage, cars, or registration just how to complete the process.

GETTING IDEAS FOR PROCESS ANALYSIS

While writing instructions for changing flat tires or ironing shirts or repotting plants provides good practice in process analysis, you will seldom be asked to write such papers. You may find yourself asked to write a series of directions to get to a location from the interstate highway, or you might be asked to write directions for movers to place furniture in your home or apartment. You might also recall the last time someone asked you to show him how to do something and write out the instructions you probably conveyed through dialogue and action.

But let's also consider a point Robert Rodale makes in his article, "Let's demonstrate how important questions are by asking what appears to be a simple one." Have you asked any apparently simple questions lately? The evening news often raises questions I would like answers for. Recent spring floods tempted me to ask, "What happens in hydroelectric plants?" Heat waves bring to mind questions about heat retention in buildings and perceived cooling from fans blowing hot as well as cold air. The space shuttle raises more questions about technology than I can possibly list here. And so on.

The point is that we are surrounded by gadgets, machines, technology, nature, and other people who function in ways we may or may not understand. But unless we ask questions, will we know what we understand? One of the more frustrating points about conversing with a three-year-old in the "Why?" phase is that our own ignorance often keeps us from answering questions about how things work. Let's explore some common household items in an effort to find a process that you might want to explore more fully.

What objects or gadgets are in the room with you? In my room, I see

fluorescent lights
radio

ballpoint pens

box of tissues

dust

books

afghan

What would you like to know about how these gadgets work or how they are made? (Do you know how ball point pens work?) I wouldn't mind knowing:

How a radio tunes in one station only?

How tissues get folded so that one pops up as another is pulled out of a box?

How dust forms?

How new printing technologies are affecting book production?

Some of the questions you've raised may not be appropriate for process analysis. My question about book production implies that I will not only look at the process of producing a book by means of new technology but also that I will compare new and old technologies and that I will focus on changes. I probably would not want to tackle such an unfocused topic for a short process analysis paper. But I would like to know about dust. As I investigate more, though, I may decide that I just can't deal with air flow, magnetic charges, and so on, but I want to learn more and so I will begin to read about dust. Then, when I have compiled information about dust, I can organize appropriate details to explain the process to someone else who doesn't know.

Try to concentrate on one of your questions as you look for answers to apparently simple questions.

What questions has Jane asked in this draft taken from her journal?

Today I went to give blood to Belle Bonfils. Giving blood is one of my favorite things to do. I get a charge out of each little step involved. I've only given blood three or four times and the routine has gone something like this. The first job is to sign up before Bonfils arrives or walk in on one of their working days. I prefer to do the latter. It's fun to just go up to the Student Center ballroom, give the lady your name and she gives you a number. I was #54 today. I like to visit a minute with the person at the door before moving on to the next station. They have two ladies, usually older, kindly women, at a typing table. These sweethearts take your vital statistics: name, address, phone and social security number. They chat with you about the weather or your mother for a moment or two; then they send you to the table where you fill out the back of the typed card. At this table they ask you to read the information about AIDS and answer questions such as, "Have you had your ears pierced in the last six weeks?" It's kind of like a test. True-false format tests have always been easy for me and I've always passed. The next step is to go over to a nurse who asks you a few more questions and pricks your finger and takes your temperature. I flunked this test once because the blood they took from my finger was too low in iron for them to take. That's when you get the heart sticker that says, "I tried." Today I passed that test with flying horses. (Not just another cliche.) The place they send you next is where you sit and wait to get a table. They ask you if you've had breakfast here and offer you cookies if you haven't. This is my favorite station. When they have a free table they call your number, and you go into a large area of white-jacketed nurses and white-faced donors. They lay you out on a reclined table-chair where they take your blood pressure and find a vein. Today my nurse had trouble finding my vein. Eventually she found one and went after it. They use a rather large needle, and I love to see it go into my arm. Today it wasn't so pleasant. She didn't get my vein, and so I didn't bleed well and my arm swelled to about twice its size and turned a lovely shade of reddish-greenish-blue. Normally they get a good vein, and in a few minutes you have given a pint of blood. If you don't faint after that part, like I did after my first donation, you get to go to the final table where these marvelous "grandmother ladies" wait on you and serve home-made cookies and MacDonald's orange juice. This is really the whole reason I give blood. Though I must admit it makes me feel physically good to give blood. I think I'm at my best when I'm running about a pint low.

—Jane A.

And finally, read this paragraph by Aldous Huxley. What is the purpose of his paragraph? Where does he state his main point?

Throw up a rubber ball with the right hand, and catch it, as it falls, in the left. Or, better, take a ball in either hand, throw up that in the right hand and, while it is in the air, transfer the ball in the left hand to the right hand, then use the left hand to catch the other ball as it comes down. By means of this rudimentary form of juggling one can impart to simple ball throwing a continuous easy rhythm, not present when a single ball is used. The eyes should be on the ball as it is thrown up by the right hand, should follow it up to the top of its trajectory and down again till it is caught by the left hand. (They should *not* stare up into the sky, waiting for the ball to appear within their field of vision.) After a long spell of close work, a brief interlude of this simple juggling will do much to loosen and relax the eyes.

—from The Art of Seeing

Writing process analysis

1. Use one of the apparently simple questions you asked to develop into a process analysis. Be sure to specify your audience so that you can use appropriate detail.

2. We often have rituals attached to certain activities. Analyze one of your rituals as a process analysis.
3. Whenever we begin new activities, we discover new ways of doing things or new things we must do. Write a process analysis for one of the activities associated with moving into new living quarters, starting a new semester of school, meeting new people in a club or at a social gathering.
4. We all have our own ways of dealing with anger. Outline your approach as a process analysis. Be sure to specify your audience.
5. Like anger, we all have ways of dealing with depression. Write your method as a process analysis designed to "sell" your approach to a national audience.

REVIEWING COHERENCE IN THE PROCESS ANALYSIS PARAGRAPH

As you recall from the discussion of narration, chronological order is not particularly difficult to maintain. Like the narrative, the process analysis relies on chronological order, and these papers often use the same transitional words and phrases. Just to help you review order before you revise your process analysis, however, look at the following paragraph:

Preparing livestock to exhibit at the Colorado State Fair has been an excellent way for our family to work together. First, my brother and I sort the lambs from the ewes; next we observe and select lambs with the greatest potential. If we both decide we like the lamb we place it into a separate pen. To decide if we like them, as we sort the lambs we keep a certain standard of perfection in mind. For example, as we sort and select the best lambs we will measure and feel for muscling on different parts of the lamb. Then we put them in pens. Periodically, we help each other weigh the lambs. Everyone helps feed the lambs and maintain health records. The last two weeks before the fair we assign different jobs to everyone. Mother is always a good sport and is happy to volunteer her help by washing and ironing the show blankets. My sister and I pitch in by mending holes and replacing missing buckles from last year's show blankets. My two brothers, Mike and Don, team up and shear all the lambs. Next they must weigh them and trim their hoofs. Finally, about the last couple of days we all get together and wash each lamb, blanket it, and put it in a clean bedded pen. At last we are ready for the fair.

—*Mary G.*

1. As you read this paragraph, where did you find that you missed the

sequence of steps? _____

_____

2. Could you rearrange parts of Mary's paragraph to make clearer how

   selecting good lambs occurs? _____

_____

_____

3. Do you suppose that mending blankets comes before ironing them?

_____

4. Are you also sure that you know how long the entire process takes?

_____

5. Would you want to know more about how often lambs are weighed

   during the initial phase? _____

6. Notice also that Mary's paragraph focuses on the process of preparing
   livestock as a process of family cooperation. Do you see any need for

   more detail on family participation? _____

_____

_____

_____

7. Where might you add details or clearer transitions? _____

_____

_____

_____

8. Now reconsider the topic sentence. Does the paragraph address a

more limited topic than the topic sentence states? How would you

revise the topic sentence? _____

_____

_____

_____

Suggest any other revisions, especially for transitional elements, that might improve Mary's paragraph.

Preparing livestock to exhibit at the Colorado State Fair has been an excellent way for our family to work together. First, my brother and I sort the lambs from the ewes; next we observe and selects lambs with the greatest potential. If we both decide we like the lamb we place it into a separate pen. To decide if we like them, as we sort the lambs we keep a certain standard of perfection in mind. For example, as we sort and select the best lambs we will measure and feel for muscling on different parts of the lamb. Then we put them in pens. Periodically, we help each other weigh the lambs. Everyone helps feed the lambs and maintain health records. The last two weeks before the fair we assign different jobs to everyone. Mother is always a good sport and is happy to volunteer her help by washing and ironing the show blankets. My sister and I pitch in by mending holes and replacing missing buckles from last year's show blankets. My two brothers, Mike and Don, team up and shear all the lambs. Next they must weigh them and trim their hoofs. Finally, about the last couple of days we all get together and wash each lamb, blanket it, and put it in a clean bedded pen. At last we are ready for the fair.

Revision checklist

1. Have you determined the audience you will write to and what they need to know? Have you considered the process analysis as one form of explanation?
2. Does the topic sentence clearly state the process and a reason for knowing it?
3. Have you listed all the tools your reader might need to complete the process?
4. Have you included all the steps your reader must follow?
5. Are the steps in clear chronological order?
6. Have you used any words your readers won't know? Have you used the most precise words?

chapter 10
Comparing and contrasting

WHAT IS COMPARISON/CONTRAST?

Every day we engage in countless comparisons: should we sleep another ten minutes or get up for one last review of test notes; should we spend money on supplies at the beginning of the month when we have plenty of money or wait till the end of the month to cover unexpected bills. Even simple decisions—should I have raisin bran or cornflakes for breakfast—generally involve comparing two items, choices, or consequences.

WHEN DO WE USE COMPARISON/ CONTRAST IN COLLEGE WRITING?

Perhaps the most common type of question on essay tests in all disciplines is the comparison/contrast question: compare treatment of the serfs under Catherine the Great and Peter the Great; compare tax revenue estimates under a value added tax and flat tax; compare metal fatigue in airplanes using two wing designs; and so on. Because we weigh information, testing our ability to present comparisons tests our understanding of concepts.

Besides the essay test, comparison/contrast appears in lab reports (of successful and unsuccessful lab techniques), in clinical notes (of two treatment plans), and in research reports (of conflicting experiments). In short, comparison/contrast helps writers in all disciplines structure their comparative evaluations of two ideas, techniques, approaches, designs, and so on.

But as you'll notice in reading the following editorial, often the comparison is not fully stated. As you read this piece, think about what comparisons the writer is asking you to make.

Parents Have Right to Use Some Force

Greg Dixon, *USA Today*

In October of 1980, a nightmare of unbelievable proportions took place for Mr. and Mrs. Darrel Trueblood of Terre Haute, Indiana. A welfare caseworker and deputy sheriff came to their home and took their 9-year-old son, Travis, from them—supposedly because Mr. Trueblood had abused him. Frightened and screaming, Travis was deposited in the back seat of a squad car, which had a wire mesh divider. The woman caseworker got into the front seat and left the terrified boy alone.

The Truebloods did not see Travis for seven days until the preliminary court hearing. The county welfare department had placed him in a foster home; his parents couldn't find out where he was. Then Travis was placed in a foster home again for two-and-a-half months, without the parents' knowledge: they were frantic. The boy's father was forced to take psychological tests at his own expense. Finally, the court, under pressure from the public and media, returned Travis to his parents. Besides public embarrassment, lost work time and mental distress, the episode cost the Truebloods nearly $4,000 in legal fees.

What was the father's crime? What terrible thing had he done to his son? He had spanked his son with a ruler for lying and had left some welts on his buttocks. Interestingly, Mr. Trueblood was never charged with child abuse.

Similar things have happened all over America since millions of dollars have been flowing into the states from Washington to set up child protection agencies. These agencies have almost total power to seize children from their homes. Phone numbers are now placed in the halls of many public schools so that children who are unhappy with discipline may simply retaliate by turning in their parents. By law, the authorities must investigate. Even a well-deserved whipping can cause children to be removed and parents charged with child abuse. And it's not unusual for a treatment program to involve the whole family and allow the state to administer drugs to hyperactive children.

The state of Indiana has alleviated this problem somewhat by amending the "child abuse" laws, by making it clear that physical abuse doesn't include reasonable corporal punishment and that mental abuse doesn't include religious instruction of their children.

The Bible and the Constitution are clear. Parents are responsible for the rearing of their children, not the state. Present laws, if enforced, are sufficient to punish the real child abuser without establishing government-funded protection agencies, which are one more blow in the destruction of the American home.

Practice—Analyzing

1. How do you define the major comparison Dixon wants readers to make? Write out what you feel is the most important comparison in

   the editorial. _____

   _____

2. Do you feel the Truebloods administered discipline or abused their

   son? What details in the editorial support your answer? _____

   _____

   _____

3. Do you see any other comparison Dixon wants readers to make?

   _____

4. Does his implied comparison of a scared nine-year-old with a criminal create sympathy for the Truebloods? If so, how? _____

_____

5. What other comparisons of values does Dixon imply, even if he doesn't address them directly? _____

_____

6. Does Dixon's description of government actions bring to mind any comparisons with other governments you know of? _____

_____

HOW DO WE READ COMPARISON/ CONTRAST?

Perhaps more than other forms we've considered so far, the implied comparison asks readers to make connections among personal experience, other knowledge, and the piece of reading at hand. While we may argue that Dixon's editorial is not effective for other reasons—such as his emotional attitude toward the topic—we must be able to fill out the comparisons in order to understand the point of his editorial. For instance, Dixon never explicitly defines child abuse or discipline, but he uses both terms in a comparison of what readers will think is reasonable parental behavior. We also must compare the "justice" of separating a child from his concerned family with the "justice" of protecting a vulnerable victim. Moreover, we must call to mind punishments we've received as children or teens from parents trying to teach us right from wrong and compare those with Travis Trueblood's punishment. And we probably also recall stories we've seen on television or read about—stories of abused children supposedly being "taught" but really being tormented by a sick adult. All these bits of information must come together as we read the editorial to help us make sense of Dixon's argument and the point he tries to make by comparing child protection laws with the traditional value of sanctity of the home.

Perhaps more than other readings we've considered so far, this editorial also suggests the complexity of thought going on below the surface because this reading calls for analysis not only of the content of the editorial but also of our experience and our attitudes toward parents' and children's rights. And if you think about it a bit, you'll probably agree that most comparison calls on not only what you read but also what you remember. Consider advertising. So many ads claim that "brand A is better than brand B" that readers must understand the content of the ad while they also remember their experiences with one or both brands. Yet, because we so constantly evaluate similarities and differences, better and worse, we accept the mental process as straightforward and ordinary.

Reading comparisons is not necessarily so complex, although readers always bring their own experience to bear on the descriptions of similarities and differences that they read. For "contrasting" means finding differences, while we use "comparing" to refer to both similarities and differences. And like other strategies for writing, the writer usually takes a position, stated in a topic sentence or thesis, and hopes to explain that position to the reader. The reader, then, must understand the position, evaluate it, and consider the points of comparison to determine if the argument lays out the most important points of similarity and difference. Let's consider Dixon's argument to see what his position is and how he explains the comparisons he feels are important in proving his point.

Using illustrations

First, Dixon adopts a strategy for writing his editorial that may prove useful in your work also. When we discussed narration, I suggested that using a specific illustration or story often grips readers in ways that statistics or other openings will not. Dixon, realizing that defining child abuse and discipline as straightforward terms would not advance his argument, chooses instead to set up his point with a story. He uses the experience of the Truebloods, suggesting especially the trauma suffered by Travis and his father, to highlight the shortcomings of new child protection laws that do not discriminate between appropriate punishment and physical abuse.

In October of 1980, a nightmare of unbelievable proportions took place for Mr. and Mrs. Darrel Trueblood of Terre Haute, Indiana. A welfare caseworker and deputy sheriff came to their home and took their 9-year-old son, Travis, from them — supposedly because Mr. Trueblood had abused him. Frightened and screaming, Travis was deposited in the back seat of a squad car, which had a wire mesh divider. The woman case-worker got into the front seat and left the terrified boy alone.

Defining terms

Dixon does not explicitly state his definitions of abuse and discipline (and perhaps you might consider working on such definitions for practice in Chapter 12). Instead, he assumes readers will agree that Travis deserved punishment for lying. Further, he assumes that readers will see that the punishment—being spanked with a ruler—is an appropriate one parents might use to reinforce their explanation of why lying is wrong.

Thesis statement and topic sentences

Dixon delays his thesis until the end of the article, although few readers would have any difficulty explaining his attitude toward the topic. He is able to wait to state his main point because the example he chooses and his word choices throughout the editorial make his position on the subject clear. In effect, he asks readers to suspend an evaluation of his argument until he has presented all of it. You can use the same technique effectively when you have clear examples and details that will paint a picture for readers that you can label later with your delayed topic sentence or thesis.

Notice that after completing the original narrative of the Truebloods, Dixon begins explaining his views. He then begins to use topic sentences, although in paragraph 3 he uses a question, paragraph 5 includes only one sentence, the topic sentence, and the final paragraph has no topic sentence because it includes the thesis for the entire essay.

Thesis: Present laws, if enforced, are sufficient to punish the real child abuser without etablishing government-funded protection agencies, which are one more blow in the destruction of the American home.

Topic Sentences—Para #3: What was the father's crime? Para #4: Similar things have happened all over America since millions of dollars have been flowing into the states from Washington to set up child protection agencies. Para #5: The state of Indiana has alleviated this problem somewhat by amending the "child abuse" laws, by making it clear that physical abuse doesn't include reasonable corporal punishment and that mental abuse doesn't include religious instruction of their children.

Supporting details

What evidence, then, does Dixon use to support his contention that parents are clearly responsible for rearing children and that child protection agencies are overstepping their bounds? He includes details that show the inhumane treatment of the Truebloods:

Travis is isolated behind "bars" like a criminal.

Travis is separated from his family for months.

Although Mrs. Trueblood had no hand in the punishment, she cannot see Travis for months.

Rather than assuming Mr. Trueblood's innocence, a fundamental tenet of our criminal justice system, the court forced Trueblood to prove his psychological soundness as a parent.

Mr. Trueblood was never *charged* with child abuse, but even so he was separated from his son for almost three months.

Dixon also generalizes about child protection laws that, he claims, pit children against parents and allow children to "turn in" parents who discipline them or try to teach them values and beliefs. Dixon doesn't include much detail except for the case of the Truebloods; instead, he relies on that story to illustrate the difference between unjust state intervention and proper child rearing. But as a reader, are you convinced that Dixon has made his case strongly enough? In this instance, implied comparisons—because they are not backed up with explicit detail—are not as effective as detailed comparisons might be. And so, in looking at comparison/contrast as a writing strategy, we will consider the detailed, explicit comparison, though you can certainly draw on your experience as readers of both explicit and implicit comparisons.

Practice—Writing

If you were asked to revise Dixon's editorial, you would probably want to add more detail to make the generalizations in paragraphs 4, 5, and 6 more concrete. First, underline the generalizations that need development. Then list several questions you would ask experts in the field to help you fill in details about parents' and children's rights, child abuse vs. discipline, state protection agencies, and so on.

Consider another essay with a more clearly defined comparison structure. This essay is an extended analogy between exercising and writing. Notice how each paragraph parallels points between the two activities.

Sweat

Everybody sweats, including me, Richard Simmons, Ronald Reagan, and probably you, too. Just what do I sweat over? I sweat over tests, over art critiques, over silly things like my car, friends, family. I sweat when I exercise, and always when I write. Just the mention of writing invariably makes me sweat because it reminds me of exercising. Writing, exercising, sweating—they're all the same in my little book of life.

"Exercise!" scream Doctor and Conscience, usually within the same agonizing moment of the yearly physical, while Face cringes and Body groans.
Generally, I shove these thoughts to the back of the mental closet and move
on to higher priority activities, but eventually I get around to thinking about
engaging in some type of physical activity. Exercising is a necessary evil in
my life, essential for better health and longevity, but no less unpleasant for
all the benefits. When the time comes for me to exercise, I have a standard
procedure I follow, rarely deviating from this well-established norm. First,
I ponder whether to jog, swim, or aerobicize, and then I set aside a specific
time for the tortuous exercise session to occur and prepare to sweat. When
the chosen time arrives, I jump into my favorite pair of worn-out sweats,
do a bit of meditation and prayer, some warm-ups and begin. The initial
moments always seem the hardest; I am torn between wanting to quit and
return to sedentary life and knowing I should keep my body in motion
because I need the work-out. I either succumb to this internal weakness and
toss the exercise notions out the window, or else call up the back-up crews
of determination and continue. Often I start and stop, and start and stop
again, indecisive about the whole thing. My heart beats faster and faster, I
sweat, and my body grows tired, quickly sapping all energy reserves, but
somehow I endure and the session ends. I always feel refreshed and re-ener-
gized after completing that final minute, swimming that last lap, or jogging
those final yards. Satisfied with my accomplishment, I am often filled with
wonder at my initial lack of enthusiasm.

Writing occurs in much the same way, with an instructor telling me,
"Write!" while I inwardly groan. Ignoring the task simply makes it all the
more agonizing and painful, until I finally face it with a thick pad of clean
paper and five or six new pens swollen with fresh ink. Before beginning to
write, I reflect on the chore and allocate a certain amount of precious time
for the writing assignment. When the time comes to write, I prepare by suit-
ing up in my favorite composing clothes—pajamas—only to find it just as
hard to start writing as to begin exercising. Fitting those first few words
together is sometimes as painful as the first few stretches and pulls I put my
body through while warming up. My brain is simply a cold and tight muscle
needing a little pushing and shoving to kick it into gear. I usually stare at
the blank page for a long time, write, scribble out, wad up, and throw away,
repeating this until I have finally made up my mind, almost like the first
few minutes of my exercise routine. At last when that final word falls on the
page, relief and satisfaction flood through me; I can breathe deep and relax
for a while in the afterglow of achievement.

This connection between writing and physical exercise developed when I
started college and discovered both activities had become important for
survival among the vicious ranks of cut-throat college kids. In my pre-col-
legiate days, writing and exercise had been fun and easy when there was less
pressure and more time for both. At college, however, I found that academic competition and pressure had increased ten-fold and my free time
for exercise had dropped ninety percent (not to mention the increased social
importance placed on being a fat-free, fashionably fit female). Doomed
from day one, my grip on both disciplines slipped away; exercise took a
back seat to studying and social obligations, while my few writing assign-

ments became engulfed in a sea of calculus problems, chemistry experiments, and biology labs. Ignoring the writing assignments led to unacceptable grades and ignoring the exercise regime led to an unacceptable state of health. Since their simultaneous demise that first fateful semester, writing and exercising obstacles have proved difficult to overcome, and consequently I think of them as malignant outgrowths of my life, eternally plodding along, hand in hand.

This analogy between writing and exercise habits helps me understand both processes, although it makes neither any easier. I realize that writing is an essential exercise of the mind, necessary for intellectual strength and growth, in much the same way that physical exercise affects the strength and health of the body. I can also see how my preference for easy forms of exercise like walking the dog, changing albums on the stereo, and opening beer bottles carries over into my favorite writing forms of crossword puzzles, letters, and unstructured, free-form rambling. I am a lazy writer in much the same way that I am a lazy exerciser.

Whether it is Dr. Brown, M.D., or Dr. Kiefer, Ph.D., goading me into sweaty action, the process and attitude are much the same. I recognize rhetorical and physical exercise as simply being painful means to a healthy end—prevention of a flabby brain and a flabby body. Unfortunately, I rarely get enough of either, spending a sad amount of time physically and mentally out-of-shape. Sure, I sweat, but when I do, there's usually a soothing shower and cold beer waiting for me in the end.

—*Jodi J.*

Practice—Analyzing

1. Does Jodi primarily compare or contrast in this essay? Why?

_____

2. Does Jodi have a thesis statement? Where is it? _____

_____

_____

3. Can you tell Jodi's stance from her thesis and wording throughout

the essay? _____ Point to specific words that tell you how

she feels about her topic. _____

_____

4. Label the topic sentences in each paragraph. How do the topic sentences help you as a reader see where Jodi's ideas are going in each

   paragraph? _____

5. Does Jodi use examples or details to develop her essay? List the most

   effective support in the essay. _____

   _____

   _____

6. Would you say that Jodi uses the block or point-by-point pattern?

   Do you think the arrangement is effective? _____

   _____

7. As you read Jodi's analogy of writing to exercise, did you make any
   mental connections between the two? Or do you equate writing with

   some other kind of activity? _____

HOW DO WE WRITE COMPARISON/ CONTRAST?

As I mentioned earlier, most writers find comparing and contrasting easier to write if they have a preference in mind so that the writing takes on an argumentative edge. While writers can simply describe similarities and differences, such objective comparisons are less common than comparisons designed to convince readers that one object, event, or decision is better, more appropriate, cheaper, wiser, and so on. So keep "argument" in mind as you consider writing a comparison.

No matter how long a comparison you want to write, you will find that it falls into one of two patterns or a mixture of the patterns. Because readers expect one of these organizational patterns, writers follow the patterns to communicate clearly. Basically, writers can choose the *block* or *point-by-point* arrangements.

Block pattern

With this organization, the writer outlines everything about one object or event and then follows with all details about the second object or event. In this pattern, the writer must be sure to arrange details in corresponding order as shown below.

Block	Point-by-Point
Item A—point 1	Item A—point 1
point 2	Item B—point 1
point 3	Item A—point 2
point 4	Item B—point 2
Item B—point 1	Item A—point 3
point 2	Item B—point 3
point 3	Item A—point 4
point 4	Item B—point 4

Point-by-point pattern

With this organization, the writer chooses corresponding points about both items and arranges the points next to each other. Generally, if the writer begins with item A and follows with B, he follows that order consistently throughout the comparison (although clear reversals of order provide a nice break from the pattern). With this scheme, since the corresponding points are adjacent in the paper, the writer need not worry about forgetting a point for one item covered for the other item. But with this pattern, the writer must take special care to provide good transitions to help readers see a smooth flow of ideas. Too often readers feel as if they are watching a tennis match—moving abruptly from side to side—when writers don't smooth out connections between ideas.

Practice—Writing

Revise the following paragraph from point-by-point pattern to the block pattern. Which do you think is the more effective pattern for this paragraph?

Fraternity members at CSU uphold the stereotype of being daily goof-offs; however, my friend Jeff is an exception. For instance, a typical fraternity person delights in viewing the hard-fought football games on Sunday while hammering down a six-pack or two. Jeff, on the other hand, prefers to sedately watch the exciting action of the sport without any alcohol in his system so that he can return to work immediately after the games. Secondly, fraternity members also watch Monday Night Football even though they have an extremely difficult test in one of their classes the following day. Jeff, in contrast to the rest of his fraternity brothers, studies for his tests regardless of who might be playing the game. For example, last Monday night the Dallas Cowboys and the L.A. Raiders played. Jeff, instead of watching the game, studied for his biology exam the following day. In addition, when weekends roll around, fraternity guys end up throwing parties or attending them, as they are sometimes indifferent to the load of homework they have due on Monday. Jeff, however, spends his precious time slaving away underneath his radiant study lamp, trying to get caught up in his school work before Monday arrives. Lastly, fraternity brothers also self-indulge in late night conversations among their peers, such as last Sunday night when Jeff's buddies from the house stayed up until three in the morning gossiping about what they had done over the weekend. Jeff, unlike his brothers, retires at about ten o'clock in the evening since he has to attend class the next morning. Observing the contrasts above, one can clearly see that my friend Jeff is an exception to the fraternity stereotype.

—George S.

Combining patterns

If you are writing a single paragraph of comparison, either pattern works well, but you can probably also imagine that the block method works especially well with a two-paragraph paper. Furthermore, if you have enough detail to fill up a paragraph with each point, the point-by-point method easily breaks into paragraphs between each new point.

If you are both comparing and contrasting, decide as well whether similarities or differences are most important for your argument. Since ideas covered at the end of a paragraph—or essay—get more emphasis because of their position, start with your less important points and finish with the most important. The following diagram suggests two possible organizational patterns with both comparison and contrast:

Block		Point-by-Point	
Item A—point 1	Compare	Item A—point 1	Compare
point 2		Item B—point 1	
Item B—point 1		Item A—point 2	
point 2		Item B—point 2	
Item A—point 3	Contrast	Item A—point 3	Contrast
point 4		Item B—point 3	
Item B—point 3		Item A—point 4	
point 4		Item B—point 4	

Especially in longer papers, you might want to mix patterns:

Compare	Item A—point 1	Block comparison
	—point 2	
	Item B—point 1	
	—point 2	
Contrast	Item A—point 3	Point-by-point contrast
	Item B—point 3	
	Item A—point 4	
	Item B—point 4	
	Item A—point 5	
	Item B—point 5	

Let's look at another comparison/contrast paper to see if its structure fits one of these patterns:

A Rebel Friend

The police once busted a good friend of mine named Rod Stoll for throwing wads of pizza dough at cars. Rod, who had stolen the odd materials for performing the stunt at a local Godfather's Pizza Parlor where he worked, had once talked to me about this original and creative idea during a high school lunch hour.

"What would that sound like?" he asked. "Think of the noise. Would it seem like you've run over a cat? Hit a person? What would the driver think?"

To be honest, I wasn't surprised he had attempted his little experiment. Rod had always lived as a rebel. I, on the other hand, lived as a dedicated student. We were opposites of sorts. With his juvenile activities (like throwing pizza dough), my decisive accomplishments, his tough background, my sheltered one, his blatant pessimism, and my straightforward optimism, Rod and I were two totally different people.

Rod and I came from two totally different backgrounds. Rod's short, stocky grey-haired father ran into a lot of failures when it came to bringing in a steady income. The burning cigarettes and clear brown liquid in the glasses the man held whenever I saw him I'm sure were of no help in his struggle. Because of her husband's low income, Rod's mother would work for a real estate agent in town. With a job on their mother's hands, Rod and his little sister did a big part of the household chores themselves including laundry, vacuuming, meal-fixing, and grocery shopping. Although they were around each other often, Rod and his sister, Kris, rarely got along well. He would constantly refer to her with very foul names. Outside the home, an older blond-haired, baseball-capped fellow named Doug, with his cruising and womanizing exploits influenced Rod's social life greatly. In contrast, my household differed from Rod's tremendously. My dad had always been a hard worker and was fortunate enough to bring in enough income to keep us well fed and our modest tri-level home paid for. My mom was an artist and her creativity seeped into my life constantly with gifts and project ideas for me to have and take part in. My brother and I grew up together and our wild, science-fiction interests grew hand in hand with our maturing bodies. Together with our friends we would play flashlight freeze-tag games in the backyards of our suburban neighborhood homes, draw Star Wars scenarios on our notebook paper in school, and read action-packed adventure comic books. While Rod's background was harsh and unsheltered, I lived in a more secure environment, usually getting a fair share of the things I wanted.

Regardless of what we received as kids, both he and I received a hardy share of conflict between his pessimistic and my optimistic attitudes. I was the guy who tried not to make enemies; I talked myself out of fights with the biggest bullies in the school. Rod, however, would look upon people whom he didn't like or people who didn't like him simply as inferior, and he would constantly bring up complaints about how stupid people infested the world. "Andy Rooney and Jane Fonda ought to be shot," he'd say. I smiled a lot; Rod often went through days on end with a frown on his face. I always looked upon school as an achievement which, although boring at times, was a necessary part of life; Rod thought it a waste of his time. While I was writing imaginary, creative poems and stories on the hopeful future, Rod typed up essays with titles like "Why Hitler was Right" or "Why I Created the World," and the girl, who floated like some unattainable angel to me, registered simply as an abusable object in his eyes. Often the only thing which kept us from halting the friendship because of such different views was that we respected each other's viewpoint; we sort of had a "law" of keeping an open mind.

Keeping an open mind would be necessary if one saw us as good friends while, at the same time, looking at the different activities we did when we were away from each other. While Rod was storing hundreds of stolen political campaign signs in his basement, I was painting banners for a community theater group in town. Just as Rod threw his pets across the room to see if they could land right, I cleaned my dog's cage out and played chase with him. Rod would only hand in homework when he felt like it; I handed it in all the time. While he was out cruising with Doug listening to acid rock, sneaking around old condemned buildings and wrapping merry-go-rounds in toilet paper and lighting them on fire, I was making short movies, listening to pop music, and going to such activities as the American Legion Boy's State (a type of summer camp only a few selected students from each high school in the state were allowed to attend). While he cruised, I studied; while he vandalized, I created. If we were to bump into one another while doing what we did separately, I doubt we'd recognize each other.

The differences we had weren't only providing bad moments in our relationship, however. Our diversity also provided dozens of humorous moments: from me going cruising with him and not realizing that the beer I was trying to twist open was actually to be opened with a can opener to his taking a girl to the senior prom and looking totally out of his element in the spiffy tuxedo he wore. Our differences, in a way, magnified our likenesses which were, of course, what we as friends focused on. These focused feelings are even found in the letters we write each other as we carry out our different occupations; while I'm a student at CSU, he's a Marine based in Japan. The differences may be there, but without them, I don't think we'd have a friendship at all.

—*Brian D.*

While Brian's paper does not argue that one personality is preferable, he does describe the most important differences between himself and his friend. Do you see where Brian sets up the major points he will cover? Then he picks up each contrast and treats it in a separate paragraph, first using a block comparison for background and then the point-by-point pattern for attitudes and activities. Notice, too, that Brian saves the most important point he wants to make until the conclusion—that he and Rod are friends because of rather than despite differences.

GETTING IDEAS FOR COMPARISON/ CONTRAST

Let's go back to the ideas that Greg Dixon brings up in his editorial on punishment. We all remember specific punishments we deserved when we were children or teens. Sometimes an unusual punishment stands out in our memories; sometimes we recall best the light punishment for a serious infraction of the rules and sometimes a punishment we felt was undeservedly severe. Focus on punishments you received from your parents as you freewrite for ten minutes.

Now look over your freewriting and find a phrase or sentence that captures the main focus of your thoughts. If you can't find a sentence in your freewriting, write out a sentence that captures your main point thus far:

_____

_____

_____

Use this sentence to guide your next freewriting loop. Write for another ten minutes. Don't stop writing if you run out of ideas on this statement, but let the ideas flow as quickly as possible while you keep them loosely connected to your guiding sentence.

Repeat the same steps once again: find a sentence that captures your main focus as much as you can now and write with that focus in mind for another ten minutes. Having completed this looping exercise, you probably have material you might be able to use in writing a paper comparing your attitudes toward discipline with your parents' attitudes. (If you find that you strayed from parental discipline to academic discipline or some other related topic, you can pursue that topic instead.) You might compare the current attitudes you and your parents have toward discipline, or you might limit your paper to a comparison of your parents' discipline with the discipline you will mete out when you have children.

APPLYING COMPARISON/CONTRAST

During my childhood, I preferred to be grounded rather than spanked as a method of being punished. Being spanked teaches a child aggressive behavioral patterns out of a form of punishment whereas grounding molds a child into a non-aggressive behavioral pattern. Another aspect of the grounding vs. spanking subject is that a spanking lasts a short period of time whereas grounding lasts anywhere from a week to a month, depending on the reasons for which the child is being grounded. A third point to be discussed is the relationship with the child and the parent. If the child is spanked everytime they do something wrong, they will definitely not be on great terms with that parent whereas with grounding a child, they know that they won't be able to do certain things for a certain amount of time. During the punishment in terms of spanking, the child has no time to discuss matters with that parent because of the spontaneity of the punishment whereas with grounding the child and the parent have time to talk matters out diplomatically. No matter which of these two methods of punishment is chosen, there are both pros and cons for both grounding and spanking that must be considered.

—Rick C.

In Rick's early draft, he compares two forms of punishment, but he closes on such an indefinite idea that the comparison seems unimportant. Can you help Rick revise by helping him focus his topic sentence on what seems to be the most important points he wants to make in comparing spanking and grounding? Then rewrite the conclusion. Add details if you can think of appropriate ones. Do not edit for mechanical and stylistic weaknesses yet.

Consider one more paragraph. What pattern does it follow? Where could you add detail?

The manner in which I would punish my sixteen-year-old son for taking my car on a road trip to the mountains without asking would be dissimilar to the way my father handled the situation with me. After being persuaded by my peers, I decided to take my father's car to the mountains without permission. Upon my arrival back at home, my father was waiting for me at the door. With firmness in his voice he shouted my punishment at me, "you will surrender the car keys to me for a week, and you will be confined to the house this weekend." If a similar situation were to arise with my own son, my form of punishment would be different. At the time of my son's sixteenth birthday, he will be informed of what will happen if he takes the car out without asking. I will state that if he is to do this the car keys will be removed from his possession forever, and if he wants to drive again he will have to buy his own car. Although my form of punishment is dissimilar to my father's, I see it as being appropriate in this situation.

—Charles V.

Writing comparison/contrast

1. Think about how your parents punished you when you broke the "rules" as a child or young adolescent. List some specific details about what you did wrong and how you were punished for each infraction. Now imagine yourself as the parent of a child or teenager much as you were. Would you punish your child the same way your parents punished you? Focus carefully on one main point that you want to make about your approach and your parents' approach to punishment or about two different methods your parents used. Write a paragraph in which you compare or contrast two of your parents' methods of punishment.

2. Or write a paragraph in which you compare or contrast one of your preferred methods of punishment with one of your parents' methods.

3. Compare and contrast two methods of discipline preferred by teachers.

4. If you have enough information, compare and contrast our culture's punishments with those of another culture. Be aware that this topic will require a longer essay rather than a short paragraph. Be sure to include specific illustrations and explanations of differences. You might also want to analyze why the differences arose between cultures.

5. In what other ways outside the criminal justice system does our society "discipline" people who don't fit our expected norms of behavior? Compare and contrast straightforward punishment with a more subtle form of discipline favored in our society. Again, note that this is an essay rather than a paragraph topic.

Revision checklist

1. Have you chosen two related ideas or things that are similar enough to be compared and contrasted?

2. Does the topic sentence or thesis statement focus adequately on the points of comparison and contrast?

3. Does the topic sentence or thesis statement reflect your stance or attitude?

4. Have you avoided vague words such as "similarities" and "differences" in the topic sentence or thesis?

5. Have you limited the scope of the paragraph so that you can develop each point in adequate detail?

6. Have you included enough detail on each point?

7. Have you chosen the best pattern to make your comparison and contrast clear to readers?

8. Have you used enough varied transitional elements to help the reader proceed smoothly through the paragraph?

chapter 11
Classifying

WHAT IS CLASSIFYING?

Another common way for human beings to deal with all the information that bombards them is to categorize it, to label it in mental file folders. We call this process division and classification because first we must decide what elements of information belong together: we must *divide* information into categories. Then we attach labels or names to the coherent groups; in short, we *classify*. Usually, though, when we mention classifying, people understand that the grouping action has to occur first, and so "classification" has come to mean the entire process.

If you think about the information you receive every day, you'll agree that we need ways to group information. Many of the labels we attach to information classify for us. For instance, if I were to give you a number such as 303–555–8768, what would you call it? Just by the sequence of numbers you would recognize it as a telephone number. And if it were important, you would remember it the way you remember other telephone numbers. You would, in effect, classify it in your mental file drawer as "telephone number."

WHEN DO WE USE CLASSIFICATION IN COLLEGE WRITING?

Whenever we have a large body of information that we need to remember, we are likely to apply some of the techniques of classification. You might, for instance, find yourself grouping the new people you meet in classes according to hair color, length, glasses, facial hair, and so on. But when writing, we use classification when it will help both writer and reader. For instance, if you have to review several articles on a single subject, you might first classify the articles so that you can group similar ones together. Your reader, then, can understand why the first three articles, the next two, and the final four are clustered logically. Similarly, in reports of research results, writers collect similar experiments or similar results into logical groups. Any analysis—in history, chemistry, engineering—with a body of data or a long list of examples can be classified to help readers understand the importance of "chunks" of the data.

As writers, we use the same techniques to help people organize information so that they can understand and remember it. Tim Tillson groups runners in the following essay, setting up what he calls, "A Running Taxonomy."

A Running Taxonomy

Tim Tillson

The 70s have been called the "decade of the individual." Many people in the United States became very concerned about their bodies and minds and did something about it: they became runners. Now it is difficult to travel the streets without being virtually stampeded by hordes of these creatures, each pursuing his or her elusive, self-actualizing high. Runners are not all the same, however. There are at least two basic categories, and the ability to distinguish between them has saved the life of many a discriminating bystander.

The largest group by far is the species Runnerus noviciae. Spanning all age groups and both sexes, these runners are those who either started yesterday or are, for one reason or another, inept. Their most identifiable features are clenched fists held at midchest and a horrible grimace. Their faces are often beet red as they attempt to run 4, 6, or even 10 miles wholly without preparation. These runners compensate for their lack of skill by wearing the most recent innovations in running apparel, including brand-new, five-star, fluorescent shoes, waterproof sweats, and brilliantly striped vests to keep pedestrians and drivers at more than a safe distance. Instantaneous identification of members of this group is seldom difficult, for a few minutes' perseverance will usually pay off: members of this species usually succumb to vomiting, collapse, or wild dogs. In short, Runnerus noviciae present no threat to property or life (other than their own).

The second species, more cunning and dangerous than the first, is Runnerus longae. These runners are usually quite thin, and their light footfalls give little warning of approach to the casual pedestrian who steps into their path. Longae are fleet, efficient, and capable of maintaining gut-wrenching speeds over long distances. Members of this species are commonly seen in down-in-the-heel running shoes (badly rain-faded, of course), light running shorts, holey T shirts sporting notices of long-distance races, and, in colder weather, stocking caps and gloves. Normally docile because of their characteristic alpha brainwave saturation, Runnerus longae can viciously attack the unprepared commuter. Many of these incidents have occurred when late model cars have unwittingly pulled out in front of Runnerus longae. Bashed side panels are common; occasionally the roof of the car itself has been trod on. Nonetheless, Runnerus longae do not become supremely dangerous until they swarm. Groups of up to 15,000 are said to yearly decimate some of the poorer sections of New York City.

Some observers feel that there is yet a third species, Runnerus fanaticus. They cite persons who run for days on end, up mountains and through blazing deserts, sometimes wearing stereo headphones. One study has even isolated runners who wear oxygen tanks at sea level to simulate high-altitude training. I am inclined to believe that members of the species fanaticus are merely an aberrant fringe of Runnerus longae who have become unhinged from the constant pounding of their feet. Fanaticus is the most frenzied and therefore most dangerous member of the genus Runnerus.

Practice—Analyzing

1. In paragraph one, how many major categories does Tillson mention?

2. Does he go on to discuss the differences between these categories?

_____

_____

3. Where does he first identify the main idea he will address in the rest

of the essay? _____

4. What categories of runners does he ultimately identify? Jot down the details that distinguish the categories.

_____   _____

_____   _____

_____   _____

_____   _____

5. Could you imagine adding any other details to the categories Tillson includes here?

_____   _____

_____   _____

_____   _____

_____   _____

6. What other ways might you classify runners? _____

_____

_____

_____

_____

7. Does the language in Tillson's article suggest his attitude toward Runnerus noviciae and longae? What specific evidence can you cite

from the article? How do the labels themselves set up the attitude

toward the groups? _____

_____

_____

_____

HOW DO WE READ CLASSIFICATION?

Especially in an essay like Tillson's, readers easily recognize the categories or groups because they are so clearly labeled, in this essay with the Latin names—Runnerus noviciae, longae, and fanaticus. Most readers, when they discover that the classification is entertaining, then go on to chuckle at the descriptions of and distinctions between classes. Having identified the essay as a classification, readers commonly judge the categories against their own experience by questioning: Have I seen these types of runners? Do I know other types of runners? Do all runners fit into these categories? Readers expect consistency and thoroughness of groupings.

Readers usually get clear clues to look for categories: often a topic sentence or thesis statement will explicitly state the groups with their labels. When we read research reports on education, for instance, the groups are clearly labeled by economic, age, or geographical tags. Surveys of working men or women often outline groups based on age, job titles, salaries, and so on. Even scientific reports, say on acid rain, group test sites by type of tree, location, or degree of damage. In all these kinds of reading, we recognize that writers have organized information for us as readers. We accept the organization, but not without question. As good readers, we examine the validity of the divisions into groups, and we expect complete details about each group so that we can be sure no members of one group could fit into another group.

Tillson's thesis: There are at least two basic categories, and the ability to distinguish between them has saved the life of many discriminating bystander.

Topic sentences: #1—The largest group by far is the species Runnerus noviciae. #2—The second species, more cunning and dangerous than the first, is Runnerus longae. #3—Some observers feel that there is yet a third species, Runnerus fanaticus.

HOW DO WE WRITE CLASSIFICATION?

Generally, classification involves at least three categories; the writer working with just two classes compares them. Like comparison, classification depends on readers seeing the common element that allows the people or objects to be clustered together and, like contrasting, classification then concentrates on distinguishing the groups from one another. You can think of it as comparison/contrast on a larger scale, though in classification we usually pay more attention to the differences between groups rather than similarities.

Being logical

However, if readers do not see a clear reason for dividing the large, related group into smaller ones to show off differences, the classification simply won't work. I could take the large class of "shoes" and divide that into boots, dress shoes, and sneakers (although unless I can be detailed or humorous the classification might seem boring because it is not focused). But I can't take as a large category "things I walk on" and talk about boots, dress shoes, and carpets as the smaller classes because I must be consistent about the common feature that divides the groups.

Being complete

Another point of consistency involves the completeness of the groups. If we want to write about university students eligible for fraternities but freshmen aren't eligible, then we shouldn't identify the first large group as "all university students." If we did so, then readers would be sure to ask why our subgroups didn't include freshmen. Thus, we must limit the large group carefully so that the subgroups take account of all elements of the large group.

Finally, no member of a subgroup should fit the description of another subgroup. Each class must be distinct.

Labels

Readers generally expect to see labels for the groups, too. In some classifications, the labels are humorous to let readers know not to take the groupings too seriously. In other classifications, say government reports, the labels are straightforward and descriptive.

Let's try another essay that could be read as a classification of TV characters. As you read this more complex essay, identify the groups Ellen Goodman sets up and think about labels you might use for each group.

TV's Hunks—Isn't Something Missing?

Ellen Goodman, *TV Guide* (July 16, 1983, pp. 6–10)

Having passed through the winter of the incredible hunk, when ripple TV replaced jiggle TV, it has finally occurred to me that nearly all of the chests being bared on prime-time television these days have hair on them.

Not that I mind, you understand. Some of my best friends have chest hair. But I had assumed that cleavage was a part of the female anatomy and that female anatomy was the prime stuff for prime time.

Now I realize that there is something odd going on, a television role reversal of massive proportions, from the piece to the hunk. We are now being treated to a star-studded, or stud-starring, cast of male sex objects.

While the film industry has tipped its hat to sexual ambiguity, with Dustin Hoffman playing Tootsie and Julie Andrews playing Victor, TV is playing it straight, superstraight, macho straight. Male sexuality is not the subject of any series; it's the object.

My first inkling of this change began with reports of the *Matt Houston* preview. In introducing Lee Horsley's character, the camera panned slowly from his $400 boots up his tight jeans and lingered longingly at what might be euphemistically called hip level. Indeed a female critic felt compelled to ask Horsley what it felt like to be featured in the "longest crotch shot" ever to grace the tube.

By now I have counted a crew of body beautifuls from the bimbo to the brutish. We have Lorenzo Lamas, a grandmama's boy in a Charles Atlas body; Tom Selleck, who has done more for a pair of jeans than Brooke Shields; and Gregory Harrison, whose bedside manner and bedroom eyes are calculated to make female viewers swoon. Add to them Pierce Brosnan in a black tux, David Hasselhoff in black leather, and you begin to get the smell of the thing. The smell is musk.

What precisely is going on in a world where all the men have *big* hard bodies to go with names like Houston and Magnum and Steele and Knight and Lance and Hooker, for heaven's sake? Is this the Woody

Allen backlash? Are these hunks eliciting drool from women, or admiration from men? Whose hunks are they anyway?

To begin with, it should be noted, and not in passing, that nearly all these beefy boys are figments of the imagination of other men: producers, agents, directors. It is at least possible that these men in high places are trying to respond to the protests of women viewers who don't want to watch the Suzanne Somerses of the world selling hardware, let alone their software.

It is even possible that they are trying in some peculiar way to respond to the women's movement by giving equal time to beefcake. This is the confused notion of equality currently being featured in the *Playgirl* centerfold and the male striptease act.

In this spirit we have seen a veritable rash of female lawyers on the air, enough to have one defend every male who could be brought up on muscle morals charges. We have also seen a minitrend of strong, powerful older women and beautiful but dumb younger men. The nighttime soaps, shows that might be catalogued as "relationship programs," are riding a wave, a "Falcon Crest" of dominating older women and younger men, notably Jane Wyman and Lorenzo Lamas.

But I don't think it's raised consciousness that has raised the pectorals. Even Lamas isn't, strictly speaking, a hunk. Biceps, triceps concepts, and he's a wimp. He's less appealing to women as a sexual-fantasy figure than a power-fantasy figure—at last, revenge on the young man who didn't call when she was 16 and he was 18. If women are powerful and men are cute when they get mad in "Falcon Crest," that really isn't so surprising. Women have always been ahead in the family business of relationships.

The true hunks are those men who star in adventure series. The antiheroes.

What I think has happened, as I watch the camera pan up Matt Houston's body and the Houston, Inc., building with equal lust, is that the men have created their own traditional fantasy figures and then beefed them up, so to speak, in accordance with their own idea of what appeals to women.

In most ways, Houston, Magnum, Knight, the late, unlamented Buck, even Steele in his mysterious way, are men's men. They are independent, handsome. . . strangers. As far as women are concerned, they are essentially loners.

Now, if the theorists are right and in hard times we return to the old mythology, the hunks are leading us back to the wonderful yesteryears of the Lone Ranger. "The Lone Ranger," you will recall, was always riding off, waving goodbye to the little lady at the ranch fence.

The steady woman in their lives is the inevitable gal Friday, who is now likely to be a gal lawyer or MBA. They are equally involved with the quirky sidekick, the male buddy or two, and more attached to the inevitable piece of equipment—preferably a car, but possibly a horse or a helicopter. But unlike the Lone Ranger, today's hunk-hero is portrayed as appealingly little-boyish. Michael Knight orders double cheeseburgers in fancy restaurants. Magnum wears a baseball cap and has to borrow a tie. Matt Houston has a passion for his boots.

What I presume is going on is that the strong man is to appeal to women's supposed instinctual need for a protector. The boyishness is to appeal to women's maternal instincts, the muscles to our prurient instincts. But would you like to be involved with a man when the other "woman" in his life is a talking car?

What these hunk heroes all conspicuously lack is a wife, paramour, significant other. They may, from time to time, look, but they don't lust; they don't smoulder; they don't love.

Now admittedly, the hunk creators have a peculiar problem. They are trying to create shows with action for men and attraction for women. They reason that the main male fantasy figure has to be sexually available in a way that, say, Robert Young wasn't. In order to be available they have to be unattached.

But in real life, fewer women are turned on by pectoral muscles and too-tight jeans than by some sense of connection—even, I blush to bring this up, a possibility of romance. I am on shaky ground here, but I'm convinced that most women are less interested in *the man* as something they want to have than in *the relationship* as something they want to have.

They are more attracted by watching a man as he interacts with women than as he sashays in front of them. Hunks don't interact, they pose. I don't want to run away with that. There's nothing nasty about a pinup or two. But I would give three Sellecks, a Hasselhoff and a baker's dozen of Lamases for one Paul Newman. He isn't tall, but he knows how to look at you.

It is my own conviction that one of the sexiest men on television is Capt. Frank Furillo on *Hill Street Blues*. Not just because I have seen him in bed (with another lawyer), but because he cares; he's involved. He is something the macho hunk is not: emotionally vulnerable.

Which bring us back to the original question: whose hunks are they?

Not mine. The hunk is to the female idea of love what male pornography is to the female idea of sexuality. Long on performance, short on emotion.

In the end, chest hair has a limited appeal. The half-life of an average hunk is likely to be as long as this month's, or this season's, centerfold.

Practice—Analyzing

1. In paragraph 1, what two major categories does Goodman mention?

   _____

   Does she go on to discuss the differences between these categories?

   _____

2. Where does she first identify the main idea she will address in the

   rest of her essay? _____

3. What categories of hunks does she ultimately identify? Jot down the
   details that distinguish the categories of hunks.

   _____   _____

   _____   _____

4. Does Goodman make clear that Newman and Furillo are hunks
   with more emotional attraction? Or does the emotional attraction

   rule out being hunks? _____

5. Yet another division Goodman brings up is that between the producers and viewers. Does Goodman identify at least three groups

   who react to hunks on TV? _____

6. Finally, Goodman suggests another division of women's roles on TV
   and as TV viewers. Again, does she identify at least three groups?

   Give some details for the classes. _____

   _____

7. Does the language in Goodman's article suggest her attitude toward
   male and female TV sex objects? What specific evidence can you cite

   from the article? _____

   _____

Reading Goodman's article undoubtedly taxed your ability to hold in your mind the several categories she mentions. And yet, because you knew she would be dealing with categories (because this chapter is about classification and the instructions asked you to look for groups in the article), you found the groups and connected pertinent details to each group.

One of the less formulaic elements of Goodman's article is that although she divides large categories into smaller ones, she does not label the groups clearly, nor does she consistently define each group she mentions. For instance, although she notes that women starred in "jiggle" TV, we never see details. Given that she is writing about "hunks," this focus on men is appropriate. But she does enrich the article by suggesting the parallel lines of development of other essays focusing on TV women, viewers, and producers.

Finally, Goodman doesn't make much of the labels she applies to her classes of hunks, but "grandmama's boy," "adventure anti-heroes," and "emotionally vulnerable" all convey her sense both of the TV roles and the woodenness of most hunks.

From reading to writing: labeling

How much would more humorous labels change the tone of Goodman's article?

1. Think of different sets of labels for her categories to see which ones make her descriptions funny, satiric, or serious.

Funny	Satiric	Serious
_____	_____	_____
_____	_____	_____
_____	_____	_____

2. Now add details for each group that will make the labels appropriate for each group.

_____	_____	_____
_____	_____	_____
_____	_____	_____

From reading to writing: paragraphing

Did you notice that Goodman's article seems choppy and disjointed? In part, the sense comes from the short paragraphs. Goodman most often publishes her editorials in newspapers, and so has adopted the journalistic habit of limiting each paragraph to two or three sentences. But when we reprint her article with wider margins, suddenly the ideas seem less tightly connected than they might be.

Practice

Look through Goodman's article again. Do you see paragraphs you can combine for more fully developed treatment of a single main point? You may have to add transitional sentences and topic sentences as you revise the article, but try to reduce the number of paragraphs by half.

1. Indicate in the margins which paragraphs you could easily combine.
2. Now pick two or three paragraphs for more detailed revision.You might want to work on the group you found most interesting in the exercise on labeling.

GETTING IDEAS FOR CLASSIFICATION

Let's try clustering to see if we can come up with ideas for classification. TV can provide many more topics in addition to Goodman's:

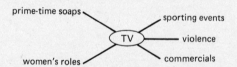

I have several large categories I might subdivide, but I'm not equally interested in working on all these groups. My next step is to decide whom I'm writing to and why. Then I can combine my interests with my readers'. I think I'll work more on violence.

Although I am occasionally amused by slapstick violence on commercials, I don't see enough material there to work with. So what point do I want to make about violence? I have nothing to add to the material written about violence on Saturday morning cartoons, but I would like to look at violence on soaps—daytime and nighttime—because I think some of the violence is so unrealistic that its presentation blurs the real violence shown as well. Hmmm. What categories of violence can I come up with?

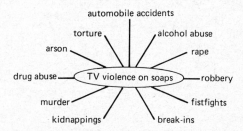

My evolving plan is to work with two major categories—violence portrayed unrealistically and realistically—but I need a third or else I will only compare and contrast. Or I can deal with three classes of each type for a more complex classification. Better yet, I will deal with categories of unrealistically portrayed crime and use the connection to real fears in my introduction and conclusion. Now I could go on and cluster details for each of the main categories I will use in my paper: violence against the self, violence against possessions, and violence against others.

In just the same way, you should set up clusters that help you narrow your focus and generate details for a classification essay.

WRITING CLASSIFICATION

1. Write a classification essay of your own in which you elaborate on classes of male and female TV sex objects, viewers, producers.
2. Write a classification essay of your own on any grouping you can support with detail.

APPLYING CLASSIFICATION

First, let's consider early drafts of student essays classifying TV sex objects.

In reading Ellen Goodman's essay about the different classifications of male hunks on TV, I am reminded of the several types of female sex symbols that grace the tube. They range from the typical dumb blonde to the mysterious and devious all the way to the rich and elegant.

The dumb blonde type of sex symbol has been around for ages. In the 50s they had Marilyn Monroe and today we have Suzanne Sommers. This type of sex symbol is popular with men because I think men like to be smarter than women. They like to be more dominant and most want to be looked to for help. The dumb blonde gives men both of these.

Another kind of sex symbol is sexy, mysterious and even a bit devious. Joan Collins who is the fiendish Alexis Carrington on "Dynasty" is just this type. Her popularity comes from man's craving for excitement and sometimes even danger. There is excitement in dealing with this kind of sex symbol because you never know what they are going to do next. They are their own people.

The last example of a kind of sex symbol is the older woman. There probably isn't a man sixteen to twenty-five who hasn't fantasized about an older woman. Characters like Sue Ellen on "Dallas" are seen more and more often. She is at the moment having a relationship (behind J.R.'s back) with a young college boy. Now this is exciting. There is probably not a man on this earth who wouldn't trade places with this young college student on "Dallas." I know I would.

So, yes, there are different classes of sex symbols, but I think each type is important in itself. They provide both pleasure and entertainment for all kinds of men with all kinds of desires. Not to mention help boost the TV stations' ratings.

—Mike A.

Mike sets forth in his thesis that sex symbols on TV range from dumb blonde to elegant women, but does he focus on these groups in his essay? He has generated groups of female characters he wants to classify, but he spends as much of each paragraph on males' reactions as he does on categorizing the sex objects. What Mike is discovering is that his thesis, though it helped him to draft this essay, now needs to be refined to reflect his real interest: he needs to indicate not only groups of female characters but also that men's reactions give rise to these groupings in the first place. Having revised his thesis, can you imagine what he might revise next? You probably noticed that each paragraph is thinly developed; each could use more detail. Even his analysis of males' reactions is now more repetitive than detailed. Though Mike has a good outline for his essay here, it needs much more work before it will be a thorough classification.

Let's see if Dan's essay has similar problems in focus and development:

The Diversification of the Female Sex Object

In the fifties when Jayne Mansfield and Marilyn Monroe starred on the silver screen, female sex objects consisted of one type—the dumb blonde. Times have changed and television has brought us a variety of sex objects.

No longer is age a factor in determining who gets the limelight. Teenager Kim Plato, star of "Different Strokes," currently has a pinup on the market and 53-year-old Joan Collins of "Dynasty" fame recently did a pictorial layout in *Playboy* magazine. These two make up the ends of a very crowded spectrum of women enhancing their careers with good looks. This group is so complex that a character does not even need to be alive to be considered a sex object. On "Jennifer Slept Here" Ann Jillian plays a very attractive ghost who is shown zipping and unzipping quite frequently.

Although sex objects have taken on new roles other than the dumb blonde image, it still exists and is considered by many to be around forever. Suzanne Somers is probably the 70s' best-known pinup to fit this category. On the other side of the intelligence spectrum women are garnering fame, too. Loni Anderson played a very well-educated secretary on "WKRP in Cincinnati" and has a new show this fall with Linda Carter in which they both play street-smart detectives.

The tough lady who can handle her own also emerged in the seventies. Carrie Fisher of *Star Wars* fame played a princess who wasn't afraid to mix it up with the bad guys.

The sex object has evolved. From its beginning as an object held in awe it has come down from its platform to partake in all styles of life. For the most part these women (or characters) are not only liked for their looks but are respected for who they are and what they do.

—Dan L.

Practice—Analyzing

1. What categories does Dan identify? _____

_____

2. Could he help readers predict more easily with clearer labels for the

groups? _____ Where might he specify the groups?

_____

3. Suggest a more precise thesis for Dan's essay. _____

_____

_____

4. Does he give enough examples and details to distinguish each category? Even if you think he has enough examples, add another example

to each paragraph. _____

_____

_____

_____

_____

5. What other revisions would you suggest Dan make?

_____

_____

_____

Practice—Revising

The following essays both have errors that a proofreader should catch, but more important are the revisions that a good editor can suggest. Revise each essay for clearer focus, more detailed development, unity, and coherent order. Use the right half of the page for your suggestions and revisions.

Psychologists have been reporting for years on the human tendency to belong to a group. It seems to be a basic human need— according to Maslow, belonging is one of man's needs which must be met before he has need of knowledge, aesthetics, etc. Media bombards us with advertisements appealing to our desire to identify with a group. It has been my observation that this need diminishes as one ages, or possibly that it is met more and more though means other than a group identity. The need for group identity seems to me to peak at the late junior high level, and continues throughout the high school period. Within a high school, it is extremely easy for an objective outsider to identify the largest and most influential parties and it is usually as easy to categorize every student into one of these groups. The first group is, and probably always will remain, the most powerful lobbyist. It is ambiguously known as 'The Popular People.' Because it is so powerful, this group incorporates the most prestigious individuals and usually some of the smaller, yet equally prestigious groups. These include: the Jocks, the Cheerleaders, the Beautiful People, the Cool People, Student Government, and occasionally a few scattered All American All Around Good Students. Membership into this large and powerful group is usually very restricted, and is usually determined by the end of junior high, or the beginning of high school. Throughout high school, however, this group retains a slew of followers who continually look longingly at its membership and who unceasingly attempt to gain admittance throughout the rest of their high school career.

The next group is 'The Hoods.' This is a significantly smaller group, but also somewhat prestigious. Like the Popular People, membership into the hoods is limited. It's members are tight, tough and wild. Repeated displays of these characteristics is necessary for admission, and the title is proudly and stubbornly borne.

Another large group is 'The Band.' This group is usually sniffed at by the Popular People and looked on with contempt by The Hoods. The Band, too, is very tight, usually because they know they have no opportunities to enroll in the other groups. The Band, however, has fun together. They work and party together, and thus become very like-minded. The group follows the Band leader's leadership faithfully. This is also typically the group that will do anything, thus the contempt from the first two groups.

Another much smaller group is 'The Brains.' They do not hold power like the

Popular People, but they, like the Band, are very tightly knit. Their emphasis does not come from partying together, but they are like-minded just the same. This group tends to be a little more individualistic than the other groups, but membership is the same.

These are just a few of the groups from which high schoolers derive their identity and it is interesting to see how these groups change or extend into adulthood. The interesting thing is that although adults are not nearly so obvious about it, their need to identify remains.

— Laurie K.

At the universities today there wander many types of people. From the cowboys to the punk rockers and wimps to beefcake. There is a classification for everyone on campus. In addition, one's appearance also can indicate the group they are associated with. The frat boys wear their bright bermuda shorts and they have a gorgeous tan. Some have more muscle than others, but nevertheless they are the 'in' crowd. Now sorority girls are dressed fairly similar and have an eye out for the parties and the boys. They always smile, socialize and run late.

The hicks are in a class by themselves. Both men and women wear boots and belt buckles from previous rodeo or riding victories. A simple T-shirt or western cut shirt and a wide belt with their name stamped into the back distinguishes them from their peers.

Straight laced and properly dressed individuals are the hardest to distinguish. If they are quiet and shy or simply modest they usually belong to one religious organization or another. Those who 'dress-for-success,' on the other hand, are usually business majors trying to impress the world.

How all these types of people and dressers end up in the same place I'll never know. I guess universities have a hidden meaning of conglomeration. Everybody welcome, no bias.

That's an important point. Although many people dress differently they all seem to tolerate each other. We all live in a certain corner of the city, yet also blend together. So, although each person has a particular dressing style, and seems to belong to a certain group, everyone is in the same melting pot, striving for the same goal. They will graduate from college with flying colors, or by the skin of their teeth.

—Heidi B.

Revision checklist

1. Have you divided your groups so that no one element could fit into more than one group?
2. Have you labeled your groups meaningfully for readers?
3. Do you have at least three groups?
4. Does your topic sentence or thesis encourage readers to read on?
5. Have you detailed each category adequately?
6. Have you kept points in similar order as you describe or explain each group?
7. Have you provided clear transitions?

chapter 12
Defining

WHAT IS DEFINITION?

To communicate with one another, we must agree on the way sentences are put together and on meanings of words. As we learn language through childhood, we constantly acquire new meanings—meanings for totally new words or new meanings for words we already know so that we can use the words more precisely. Especially as adults, we learn new words because of specializations: psychologists use a vocabulary different from that of engineers; computer scientists use words with meanings different from that of language teachers. An important job of writers, then, is to assure that readers share a common definition for words.

WHEN DO WE USE DEFINITION IN COLLEGE WRITING?

As you think about unfamiliar terms you come across in lectures or readings, you can undoubtedly recall several instances when you had to write definitions for new terms in your classes. Almost any introductory class in any field takes as one of its responsibilities the definition of terms in the field, and so students in those introductory courses repeatedly copy down or decipher definitions. Moreover, when we write papers explaining our fields of specialization to people outside that field, we usually include definitions of unfamiliar terms. Finally, in lab reports, a writer might define mechanisms, tools, techniques, procedures, or other unusual terms that might appear in the lab report.

Consider what definition Michael Demarest wants his readers to share from this article on "long weekends."

In Praise of the Long Weekend

Michael Demarest, *United Airlines Magazine* (June 1983, p. 136)

There is one European institution, the American correspondent abroad soon learns, that is sacrosanct and immutable: the weekend, *aka, le weekend, het weekend, die weekend.* Not the correspondent's weekend, but that long lacuna of leisure connecting Thursday to Tuesday during which no Important Source will be available from Lyons to Leeds. This fact of lifemanship used to inspire bitter mirth among hardworking American newsmen, who had to be available to their editors at all hours and shared their countrypeople's reverence for the old-fashioned Monday-Friday work ethic. After all, we reasoned, what head of a major American corporation would totally disappear on a grouse moor or an alp during regular working hours? What U.S. government official would dare absent himself from his desk before his secretary had cleared hers?

Or so it used to be.

In the past decade growing numbers of Americans have come to cherish the long country weekend, European style. Many big offices let their employees leave at noon on Friday in summertime; many corporate corridors have a cathedral hush on Monday mornings. More and more, executives plan business trips that will leave them close to seashore, trout streams, or ski slope as the workweek ebbs.

Another sign of the new Friday-to-Monday weekend, if you look carefully, is the sartorial camouflage that increasingly is being affected by the long-weekend-bound senior executive. He will not, you will note, come to the office on early Friday or late Monday mornings in the gray tickweave or blue pinstripe that has been his uniform of bondage since he had his first expense account. Instead, he will sport a subtly ambiguous outfit that in winter may include a restrained tweed and in summer a linen or silk ensemble; either, with a few deft substitutions—shirt, tie, shoes—will be as much at home in woodland or patio as in the executive suite. The English invented this sly form of costuming, as indeed they invented the long country weekend. Or what they call the house party.

The house party has universal appeal. For almost anyone except besotted lovers and dedicated misanthropes, the liveliest weekends are those that are shared with other people, away from the city, for better or for worse. (As the adage has it, there is no faster way to make friends or lose them than on a long weekend.)

We have, fortunately, graduated from the superorganized weekend in which every last minute was earmarked for some specific activity, like an astronaut's agenda. The best weekends, we have come to realize, are not those that are single-mindedly attached to beach or boat or court or course. Rather, they are open-ended, ad hoc, laid-back, pickup affairs in which there will be a whole range of optional, self-starting outdoor pursuits, from knockabout tennis, bird-watching, berry-picking, stalking the wild asparagus, bicycle riding, log splitting, and sun worship, to such indoor pastimes as shelling peas, shucking corn, Monopoly, backgammon, communal crossword-puzzle-solving, storytelling, The Game, slander, ping-pong, or singing barroom ballads off-key. (Two of the great weekend liberators have been the dishwashing machine and the food processor, which have freed guests of drudgery or guilt.)

As the gifted Lee Bailey makes clear in his new book, *Country Weekends,* weekend guests not only have to be lubricated and nourished, they also have to be kept out of mischief (public, anarchic mischief, that is; any other kind goes). And there is really no excuse for boredom on a weekend. Or at least no host or hostess can be excused for having bored guests on hand. It does, of course, take a certain flair to pick a combination of people who will sparkle rather than sputter, a mixture, perhaps of interests, accents, ages, and backgrounds, with no two couples too well known to each other in advance, and a maximum of ten guests.

This kind of selection can take genius, but with good luck and that "illusion of effortlessness" propounded by Bailey, the long weekend can go faster than you can say salut! The secret, he suggests, is to keep everyone so well fed and salivating for the next round of rations that there is no time for malice or mutiny. On a great gustatory weekend there is no time, thank goodness, even for jogging. Frivolities like physical exercise can be well taken care of during the long Monday-through-Friday week.

Practice—Analyzing

1. How does Demarest define the long weekend? _____

_____

2. How does his definition differ from your usual understanding of the

term? _____

_____

3. Does Demarest define any other major terms in this article? _____

_____

4. Demarest also uses several uncommon or unfamiliar words. Could
you discover their meanings as you read through the article? If not,
look again at paragraph 4 for clues to the meanings of unfamiliar

words. Use the dictionary for any other elusive meanings. _____

_____

_____

_____

5. Do you sense in your community a move toward the long weekend

this article discusses? What evidence can you give? _____

_____

_____

6. What does this definition suggest about the American culture compared with European societies where the long weekend is well

established? _____

_____

_____

7. Describe your typical long weekend, as you use the term. _____

HOW DO WE READ DEFINITION?

As you can see from Demarest's article, not only technical language needs to be defined clearly. No matter how common the topic—and "weekends" clearly qualify as common subject matter—writers must define any terms that readers might misinterpret. If not, writers and readers do not communicate in the same way that people arguing about politics or religion might finally say, "We really agree, but we've been using different words for the same concepts." Had Demarest not defined the special sense of long weekend that the article focuses on, American readers might easily have interpreted his article in the context of our ordinary "long weekend," that extra Monday off because of a national holiday.

A concept from reading research helps explain why definitions are so important to readers. In other chapters, we've considered the essential role of predicting the course of an essay. But when we read definitions, we must use the information in the definition as the starting point for our predictions. In short, writers tell readers specifically what a concept means in that piece of writing. Predicting is less important, then, because writers take the some of the guesswork out of reading.

Networks of meaning

What becomes more important is the definition itself. We know that as we learn new ideas—embodied as words or more abstract concepts— we connect the new ideas to existing ideas we already understand. We create networks of meaning. Think of your understanding of "restaurant," for example. Until you go to an expensive restaurant with maitre'd, wine steward, waiter, server, and so on, you may have "expensive restaurant" in your network for "restaurant," but you are more likely to think of the most common "restaurants" you patronize. Similarly, before I moved to a quiet town with so many young families, I didn't divide restaurants into those where young couples bring infants and those where only adults eat. Now I divide restaurants into those new divisions in my network of images for restaurants, even though my fundamental definition of "restaurant" hasn't changed.

When we read definitions, then, we take the information conveyed by the writer and relate that information to other more familiar concepts. In addition, every connection a writer helps readers make between the new definition and other related concepts enriches readers' networks of ideas and experiences. Demarest makes several connections that help readers see the distinction between the long weekend he means and the one we usually think of. He discusses social gatherings, clothing, food, activities, reactions in the office, and so on, all to help his readers make connections to ideas they already have. The more detailed a network of images, the more successful readers will feel in understanding a new term.

Of course, reading definitions of completely new terms is more demanding than reading about variations on an idea we already know. Depending on the fullness of the networks to which they can relate a new idea, readers may have more or less difficulty "reading" the definition. That's where writers must help readers by evaluating what readers are likely to know and what they probably need more detail for.

Practice—Reading

Consider this short definition from a *Scientific American* article. Pay special attention to the way Paul Buisseret helps you tie into your networks of meaning:

Allergy

Paul D. Buisseret, *Scientific American* (August 1982, p. 86)

It is best to begin a discussion of allergy by defining the word and establishing the scope of its meaning. "Allergy" is from the Greek *allos* (other) and *ergon* (work). The derivation implies an unusual or inappropriate reaction to a stimulus. Not every adverse response to a normally harmless external stimulus is an allergy, however, and the distinction is not always clear. One person may develop an itchy rash after an injection of penicillin, another whenever he wears a certain wristwatch. Hay-fever victims sneeze in certain seasons. Some women are nauseated by oral contraceptives. A person may have abdominal cramps and diarrhea after eating a certain food. Are all these people "allergic"? Some are indeed, but some may not be. For example, many people have an unusual or exaggerated response to a drug, but they are not necessarily allergic to the drug.

Allergy is a disorder of the immune system; it is immunity gone wrong. In the immunological world of a vertebrate organism the great divide is between the self and the nonself. The organism distinguishes nonself tissues, cells, proteins and some other large molecules from those of the self; it identifies them as being either harmless or potentially harmful and thereupon either ignores them or defends the organism against them. The cells with the capacity for recognizing, evaluating and neutralizing or eliminating nonself material constitute the immune system.

Practice—Analyzing

1. Whom is Buisseret writing to? Outline the potential audience as carefully as possible. _____

_____

_____

_____

2. How do the examples in paragraph 1 help you understand allergy?

_____

_____

3. Does Buisseret choose examples and details that help you relate "allergy" to your own experience? _____

_____

_____

4. How does the definition in paragraph 2 make more precise what

Buisseret sets up with his examples in paragraph 1? _____

_____

_____

5. How do you expect the article to continue? Can you see how definition fits into other patterns of writing to give readers a full sense of

the topic? _____

_____

_____

_____

HOW DO WE WRITE DEFINITION?

Let's consider the "long weekend" definition again. The essay opens with a short definition and synonyms:

> There is one European institution, the American correspondent abroad soon learns, that is sacrosanct and immutable: the weekend, *aka, le weekend, het weekend, die weekend.* Not the correspondent's weekend, but that long lacuna of leisure connecting Thursday to Tuesday during which no Important Source will be available from Lyons to Leeds.

Had Demarest begun with his examples rather than a definition, most readers would probably not see the point of the article. But by beginning with a definition, Demarest asks readers to compare their notions of what a weekend is with his emerging definition of the "long weekend."

Perhaps more important to him as a writer, Demarest had to determine what his readers probably know and don't know. Who is likely to read *United Airlines Magazine?* Demarest knows that many travelers are business executives, but many fliers are vacationers as well. He needs to be entertaining without making the article too difficult (because those magazines are made available to take travelers' minds off the flight and to advertise for the airlines). Demarest must conjure up an image of relaxation that will appeal to most of the readers he expects to glance through the magazine.

Practice—Determining audience for definition

Has Demarest successfully identified his audience? Has he overestimated the educational background and social interests of readers? What might you change in the opening paragraph?

There is one European institution, the
American correspondent abroad soon learns,
that is sacrosanct and immutable: the
weekend, *aka, le weekend, het weekend, die
weekend.* Not the correspondent's weekend,
but that long lacuna of leisure connecting
Thursday to Tuesday during which no
Important Source will be available from
Lyons to Leeds. This fact of lifemanship
used to inspire bitter mirth among
hardworking American newsmen, who had
to be available to their editors at all hours
and shared their countrypeople's reverence
for the old-fashioned Monday-Friday work
ethic. After all, we reasoned, what head of a
major American corporation would totally
disappear on a grouse moor or an alp during
regular working hours? What U.S.
government official would dare absent
himself from his desk before his secretary
had cleared hers?

If you were to define a term for such a general audience, how would you characterize the audience and what terms might you define?

_____

_____

_____

Writing definitions with detail

Demarest does succeed, I think, in giving readers a context for the definition and in filling in detail to enrich readers' notions of "weekend."

Both these elements are critical in writing definitions. Moreover, among the common techniques he uses, Demarest illustrates, compares, negates (saying what something is not), and replaces the key term with synonyms. Each of these techniques helps readers build up a web of meanings connecting a new term with ideas they already know.

What other techniques might he have used? Other common approaches to definition include giving a history of the term. Many common words today began with specialized definitions; still other terms have come to mean almost the exact opposite of their original definitions in the language. A related technique is to examine the origin of a word. If we borrow a word from another language or if it relies on root words taken from another language (as does "allergy"), we can use that information to help readers see how the word is like and unlike related words of similar origin. We can also take more practical approaches in defining: we might explain the function associated with a new word or we might explain the process it refers to. Finally, we might illustrate how the word relates to other words, specifically how it is part of a larger concept. The table on p. 284 summarizes the most common techniques for defining.

Practice—Identifying methods of defining

1. What methods does Jennifer use in defining "super deluxe"?

> The term "super-deluxe" may have come from the old hamburger stand our parents used to go to when they were youngsters. The plain hamburger became something special after adding "the works" (mayo, pickle, lettuce, tomato, onion, and cheese), and an order of french fries. That is what made the hamburger super-deluxe, all the extra added features. Members of the CSU athletic department have derived a new meaning for the term "super-deluxe"—a tape job with special added features for support. In athletic training there are many different ankle tape jobs, such as semi-deluxe, deluxe, and the support wrap. The super-deluxe tape job is used on athletes who have recently damaged the ligaments in their ankles. The athletes usually have massive amounts of swelling, pain, and have very little ankle support. An athlete will hobble into the training room and ask for a super-deluxe, and the trainer will know exactly what needs to be done. The super-deluxe uses almost a whole roll of Elasticon tape to anchor the foot in the normal flex position. Then a roll of adhesive tape, like that used for a regular tape job, is applied on top of the Elasticon. This super-deluxe tape job enables the athlete to resume activity at full capacity. From now on, think of an athlete getting a super-deluxe like the hamburger, a tape job with the works.
>
> —*Jennifer H.*

Common ways of defining, illustrated by defining *writing*

Methods	Examples
Illustrating	Writing is a form of communication as when we share our experiences with friends in letters.
Comparing	Writing is like speaking in that both require active participation; it is unlike speaking in that feedback from the reader is not immediate as is feedback from a listener.
Negating	Writing is not a simple linear process that we follow from beginning to end.
Synonyms	Writing is *composing* meaning, just as in music, painting, and other forms of design.
History	Writing began with advanced ancient civilizations that needed record keeping for taxes and other official functions.
Origin	Writing comes to use through Old English from a Germanic word meaning to tear or scratch, appropriate for the stylus that scratched letters on paper or parchment and even for many contemporary writers' handwriting.
Function	Writing has several functions, of course, but it serves mainly to capture and communicate ideas over time and space.
Process	Writing does not follow a single process, although most writers recognize their own common, repeated patterns of prewriting, drafting, and revising.
Part-to-whole	Writing is part of a larger set of cognitive problem-solving processes whereby we learn and communicate our insights to others.

Technique 1 _____

Technique 2 _____

Technique 3 _____

Technique 4 _____

2. Now read carefully K. C. Cole's essay on "understanding." Look again for techniques of definition.

The Essence of Understanding

K. C. Cole

No layman, it is probably safe to assume, really understands Einstein's theory of general relativity—the idea that gravity is an unseen curvature of space caused by the presence of matter. Yet it is somewhat unnerving, to say the least, when somebody like MIT's Victor Weisskopf, a National Medal of Science winner, claims not to understand it either. "It's like the peasant who asks the engineer how the steam engine works," Weissskopf says. "The engineer explains exactly how the steam moves through the engine, how all the parts move, and so on. And when he's finished, the peasant says, 'Yes, I understand all that. But where is the horse?' That's how I feel about general relativity. I know how it works in great detail, but I don't understand where the horse is."

Knowledge is not the same as understanding, of course. Doctors know how to treat what ails the human body, but rarely do they understand in detail how or why their treatments work. Many people (scientists included) know a great deal about quarks and quasars, dinosaurs and jumping genes, without claiming to understand them in the least. Everyone knows that objects fall toward the earth. But understanding *why* they fall is quite another matter.

Even Isaac Newton admitted that he never understood gravity—something that later earned him Einstein's greatest respect. Newton wrote: "It is inconceivable that inanimate brute matter should, without the mediation of something else which is not material, operate upon and affect other matter without mutual contact. That gravity should be innate, inherent, and essential to matter, so that one body may act upon another at a distance is to me so great an absurdity that I believe no man who has in philosophical matters a competent faculty of thinking can ever fall into it."

Newton was the first to see that the fall of the apple and the orbit of the moon were propelled by the same force: gravity. He even invented calculus the better to predict the pull of that force at various distances from the earth's center. Newton knew precisely how gravity behaved; he just did not understand how it worked. But if Newton did not understand gravity, who did? What does understanding mean, anyway? It turns out that there is no single answer to that question. The philosopher Kant said there were twelve "forms of understanding"; in science, there may be even more.

In the first place, understanding means literally coming to terms. Confucius said, "The beginning of wisdom is calling things by their right names." To a biologist or a paleoanthropologist, giving something a name means putting it in its proper place among species—defining, quite specifically, what it is. Rose is a rose is a rose, but Homo erectus and Homo habilis are very different indeed.

Yet names alone are hardly enough. As Paul Hewitt, author of the popular college text *Conceptual Physics,* tells his students, "We understand many things, and we have names and labels for these things. And there are many things that we do not understand, and we have names and labels for these things also." It is easy to answer the question "Why do things fall toward the earth?" by giving the phenomenon a name, like gravity. Or even curved space. Whether or not this suffices for understanding depends entirely on how well you understand what the name represents.

Nobel laureate Richard Feynman, for example, recalls a boyhood encounter with a friend who teased him because he did not know the name of a particular bird. Feynman went to his father, who had taught him many things about nature. His father answered, "Do you know what that bird is? It's a brown-throated thrush—but in Portuguese it's a ————, in Italian it's a————, in Chinese it's a————, et cetera. Now you know all the languages, and when you've finished with all that you'll know absolutely nothing whatever about the bird. You only know about humans in different places and what they call the bird."

One of the prime tasks of understanding is to sort out the true nature of things from the names and labels that human beings attach to them. Astronomer Sir James Jeans told the story of the man who complained that a lecturer had explained beautifully how the astronomers had discovered the sizes and temperatures of the stars, but had forgotten to explain how they found out their names. It may seem obvious that people project their own ideas onto nature when they name stars and birds. But it is not so obvious that the entire evolution of scientific understanding has reflected similar projections. Aristotle imprinted his image of perfect symmetry onto the motions of all heavenly bodies, proclaiming that they could orbit only in circles. This "knowledge" was uncritically accepted for more than two thousand years, even by Copernicus. In the same way, people knew in the third century B.C. that the earth orbited the sun and not vice versa. Yet the familiar image of the rising and setting sun blurred their understanding for more than 17 centuries—until Copernicus discovered (really, rediscovered) the heliocentric universe. Even today, most people can "see" the sun moving across the sky far more easily than they can accommodate the notion of hanging upside down by their heels as they pass through the shadow of night.

Understanding obviously embodies an element of getting used to things. This remains one of the major obstacles facing those who wish to understand time dilation, curved space, and other consequences of relativity. Even when you know about them, they are very hard to get used to. Understanding takes an intuitive feel for things—like that required for riding a bike. The trouble is that this understanding becomes so internally entrenched that it is almost impossible to *un*learn. And in the end it may be the difficulty of unlearning the old ways of thinking about time and gravity that stumps people trying to master relativity. James Trefil, a physics professor at the University of Virginia, came to the conclusion that people often have trouble understanding quantum physics for the same reason—because they have become so accustomed to the old Newtonian view. At first, he said, he was surprised to find that his Physics 101 students were not bothered by the paradoxes that pervade quantum theory. Then he recognized why: "They had no reason to expect that a photon or an electron would have to be either like a baseball or like a ripple on a pond, so they weren't surprised when it wasn't."

Understanding goes far beyond knowing in that it requires a certain degree of acceptance. To say you "understand" something implies a sympathetic point of view. In a very real sense, the evolution of species is no better understood by the creationist than elliptical orbits were by Copernicus. Indeed, what people understand to be self-evident and what they dismiss as absurd are often matters of faith. The English astronomer Sir Arthur Eddington said in the early part of this century that it was absurd to think that the speed of light could be infinite—as absurd as it was to think of it as hexagonal or blue or totalitarian. Yet until the seventeenth century, almost everyone regarded the infinite nature of the speed of light as self-evident.

People often try to understand things in terms of familiar analogies—ideas that are easily acceptable. "Knowledge is gained by establishing relations between an inner process of understanding in our private minds and the facts of that public outer world which is common to us all," said Jeans. Yet analogies are by definition only partial truths, and an analogy that works for one person may not make sense to another. To "come to an understanding" means, colloquially, to agree. Perhaps that is why mathematics is the favored form of understanding among scientists: equations are more nearly universal than analogies crafted from everyday things. Naked numbers are less prone to cultural and perceptual prejudices. But quantitative understanding (like raw historical facts) is rarely satisfying. Knowing that gravity decreases by the inverse square of the distance is important; yet it tells you no more about the essence of forces than knowing how many bricks it takes to build a cathedral tells you about the essence of Notre Dame.

Most laymen, at least, think of understanding in terms of ultimate answers to cosmic questions: not only What makes the apple fall? but also Why is there gravity? Why should space be curved? and if the source of the curvature is mass, Why is there mass? Such questions teeter on the brink between physics and metaphysics. Once Weisskopf was talking to some students about the origins of the universe, when a girl asked, "But WHY did the Big Bang happen?" His answer was one that he often gives to such questions. "Physics isn't always giving reasons. It's showing that everything comes from a few fundamental laws. If you keep asking why, you come to God, and that's not our business." Or as Lincoln Barnett concludes in his classic *The Universe and Dr. Einstein,* "Most modern physicists consider it naive to speculate about the true nature of anything."

Surprisingly enough, the true cosmic understandings usually come from asking more limited questions. As long as people asked grand fundamental questions about the nature of the universe (What is life? What is matter?) they did not get very far. As soon as they began to ask more focused questions (How does blood flow? How do the planets move?) they were rewarded with more general answers. Senator William Proxmire often bestows his Golden Fleece awards on what he considers to be wasteful scientific research aimed at unimportant answers to silly questions. But it is not always that easy to tell which small pieces of knowledge will eventually accumulate into the mosaic of interlocking fact that is the essence of understanding.

Newton's understanding of gravity was no less valuable because it was incomplete. As he answered the critics who accused him of introducing occult qualities into what was then called natural philosophy, "To understand the motions of the planets under the influence of gravity without knowing the cause of gravity is as good a progress in philosophy as to understand the frame of a clock, and the dependence of the wheels upon one another, without knowing the cause of gravity of the weight which moves the machine."

The main thing that sets scientific understanding apart is its very tentativeness. By definition, it is always incomplete, much like our understanding of understanding itself. In 1922, so the story goes, Werner Heisenberg asked fellow physicist Niels Bohr how anyone could hope to understand the atom, given the lack of an appropriate language or imagery. Bohr replied that understanding the atom would first require a fresh look at what understanding really means.

Technique 1 _____

Technique 2 _____

Technique 3 _____

Technique 4 _____

Structure and precision in definitions

Notice that most of the definitions in the table on page 284 follow a similar sentence pattern:

Writing is . . .
or
Writing means . . .

Definitions, especially dictionary definitions, often fall into this pattern. First, we state the term being defined; then we equate that term with what follows the verb. Most often we use "is" or "means" to set up the equation between the two parts of the sentence. The second part of the sentence then tells us the class of objects or ideas that the term falls into and distinguishes the term from other elements in the class. For example, were we to define orphans, we could simply say:

Orphans are children.

But we need to be more precise because any person, not just children, whose parents have died is technically an orphan. Moreover, not all children are orphans, and the preceding statement could syntactically appear as "Children are orphans." So we set up the definition to state the category, "children"or "persons" and then we distinguish "orphans" from other members of that category:

Orphans are persons whose parents have died.

Now our definition is accurate, but it doesn't reflect our cultural limitation that orphans are usually children under legal age to sign and execute binding contracts. To be more precise,

Orphans are minors whose parents have died.

Now we have been as precise as necessary to explain to someone unfamiliar with the word "orphans" what the term means to English speakers. Only *precise* word choice conveys an exact meaning to readers. And don't hesitate to use the formula outlined here since readers will immediately recognize that you are defining for them.

One other point I've mentioned in passing is that readers learning new definitions benefit from more rather than less detail. Just as in other kinds of writing, readers need detail to create the meaning writers intend. With definition, since predicting is less important, readers need detail to make the appropriate connections to other concepts and experiences. Only a good writer can help readers make these connections by supplying detail. Certainly, someone learning to read English might want to know what "orphan" means, but your writing involves more than dictionary definitions. Usually when you write, your definitions will help a reader make sense of a larger concept than simply the word defined, just as Demarest tries to make his readers aware of different cultural values and life-styles embodied in the notion of the "long weekend." Perhaps our society is wrong to think of only minors as orphans, and you might write about how adults losing their parents feel as betrayed and alone as the youngster suddenly orphaned. If you wanted to explore the social consequences of our definition, you would have to provide details of adults' emotions when their parents die. As a writer, you must determine the needs of your readers and then define in adequate detail to make readers see just what you mean.

Let's consider a sample to see just how detail clarifies the writer's definitions:

> Induction is the process of drawing general conclusions from particular instances; it is, I think, the basic process whereby learning takes place. We have not proved a conclusion, however, since there is always the possibility that a counterexample will be found. For this reason inductive reasoning, as all the scholastic philosophers of Galileo's time knew, cannot lead to indubitable truth.
>
> Deduction is another matter. Given true premises, a conclusion reached by valid deduction must be rigorously true. (from Owen Gingerich, "The Galileo Affair," *Scientific American,* August 1982, p. 137.)

Each of these paragraphs defines a term, but I have deleted details written to make the definitions more comprehensible. Without the detail, most readers who don't already know the difference between induction and deduction will not see the difference now. But consider the details Gingerich includes in his article on Galileo:

> Induction is the process of drawing general conclusions from particular instances; it is, I think, the basic process whereby learning takes place. Consider the reproduction of birds: chickens lay eggs, robins lay eggs, ostriches

lay eggs, and so on, and thus we generalize that all birds reproduce by laying eggs. We have not proved this conclusion, however, since there is always the possibility that a counterexample will be found. For this reason inductive reasoning, as all the scholastic philosophers of Galileo's time knew, cannot lead to indubitable truth.

Deduction is another matter. Given true premises, a conclusion reached by valid deduction must be rigorously true. Consider this syllogism:

A. If it is raining, the streets are wet.
B. It is raining.
C. Therefore the streets are wet.

Now consider the converse:

A. If it is raining, the streets are wet.
B. The streets are wet.
C. Therefore it is raining.

To students of logic this procedure of confirming the consequent was a well-known fallacy. After all, the streets could be wet for other reasons: the winter snow could be melting, the street-cleaning department might be out in force, or the Lippizaner horses might have been on parade.
(Owen Gingerich, "The Galileo Affair," *Scientific American,* August 1982, p. 137.)

In paragraph 1, Gingerich cites an illustration that allows readers to go through an inductive process themselves. In defining deduction, Gingerich also shows us the process by outlining two illustrative syllogisms. Moreover, the section as a whole uses comparison to highlight the distinctions between deduction and induction. But without the detail, most readers would have to take Gingerich's word for the less rigorous generalizations possible with induction. And not all readers are obliging enough to take a writer's word for definitions and concepts. Most readers need to understand distinctions to be able to continue comprehending and enjoying their reading.

GETTING IDEAS FOR DEFINITION

We all use words in specific contexts that people unfamiliar with those contexts will not understand. For instance, as a university student, you use terms related to registration procedures, courses, policies, and so on, that parents or friends not in school don't know. As you become a specialist in your chosen field, you also learn words that nonspecialists don't know. Finally, just because you are a certain age living in a certain part of the country, you probably have some slang expressions older and younger people or people your age from another part of the country don't know.

First, brainstorm for words that you use in some way unlike the common definition or for words nonspecialists wouldn't know. (You might also include words associated with hobbies.)

_____   _____

_____   _____

_____   _____

_____   _____

Now choose a word you might want to define and let's work through the following heuristic to get more ideas for writing a definition. These questions are based on classical topoi, or commonplaces, from Aristotle's *Rhetoric*.

Notice, though, that before you can complete these questions you must consider your potential readers. Just whom are you writing to? Why will they want to know this definition? Don't simply write for yourself or for your teacher, but describe some nonacademic audience you feel comfortable writing for.

1. Can you give synonyms for the term? Do the synonyms subtly change the meaning of your term? How?
2. What is the formal definition of your term? What elements of a dictionary definition are helpful to you in defining your term for your audience?
3. Can you think of an analogy that describes or exemplifies your term?
4. What does the term mean to *you?* How does your definition differ from the dictionary definition?
5. Can you divide the term into categories? If so, how do the categories reflect on the meaning of the term?
6. Does the term change over time? If so, how do the changes reflect on the meaning of the term?
7. Can you give examples of the term? Do so with as much detail as necessary for your audience.

Practice—Writing

As you draft your definition, keep in mind that writers must accommodate readers' needs. If the audience is looking for information, the writer must provide it. If the audience is looking for entertainment, then the writer must provide that. While writers can combine entertainment with information-sharing, they must never lose sight of why readers pick up reading material. Readers have goals, too. Put yourself into the position of reader for a moment. If you picked up *Psychology Today* and started reading this article, would you continue?

> The Affectionate Machine
>
> The ideal companion machine would not only look, feel and sound friendly but would also be programmed to behave in a congenial manner. Those qualities which make interaction with other people enjoyable would be simulated as closely as possible, and the machine would appear to be charming, stimulating and easygoing. Its informal conversational style would make interaction comfortable, and yet the machine would remain slightly unpredictable and therefore interesting. In its first encounter it might be somewhat hesitant and unassuming, but as it came to know the user it would progress to a more relaxed and intimate style. The machine would not be a passive participant but would add its own suggestions, information and opinion; it would sometimes take the initiative in developing or changing the topic and would have a personality of its own.
>
> —Neil Frude, *The Intimate Machine*

Chances are that if you have any interest in computers or futuristic projections, you would keep reading as Frude defines the characteristics of friendly, humanlike machines. Has he targeted his audience well then? Yes he has because he has whetted their appetite to read more. Like good definitions, this one sets out its goals early—to define the "ideal companion machine"—and it follows with the details that create clear images for readers, especially those details that suggest memories of contacts with reserved but intelligent human beings. As you compose your definition, keep asking yourself, "If I were reading this paper, would I want to keep reading?"

Practice—Details for the audience

Read Howard's paragraph and suggest revisions.

> Millions of Americans suffer from the recurring, incurable affliction known as "cottonmouth." "Cottonmouth" is a condition of the mouth and throat characterized by a total lack of moisture in those areas. It is a temporary condition (usually lasting two to four hours) brought about by various causes including strenuous exercise and smoking marijuana. It's as if the saliva glands dry up and fail to produce any more liquid. A sticky, pasty film is left in the mouth which has a tendency to collect in the corners of the lips. The aspect of "cottonmouth" that distinguishes it from other forms of mild dehydration is that the thirst cannot be quenched. The dry feeling persists no matter how much a person drinks. The word "cottonmouth"

contributes much to the understanding of its meaning. Chewing on balls of dry cotton is probably very similar to having "cottonmouth." "Let's stop and get something to drink 'cause I've got cottonmouth to the max," is an oft-heard remark around parties and tennis courts.

—*Howard W.*

1. Whom is Howard writing to? _____

_____

2. What details could he add to appeal to his readers? _____

_____

_____

_____

_____

APPLYING DEFINITION

Consider two other sample paragraphs of definition. Be sure to note what these writers have included as appropriate details to appeal to their readers.

During my high school days in Southern California, slang terms and expressions were constantly entering the teenage vocabulary. My favorite was "rad," an abbreviation of "radical." Both terms were used in nearly every conversation when the skateboarding and surfing craze hit California in the early 70s. Any skater or surfer who would do moves that risked injury, such as riding vertical on the tiles of a swimming pool, or getting air off a wave, was "rad." One could "get rad" if he rode all out and pushed his limits, even if it meant sacrificing flesh and bones. The terrain that one rode on could be "rad" if it was insanely steep or had over-vertical walls—like a huge wave or a deep swimming pool or pipe. When "rad" was first coined, it was almost exclusively used among groups of friends in the skateboarding and surfing circles. As it spread somewhat to other people, its meaning broadened. Rock music became "rad" if it was especially loud or heavy. Even a car with a screaming engine or an eye-catching paint job was "rad." In general, we used "rad" to mean anyone who had a fast-paced, positive attitude toward life, who constantly pushed his limits trying to go as far as possible in anything he did.

—*Curt C.*

If you are knowledgeable about cooking, the word "dredge" will mean both to cover or coat meat in seasoned flour or a crumb mixture, as well as to dig a deep hole. Most likely you have dredged in the cooking sense, both pot roast and chicken, for example, and never realized it. Perhaps you will recognize one of the two methods of dredging after I explain them. First it is important to moisten the meat to be dredged with water, milk, or raw egg. This is so the flour or crumbs will cling to the meat. The first method is to place flour, salt, and pepper or a crumb mixture in a large bowl, and dunk the meat in until it is completely coated. The second method is to take a plastic or paper bag and put both the seasoned flour and the meat inside. Shake the bag vigorously until the meat is thoroughly covered. Now you are ready to cook. The result of dredging will be seen when the meat comes out of the oven, and when you cut into it. A light golden crust will surround the outside of the chicken or roast; as you cut into it, the juices will ooze out. Dredging locks in those precious juices instead of letting them bake away.

—Susan C.

WRITING DEFINITION

1. Choose some slang term that you use in your everyday conversations with friends. Define that term for adults unfamiliar with the term. Be sure to use sufficient examples and details to make the definition clear for the audience.
2. Choose a technical term that someone unfamiliar with your academic specialization or hobby might not know. Define that term so that a general reader of *Science* or *Discover* magazines would understand its technical significance.
3. Consider "In Praise of the Long Weekend." Do you use some unusual definition of a common term? Write a paragraph developing a term's new meaning or defining a common term as you use it.

Revision checklist

1. Have you identified the audience and purpose of your definition?
2. Have you chosen a personal perspective if you are defining a general word?
3. Have you chosen the best method or combination of methods to develop your definition?
4. Have you checked your paragraph for adequate detail?
5. Have you checked for adequate transitions?

chapter 13
Analyzing causes

WHAT IS CAUSAL ANALYSIS?

Because human thinkers want to make connections between events and the causes that led to them or the consequences that resulted from them, we often analyze causes and effects. Whenever we ask "what led the chemical tank to explode?" or "what happened after the virus was released into the atmosphere?" we are engaging in causal analysis. More broadly, whenever we ask "why?" we are engaging in causal analysis.

Most of our understanding of causal analysis is based primarily on physical causation. That is, we know from physics that if I throw a ping-pong ball against my kitchen wall, it will bounce back, not because I want it to but because of laws of energy and motion. We needn't limit ourselves to physical causes and effects, though. We can also inquire about the reasons for my throwing that pingpong ball. Have I started a new game? Am I playing with my cats? Have I been working so hard that I don't know the difference between a kitchen wall and a pingpong table? All these questions investigate *why* I perform an action; all these questions analyze causes or reasons for my behavior. We can ask parallel questions about effects: Does the new game improve my reflexes? Have I taught my cats to jump higher than the average cat? Have I challenged visitors to wall pingpong games in my kitchen? Each of these questions suggests effects that an interested observer might want to analyze.

WHEN DO WE USE CAUSAL ANALYSIS IN COLLEGE WRITING?

Think again of lab reports. In a typical report of a biology, chemistry, or other experiment, we explain the results we obtained in the lab. This is a causal analysis. But we can also go outside the lab. In a history course, we might analyze causes or effects of World War I. In a geology course, we might analyze causes or effects of land mass movements. In art, we might ask causes or effects of a particular technique or art form. In economics, we might ask causes or effects of a stock market shift. In computer science, we might ask causes or effects of a new chip design. Because causes and effects are so important to human beings—who like to understand the logic behind events and actions—causal analysis is a common form of writing we practice frequently in college writing.

But because we expect the causes and effects to be reasonable, when writers become unreasonable, readers are often amused. As you read the following humorous explanation of Reagan's causal analysis of education, ask yourself not only why education needs help but also why we find this editorial funny.

Schools Failing Pupils; Reagan Failing Schools

Art Buchwald, *Dayton Daily News*

"The Rising Tide of Mediocrity threatens our very future as a nation." Thus sayeth the recent report by the National Commission on Excellence in Education.

Here are a few statistics they uncovered. There are 23 million functionally illiterate adults in the country, and 13 percent of all 17-year-olds cannot read, write or comprehend. The average teacher in America makes $17,000 a year and must moonlight to stay out of the poorhouse. There are severe shortages of instructors in math, science and foreign languages. Half of those now teaching these subjects are not qualified.

President Reagan, in his radio address, blames the U.S. government's role in the past 20 years for the country's educational problems. If parents would just get involved in their children's learning process and we turned our education back to the local communities, all would be well again, the president said. He was adamant that the government not increase its activities in education for any reason.

If anyone needs remedial education now, it's the president of the United States.

"All right, Mr. President. Here is a graph. The red line shows where the Soviets are in education, and the blue line shows where we are. Note the blue line is going down every year and the red line is going up. What does that mean for the nation?"

"American parents aren't doing their job."

"It could mean that. It also could mean the country is not spending enough on education to meet the Soviet threat. Now, Mr. President, here is another chart. It indicates that if we keep turning out people not equipped in the sciences, commerce or technology, we will soon be overtaken by our competitors throughout the world. As the nation's leader, what should you do about it?"

"Work for a constitutional amendment to bring back prayer in the schools."

"I'm not certain that's the correct answer. Would you consider raising teachers' salaries and getting more qualified instructors to make sure our students are equipped to deal with the tasks that lie ahead?"

"*Are you crazy?* I need every dollar I can get for defense. Bigger budgets for education are not the answer."

"But where are you going to get the people to build your weapons and learn how to use them if they are illiterate?"

"I don't know the answer to that one. Go on to the next question."

"Do you know what it costs the country in unemployment, welfare and crime because Americans can't read and write?"

"I didn't know I was supposed to study that."

"Don't you think it's your duty as president to be concerned about the quality of education in the United States? Isn't it a question of national security and survival?"

"I've advocated tax breaks for parents who want to send their kids to private schools."

"That isn't the right answer, Mr. President. You have to consider the illiteracy bomb in this country with the same seriousness you consider the threat from Central America."

"You don't expect me to appear before a joint session of Congress just because Americans can't read and write?"

"It could eventually become a bigger threat than El Salvador."

"If I did that, Congress would take away my tax cut for this year. Are you seriously asking me to choose between the education of our children and a 10 percent tax cut?"

"Mr. President, your homework assignment was to read the report of the National Commission on Excellence in Education last night. Apparently you watched television instead."

"It's not my fault. I didn't know I was going to have a test today."

Practice—Analyzing

1. What is the main cause-effect connection Buchwald wants his read-

   ers—and Reagan—to consider? _____

   _____

2. Buchwald claims that Reagan has identified several causes for the

   decline in education. What are they? _____

   _____

   _____

   _____

3. Do you agree with Reagan that lack of parental involvement can cause a decline in literacy for youngsters? How does Buchwald respond to the notion that parental involvement will improve

   education? _____

   _____

   _____

   _____

4. What techniques does Buchwald use to show his attitude toward Reagan's ideas on defense, tax cuts, and education? _____

_____

_____

_____

5. Is Buchwald making a serious point through his satire of Reagan's radio speech? Why do you think so? _____

_____

_____

6. Do you find Buchwald's approach funny? Why? _____

_____

_____

HOW DO WE READ CAUSAL ANALYSIS?

Because we have asked "why" long enough to understand causes and effects well, readers quickly note the clues to causal analysis; "because" is one of the most common connecting words in our language, followed by others that suggest cause and effect:

due to	therefore
as a result of	thus
resulting from	consequently

Moreover, when we read analysis, we can identify the attempt to explain *relationships*. Causal analysis can never occur without the writer, and thus the reader, establishing relationships between conditions (the causes or effects) and an event. If a writer focuses on only the event, we generally see a narrative or perhaps a process analysis. And we can see descriptions of conditions or scenes; or we might read definitions of one item or idea. But causal analysis requires a relationship—between parents' help and students' progress in school, between good teachers and better-prepared students, and so on.

As we read causal analysis, then, we establish the main focus of the analysis. If it is a cause or several causes, then we know that the explanation will eventually make a relationship to the event caused or perhaps to specific effects. Similarly, if we focus on effects, we must understand the relationship to the causes.

Perhaps more importantly, as we read causal analysis we constantly weigh the proposed causes and effects against those we would support as most central. One reason we find Buchwald's satire humorous is that the causes he attributes to Reagan are clearly not major causes for the decline in education. We can't help asking ourselves, "Just how would prayer in the schools improve academic achievement?" Prayer might contribute to other aspects of education or personal growth, but most of us can't see a direct connection to academic excellence. Reading causal analysis, thus, draws on our reasoning skills to evaluate the directness of the link drawn between cause and effect.

Practice—Working with causes and effects

Take a few moments to choose some decision you made in the last few hours. Why did you decide to do what you did? List two or three main causes or reasons. Now list the most far-fetched reasons you can think of for the decision you made. Do the same with effects. You might work in groups to devise humorous causal analyses.

Decision _____

Cause _____   Effect _____

Cause _____   Effect _____

Cause _____   Effect _____

Cause _____   Effect _____

HOW DO WE WRITE CAUSAL ANALYSIS?

When writing causal analysis, focusing on the most important causes or effects is critical. Your readers will evaluate your selection of causes or effects just as carefully as you do when you read. Although loosely related causes and effects might be interesting to consider, most readers prefer to see explanations of what you think are the main causes or effects. In your prewriting, then, be sure to include all those causes or effects that you might use, but choose carefully which ones to develop in your paper.

Choosing major causes

Even as children, human beings want to know why things happen. As they gain experience with the world, they understand that few complex events happen for simple reasons, and so their causal analyses take account of the complexity of causes and effects. One "mistake" in causal reasoning that most of us outgrow early on is to identify a single cause as the root of an event. For instance, most students who study American history of the 1930s and 1940s understand that Pearl Harbor alone did not get this country into World War II. But at the same time, we recognize that Pearl Harbor—the sneak attack that killed thousands of GI's—sparked our entry into the war as few other causes could have. And so we also recognize that some causes are more central or more important in bringing about an event than are others. The same is true of effects: we try to identify the most important ones, but we rarely suggest that only one effect results from any action.

Practice—Reading

A well-known science writer explores some far-fetched and realistic causes for the extinction of dinosaurs in the following essay. Read it carefully to understand his causal analysis.

Sex, Drugs, Disasters, and the Extinction of Dinosaurs

Stephen Jay Gould, *Discover*

Science, in its most fundamental definition, is a fruitful mode of inquiry, not a list of enticing conclusions. The conclusions are the consequence, not the essence. My greatest unhappiness with most popular presentations of science concerns their failure to separate fascinating claims from the methods that scientists use to establish the facts of nature. Journalists, and the public, thrive on controversial and stunning statements. But science is, basically, a way of knowing—in P. B. Medawar's apt words, "the art of the soluble." If the growing corps of popular science writers would focus on how scientists develop and defend those fascinating claims, they would make the greatest possible contribution to public understanding.

Consider three ideas, proposed in perfect seriousness to account for the greatest of all titillating puzzles—the extinction of dinosaurs. These three notions involve the primally fascinating themes of our culture—sex, drugs, and violence—and I want to show why two of them rank as silly speculation, and why the other represents science at its grandest and most useful.

1. Sex: Testes function only in a narrow range of temperature (those of mammals hang externally in a scrotal sac because they need to be cooler than the body). A worldwide rise in temperature at the close of the Cretaceous period caused the testes of dinosaurs to stop functioning and led to their extinction by the sterilization of males.

2. Drugs: Angiosperms (flowering plants) first evolved toward the end of the dinosaurs' reign. Many of these plants contain psychoactive agents, avoided by mammals today because of their bitter taste. Dinosaurs had neither the means to taste the bitterness, nor livers effective enough to detoxify the substances. They died of massive overdoses.

3. Disasters: A huge asteroid struck the earth some 65 million years ago, lofting a cloud of dust into the sky and blocking sunlight, thereby suppressing photosynthesis and so drastically lowering world temperatures that dinosaurs and hosts of other creatures became extinct.

Before analyzing these three tantalizing statements, we must establish a basic ground rule often violated in proposals for the dinosaurs' demise. *There is no separate problem of the extinction of dinosaurs.* Too often we divorce specific events from their wider contexts and systems of cause and effect. The fundamental fact of dinosaur extinction is that it coincided with the demise of many other groups across a wide range of habitats, from terrestrial to marine.

Speculations limited to dinosaurs alone ignore the larger phenomenon. We need a coordinated explanation for a system of events that includes the extinction of dinosaurs as one component. Thus it makes little sense, though it may fuel our desire to view mammals as inevitable inheritors of the earth, to guess that dinosaurs died because small mammals ate their eggs (a perennial untestable speculation). It seems most unlikely that some disaster peculiar to dinosaurs befell these massive beasts—and that the debacle happened to strike just when one of history's five great dyings had enveloped the earth for completely different reasons.

The testicular theory, an old favorite from the 1940s, had its root in an interesting and thoroughly respectable study of temperature tolerances in the American alligator, published in the staid *Bulletin of the American Museum of Natural History* in 1946 by three experts on living and fossil reptiles—E. H. Colbert, my own first teacher in paleontology, R. B. Cowles, and C. M. Bogert.

The first sentence of their summary reveals a purpose beyond alligators: "This report describes an attempt to infer the reactions of extinct reptiles, especially the dinosaurs, to high temperatures as based upon reactions observed in the modern alligator." They studied, by rectal thermometry, the body temperatures of alligators under changing conditions of heating and cooling.

Colbert, Cowles, and Bogert compared the warming rates of small and large alligators. As predicted, the small fellows heated up (and cooled down) more quickly. When exposed to a warm sun, a tiny 50-gram (1.76-ounce) alligator heated up one degree Celsius every minute and a half, while a large alligator, 260 times bigger at 13,000 grams (28.7 pounds), took seven and a half minutes to gain a degree. Extrapolating up to an adult ten-ton dinosaur, they concluded that a one-degree rise in body temperature would take 86 hours. If large animals absorb heat so slowly, they will also be unable to shed any excess heat gained when temperatures rise above a favorable level.

The authors then guessed that large dinosaurs lived at or near their optimum temperatures; Cowles suggested that a rise in global temperatures just before the Cretaceous extinction caused the dinosaurs to heat up beyond their optimal tolerance—and, being so large, they couldn't shed the unwanted heat. (In a most unusual statement for a scientific paper, Colbert and Bogert explicitly disavowed this speculative extension of their empirical work on alligators.) Cowles conceded that this excess heat probably wasn't enough to kill or even to enervate the great beasts, but since testes often function only within a narrow range of temperatures, he proposed that this global rise might have sterilized all the males, causing extinction by natural contraception.

The overdose theory has recently been supported by UCLA psychiatrist Ronald K. Siegel. Sigel has observed, he claims, more than 2,000 animals that can give themselves various drugs—from a swig of alcohol to massive doses of the big H. Elephants will swill the equivalent of 20 beers at a time, but do not like alcohol in concentrations greater than 7 per cent.

Since fertile imaginations can apply almost any hot idea to the extinction of dinosaurs, Siegel found a way. Flowering plants did not evolve until late in the dinosaurs' reign. These plants also produced an array of aromatic, amino-acid-based alkaloids—the major group of psychoactive agents. Most mammals are "smart" enough to avoid these potential poisons. The alkaloids simply don't taste good (they are bitter), and in any case we mammals have livers happily supplied with the capacity to detoxify them. But, Siegel speculates, perhaps dinosaurs could neither taste the bitterness nor detoxify the substances once ingested. Speaking of the extinction, he recently told members of the American Psychological Association: "I'm not suggesting that all dinosaurs OD'd on plant drugs, but it certainly was a factor." He also argued that death by overdose may help explain why so many dinosaur fossils are found in contorted positions. (Do not go gentle into that good night.)

Extraterrestrial catastrophes have long pedigrees in the popular literature of extinction, but the subject exploded again after a long lull three years ago when the father-son, physicist-geologist team of Luis and Walter Alvarez proposed that an asteroid, about six miles in diameter, struck the earth 65 million years ago. Most asteroids circle the sun in an orbit between Mars and Jupiter but some, the so-called Apollo objects, take a more eccentric route, actually crossing the earth's orbit in their path around the sun. The chance of a collision at any crossing is minuscule, but the number of Apollo objects and the immensity of geological time virtually guarantee that impacts will occur once in a great while.

The force of such a collision would be immense, greater by far than the megatonnage of all the world's nuclear weapons. In trying to reconstruct a scenario that would explain the simultaneous dying of dinosaurs on land and so many creatures in the sea, the Alvarezes proposed that a gigantic dust cloud, generated by particles blown aloft in the impact, would so darken the earth that photosynthesis would cease and temperatures drop precipitously. (Rage, rage against the dying of the light.) The single-celled photosynthetic oceanic plankton, with life cycles measured in weeks, would perish outright, but land plants might survive through the dormancy of their seeds (land plants were not much affected by the Cretaceous extinction, and any adequate theory must account for the curious pattern of differential survival). Dinosaurs would die by starvation and freezing; small, warm-blooded mammals, with more modest requirements for food and better regulation of body temperature, would squeak through.

All three theories, testicular malfunction, psychoactive overdosing, and asteroidal zapping, grab our attention mightily. As pure statements, they rank about equally high an any hit parade of primal fascination. Yet one represents expansive science, the others restrictive and untestable speculation.

How could we possibly decide whether the hypothesis of testicular frying is right or wrong? We would have to know things that the fossil record cannot provide. What temperatures were optimal for dinosaurs? Could the beasts avoid the absorption of excess heat by staying in the shade, or in caves? At what temperatures did their testicles cease to function? Were late Cretaceous climates ever warm enough to drive the internal temperatures of dinosaurs close to this ceiling? Testicles simply don't fossilize, and how could we infer their temperature tolerances even if they did? In short, Cowles's hypothesis is imply an intriguing speculation leading nowhere.

Siegel's overdosing has even less going for it. At least Cowles extrapolated his conclusion from some good data on alligators. And he didn't completely violate the primary guideline of explaining dinosaur extinction in the context of a general mass dying—for rise in temperature could be the root cause of a general catastrophe, zapping dinosaurs by testicular malfunction and different groups for other reasons. But Siegel's speculation cannot touch the extinction of ammonites or oceanic plankton. It is simply a gratuitous, attention-grabbing guess. It cannot be tested, for how can we know what dinosaurs tasted and what their livers could do?

The asteroid story, on the other hand, has a basis in evidence. It can be tested, extended, refined and, if wrong, disproved. The Alvarezes did not just construct an arresting guess for public consumption. They proposed their hypothesis after laborious geochemical studies with Frank Asaro and Helen Michel had revealed a massive increase of iridium in rocks deposited right at the time of extinction. Iridium, a rare metal of the platinum group, is virtually absent from indigenous rocks of the earth's crust; most of our iridium comes from extraterrestrial objects that hit the earth.

The Alvarez hypothesis bore immediate fruit. Based originally on evidence found in rocks at two sites in Europe, it led geochemists through the world to examine other sediments of the same age. They found abnormally high amounts of iridium everywhere—from continental rocks of the western United States to deep sea cores from the South Atlantic.

Cowles proposed his testicular hypothesis in the mid–1940s. Where has it gone since then? Absolutely nowhere, because scientists can do nothing with it. It merely stands as a curious appendage to a solid study of alligators. Siegel's overdose scenario will also win a few press notices and fade into oblivion. The Alvarezes' asteroid falls into a different category altogether, and much of the popular commentary has missed this essential distinction by focusing on the impact and its attendant results, and forgetting what is really important to a scientist—the iridium. If you talk just about asteroids, dust, and darkness, you simply tell stories no better and no more entertaining than fried testicles or terminal trips. It is the iridium—the source of the testable evidence—that counts and forges the crucial distinction between speculation and science.

Practice—Analyzing

1. What three explanations does Gould examine as possible causes for

   the extinction of dinosaurs? _____

   _____

2. How does Gould set up readers for the three causes? _____

   _____

   _____

3. Does he treat all three causes fairly? _____

   _____

   _____

4. Are you convinced by his analysis of why causes 1 and 2 are less

   plausible explanations of the mass extinction? _____

   _____

   _____

   _____

5. Are you convinced by his analysis of why cause 3 is a plausible

   explanation? _____

   _____

   _____

6. Does Gould address the issue of choosing a primary cause, and if so,

   how? _____

   _____

The topic sentence or thesis statement

Like Buchwald's and Gould's analyses, your causal analysis also commits you to a position. Just by writing the causal analysis, you tell readers that you believe these causes or effects are the most important ones to concentrate on. Your paper, whether it be a single- or multiparagraph essay, must stake out the territory you will cover; it must identify its purpose and scope early on. Then you must provide adequate details to support your contention that the causes or effects you've identified are the most crucial. In other words, you must carefully focus and then support your topic sentence or thesis statement.

Practice—Revising topic sentences

The following topic sentences are taken out of the context of the paragraphs they controlled, but you should be able to analyze each to determine if it is adequately focused and what it predicts about the paragraph. Revise those topic sentences that are not focused.

1. Because of the strain it causes on my eyes, I constantly get migraine headaches after viewing television for prolonged periods of time.

   Revision: _____

   _____

2. Because my parents treated my twin sister and me as individuals, my role as a twin has had little influence on my life.

   Revision: _____

   _____

3. When I became a mother I found out that I had to have a schedule to get anything done.

   Revision: _____

   _____

4. As a nurse, I act differently to a lot of people all the time.

Revision: _____

_____

Practice—Revising thesis statements

The following thesis statements are taken out of the context of the essays they controlled, but you should be able to analyze each to determine if it is adequately focused and what it predicts about the essay. Evaluate essay maps as well. Revise those thesis statements that are not focused. You might try adding an essay map if it would help to focus the thesis.

1. From this experience I found that infringement on my seclusion, such as having the bathroom door kicked in, being needlessly awakened, and having constant interruptions while writing make my anger mount to the physical level.

    Revision: _____

    _____

    _____

    _____

2. Anorexia nervosa is a self-mutilating disease that affects its victim both physically and mentally.

    Revision: _____

    _____

    _____

3. Angry arguments with my father now stem from those differing views regarding world politics, my career goals, and my personal life.

    Revision: _____

    _____

    _____

Structure in the causal analysis paper

Most often, the purpose of your paper will determine whether you should focus on causes or effects. Seldom can a short paper include both causes and effects, and so focusing on one or the other is most appropriate for the single-paragraph essay. As you organize your paper, you can use the following visual schemes to help you focus your attention on causes or effects:

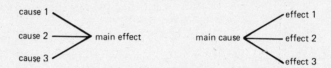

If you choose to look at two or more causes, you would state the effect and probably the causes or a generalization about the causes in your topic sentence. Then the bulk of the paragraph would develop the causes in detail, often by using examples, facts, or other details to flesh out the analysis. If you choose to look at two or more effects, you would likewise identify the cause and probably the effects in your topic sentence and develop the effects in the paragraph. Remember, though, that such a paragraph or essay is not simply an illustration paper. You must demonstrate the *relationship* between the causes and effects by analyzing the causes or effects.

If you want to focus on a single cause-effect chain, having picked a major cause and effect but noting that other causes and effects contribute to the relationship, you might use the following scheme:

major cause ▪━━▶ major effect

In this paragraph, you might divide the paragraph into equal portions to develop each part of the chain adequately.

For longer papers, you might decide to explore a longer chain of causes and effects, organized somewhat like this:

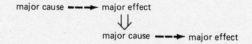

In this arrangement, each effect becomes the cause of the next effect, and the chain can extend through several effects becoming causes of subsequent effects. Do not, however, attempt to explain a causal chain unless you have enough time and space to convince readers of the several connections.

Let's look at one student paper that illustrates the simple single cause-effect chain:

Because college freshmen at CSU misread newspaper articles, they receive poor grades when using them in classes. For example, two weeks ago a freshman student in my composition class who had carelessly taken a quote out of context from a newspaper article he had read received a "C" on his paper for failure to use the quote directly and keep it in the correct context. In another class, Speech 100, a freshman stood before the entire class last Wednesday and proclaimed that, according to a newspaper article he read in *The Denver Post,* President Reagan had cut the spending budget for defense when in fact Reagan had previously spoken the night before stating the exact opposite. Needless to say, the student was quite embarrassed and received a "D" on his badly-prepared speech. Finally, after thinking that misread newspaper articles couldn't actually be a trend in the freshman class, I was surprised to find that a girl in my macroeconomics class had written an essay concerning the six month's economic forecast and had turned around every statistic which in effect resulted in conclusions totally the opposite from what the article had implied. She had carelessly misread the article and received a "D" for the little effort she put forth to get the facts straight. Because of these instances of personal experience, it is quite common to find that freshmen misread newspaper articles and unfortunately receive poor grades because of it.

—Julie R.

As you can see, Julie sets up a specific relationship, carefully focused so that she can use her personal experience to support her position. We could show the visual scheme of her paper like this:

freshmen misread newspapers --------------------→ poor grades

comp class	C
speech	D } examples
economics essay	F

But when prewriting, Julie probably started out with a messier map of her ideas, jotting down causes and effects of the decline in education in general and then focusing on her own experiences that explained poor academic achievement.

GETTING IDEAS FOR CAUSAL ANALYSIS

To get started generating ideas for causal analysis, why not map out a few general causes of low academic performance, with effects on the other end of the map line. We can begin with the causes and effects Buchwald brings up:

Causes   Effects

parents not involved ----------------------→low academic achievement
shortages of qualified teachers
low teacher pay
low government spending

low academic achievement --------------→US overtaken by competitors
                                              not know how to use
                                                 weapons
                                              unemployment and crime
                                                 rise
                                              higher welfare costs
                                              threat to national security

Because Buchwald doesn't include many details, you might want to work first with the causes and effects he cites. If you can, add more specific causes or effects. For instance, you might add to the first general cause some of the specific causes for parents not being involved in their children's education, such as the pervasive influence of television, both parents working, parents' lower skills making them feel unqualified to help children, and so on. And you can then add specific examples.

Now you can look closer to home and ask yourself about the academic skills of your peers. Do you agree that you and your classmates have achieved academic excellence? If so, cite causes for and effects of your achievement. If not, list specific causes—much as Julie did before she wrote her paper—and effects for your less-than-excellent skills. Make your maps as complex as necessary by grouping related causes under a more general label. Julie's map might have looked partly like this:

.   Causes   Effects

poor reading skills ---→poor grades
    misread texts
    misread newspapers
    read few magazines
    little reading for pleasure

WRITING CAUSAL ANALYSIS

1. Reread Art Buchwald's musings on the report issued by the National Commission on Excellence in Education. List the statistics he cites from the report. What does he feel are legitimate causes of the decline in American students' skills? What causes does he dismiss as shortsighted or irrelevant? Do you agree with him? What do you think are the main causes

of the decline in students' ability to read, write, and calculate? List those causes or reasons you think are most important. Now list the major effects you see, both for our educational system in the next few years and for our country in the next ten years. Which of these effects are most serious?

For your paper, pick either the most significant reason or effect you have listed. Develop a main point clearly, and then develop the paper with specific facts, examples, and analysis.

2. Reread "Grandma Junkies" (in Chapter 3) and consider why our culture encourages people to become addicted to various drugs—coffee, cigarettes, aspirin, other medications, marijuana, and so on. Now focus on specific groups. Why do those groups seem addicted to drugs they take? What causes do you see? What effects? Choose just one group and make it as specific as possible. Refine the causes and effects you've listed. Now choose one major cause or effect and write a paragraph on "drug" addiction for that specific group.

3. We all read about cause-effect relationships in newspapers or news-magazines. But we may often disagree that pollution causes eye irritation, that high interest rates cause decline in the housing industry, that caffeine causes headaches, that higher tuition causes expansion of services on campus. Choose any such relationship that you have read or heard about. Decide whether you think the relationship is valid or not. If you agree that a cause-effect relationship exists, explain the cause and the effect. If you disagree that a cause-effect relationship exists, explain your reasons. You might use Gould's essay as a model.

APPLYING CAUSAL ANALYSIS

Before you begin to draft your own paper on this topic, you should review the original and revised samples below. Notice that Matt strengthens his revision by focusing on personal experience so that he can develop his supporting details fully. Should you decide to pursue a more general cause or effect in your paper, you may need to do some library research to collect supporting details for your position.

Original

Many reasons can be found for the lack of preparation in college fresh-men, but none as relevant as the lack of basic educational skills. In math, for example, many basics should have been taught in high school but were not. Some of these are factoring, the use of exponents, word problems and others. In high school, math was only required through the sophomore year, thus letting slower students quit after only basic algebra. Then when they get to college and find they need more math they have to start in remedial classes. The same also holds true for English. Although students do go all four high school years, they still lack basic skills. The biggest problem is that they cannot write a paragraph. Too much time is spent on reading instead of writing in high school English courses. Because of this college freshmen spend their valuable class time learning how to write fundamental paragraphs. These are just a couple of the problems in the lack of college preparation in high school students.

—*Matt R.*

Revised

Many reasons can be found for the lack of preparation in college freshmen, but none as relevant as the lack of basic educational skills such as math and English. In math, for example, many basics should have been, but were not, taught in my high school. Some of these basics are factoring, the use of exponents, word problems and others. In high school, math was only required through the sophomore year, thus letting slower students quit after only basic algebra. Although able to quit, I continued through my senior year, completing calculus. But soon after entering college I found my math skills to be only average. Not only had I forgotten how to factor, but it took me over a week of studying to regain the confidence needed to test out. The same holds true for English. Although students do go through English all four years of high school, the basic skills are still lacking. The biggest problem is that of writing paragraphs. For instance, during my senior year I wrote a five-page term paper for which I received an A grade. But when I wrote a simple paragraph for English Composition 101, I could not believe all the mistakes pointed out. Because of this problem college freshmen spend their valuable class time learning how to write fundamental paragraphs instead of full-length papers. Thus, the first year of college is wasted because skills that should have been learned in high school must now be taught. College freshmen seem to be terribly ill- prepared.

Practice—Revising

1. How did Matt improve his focus in his revision? _____

_____

2. Can you suggest a more precise topic sentence than the one in his

revised version? _____

_____

3. What examples did Matt add to the revision? _____

_____

_____

_____

4. How did the examples strengthen his paragraph? _____

_____

_____

5. Can you think of other possible examples Matt might include in his

   paragraph? _____

_____

_____

_____

_____

Now consider Lisa's essay analyzing the causes of her arguments with her father:

Original

Dad and I used to play "horsey," and he also helped me pull in my first big fish. He'd tell funny jokes at dinner, and my friends just loved to visit my house to listen to him. But those years are gone and with those years went that total fatherly control he had over me. Now in college, I've seen, heard, and learned much more about the rest of the world and have formed my own opinions based on this knowledge and my experiences. But the opinions I hold and my father's opinions usually conflict. Angry arguments with my father now stem from those differing views regarding world politics, my career goals, and my personal life.

The one subject guaranteed to cause conflict is politics; no matter what my view, his always seems the opposite. After the horrifying Korean Airlines incident in the Sakhalin Islands, Round 1 of the boxing match began.

In the far corner weighing 190 pounds and believing we should cut off all shipments of grain to the Soviets is Pa K. And in this corner wearing blue trunks and saying that the grain has absolutely nothing to do with it is Little Lisa. At the dinner table, which used to be the place for daily stories and ethnic jokes, Round 1 commences. We sparred for a while and tried to find out exactly what the other's position was. Finally, after Lisa couldn't stand the growing tension anymore, she burst out with a hard right punch and said, "You're not listening to a thing I've said!!!" Pa K just keeps saying over and over, "Quit sending them grain and then they'll quit blowing innocent commercial airliners out of the clear blue sky." Round 2 action is shifted to the living room where my father and I entertain my aunt and uncle with our political boxing antics. At the sound of the bell, we start again, the arguing at almost a peak level. As the noise raises higher and spills over into the next rooms, my aunt quietly tugs my uncle's coat and mentions something about needing to wash the cat. They're afraid of watching World War III start in the home of their relatives. Finally, I give in. The redundancy of his statements batter me until I fall to the mat. But the judges don't award a Technical Knock-out; it's a draw, as usual, and we don't speak to one another for about three days. When we finally do start talking again, it's a light subject, not the forbidden politics of the world that get us both in trouble.

Recently, comments regarding working women have been cropping up all too often at our house. These remarks, such as "if you'd stay home and out of the workforce, maybe you wouldn't wonder where all your dishes disappear to," are mostly directed at my mother, but are also little arrows shot my way as my father realizes the steps I'm taking toward a real career, not just another job. The plain fact is that my father has not yet succumbed to the 80s and the idea of liberated career women; he still believes women should stay at home, have and care for the kids, and create a perfect environment for the man of the household. This is contrary to what I believe in, obviously, or I wouldn't be in college working toward a degree in accounting. The comments enrage me, and I try to control myself as I calmly tell him that the world would not be in such good shape today if not for working women; their contributions have been tremendous. The arguing starts again and my father and I go around and around, and once again, I find it hard to fight my battle when I'm talking to a brick wall without ears. Afterwards we don't speak for several days, and the tension between us is almost tangible. All I want is for him to respect the strides I'm making toward being a working woman and recognizing them for what they're worth to me, as well as recognizing my potential to be a good wife and mother at the same time.

After breaking up with an old boyfriend I found out that my father disagreed with my decision to end the relationship. But he didn't know the whole story and wouldn't listen when I tried to explain. Paul was tall, 6' 8", dark and handsome with deep ocean-colored eyes. Any girl's dream! My father saw him as a fairly handsome, well-educated, well-mannered, house-owning engineer. But what he didn't see was that Paul also fit the personality of the stereotyped engineer—boring. My father wasn't the one who had to spend evenings with him so there was no way he could, or would, ever understand why I no longer desired to see Paul. I explained to Paul that I preferred to keep our relationship friendly, and I also asked him not to surprise me by dropping by. Under the circumstances, Paul was not very understanding. The phone rang off the hook for weeks after the breakup, and I'd instruct whoever answered to tell Paul that I wasn't home. My father clearly couldn't comprehend my decision to do what was best for me, breaking up, and let his opinions be known loud and clear. My father blew up with anger at me, which was reciprocated, and demanded that I be totally honest with Paul and tell him to "bug off." We argued over and over until once again, the unlistening wall defeated me. As with my career decisions, he couldn't understand that what I was doing I was doing to please myself, not my boyfriend or others.

When we aren't arguing about politics, my dream career, or my handling of my personal life, my father and I get along fairly well. But when these subjects do arise, the barriers are erected and my father's lack of listening skills start my blood boiling until the anger surges outward. Instead of arguing, maybe I'll find a better way of deal with this anger and never have to face the earless wall again.

—*Lisa K.*

If you had to suggest revisions, what would you have Lisa begin on? Would you suggest she refocus her thesis to reflect the most important impression she makes throughout her essay? Would you have her continue to use the boxer image in paragraph 2? Would you ask for more details in paragraph 3? Would you improve paragraph hooks? Would you have her relate details to causes and effects throughout the paper? Consider what she actually revised:

Revised

Dad and I used to play "horsey," and he also helped me pull in my first big fish. He'd tell funny jokes at dinner, and my friends just loved to visit my house to listen to him. But those years are gone and with those years went that total fatherly control he had over me. Now in college, I've seen, heard, and learned much more about the rest of the world and have formed my own opinions based on this knowledge and my experiences. But the opinions I hold and my father's opinions usually conflict. Angry arguments with my father now stem from the deaf ear that he turns during our disagreements regarding world politics, my career goals, and my personal life.

Lately I never discuss politics with my father unless I know that our views are 100% the same, in other words, hardly ever. After the horrifying Korean Airlines incident in the Sakhalin Islands, Round 1 of the boxing match began. In the far corner weighing 190 pounds and believing we should cut off all shipments of grain to the Soviets is Pa K. And in this corner wearing blue trunks and saying that the grain has absolutely nothing to do with it is Little Lisa. At the dinner table, which used to be the place for daily stories and ethnic jokes, Round 1 commences. We sparred for a while and tried to find out exactly what the other's position was. Finally, after Lisa couldn't stand the growing tension anymore, she burst out with a hard right punch and said, "You're not listening to a thing I've said!!!" Pa K just keeps saying over and over, "Quit sending them grain and then they'll quit blowing innocent commercial airliners out of the clear blue sky." Round 2 action is shifted to the living room where my father and I entertain my aunt and uncle with our political boxing antics. At the sound of the bell, we start again, the arguing at almost a peak level. As the noise raises higher and spills over into the next rooms, my aunt quietly tugs my uncle's coat and mentions something about needing to wash the cat. They're afraid of watching World War III start in the home of their relatives. Finally, I give in. The redundancy of his statements batter me until I fall to the mat. But the judges don't award a Technical Knock-out; it's a draw, as usual, and we don't speak to one another for about three days. When we finally do start talking again, it's a light subject, not the forbidden politics of the world that get us both in trouble.

Heated discussions now arise at home because of remarks my father makes about working women. These remarks, such as "if you'd stay home and out of the workforce, maybe you wouldn't wonder where all your dishes disappear to," are mostly directed at my mother, but are also little arrows shot my way as my father realizes the steps I'm taking toward a real career, not just another job. The plain fact is that my father has not yet accepted the idea of liberated career women; he still believes women should stay at home, have and care for the kids, and create a perfect environment for the man of the household. This is contrary to what I believe in, obviously, or I wouldn't be in college working toward a degree in accounting. The comments enrage me, and as my blood begins to boil, I tell myself that it's not worth fighting about and that, as usual, he won't listen to what I have to say. But I try to control myself as I calmly tell him that the world would not be in such good shape today if not for working women; their contributions have been tremendous. The arguing starts again and my father and I go around and around, and once again, I find it hard to fight my battle when I'm talking to a brick wall without ears. Afterwards we don't speak for several days, and the tension between us is almost tangible. All I want is for him to respect the strides I'm making toward being a working woman and recognizing them for what they're worth to me, as well as recognizing my potential to be a good wife and mother at the same time. If only he could really listen, not just pretend to hear.

As for my personal life, we also argue about that. After breaking up with an old boyfriend I found out that my father disagreed with my decision to end the relationship. But he didn't know the whole story and wouldn't listen when I tried to explain. Paul was tall, 6′ 8″, dark and handsome with deep ocean-colored eyes. Any girl's dream! My father saw him as a fairly handsome, well-educated, well-mannered, house-owning engineer. But what he didn't see was that Paul also fit the personality of the stereotyped engineer—boring. My father wasn't the one who had to spend evenings with him so there was no way he could, or would, ever understand why I no longer desired to see Paul. I explained to Paul that I no longer wanted to date him. The phone rang off the hook for weeks after the breakup, and I'd instruct whoever answered to tell Paul that I wasn't home. Not liking my response to any ringing phones, my father let his opinions be known loud and clear. My father blew up with anger at me, which was reciprocated, and demanded that I be totally honest with Paul and tell him to "get lost." We argued over and over until once again, the unlistening wall defeated me. As with my career decisions, he couldn't understand that what I was doing I was doing to please myself, not my boyfriend or others and, in the end, he wouldn't listen.

When we aren't arguing about politics, my dream career, or my handling of my personal life, my father and I get along fairly well. But when these subjects do arise, the barriers are erected and my father's lack of listening skills starts my blood boiling until the anger surges outward. Instead of arguing, maybe I'll find a better way of deal with this anger and never have to face the earless wall again.

—Lisa K.

REVISING TO IMPROVE LOGICAL DEVELOPMENT

A common difficulty with causal analysis is thoroughness of analysis. Often writers expect readers to follow exactly the same chain of logic without spelling those steps out. Unfortunately, readers are not always willing to do so, and so writers must revise carefully to insure that all logical connections are detailed. Suggest revisions for logical development in the following paragraph.

Original

When students show up for class unwillingly, they should show respect by not talking so that the students who want to be there can learn something. I go to class to learn but I can't learn anything if other people are talking all the time. To be put another way, if the students didn't want to learn anything, then why are they in school in the first place? Moreover, instead of listening to the professor, the students, with a lack of respect and interest for the class, tend to entertain themselves by talking to their buddies. As a result, the talking persists, which provokes me to get upset because I lose my concentration.

—Scott W.

What should Scott work on first? If he improves his focus, what will he need to make a convincing argument? Look at what he revised and suggest still other improvements.

Revised

When students show up for class and do nothing but talk, it annoys me because I lose my concentration in taking notes on the lecture. In physiology, for example, it's difficult to concentrate on what the professor is saying when students are talking louder than the professor who's using a microphone. This situation irritates me because when I lose my concentration in class I miss some of the notes, which in my case always end up to be the important questions that I miss on the test. For instance, one day when discussing all of the parts of the inner ear, which requires a lot of concentration because it's so detailed, I was distracted by the students sitting behind me, who were talking about their weekends at home. For me, it's hard to take notes when the only voices that are heard are everyone's except the professor's. Well, in the process of listening to the professor, as well as the irrelevant chanting of the students, I missed some of the notes during the lecture. The following day was the test and I was psyched and confident going into it but a little shaky about the parts of the inner ear. Afterwards, I received a score of "C" on the test. Later, when I was going over the test, I found out that most of the questions missed were related to the inner ear. This wasn't pleasing to the eye because the only reason why I missed them was because on the day of the lecture about the inner ear, I missed some of the notes due to the fact that students were talking all around me. In other words, I wouldn't have missed those questions if the students weren't talking.

—*Scott W.*

Revision checklist

1. Have you concentrated on major causes or effects in your paper?
2. Does your topic sentence or thesis statement identify clearly the cause-effect relationship and your position?

3. Does your topic sentence or thesis statement focus adequately on causes or effects you can develop fully in your paper?
4. Does your paper develop the cause fully?
5. Does your paper connect cause to effect adequately?
6. Have you helped the reader see each logical step in the analysis by providing full detail, clear transitions, and repetition of key words?

UNIT FOUR

Persuading

Although this unit contains only one chapter, that chapter
addresses one of the most important kinds of writing we do. If
we want readers to agree with us and act with us, we must
persuade them of the correctness of our position. This unit
covers the principles of persuading readers. You'll also have the
chance in this unit to combine methods of development you've
practiced up till now, for persuasion uses examples, description,
comparison, definition, and all other patterns.

chapter 14
Persuading

WHAT IS PERSUASION?

Our argumentative strategies change as we grow older because as youngsters we often argue by name-calling and taunting. As we learn more about language and about writing, though, we discover that persuasion means much more than juvenile "arguing" and that most of our writing is persuasive to some extent: we ask readers to adopt our points of view as writers, even when we are not making specific recommendations or trying to prove a point. But some writing is clearly *persuasive* in that we, as writers, try to change our readers' attitudes and opinions on a topic. Every editorial we read—and even many apparently objective news reports—are primarily persuasive. In this chapter, we'll examine techniques that make persuasive writing more convincing.

WHEN DO WE USE PERSUASION IN COLLEGE WRITING?

Although in one sense all academic writing attempts to persuade instructors that students know and understand the material, some writing is clearly persuasive in that it argues for a position. If a professor asks on an essay test which of two competing explanations is better, that professor gives you the opportunity to persuade. Similarly, when students write editorials or letters to the editor of the college paper, those are persuasive pieces. Students who lobby for a bill in the student senate attempt to persuade their constituents and colleagues.

Moreover, some academic assignments are clearly persuasive. One of our mathematics courses requires students to write an essay in which they explain a mathematical model for taxation, crop rotation, or some other practical matter. But the bulk of the paper is an argument or an attempt to persuade readers that appropriate action should be taken on the basis of mathematical predictions. Such assignments are not uncommon in other disciplines as well, especially in the liberal arts.

The most common persuasive writing that all students will eventually practice is the job application letter. Although few schools teach this kind of persuasion, assignments in other areas help prepare students to convince readers that they are "right for the job." Persuasion, then, has practical uses that more than justify time spent on persuasion in a writing class.

Let's begin by considering two opposing viewpoints on a controversial issue:

Women Deserve Absolute Equality
USA Today

The phrase is by now a cliche: "You've come a long way, baby." Indeed, women have made great strides. We are constantly reminded of women's 'firsts': the astronaut, Sally Ride; the movie studio head, Sherry Lansing, and the U.S. Supreme Court Justice, Sandra Day O'Connor.

It has been years since bras were burned in anger. Today, women demonstrate in more constructive ways that their own potential can change society. Their growth has altered police forces and fire departments, introduced men to dishes and diapers, and even changed the way people refer to the sexes and occupations in ordinary conversation.

But if women have begun to get men to accept them as equals, their gains still mask deep inequalities:

- Last month Congress reported that 80 percent of women still are in the lowest-paid jobs. In 1955, a working woman earned 64 percent of a man's salary; by 1980, just 60 percent. Women's median pay is $12,000; men's $20,000.
- Although 52 percent of college students are women, and many enter non-traditional fields, these gains haven't been matched by higher salaries and promotions. Over a lifetime, a male college graduate can expect to double the earnings of a female. And women today hold only 28 percent of management positions.
- Women are America's fastest growing poverty group. Because women have lower lifetime incomes and raising families doesn't qualify them for benefits, Social Security pays elderly women less than men. Elderly women's median income is $4,600, half that of men's. Women head 16 percent of all families, but 50 percent of poor families.

Even though women make up 51 percent of our population and 42 percent of our workers, it is clear many aren't being treated equally or fairly. Congress is considering legislation to correct some inequities, but a lasting solution must be broader-based.

Next month, Congress will begin hearings on a new push to ratify the Equal Rights Amendment to the Constitution. It fell three states short in 1982, even though polls showed a majority of Americans favored it. Opponents say ERA is unnecessary—present laws will do. But the evidence is overwhelming that existing laws haven't done the job.

Unfair pay and promotion practices for women are deeply ingrained in society. Only a Constitutional amendment will provide the broad base that is needed to attack all these pernicious practices. And there should be no time limit on ratification, as there was last year.

A few firsts, in a courtroom or a space shuttle, make it easy to swallow phrases about progress. The truth is that women still have a long, long way to go, and the nation owes them absolute equality under law to help them get there.

ERA is Redundant, Will Create Problems

Phyllis Schlafly, *USA Today*

Anybody who thinks that the Equal Rights Amendment will raise women's wages is a person who would believe in the tooth fairy.

It is deceptive and unfair to mislead women into believing that ERA can solve their financial or other problems.

We already have a Equal Employment Opportunity Act, which prohibits sex discrimination in jobs, pay and promotion. Passing a redundant law will do nothing at all to correct violations of the existing law—that's an enforcement problem.

On the other hand, ERA will immediately require the draft registration of 18-year-old girls, just as 18-year-old men are now required to register. This effect has never been denied by leading ERA advocates.

The ERA-draft connection proves that ERA is a grievous take-away of young women's traditional rights.

In 1980, Congress decisively rejected, in both houses, the Carter plan for the draft registration of women. In 1981, the Supreme Court, in Rostker vs. Goldberg, upheld the exemption of all women from the military draft under the present Constitution.

ERA would reverse that decision.

ERA will require the payment of federal tax funds for abortion, by making the Hyde Amendment unconstitutional. The American Civil Liberties Union and other pro-abortionists have already made this argument in court in three states that have state ERAs: Hawaii, Massachusetts and Pennsylvania.

Their theory is that, because abortion is a medical procedure performed only on women, it is discrimination "on account of sex" to deny tax funds for abortion. Because of the pro-abortion bias of the federal courts, ERA would put abortion funding in the Constitution.

ERA will mandate "gay/lesbian rights" because the word used in ERA is "sex," not "women."

In a landmark analysis of this subject, the *Yale Law Journal* stated: "The stringent requirements of the proposed Equal Rights Amendment argue strongly for removal of this stigma by granting marriage licenses to homosexual couples who satisfy reasonable and non-discriminatory qualifications."

This ERA-gay connection is admitted by many other pro-ERA lawyers.

Some ERAers claim that ERA won't do these things. But who knows how the federal courts will rule when presented with these issues?

The burden of proof is on the ERAers to prove these things won't happen, and they cannot prove that. There is only one way to be sure ERA won't do these things, and that is by including specific prohibitions in the text of ERA itself.

Practice—Analyzing

1. Where do you find a statement that expresses the authors' opinions on ERA?

   USA Today editor   Schlafly

   _____   _____

   _____   _____

   _____   _____

   _____   _____

2. Do both editorials seem equally objective? Cite examples of words and arguments that set the tone of each editorial.

   USA Today editor   Schlafly

   _____   _____

   _____   _____

   _____   _____

   _____   _____

3. What kind of evidence does each author use? Be specific as you create categories for evidence.

USA *Today* editor   Schlafly

_____   _____

_____   _____

_____   _____

_____   _____

4. Did you have an opinion on this issue before you started reading? Did one editorial express your opinion? Did the other editorial sway you? If you had no opinion when you began reading, do you have

   one now? Why? _____

   _____

   _____

5. What persuasive techniques do these authors use that you would like to practice in your own writing?

   USA *Today* editor   Schlafly

   _____   _____

   _____   _____

   _____   _____

   _____   _____

6. Do any words or phrases create negative attitudes without facts to base them on? Cite examples.

   USA *Today* editor   Schlafly

   _____   _____

   _____   _____

   _____   _____

   _____   _____

7. Which editorial is more convincing? Why? _____

_____

_____

_____

HOW DO WE READ PERSUASION?

Although most of what we read captures our attention as it expresses a writer's viewpoint, some writing is strictly persuasive. As readers, we recognize persuasion by the clear statement of a problem and the writer's position in the controversy. Moreover, persuasion is characterized by strategies designed to convince readers—accumulation of facts, examples, description, and expert testimony as evidence; analysis of positive evidence to support the position; and refutation of the opponent's evidence. Let's consider these points more fully.

Readers organize arguments

Recognizing and reacting to persuasion is not difficult for readers. Most readers react immediately to one of two main patterns of organizing arguments. Writers typically express their positions either at the beginning or the end of the argument. If stating the position early will help the writer convince readers, then the thesis appears near the beginning of the editorial.

Notice that Schlafly states her main point with a slightly humorous comparison in the first sentence and then restates that view more objectively in the second sentence. Readers know immediately what position Schlafly will defend in her essay.

> Anybody who thinks that the Equal Rights Amendment raise women's wages is a person who would believe in the tooth fairy. It is deceptive and unfair to mislead women into believing that ERA can solve their financial or other problems.

Similarly, the *USA Today* editor states a main point in the third paragraph, but he saves his strongest recommendation for the end of the editorial. Readers react to the early statement of the controversy and begin comparing what they know about the issue with what the writer tells them.

> But if women have begun to get men to accept them as equals, their gains still mask deep inequalities. . . . The truth is that women still have a long, long way to go, and the nation owes them absolute equality under law to help them get there.

Readers begin accumulating their own arguments, hoping to see the writer take account of their objections to the stated position. Each piece of evidence and analysis is weighed against the reader's personal experience and knowledge.

For this reason, some writers prefer to state the controversy early in the paper but not to state their own positions until later. When using this technique, writers can outline arguments on all sides of the issue, define terms, and evaluate more objectively until the strength of one position emerges. Then that position becomes the stance the writer adopts. Readers faced with this approach again recognize the objective description of the problem as a prelude to the specific arguments. They weigh the writers' descriptions against their own knowledge of the issue and scrutinize the paper for inherent bias. Though this technique can help readers objectively review arguments for and against highly emotional or controversial subjects, writers must be extremely careful not to ignore evidence or weight arguments in favor of one position.

Readers expect "fair play"

Readers, then, become involved in argumentation, just as they would if the argument were happening in conversation. And, just as in conversation, readers expect clarity of definitions, reliability of evidence, and honesty in treating the opposing view. Readers depend on trustworthy presentation of arguments; if writers expose their bias or argue unfairly, even on relatively unimportant points, readers often refuse to continue reading arguments. If they do read on, they will generally downplay strong evidence because they feel the writer is untrustworthy.

Readers expect complete evidence

Readers understand the importance of evidence and fair analysis of just what the evidence means. So readers match their knowledge and experience against what persuasive writers present. Readers look for facts and statistics, clear personal examples, quotations from authorities as well as treatment of evidence that would support the opposing view. If readers see all positive evidence but no explanation of data that support opponents, readers will reject the argument as incomplete or biased. If readers see unreasonable conclusions drawn from evidence presented, readers reject the logic of the argument. If readers see no evidence and only an emotional appeal, they again reject the argument as overly emotional.

In short, readers apply stringent criteria to arguments before they will be persuaded to writers' views. Writing successful arguments, then, requires the ability to put oneself in readers' shoes to project readers' reactions to the persuasive appeal of a paper.

Practice—Reading

The following article was intended as an objective evaluation of data on working women. But can you see a persuasive edge in the article?

Survey: Work in the 1980s and 1990s

Julia Kagan, *Working Woman*

Drawn from an American project conducted by Public Agenda research analyst Harvey Lauer in August and September, 1982, through personal interviews, a study reveals striking differences between men and women who work. Even more surprising—given these differences—are the similarities. More women than men have "an inner need to do the very best" they can "regardless of pay," and women seem to be more motivated. Among the most significant findings—particularly for our national debate on productivity—is the difference between job motivators (rewards people want that make them work harder) and job satisfiers (benefits that make people happier but don't affect their output).

Perhaps the most astonishing revelation in the survey concerns job satisfaction. Despite a decade of protest against the low salaries and limited opportunities that women encounter in the job market—inequities that show up as clearly in this questionnaire as they do in occupation and income data from the census—it turns out that women are not more dissatisfied with their jobs than men are. In fact, the majority seem quite satisfied.

To begin with, people are remarkably happy with the kind of work they do. An overwhelming 75 percent of men and women say that—aside from how much they earn or how they feel about the job they have at the moment—their current occupation is "right" for them, that there is a good match between their interests, temperament and abilities, and the type of work they do. Nearly 90 percent of professionals and managers feel this way, as do two-thirds of blue-collar workers and three-quarters of women with clerical jobs.

When asked, "If you had a choice, would you prefer to remain in your present job, change jobs but remain in the same occupation or change occupations?" the majority (51 percent) of the work force said that they would like to keep their present jobs. Only a quarter (26) percent want to change fields. Obviously, there are differences according to occupation—56 percent of white-collar workers would keep their jobs, while 45 percent of blue-collar workers would. But within occupations, there virtually is no sex difference.

But these are bad times, skeptics reading this might say, pointing to the timing of the survey—late last summer during a major recession. We don't think the economy has anything to do with the results. The question was not *will* you leave your job, but *would* you "if you had the choice." And most people would stick with their jobs. The only major deviation from the pattern is by age—34 percent of those under 30 would keep their jobs, while 80 percent of those over 55 would.

The mystery is why women are so satisfied. People were asked a long list of questions about various positive characteristics that jobs can have, and whether these describe their jobs "fully," "partly" or "not at all."

Looking at their occupation and educational background provides a better picture of the different conditions and attitudes that exist. Female professionals and managers are the only group of women to exceed the average "good pay" level of everyone who answered the survey, and they exceed it by only 1 point. The difference between male and female college graduates is particularly striking (26% of female and 50% of male college graduates report earning good pay). Women managers and professionals are again the only women who report that their jobs give them "a say in important decisions" and "a good chance of advancement." All the men except blue-collar workers respond positively to these questions.

Are women happier than one would expect because those in the survey were doing so extraordinarily well? They don't seem to be. The men—92 percent of whom work full time—have a median income of $18,885. For women, the number is $10,674. However, 24% of the women work part time; the median income of the full-timers is $11,720, still only 62 percent of men's. Female college graduates earn only 61 percent of what male grads earn ($15,000 compared to $24,444).

To find an answer to the paradox of why women are as satisfied with their jobs as men, you have to look at research on what makes people feel satisfied about their work. It turns out that people at different levels have different reasons for feeling good about their jobs.

Sociologists Nancy C. Morse and Robert S. Weiss noted in 1955 that "people in different occupations do not vary as greatly in whether or not they are satisfied with their jobs as they do in their reasons for their satisfaction." When discussing these reasons, managers mentioned salary much more frequently than did professionals and salespeople, who stressed the content of their work. People in service occupations—among the lowest paid—stressed that the jobs they had were the only ones they could get and that they derived pleasure from the people they worked with and met. In short, people emphasize the positive.

They also compare themselves to others at their level or among their friends. Researchers call this phenomenon "relative deprivation." In a major study published last year (*Relative Deprivation and Working Women*), psychologist Faye Crosby, Ph.D., notes that women in pink-collar jobs are least likely to express discontentment over the way things are at work, while executive and professional women who compare themselves to their male colleagues are much more disgruntled.

Crosby is not the first to observe that people who are doing very well often feel more unsuccessful and dissatisfied than others much lower down on the ladder. Looking at studies of men in 1969, psychologist Victor H. Vroom noted that first-line supervisors making over $12,000 were more satisfied than were company presidents making under $49,000.

Consider again the "good pay" issue: college women are much less likely to say that their jobs pay well than women as a whole are. Women with clerical jobs (median income: $11,702) are as likely to say they are well paid as women managers and professionals (median income: $14,111) are. And the managers and professionals, who earn less than college graduates (median income: $15,000), feel much better paid. (Not all managers and professionals are college graduates, of course.)

The answer seems clear. Money, power, and career prospects are not what make women feel good about their jobs. But women do report other rewards.

A number of job characteristics are related strongly to job satisfaction. We'll call these characteristics job-satisfaction factors. It's important to note, by the way, that the correlations we've found don't prove that these factors *cause* job satisfaction. But the differences in benefits that men and women point to in their jobs can permit us to make some guesses about what pleases them. Most of these factors are equally prevalent in men's jobs and women's jobs. Among the most important: managers who listen, recognition for good work, feeling informed, a company that does high-quality work, and a job with good procedures for getting work done.

The amazing difference is that men report having only two important job-satisfaction factors in higher numbers than women—good pay and a say in important decisions. Women report having eight.

The differences between men and women in these eight areas are striking—and substantial. Women are much more likely than men to say that their jobs fill certain "human relations" needs. For example, 59 percent of women report that their jobs allow them to work with people they like, compared to 43 percent of men. These feelings are even stronger from women managers and professionals (66/43) and college graduates (62/37). Women also are much more likely to say that they feel like part of a team at work and that the people for whom they work treat them with respect and care about them. Women are prouder of their companies than men are and more likely to say that they never are asked to do anything they consider improper or immoral—an element that turned out to correlate highly with people's job satisfaction. And women managers and professionals and those with high incomes are more likely than their male counterparts to say their jobs are challenging and let them learn new things.

What does all this mean? Are women revealed as patsies or simply reconciled to their fate? Are women's jobs really more humanly satisfying or are women just more likely to be satisfied by the human components in them? Crosby points to the danger inherent in accepting "psychic income" in lieu of financial rewards. This well may be what women are doing. What is clear is that the inequities women encounter—and report—are not alienating the majority from their jobs, at least not yet.

Practice—Analyzing

1. Is Kagan's main emphasis on information or persuasion? Why?

   _____

   _____

2. What word choices suggest her attitude toward the subject?

   _____

   _____

3. Could you imagine a more effective argument with a clearer structure for persuasion? Outline a thesis and possible arrangement.

   Thesis _____

   _____

   Possible order of arguments: _____

   _____

   _____

   _____

HOW DO WE WRITE PERSUASION?

Determine your audience

The first and most important key to writing successful arguments is knowing the audience. If readers weigh presented evidence against their own knowledge and experience, then writers must estimate just what readers know. If I were writing to a congressional committee on world hunger, I would include different evidence than if I were writing for a church group in a Midwest agricultural town. Similarly, if Schlafly and the *USA Today* editor were writing for *Working Woman* magazine, they would tailor their arguments differently. Sex, age, educational background, travel experience, political views, religion, and so on, can all be important factors when defining just what readers know. And before writers can persuade readers by analyzing evidence, writers must anticipate how much readers need information to form an opinion and how much readers are already committed to an opinion. One good technique for defining your audience is to pick a representative person from the group and describe that character in as much detail as possible. Then your argument will address that reader's need just as if you were in heated conversation.

Practice—Writing

Use the following chart to define three different audiences you might write to about some national controversial issue you're concerned about:

	Audience 1	Audience 2	Audience 3
Age			
Sex			
Education			
Occupation			
Place born			
Place raised			
Local attitudes			
Income			
Marital status			

Can you think of other variables that you would want to consider as you prepare an argument for these audiences?

Now use the chart again to define three audiences for a local controversy. For instance, at my school last year we had a major argument about censorship by our newspaper editors. We also have ongoing arguments about natural resources versus development in our county. Pick some issue important at your school or in your community. What elements of the chart must you change to help you determine your audience? (Remember to focus on one person who might read your essay were you to write it.)

	Audience 1	Audience 2	Audience 3
Age			
Sex			
Education			
Occupation			
Place born			
Place raised			
Local attitudes			
Income			
Marital status			

Know your own mind

Oddly enough, many writers discover when they begin working on an argument that the opposing view has more merit than they thought. Nothing can confuse readers more than a persuasive paper that shifts from its initial position to the opposite view. Always work through an argument thoroughly before you begin drafting your paper so that you can be consistent about your position.

Become an expert

One reason writers shift from one side of an argument to the other is that they *discover* important information as they research the controversy. Although you may be temporarily embarrassed by your inconsistency in viewpoint, learning enough about the subject to argue persuasively should help you maintain a view while you write.

Obviously, if readers evaluate the completeness and objectivity of evidence writers present, then writers must know as much about a topic as possible. Especially as they choose evidence appropriate for different audiences, writers must be aware of the range of information they can assume readers have and need. Only by being an expert can writers select appropriate detail.

Furthermore, a typical argument relies on expert testimony. As writers review material, they read about scholars and other experts who can contribute to their own arguments. But writers who are becoming experts themselves know how to evaluate the experts they quote. Should a writer quote someone claiming to be an expert who is known to be biased, then the "expert testimony" can backfire with readers. Writers must also evaluate more than the expertness of authorities. For instance, at a recent conference, a colleague pointed out that Edward Teller is clearly an authority on nuclear physics but asked if we would want Teller as our "expert" for a computer-aided system teaching advanced research methods in nuclear physics. Because of his political views, many educators would not want to rely on Teller's authority, even in an educational setting. Similarly, other experts may indeed know more than anyone else working in the field, but because of political, religious, moral, educational, or other biases, these experts may not be reliable authorities for the argument you want to present. Without knowing enough about the field and its authorities, you could undercut your argument by citing an expert your readers reject.

As you become an expert, then, do not ignore the motives other experts might have as they espouse their views. Choose authorities you and your readers will trust.

Practice—Reading

Analyze the evidence presented by this author. Given his position as President of the Therapeutic Communities of America and of Samaritan Village, Inc., is he a trustworthy expert?

Vocational Drug Use Costs Industry Billions

Richard Pruss, *USA Today*

> "The drugs had a lovely effect. They were doing everything they were supposed to, giving me untold energy." I said to myself: 'I can work here 13 hours a day and not even feel like I worked.'"

That's how Naomi, a crack legal secretary who was a conscientious worker, described her use of drugs on the job. Her routine use of drugs helped with the pressure, made the job satisfying, even exhilarating—until she collapsed.

Matty was in charge of a 25-man maintenance crew at a New York City apartment complex. He was proud of his responsibilities. The cocaine and the methadone he took helped make even the routine jobs interesting. But after a while, he didn't care anymore. "I'd do a lot of jobs myself—like plumbing. Then I'd go in the next day and see what I did when I was high the day before. The pipe wasn't level; the soldering was sloppy. It was like a completely different person had done it."

And for Ian, cocaine was one of the rewards of success. In his best year, he sold more than 200 luxury cars. He was 25 years old. "I felt I had more or less made it in life. I had reached the top of my profession, and cocaine and quaaludes went hand-in-hand in that type of lifestyle. I thought: 'It's time to start using cocaine; I can afford it now. I felt I owed myself cocaine.'"

There is no longer anything unusual about these stories—which come from clients at Samaritan Village, a drug rehabilitation program in New York City. In America in 1983, illicit drug abuse is no longer merely "recreational," it is now vocational. It is a multi-billion disaster for American industry and labor and a new formidable challenge to drug-abuse rehabilitation.

Insights gained by drug rehabilitation programs like Samaritan will help develop programs for the addicted or drug-dependent worker. There won't be any swift solutions.

And if employers and union leaders want results, they are going to have to think hard about how they handle people. If on-the-job pressures can produce drug abuse, is the best answer trying only to interdict drugs, or trying to relieve the pressures? As Ian told us: "When you are dealing with other sales people, and you are dealing with a boss who's bearing down on you, it might not be such a bad idea to run encounter groups, give people time to voice their opinions, give people a chance to know and express their feelings."

Encounter groups, expressing feelings frankly and fully, "ventilation"—these techniques have been part of drug rehabilitation for years. They can be one of the most effective means of fighting drug abuse on the job and off.

Practice—Writing

Jot down all the pro and con arguments you can think of for your local controversy. Now compare your list with your classmates'. What information would you have to find to become an expert in the field? Does your list suggest gaps in your understanding of the problem? Can you pool your knowledge for your group to become an expert?

PRO   CON

_____   _____

_____   _____

_____   _____

_____   _____

_____   _____

_____   _____

Now list sources you might go to for expert testimony. Who has experience with this issue? (Don't ignore personal experience as well.) List some sources who might be biased and thus not good authorities. Star those names. Again compare lists.

_____

_____

_____

_____

_____

Anticipate opposing arguments

After becoming an expert, persuasive writers know pertinent evidence both for their own positions and for the opposition. Writers must take account of the opposition because our culture expects writers to refute the major arguments opponents cite in their favor. Unless you know the topic thoroughly, you might not identify the most important opposition arguments. If you focus on minor points, your readers might suspect that you have no refutation for the opposition's major points. Once again, you must put yourself in your reader's shoes to evaluate which arguments must be refuted. Furthermore, while working on refuting your opponent, you will probably discover ways to strengthen your own arguments, a useful side-effect of anticipating the opposition.

Argue fairly

I've already mentioned that readers judge the trustworthiness of writers and that they evaluate writers' expertness, use of authorities, and treatment of the opposition. All these elements go into fairness in persuasion. But writers can also stumble into other traps. Let's review quickly some of the most common argumentative mistakes writers make.

Incomplete arguments

If we look again at Schlafly's editorial, we find arguments based on incomplete evidence. She cites the "Equal Employment Opportunity Act, which prohibits sex discrimination in jobs, pay and promotions." Yet, in July 1984, several years after Congress passed this act, the Supreme Court ruled that because there is no Constitutional guarantee of equal pay, women need not be paid the same salary for performing the same job as men. Schlafly gives us pertinent information, but not all of it. A congressional act does not have the force of Constitutional law, and states are free to enforce acts as they wish.

Arguments ad hominem

Unfortunately, we see many of these arguments, especially in political debates. Literally, this fallacy means arguing "to the man." If a person has some shortcoming, using that flaw as an argument against the position he or she holds is illogical. For example, just because a politician was once treated for depression does not make the laws he proposes bad laws. A similar fallacy, *ad populum,* draws on the general prejudices of a group as an argumentative technique. Flag-waving or calling an opponent a "Commie" are both illogical and ineffective techniques. (We could consider Schlafly's "gay rights" argument as an *ad populum* argument against ERA.)

Bandwagon

"Just because everyone else is doing something, so should you." We all try this argument on our parents, but it generally doesn't work. Don't try it on readers.

Cause-effect

When one event causes another, then we can argue about causes and effects. But we must be careful not to call one event a cause just because it happens *before* a second event. Just because I tripped over the telephone cord ten seconds ago doesn't cause the phone to ring now. We recognize the illogical relationship in simple cases like this one, but we need to see the same fallacy in some cause-effect relationships dealing with more complex or distant events.

Hasty generalization

We need to avoid drawing a conclusion from just one or two examples that do not represent the range of possibilities. For instance, if we have gone to a grocery store twice and it was out of an item, we cannot conclude that it never has that item. This logical problem often occurs when we group people together or label them unfairly. Although some politicians are unscrupulous, we cannot argue that all politicians cheat their constituents.

Faulty analogy

Often we can compare less familiar objects to more familiar objects to help readers understand the less familiar. But when we make analogies, we must take care to compare only those objects, persons, or events that are similar. Most analogies break down when pushed to the limit, but we should argue only with analogies that help explain. And where the analogy does not represent a true comparison, we should say so.

Circular reasoning

Schlafly again demonstrates this fallacy when she argues that the ERA will "mandate" gay/lesbian rights. Because this is a point of the controversy, Schlafly should prove that the ERA will have this effect, but instead she assumes the result and then claims she has proven it. Proving what you assume in the first place is not good argumentative technique.

Other traps

Most readers recognize quickly other flaws in reasoning that might appear in arguments. Among the most straightforward are conclusions that don't follow from the premises of an argument, polarization of an argument into two possible solutions when more than two are reasonable, and claiming that people are experts when they have no special claim to authority. Commercials that use stars to sell products as if the stars were authorities exemplify this final category.

Practice—Finding faulty arguments

Read this satirical piece on ERA. If this were a serious argument, what logical flaws would you identify?

Who'd Trade 'Primp Time' for Overtime?

Edgar Berman, *USA Today*

Just a hundred years or so ago, it was a toss-up whether a man would hitch his jackass or his wife to the plow. Yet the feminists are already nagging to compete with the male—not the mule.

In that short time, they claim to have "come a long way." But they're still grumbling that punching a typewriter doesn't pay as well as welding a girder 60 stories up.

They just don't know when they're well off. All the wonders of consciousness-raising and assertiveness training will never replace the sacrifices in femininity women will have to make to play in the male money league.

Sure, the female worker has lost her horse collar callouses. But they're now replaced by scars on her belly from slithering along five miles down in a West Virginia coal mine. So she's getting equal pay as she scrubs equal scads of soot from her equally clogged pores—that treatment won't produce the Oil of Olay skin you love to touch.

As a bonus, she can now be equally trapped with her male competitors when the mine disaster strikes.

It's even worse when she gives up waitressing and filing to hustle on an assembly line. I would guess that the average office female makes 509 visits to the lavatory to a male's 230, and spends 10.7 minutes there to a male's 2.5. What management is going to put up with this 'primp time' featherbedding at equal pay?

In another field, former followers of Jimmy Hoffa admit that the female can jackknife a tractor trailer with the best of them, but how would she stack up working on the goon squad? Can the union expect explosive results from her when her hormones are raging?

To top it all off, what real woman is going to give up that most pleasurable overtime of office work—the joy of harassment—just to earn more money as a pipe-fitter? After all, 85 percent of all office affairs start on the boss's lap. And though Steinem may run workshops against it, what is one secretary's harassment is another's ecstasy.

So ladies, if you take your money, you'll pay the price. But which is better: getting equal pay while bulldozing a foundation on an icy January morning, or selling Jim Palmer his jockey shorts behind a nice warm counter in Bloomingdale's?

Now read this serious article on censorship. Does it contain any flaws in logic?

Ignorance of Censors Never Varied

David Rossie, *USA Today*

The news from Texas that representatives of an organization called People for the American Way has been able to battle the gabbling Gabblers to a standstill is encouraging. But to celebrate it as a major victory over book censorship would be premature, not to mention dangerous. The spiritual descendants of Anthony Comstock have been with us for a long time in one guise or another, and they are not about to strike their colors after one skirmish.

In a previous incarnation as an education writer, I covered countless confrontations between school librarians and English teachers on one side and self appointed censors on the other. The books at issue varied from *Brave New World* to a kindergarten tome that featured two rabbits, one black, the other white, and all that seemed to imply. One thing didn't vary, however: The ignorance of the censors and their eagerness to share it.

My favorite encounter pitted a local parent group against a high school English teacher who had assigned his class the book *Hog Butcher*. *Hog Butcher,* a quick reading convinced me, would not make it onto anyone's great books list. But I suppose it is a fair description of what it's like to grow up poor and black on the South Side of Chicago. The confrontation took place in the school library, and that alone seemed to make the protesters restive, as if they were surrounded by evil. Their chief spokesman was a truculent fellow who spoke of the continuing struggle to preserve his daughter's chastity and the danger such books posed to it. Should his fair flower be forced to continue to read such filth, the man declared, he would withdraw her from this sinkhole of permissiveness.

The board of education eventually struck a compromise that allowed the teacher to continue using the book, while making other books available to children who were uncomfortable with *Hog Butcher*. That seemed like an equitable solution, but it wasn't the end of the story. A couple of weeks later, the man who had fretted so long and loud about his daughter being corrupted by *Hog Butcher* was arrested by state police for sexually harrassing a young woman hitch-hicker he had picked up.

I figure he got the idea out of a book.

Use emotional appeal carefully

Although emotional appeal can sometimes convince readers, such appeals have little lasting influence on the thinking reader. Overusing an emotional appeal can influence readers negatively, in fact, if they perceive that emotion substitutes for logic in a writer's analysis. Schlafly, unfortunately, again provides examples of this technique. She claims that ERA would require women to register for the draft. In fact, that claim is true. But she goes on to say that draft registration is a "grievous take-away of young women's traditional rights." The emotional appeal to the sanctity of womanhood covers up the logical argument that draft registration perhaps infringes on men's rights. Our government has traditionally looked upon exemption from military service not as a "right" but as a "privilege" for women. Countries like Israel have long included women in the military, and we allow women to volunteer for military service, so women are capable of serving. How then is exemption from registration a "right"? Moreover, even if registered, women need not be drafted. We might then argue that draft registration currently discriminates against men, but Schlafly makes an emotional appeal to the view of women as dainty, tender, and unable to defend themselves and their country. The emotional appeal is not effective when scrutinized.

How can writers use emotion effectively? Let us recall some advertisements that show starving children. Those emotional appeals often effectively open people's pocketbooks. Similarly, a striking incident can create an emotional atmosphere that encourages readers to think well of your argument. But writers must consider readers carefully. A student on our campus wrote an editorial calling for more lighting on heavily traveled sidewalks where women were subject to late-night attacks. He opened with a description of a particularly brutal rape. While he convinced some readers, others quit reading before the end of the first paragraph. Vivid incidents used for emotional impact rather than logical analysis can turn readers off.

Consider, though, the other editorial at the beginning of this chapter. In "Women Deserve Absolute Equality" the author includes several statistics that together create a picture of female poverty. Without the overt emotionalism of Schlafly's editorial, these statistics create a logical argument balanced with a humanitarian, emotional appeal. When writers balance logic and emotion, their arguments are more effective in convincing readers.

Practice—Using emotional appeal

1. Find an editorial that overuses emotional appeal. Be prepared to discuss with classmates why the emotional appeal is not effective. What logical flaws does the emotional appeal mask?

2. Read Shawn's essay to consider its use of emotion.

Medicaid: A Worthwhile Savings?

In an era of rampant inflation, where national deficits soar past the one trillion dollar mark with hardly a murmur of notice from the populace, it is of little surprise that the important ideas are often overlooked. When the government becomes preoccupied with spending more and more money on defense, private industry, and foreign intervention, all too often it ignores the common man. One of the most easily forgotten segments of our population is the elderly. Specifically, those often ignored are the elderly who, for one reason or another, are forced to live in nursing homes. Many of these people live on income provided by such organizations as Medicaid. A few people abuse the privilege of these benefits, but most nursing home residents on Medicaid need this help to cover the costs of living. Surprisingly, in light of this definite need, Medicaid remains one of the first organizations to receive cuts in funding by the same government that constantly increases spending in most other departments. Our elderly have already paid their debt to society. They have lived full lives, defended our nation, and paid a lifetime of taxes in support of government programs. And yet, this same government now seeks to deny them aid during the time that they need help the most. The government now asks the families of these nursing home residents to take up the load left by Medicaid cuts. The advantages to these budget cuts have not been documented. The disadvantages are obvious. The Federal Government should immediately increase the funding to the Medicaid program for the institutionalized elderly until its budget returns to the pre-cut level.

The lawmakers in favor of continued Medicaid cuts invariably cite one reason for continuing to decrease funding to the program. This reason is that by making funding cuts to the program they will somehow alleviate the financial deficits of both state and federal governments. This argument proves not entirely true, as I will examine later. Accepting its validity for the moment, however, we can examine the rest of their argument. The proponents of this argument rationalize the cuts to elderly Medicaid patients by stating that children of these nursing home residents should be responsible for helping to settle their parent's health care expenses. The history of this country, they point out, is filled with a rich tradition of children taking care of their sick or disabled parents. In addition, lawmakers such as governer Dick Lamm of Colorado maintain that the government shouldn't be responsible for paying the health care costs of families that make $100,000 a year.[1] By forcing children of nursing home patients to take up some of the slack left by Medicaid cuts, more Medicaid money will remain for the truly indigent living in these homes.

When we examine the previous arguments in an enlightened way, we find them highly misleading at best. The main point that these Medicaid budget cuts will save government money is somewhat true, but not to the degree that the argument's originators would like us to believe. From the period of 1974 to 1980, Medicaid budget increases grew at a level approximately equal to the general cost of living increase of the same time.[2] The Reagan Administration began to cut the Medicaid Program as soon as President Reagan gained office in 1981. For fiscal year 1982, the Federal Government allocated 29.9 billion dollars to the Medicaid program, of which 8.3 billion went to the medically needy in nursing homes.[3] Reagan himself is not sure how much money the cuts will actually save, but he estimates the savings to be less than 500 million per year.[4] A few quick calculations show that these projected savings will comprise less than a 1.7% decrease in the Medicaid annual budget. Viewed somewhat differently, this decrease is a mere one-twentieth of one percent of the national deficit. Clearly if capital savings are the primary motive behind Medicaid cuts, the government can find much bigger budget reductions elsewhere.

The idea that the children of nursing home residents can help defray the costs of health care left from these Medicaid cuts is also false. When Congress first established Medicaid, the primary intent was to preclude making relatives other than spouses contribute to the cost.[5] In addition, national statisticians have determined that fifty percent of institutionalized elderly are childless.[6] Obviously Medicaid budget reductions will affect these elderly as well as those with children. Even among those nursing home residents who do have surviving children, the same statistics show that sixty-six percent of these families earn less than $14,999 per year. Of these, forty three percent earn less than $10,000.[7] Apparently the independently wealthy families who can support their elderly parents form a small minority. An additional consideration is that many nursing home patients are in their seventies or eighties, and their children, in their fifties or sixties, are spending their limited funds in preparation for their own future health care.[8]

Even if children were able to support their elderly parents, difficulties inherent in the system of collecting the funds negate any proposed Medicaid savings. The five hundred million dollar savings projected by President Reagan fails to consider the cost of initiating and maintaining a complex program to collect the money from widely scattered and probably unwilling relatives.[9] Another consideration advanced by such experts as Elma Holder, Executive Director of the National Citizens Coalition for Nursing Home Reform, is that the detailed financial information necessary for such a program would constitute an invasion of privacy for the families involved.[10]

The average nursing home resident must pay a cost of between $1200 and $1400 per month, or up to $17,000 per year.[11] These costs are just the beginning, as most elderly accrue additional medical and personal costs which can easily push the total over $25,000 a year. Clearly a healthy Medicaid budget, unhampered by needless cuts, is required to help cover these tremendous costs. If the elderly patient even has a surviving family, chances are they are already helping out in various supplemental tasks such as purchasing clothing and medication, or doing laundry, etc.[12] Most families can't afford to cover the losses caused by careless bureaucratic cuts, and logically, there is no reason why they should have to. If government officials merely consider the potential harm involved in cutting this needed program, perhaps they will decide to divert some of the funds used to destroy life into a department where the money can be used to preserve life.

—*Shawn H.*

Notes

[1] "Bill Children for Parents' Nursing Care?" *U.S. News and World Report,* August 15, 1983, p. 51.

[2] Robert Pear, "Medicaid Cutback Proposed," *New York Times,* April 2, 1982, p. 1-A.

[3] Ibid.

[4] Ibid., p. 12-A.

[5] "Bill Children for Parents' Nursing Care?" p. 51.

[6] Abigail Traford, "Are Medicare, Medicaid Going Belly Up?" *U.S. News and World Report,* Sept. 6, 1983, p. 37.

[7] Ibid., p. 37.

[8] Pete McWilliams, "Important Information," *Concerned Relatives and Friends of Nursing Home Residents,* Sept. 11, 1983, p. 2.

[9] Ibid.

[10] "Bill Children for Parents' Nursing Care?" p. 52.

[11] Traford, p. 2.

[12] "Bill Children for Parents' Nursing Care?" p. 52.

Focus your argument

As you will have discovered by now, by becoming an expert and by outlining all the opposition arguments, you have accumulated more evidence and analysis than you can probably use in a short paper. Concentrating on your readers will help you select the most pertinent information for them, but you will probably need to focus still more to persuade fully. Because details convince more readily than generalities do, writers must begin their arguments from a reasonably focused position or else they cover too much territory without enough detail to persuade. Thus, focusing improves your ability to convince readers. Let's consider another pair of editorials on scholastic standards to see if these writers have focused enough to be convincing.

Practice—Reading

Passing Kids Along Does Them No Favor

USA Today

With pomp and ceremony, 2.8 million young men and women are graduating from high school this spring. If past performance is a guide, 12 percent of those graduates are functionally illiterate—but every one will have a diploma. Thousands won't be able to write a letter or to balance a checkbook—but every one will have a diploma. Thousands more won't have even the basic skills needed to fill entry-level jobs—but every one will have a diploma. When prestigious private colleges as well as wide-open public universities have to teach poorly prepared freshmen what they should have learned in high school, something is wrong. When three out of four businessmen say they have to provide remedial instruction to prepare high school graduates to start work, something is wrong.

When thousands of pupils are moved in lock step through 12 years of school and handed diplomas without reasonable standards, something is radically wrong.

Even so, there is resistance to doing anything about it. When New York and Florida sought to impose minimal standards for high school diplomas, they had to fight off lawsuits implying that students have a right to a diploma after keeping their chairs warm for 12 years. Minneapolis tests kindergarteners to see if they're ready for first grade and provides summer school for those who aren't. The notion of flunking 5-year-olds draws flak, but it makes more sense to deal with learning problems when they appear, rather than passing them on untreated.

If we're serious about improving education, we've got to get over the notion that all 5-year-olds, all 12-year-olds, all 17-year-olds are alike— and must be treated alike. There is no magic in moving youngsters in blocks through 12 one-year units from age 6 to 18. Here and abroad, alternatives abound: Children can start school when they're ready and go as fast as they can. If we want quality education, we must be willing to back a system based on performance, not social promotion. Educators who bemoan the lack of citizen support for school budgets would probably find taxpayers more supportive if they were convinced that schools were demanding reasonable standards of performance. Equal opportunity requires that slow learners and the learning disabled be given help and extra time to develop their abilities. Common sense demands that academic achievers be stimulated to progress as far as they can. But schools that give diplomas to illiterate 18-year-olds do no favor to those young people or to society. Meaningless diplomas are an abuse that distorts education, misleads employers and cheats our children.

Keeping Kids Back Can Ruin Young Lives

Milly Cowles, *USA Today*

Listen to most educators and editorial pages these days, and you'd think America's schools should look like the assembly line at General Motors. At every stage of production, they seem to say, children must be hammered and tested and bolted down alike. And if they come down the conveyor belt anyway, weed them out and throw them back. To our academic efficiency experts, that's quality control. Defective products, they say, shouldn't be promoted. So maybe it's time to restate the obvious, even if these days it sounds like heresy: Children are not products. They are individuals who are different and who grow and learn at different speeds. If we turn our schools into factories and our curriculums into one long standardized test, we won't make our children smarter—but we will ruin a lot of them trying.

Here's the way you program a child for failure. First you decide that when he is 6 years old he must read by September, whether he's ready or not. If he can't, he flunks kindergarten. It would be cruel to pass him, you say; that would be "social promotion." Never mind that making him repeat a grade makes him feel ashamed and stupid. Never mind that studies show that when most children are held back, they don't do any better the second time around. You ignore all that and establish competency tests to make sure that no child slips through the failure net. You label them "developmentally slow" and put them in classes for the "learning disabled."

But what do you do when they go to learning disability classes forever? What do you do when they stay in the second grade five years? We all want children to learn more. We all want school to be better. But the way to do it is not to make every child conform to one artificial standard. It is to design schools that meet the needs of real children. It can happen. It doesn't cost much money. It is a matter of attitude. We need to recognize that classrooms shouldn't be pressure-cookers. We need to understand that just because a child can't read by age 6 doesn't mean he's a "failure." It does mean that we think of a child's progress as continuous. We don't arbitrarily measure it once a year as a way to hold him back; instead, we help him go forward. Treat children as individuals and they will flourish—and become healthy, well-rounded achievers. Treat them as products and you will produce unhappy children—and a dead level of mediocrity.

Practice—Analyzing

1. Where do you find a statement that expresses the authors' opinions on passing children?

USA Today editor	Milly Cowles

_____   _____

_____   _____

2. Do both editorials seem equally objective? Cite examples of words and arguments that set the tone of each editorial.

       USA Today editor   Milly Cowles

_____   _____

_____   _____

_____   _____

_____   _____

_____   _____

3. What kind of evidence does each author use? Be specific as you create categories for evidence.

       USA Today editor   Milly Cowles

_____   _____

_____   _____

_____   _____

_____   _____

4. Did you have an opinion on this issue before you started reading? Did one editorial express your opinion? Did the other editorial sway you? If you had no opinion when you began reading, do you have

one now? Why? _____

_____

_____

_____

5. What persuasive techniques do these authors use that you would like

to practice in your own writing? _____

_____

_____

6. Do any words or phrases create negative attitudes without facts to
base them on? Cite examples.

USA Today editor	Milly Cowles
_____	_____
_____	_____
_____	_____

7. Which editorial is more convincing? Why? _____

_____

_____

Finding a focus for an argument

You can consider all the reading and thinking you do to become an expert as part of your prewriting. Listing the characteristics of your audience and the pro/con arguments certainly contributes to prewriting. With this prewriting, you can focus by asking yourself how much time you have to develop an argument (2 pages, ten pages, sixty pages?) and which arguments are most important to you and your readers. Although you are concerned with the social stigma and psychological stress attached to failing in school, your own arguments have more to do with the consequences for society when high-school graduates cannot find jobs because they lack basic skills. Or perhaps you have been touched by the unfairness of grades assigned to you and school athletes. If so, you might want to focus on scholastic standards for competing athletes. Or you might focus on academic honesty. Let your own experiences and interests determine the focus of your argument. But be sure to consider what an opponent would say about the specific evidence and analysis you present so that you match your arguments and refutation on the same points.

Practice—Revising topic sentences

The following topic sentences are taken out of the context of the paragraphs they controlled, but you should be able to analyze each to determine if it is adequately focused and what it predicts about the paragraph. Revise those topic sentences that are not focused.

1. I think it's a good idea for high school students to hold part-time jobs because it gives them the independence of having their own hard-earned money to do as they want with rather than having to depend on their parents for funds.

   Revision: _____

   _____

2. Basic Writing should be changed for me and others who want to wait and maybe decide that we don't need it.

   Revision: _____

   _____

3. I feel that Basic Writing should be kept in the requirements because it is a good review in writing and mechanical skills that will help the students in other courses.
   Revision:

   _____

   _____

4. While in high school, I found it essential to maintain a part-time afternoon job to save me from small emergency situations.

   Revision: _____

   _____

Practice—Revising thesis statements

The following thesis statements are taken out of the context of the essays they controlled, but you should be able to analyze each to determine if it is adequately focused and what it predicts about the essay. Evaluate essay maps as well. Revise those thesis statements that are not adequately focused for a short persuasive essay. You might try adding an essay map if it would help to focus the thesis.

1. In necessary attempts to combat alcohol and drug use, poor grades, and poor attendance, school boards have begun to use suspension from athletics as a deterrent.

   Revision: _____

   _____

   _____

2. The bill authorizing the appropriation of funds for research and development of chemical weapons should be repealed.

   Revision: _____

   _____

   _____

3. The president's budget cuts in youth employment programs are definitely not the solution to reducing the federal deficit.

   Revision: _____

   _____

   _____

4. The federal government should increase allocations for education from the federal budget, satisfying the want and need for merit pay, plus improving teaching with incentives for improved productivity.

   Revision: _____

   _____

   _____

   _____

GETTING IDEAS FOR PERSUASION

Jot down all the pro and con arguments you can think of for passing students whether or not they have mastered basic skills. Now compare your list with your classmates'. What information would you have to find to become an expert in the field? Does your list suggest gaps in your understanding of the problem? Can you pool your knowledge to become a group expert?

PRO	CON
_____	_____
_____	_____
_____	_____
_____	_____
_____	_____

Now list sources you might go to for expert testimony. Who has experience with this issue? (Don't ignore personal experience as well.) List some sources who might be biased and thus not good authorities. Star those names. Again compare lists.

_____

_____

_____

_____

APPLYING PERSUASION

Read the following persuasive essays and consider the focus, development, and arrangement of arguments.

The Payment-in-Kind Program is Very Kind . . . to Farmers

It appalls me to think of starving people around the world that could be fed with the U.S. government's surpluses of grain. The amount of surplus grain our country is holding is phenomenal. But now, as well as others around the would, our farmers are hungry. The government has adopted the PIK Program to solve the problems of the farm commodities surpluses and of the poor financial status of the nation's farmers. The federal budget allotment for the PIK program of $21 billion dollars is a justified expenditure in order to get the farmers of our nation back on a steady financial basis while decreasing surplus grain at the same time. It helps the farmers and the government by decreasing the surplus, decreasing farm expenses, and decreasing grain exports.

The issue in the forefront of PIK is the government surplus of commodities such as wheat, corn, sorghum, and cotton. What PIK is trying to accomplish is to get rid of the government surplus that just keeps growing while helping farmer's financial status by raising overall farm commodity prices. The surplus figures speak for themselves: the Department of Agriculture states that in 1974, the surplus of corn in millions of bushels was only 484 but the estimates for the 1983 surplus stand at 3447 million bushels. As for wheat, in 1974 the surplus was at 340 million bushels, while in 83 the estimates again are considerably higher at 1461 million bushels.[1] Opponents to PIK believe that giving away this grain to farmers who set aside crop acreage won't even make a dent in the surplus. History, however, helps to show this is not the case. The basic PIK formulation came about in the late 20s and early 30s in the midst of the Great Depression. In the 30s, this kind of program curbed cotton planting and in the 60s, reduced feed grain production with good results.[2] As an example, the government asks Farmer Joe, a wheat farmer, to set aside 20% of his acreage. For compensation, the government gives him cash and continued price support protection. For any amount of acreage over 20%, Farmer Joe receives government surplus crops as extra compensation.[3] This decreases the amount grown, makes an obvious dent in the government surplus, and increases farm commodity prices as well as Farmer Joe's amount of relaxation time.

Another point of the opponents is that President Reagan is spending too much on PIK. Reagan's budget proposed that the government spend $21 billion on PIK to get rid of this surplus. The reason for spending is sound: it will get rid of a $5 billion dollar expense that the government pays every 2 years to store and maintain the quality of the surplus grain.[4] It will help raise farm commodity prices by decreasing the overall supply. It will bring in income tax to the government from the farmers who will pay these taxes on the free grain they choose to sell. It will slash farm expenses, save on seed, herbicide, fertilizer, and equipment costs, just to name a few. This will then enable them to start paying off loans and help bring down the 1983 projected national farm debt of $218 billion.[5] By paying off their loans and helping to decrease the farm debt, this will get them "out of the red" with their creditors.

Opponents also claim that the PIK program will reduce national export figures. Although food is the number one United States export, the demand for it has slackened in foreign markets. One of the main causes in the decline in U.S. grain exports was the Carter Administration's USSR grain embargo. In 1979, the Soviets purchased $2.1 billion worth of grain from the U.S. After the embargo was instated, their purchases dropped by $700 million to $1.4 billion dollars a year.[6] Instead of being dependent on the U.S. for grain, they chose alternate suppliers such as Canada, Australia, and Argentina. The grain that is no longer being sent there is causing government expenditures for storage, and economic havoc due to low farm prices. Since the export figures are not being lowered by overproduction but by governmental actions, using PIK to maintain a lower surplus and higher farm prices is beneficial.

The opposition also believes that few farmers would be eager to participate and that changes in economic figures would not be seen for a long while. As for the eagerness to join, one example is from Panola County, Mississippi (693 square miles and a 1980 population of 28,164)[7], where every cotton and wheat farmer opted to sign up for the PIK program. They knew that they would make more money by selling government surplus at higher prices rather than helping to create more of a surplus at lower prices. As for economic changes, in January of 1983, when the program was officially installed, the going price for a bushel of corn was around $2. By the end of May, 1983, the signs of progress were beginning to show since the price per bushel had risen to $3 over six months.[8] One of the goals of PIK was to increase farm prices.

If the PIK program continues to go as planned, it will help the government and the farmers of our country. Although the opponents do have valid arguments, the evidence supports Reagan's decision to spend the $21 billion to help our nation's farmers.

—*Lisa K.*

Notes

[1] "Reagan Revives 50-Year-Old Crop Swap," *U.S. News and World Report,* 94 (January 14, 1983), 7.

[2] Ibid.

[3] Ibid.

[4] Ibid.

[5] "Going Against the Grain," *Time,* 121 (April 4, 1983), 29.

[6] "The Golden Glut," *Nation's Business,* 71 (March 1983), 34–36.

[7] 1983 *Commercial Atlas & Marketing Guide,* 114th edition (Chicago: Rand McNally, 1983).

[8] "A Turnaround Year for America's Farmers?" *U.S. News and World Report,* 94 (May 30, 1983), 49–50.

Public Television Funding

Big Bird bounces happily across the screen while the announcer states the preceding program has been brought to you by the letter A and the number four. In one year, if budget cuts continue, "Sesame Street" may have a real sponsor such as Coco-Puffs or may not even continue on the air. Congressman Timothy Wirth of Colorado, as Chairman of the Subcommittee on Telecommunications, Consumer Protection and Finance has stated that further cuts in public broadcasting "do not seem to me to be fair nor to be appropriate to the fabric of public broadcasting and the role that public broadcasting plays in the United States." I, too, feel that further cutting of funds from 137 million to 116.5 million could end public broadcasting as we know it within five years. Public broadcasting needs this level of funding for many reasons including its lack of advertisements, the different audience focus that it offers, and because putting public T.V. on cable to receive money would only hurt viewers.

Many on the side of budget cuts, including President Reagan, feel public broadcasting, although necessary, can receive funding elsewhere through such sources as corporate sponsors, cable pay television, and more extensive fund drives. In 1982, one sponsor, American Telephone and Telegraph, contributed a record $10 million to the MacNeil/Lehrer Report, a Public Broadcasting Service program devoted to news. Proponents for cuts feel sponsors like AT&T can receive longer "plugs" between programs, thereby bringing in the $20 million shortfall for PBS. Michael Kinsley in *Harper's* magazine states that with the advent of pay cable television public broadcasting can eventually receive funds by adding stations to the booming cable market. Another viable alternative already in use for raising the necessary funds from sources other than the government—fund raising drives—has also received mention by those in favor of cuts.

Advertisements, so annoying and time consuming on commercial television, have yet to invade the Public Broadcasting System. Keeping corporate advertisements off public broadcasting remains not just important from the annoyance standpoint but from the fact that corporate sponsors can and will influence programming. In a series aired last year on PBS, "Creativity," Chevron, the sponsor, influenced the program so much that it became sappy and non-controversial. During one segment, the interviewer asked Jerry Brown, a controversial figure, idiotic questions including queries about his childhood, while leaving other questions unasked. Chevron, wanting to sidestep controversy and build a favorable corporate reputation, became the sole reason for the show. This clearly illustrates the unneeded influence corporate sponsors can have on a possibly good program. Sponsors such as Mobil, Gulf, and Chevron have led many to call PBS the Petroleum Broadcasting System; but the undue influence these corporations have has not yet severely hurt public broadcasting, but with further federal cuts corporations can gain more influence and possibly ruin public broadcasting.

According to a survey by WNET, a public broadcasting station in New York, the average median income of a PBS viewer, $43,000 a year, shows that most of the viewers have an above average intelligence, watching PBS for its intellectually stimulating programming. Since a certain viewer watches and listens to public broadcasting, decreasing funding for it could possibly leave these viewers with little or no stimulating programming on commercial television. Network programs such as "Love Boat" and "Three's Company" offer little stimulation for the mind. The argument given by budget cut proponent Jeff Blydal of *Forbes* states that since the median income is so high, the viewer ought to be able to afford donations during special viewer "appreciation" weeks and annual auctions given by the public stations. The money taken by these auctions on the average makes up 28% of the operating budget of the public stations, and if federal budget cuts went into effect next year, these stations, because of saturation, would have trouble squeezing more money out of these auctions. WNET now has three pledge weeks a year plus an annual auction, but with federal cuts they would need up to two or three more pledge weeks. These weeks defeat the purpose of noncommercial television because, like commercials, they interrupt regular programming and can become an annoyance. Another negative point of these weeks is the programming that sometimes eliminates regular viewers of PBS because it gears itself to a popular audience by showing old movies such as "Bonzo Goes to College."

Another opponent's argument favors cable as a method to supply funds for public television stations, but this too has many flaws that can't be overlooked. Jeff Blydal states that PBS cable, a new system being proposed could produce a good flow of new operating income for stations. Unfortunately, Blydal fails to mention the lack of cable facilities in such remote places as Butte, Montana, or Laramie, Wyoming, which both right now have public broadcasting but, with Blydal's proposal, would lose these stations. Since public broadcasting is just that—public—consideration must be given to everybody, not just city dwellers. Another point budget cut proponents fail to mention, the time factor, Congressman Wirth feels must receive consideration. Wirth's research indicates that a town such as Butte would have a four to eight year delay in getting cable while many people in large cities, including Denver, still have not received cable service and may not for up to five years. If public stations, because of budget cuts, become forced to move to cable, the viewers who previously had PBS could lose their stations either temporarily, or in some places, permanently.

The three front range stations in Colorado now receiving funds from the federal government—KRMA TV in Denver, KBDI TV in Broomfield, and KCFR radio in Denver, all would have to use at least one of the the previously outlined funding solutions if budget cuts were enacted. All three solutions, though, could hurt programming at the stations or even worse end all programming. A survey taken in January showed that 58% of all American homes watched public television, while spending on public television amounts to only 20% of a commercial network's annual revenues. Federal budget cuts may not destroy public television's diverse programming, but they would definitely hurt many shows. Replacing the whimsical sponsors such as the letter A and the number four with Coco-Puffs on "Sesame Street" will bring in money, but will this money only destroy a once educational and high quality children's program?

—Greg H.

REVISING TO IMPROVE LOGICAL AND PERSUASIVE DEVELOPMENT

Look at Paul's attempt at arguing against keeping a fundamental writing course. What does he focus on? Is his argument logical?

Mr. Jenkins,

Being a student presently enrolled in fundamental writing, I feel that the class has no purpose, positive learning effects, and it is also a waste of students' time and it should be abolished. After completing twelve weeks of the course, I have found that all the material has been a boring review and a waste of my time. I am not the only one who feels this way. After talking to other students in the class, I have found that there are no positive views by any of the students. All agree that the class has no purpose and would rather be in freshman comp. After being asked what they had learned, many students replied "nothing" or "how to waste good time." Perhaps if workshops were set up for those needing help in freshman comp, the students would not feel so disagreeable. Still many other pitfalls remain in fundamental composition. The pass/fail grading is one area where students get discouraged. The fact that "A" work is the same as "C" work makes it difficult to put out any more effort than is needed. This lack of effort may be reflective of the amount of planning that went into making the course. With these reasons, I feel that the course should be abolished and taken out of the program.

—*Paul W.*

As you discovered, Paul hasn't focused on a single point, and as a result his paragraph jumps from idea to idea without developing any one in detail. Do you notice, moreover, any illogical arguments in Paul's paper? What would you suggest Paul do to improve the logical structure of his paper? Right now, Paul sounds unhappy but not convincing. After he thought about the point he was most concerned about, he revised his paragraph:

Mr. Jenkins,

As a student presently enrolled in fundamental writing, I have found the grading to be very discouraging and confusing. The fact that a pass/fail system is in effect creates many negative thoughts and feelings. With a pass/fail system, the student has no real goal to strive for. It is difficult for one to accept that "A" work is the same as "C" work. This grading makes it discouraging and creates a lack of effort among students. Not only is it discouraging, but many pupils find it confusing. There is no logic behind this type of grading. With no in-betweens, many normally below-average students don't pass. This grading is foolish and is another reason to abolish this course.

Now Paul focuses on just one reason to abolish the fundamental course, but he doesn't give enough examples and details to develop his idea concretely. Can you suggest specific revisions Paul might now make? What other changes would you make in this paragraph?

Now analyze the following paragraph that also considers the value of the fundamental writing course:

Dear Mr. Jenkins,
I would like to encourage you to keep the course entitled CO101 for the simple reason that it gives the struggling writer an opportunity to improve the different techniques required in writing paragraphs. Among these is the narrative paragraph in which the student learns to organize his ideas into a story. He learns to organize his paper in a flowing, easy-to-read manner. Another paragraph he writes is the persuasive, where he organizes his ideas in an attempt to change or persuade the readers' feelings on a particular subject. This gives the writer a chance to express his feelings in an authoritarian way. Finally, the student takes two ideas and examines them closely to write what is known as a comparison/contrast paragraph. Here he formulates his paper in an almost persuasive manner to prove his point. All these techniques together help the student in improving his writing ability and helping to express himself clearly as well as form his own style.

—*Mark R.*

If you had to choose one skill Mark should continue working on, what would you tell him? What other revisions would improve his paragraph, especially to make it more convincing?

WRITING PERSUASION

1. Read the conflicting views on high school standards presented in "Passing Kids Along Does Them No Favor" and "Keeping Kids Back Can Ruin Young Lives." After listing pros and cons for giving diplomas to all students who attend high school, whether they learn mate-

rial or not, write a paragraph or short persuasive essay arguing for the main reason you feel students should or should not be given diplomas based on their mastery of basic skills.

2. Read the excerpt from "Survey: Work in the 1980s and 1990s," published in *Working Woman,* April 1983, pp. 26–28. Keeping in mind that women work for less money but report greater job satisfaction and that men apparently need less "psychic income" to be happy with jobs, write a paragraph or short essay arguing for the main reason you instead of another equally qualified person should be hired for a job you are both seeking. Direct your paragraph to the head of personnel of the firm you are interviewing with.

3. Should a high school student hold a part-time job? Assume that you are persuading your younger brother or sister to look for or turn down a job. Write one paragraph in which you explain one main reason for the position you state clearly in your topic sentence. Use facts, examples, incidents, or comparison/contrast to support your position.

4. Most college students immediately notice things about their institution that they would change if they had the chance. Think of the things you would change if the administration would listen to you—food, dorm life, class schedules, and so on. Decide on one thing you would like to see changed. In one paragraph, explain to the president of the university (or the appropriate official) what you would like to see changed and why. In your topic sentence, state the major reason you would make this change. Then in the body of the paragraph explain your reason with specific examples or details.

5. Write a short persuasive paper arguing for one position in the local controversy you outlined earlier.

Revision checklist

1. Have you identified the audience for your persuasive paper?
2. Have you taken a clear argumentative stance in your topic sentence or thesis statement?
3. Have you chosen specific facts, details, and examples to convince your readers?
4. Have you evaluated your experts to choose only the most convincing?
5. Have you arranged arguments effectively?
6. Have you anticipated and refuted the major opposing arguments?
7. Have you avoided flawed logic in your arguments?
8. Have you used emotional arguments carefully and effectively?

UNIT FIVE

Revising and editing

In this unit we'll take up specific problems students often have in editing their own work. By editing, I mean fixing punctuation, spelling, pronoun use, and so on. Editing also includes changing words for precise usage and even rearranging sentences for more effective structure. Revising, on the other hand, means looking again at readers and their needs to be sure that you have stated your points clearly, developed ideas fully, provided adequate connections between ideas, and arranged details and arguments effectively. Revising means reworking your papers on a larger scale to make your paragraphs and essays as effective as possible. Do not hesitate to revise any of the exercises in this unit—because that's good practice—even when the exercises ask you to edit only. And be sure to apply the editing techniques you learn here in your own writing process as you prepare papers for your readers.

chapter 15
Editing for sentence punctuation errors

As we've discussed the writing process so far, I've assumed that writers include editing as a major step in the final preparation of a paper. Although readers caught up by the ideas of a piece of writing may tolerate some errors, most readers find errors distracting. In fact, some errors are so distracting that readers find they cannot follow the ideas when they have to untangle sentences. Readers find sentence punctuation errors particularly distracting. In this chapter we will review the kinds of errors in sentence punctuation that good writers edit for.

Defining the sentence

Just what is a sentence? We can define sentences in any number of ways—as a statement of an idea, as one or more words, as a complete thought that can stand alone, as a subject and verb. The numerical definition is correct in part because "Run." is a complete sentence in English. The definition of a sentence as a subject and verb is also accurate because we look for *subjects* to state the *who* or *what* the sentence is about and *verbs* to show the action or state of being of subjects. Unfortunately, in

English we can also identify subjects and verbs in *parts* of sentences that are not complete sentences by themselves. Similarly, the definition of a sentence as a complete idea creates some problems because in response to a direct question a single word or a short phrase may communicate a complete idea although not in a complete sentence. Let's look at some sentences to build up an idea of sentence parts and a thorough definition of a sentence.

Consider these sentences:

The wind is blowing hard today.

I listen to "Morning Edition" every day as I eat breakfast.

Youngsters taken to tennis camps every summer often develop knee and elbow injuries.

After the river rose above flood stage, the rains seemed even more vicious than before the flood.

All of these are complete sentences. What differs among these sentences? First, each sentence is *about* something different—"the wind," "I," "youngsters," and "rains." Each sentence has a different *subject*. Every written English "sentence" has a grammatical subject—that person, place, or thing that the sentence asserts something about. Subjects can be proper names—Carl, Becky, Dayton—or common names for people or objects—dog, chair, girl, clock—or pronouns that stand for naming words—I, you, he, we, they, and so on. We can also use more complicated words and phrases as subjects:

Singing in the shower exercises my vocal chords.

To be on time impresses prospective employers.

Whoever comes to the party will have a good time.

In these sentences, "singing in the shower," "to be on time," and "whoever comes to the party" are the subjects. We'll talk about these forms again later, but for now remember that *-ing* forms, *to* + verb forms, and some clauses can also be subjects of sentences.

But in three of these sample sentences we also have sentence parts that have subjects. We have both *independent* and *dependent* clauses. Every clause has a subject and verb, but not every clause is a sentence. Look again at these two sentences:

I listen to "Morning Edition" every day as I eat breakfast.

After the river rose above flood stage, the rains seemed even more vicious than before the flood.

Can you find two subjects and two verbs? In the first sentence, "I listen" is the subject-verb pair of the *independent* clause, and "I eat" is the subject-verb pair of the *dependent* clause. In the second sentence, "river rose" is the subject-verb pair of the *dependent* clause, and "rains seemed" is the pair for the *independent* clause. What distinguishes independent from dependent clauses? All dependent clauses do just that—depend on another clause, an independent clause, for support. All dependent clauses begin with one of two kinds of words: words like *although, because, before, after, whenever,* that indicate space, time, and manner relationships or words like *who, whose, that, which,* that generally replace rather than repeat a word from the independent clause.

REMINDER: All clauses have a subject and verb.
Independent clauses can stand alone.
Dependent clauses rely on independent clauses.
Dependent clauses begin with words such as

although	before	after	when
where	if	as	until
who	which	that	whoever

Verbs

Now we know what subjects and clauses are; what about verbs? Verbs show time in sentences so that we know when an action takes place. Verbs also show action or assert a state of being. Can you find the verbs in the seven sentences we looked at before?

The wind is blowing hard today.

I listen to "Morning Edition" every day as I eat breakfast.

Youngsters taken to tennis camps every summer often develop knee and elbow injuries.

After the river rose above flood stage, the rains seemed even more vicious than before the flood.

Singing in the shower exercises my vocal chords.

To be on time impresses prospective employers.

Whoever comes to the party will have a good time.

"Is blowing," "listen," "develop," "seemed," "exercises," "impresses," and "will have" are the verbs in the *independent* clauses. (Remember that we called "whoever comes to the party" a dependent clause; "comes" is the verb in this *dependent* clause.) Verbs include helping verbs like *may, can, might;* action words like *run, jump, talk;* and words expressing being like *am, is, were,* and so on.

Finding subjects and verbs is usually not a major problem for writers editing their work; however, if you are having problems punctuating sentences, you would probably benefit from more practice in identifying subjects and verbs. Go through any of the sample paragraphs in this chapter and underline subjects once and verbs twice and bracket dependent clauses.

Why recognize sentences?

Why must writers know how to find subjects and verbs? As writers mature, they use more and more complex sentences to convey more and more complex ideas. Sometimes when they try a new type of sentence for the first few times, they punctuate part of a sentence as a complete sentence. Readers expect sentences beginning with a capital letter and ending with a period to be complete sentences. If writers mark part of a sentence as a complete sentence, they create sentence fragments, bits and pieces of sentences that can confuse readers relying on standard signals. Because sentence fragments confuse readers—and thus slow them down—writers should always check their writing to eliminate sentence fragments.

EDITING FOR FRAGMENTS

Dependent clause fragments

Sentence fragments occur most frequently when a writer punctuates a dependent clause as if it were a complete sentence. Remember to check for all subjects and verbs in sentences. If you see a word that introduces a dependent clause, make sure you have that clause connected to an independent clause. Also, we use commas to help readers spot dependent clauses when they come first in the sentence. For example:

If you can, bring some salad dressing to the picnic.

Without the comma, this sentence sounds like a fragment: "If you can bring salad dressing," then what. With the comma, the writer separates even the short dependent clause from the beginning of the independent clause.

Here's the rule for commas with dependent clauses:

dependent clause, independent clause
independent clause dependent clause (no comma)

-ing fragments

Another common fragment occurs when a writer mistakes an -ing form of a verb for a complete verb. Any verb ending in -ing must have a form of to be with it to act as a complete verb for a sentence. Otherwise, the -ing form acts like something other than a verb in the sentence. Compare these sentences:

> As the dog ran around the yard, it <u>was hobbling</u> because of a sore foot.
>
> He <u>being</u> such a crass materialist.

In the first sentence, "hobbling" takes "was" to complete the verb; in the second example, a fragment, the -ing form has no accompanying form of to be. Although "being" is a form of to be, it too must have another form of to be showing time so that it is a complete sentence rather than a fragment. Remember, as sentences get more complex, check for a complete verb with a form of to be and an -ing word.

Other kinds of fragments are possible but less likely to appear in writing. If you have trouble with fragments, reading your papers aloud will often help you spot problems so that you can check for subjects and verbs.

REVISING TO IMPROVE COHERENCE AND TO ELIMINATE SENTENCE FRAGMENTS

Practice your skill in finding fragments in the following early version of a narrative paragraph. Because Carla is just starting on the paragraph, she has several sentence fragments. If she were working on this paragraph, she would probably not yet worry about editing for fragments because she needs to concentrate more on the story. But you can look for fragments, and you can also suggest other ways to improve her paragraph.

Grandmother Story's funeral, July 31, 1981, in Miller, South Dakota. A critical decision tied together two sisters. Grandmother Grey and her sister Ruby by the sharing of sorrow and compassion. While making a critical decision. After the funeral on an overcast, chilly day my grandmother Grey and her sister Ruby both in black. The two sisters sat at the table clinching each other's hands in sorrow. They had to decide

how to get Grandmother Story to Kentucky.
My grandmother Story had wanted to be
buried in Kentucky, but the morning of the
funeral the air traffic controllers had gone on
strike. Facing this decision together. They
realized how much they needed and loved
each other.

> —*Carla F.*

Carla wants to tell the story of how a crisis in the family brought her grandmother and aunt closer together. Has she filled in all the necessary details yet? Can you imagine what else she might add? How would you make the details flow coherently? As you add details in a coherent order and as you add transitional devices, correct the sentence fragments.

Now consider what Carla did in a later version of her paragraph:

At my great grandmother Story's funeral,
July 31, 1981, in Miller, South Dakota, a
critical decision bonded two sisters with
love. After the funeral on an overcast, chilly
day, my grandmother Grey and her sister
Ruby, both dressed in black, with tear-
streaked faces, sat at a table in the pastor's
office. Clinching each other's hands in
sorrow, they faced the decision of how to get
grandmother Story to Kentucky. My
grandmother Story had wanted to be buried
in Kentucky, but the morning of the funeral,
the air traffic controllers went on strike. The
two sisters sat in sorrow, considering other
ways to get grandmother Story to Kentucky.
After considering all the alternate routes and
deciding to rent a car, the two sisters looked
into each other's eyes and realized how much
they needed one another. They had achieved
a feeling of togetherness and love by facing
the decision together.

And now revise yet another paragraph. Suggest improvements for the paragraph and then edit fragments to make complete sentences.

Motivated by grief, I learned to physically
express care for my hardened brother at our
mother's funeral. As I leaned weak-kneed
against the gray casket. I glanced at my

brother Mike, impeccably suited. Hands clasped rigidly behind his back, his eyes staring fixedly ahead. The skin drawn tight across his jaw, his face like a tough mask to protect him from the pathos of the situation. I felt I wanted to hug him, comfort him, soften him. Thereby softening myself. However, any show of emotion had never been easy for me; so I grew embarrassed in spite of my sadness. And looked away, seeking sanctuary in perusing the casket. But escaping into myself was not to be my sort of sanctuary. I started to remember the times in the past when my mother asked me, pleaded with me in fact, to touch Mike, hug him, as if always solidifying the spoken words of caring. These bitter memories brought silent tears to my eyes; I was crying both over the loss of her and the realization that I'd always procrastinated giving both her and myself our wish. Now, it was too late for her. "Well," I thought, "this is as good a time as any for me." I again looked at Mike. Feeling awfully awkward but refusing to quit what I was determined to do. Perhaps feeling my eyes on him, Mike met me eye to eye, his mask as hard as ever. I took the long walk (3 paces) to him and spread my arms. He accepted my hug and returned it with a stronger one. It seems ironic that we finally touched each other over our mother's casket, but not so ironic is that from death sprang a feeling of new life in me.

—*Rod G.*

EDITING FOR COMMA SPLICES AND FUSED SENTENCES

We have already considered an error most readers find distracting—the sentence fragment. Now, let's consider other major flaws in sentence punctuation—the comma splice and fused sentence.

Let's review definitions once more. Every *clause* has a subject—the person, place, or thing the clause is about—and a verb—the word or phrase showing action or a state of being. Clauses that are not introduced by *subordinating* words are independent clauses; they can be punctuated as independent sentences. Clauses introduced by subordinating words are *dependent* clauses; these clauses depend on an independent clause for complete meaning. We can combine independent and dependent clauses in one sentence, but every sentence punctuated as such must have an independent clause.

Coordinating sentences

How can we connect independent clauses? If we were to punctuate every independent clause as a separate sentence, we might find that we have choppy paragraphs. Changing independent clauses to dependent clauses often helps because the subordinating words show the logical relationship between ideas in the clauses. But a subordinating word does make the dependent clause less important than the independent clause. Perhaps we have two equally important ideas, but we don't want to write them in separate sentences. We can combine independent clauses by using a coordinating word (*co*-ordinate to show equality between the clauses):

> The wind squealed through the cracks in the wall, and the chintz curtains rustled constantly.

> After nodding politely, the cement-truck driver still backed up over the compact car in its way, but the car owner only stared.

To coordinate independent clauses, use these words:

and	but
or	nor
for	yet
so	

And remember, if you use these words to connect two independent clauses, use a comma before the coordinating word.

Using semicolons

How else can we connect independent clauses? We can use a semicolon (;) either with or without a connecting word that expresses the logical connection between the clauses. We could rewrite the two preceding sentences:

> The wind squealed through the cracks in the wall; the chintz curtains rustled constantly.

After nodding politely, the cement-truck driver still backed up over the compact car in its way; however, the car owner only stared.

Semicolons separate only independent clauses. If you use a semicolon to separate a dependent clause from an independent clause, you create a sentence fragment.

Recognizing comma splices

Although it is possible to create fragments by misusing semicolons, an even more common error is to use only a comma in place of a semicolon. The following error is a comma splice because a comma alone tries to splice or hold together two independent clauses:

The wind squealed through the cracks in the wall, the chintz curtains rustled constantly.

Why is such an error confusing to readers? Readers learn early that marks of punctuation are like road signs for drivers. With periods, semicolons, and commas, writers tell readers what kinds of phrases and clauses to expect. If a writer uses an incorrect mark of punctuation, the reader must stop, figure out the wrong direction signal, and then reread the sentence to puzzle out the meaning. When we use commas in place of semicolons, or commas only when we need a comma *and* coordinating word, we tell readers to expect structures other than combined independent clauses. In our sample sentence, for instance, the comma tells readers to expect to see a series of items that the wind squealed through (because we use commas to indicate a series of words or phrases):

The wind squealed through the cracks in the wall, the chintz curtains, and the fireplace opening.

Readers who expect one structure but then are presented with a different one find themselves distracted if not completely lost. Often, a confusing sentence forces readers not only to puzzle out the offending sentence but also to return to the beginning of the paragraph to recapture the train of thought.

Although not all comma splices are equally confusing, some are almost impossible to interpret:

Have some spaghetti, if you want tea it's in the pot on the stove.

On first reading, most readers assume that "if you want" goes with "spaghetti" when, in fact, the next clause begins, "if you want tea." Such errors slow readers. Moreover, if readers find enough of these errors, they may simply stop reading, and no writer can afford to turn off the audience.

Practice—Eliminating comma splices

In the following essay, the writer has missed several proofreading errors involving commas. Correct comma splices by adding coordinating conjunctions or replacing the comma with a period or semicolon.

A romantic haze enhances the setting for this idealistic Taster's Choice commercial. The wife anxiously awaits her husband's arrival from work, through the window she stares out into the rainy evening with a worried expression. At last! "He" is home. They embrace and spend the rest of the evening by the toasty fireplace sipping Taster's Choice. Although this evening could be imaginable by husband and wife, spouses very rarely have time to share romantic evenings of this sort together.

It is unlikely that a housewife would be doing nothing but watching out the window for her husband to drive up from work. In the commercial, however, the wife concerns herself with nothing more than seeing her husband arrive safely home, her anxiety intensifies with each passing moment as the rain pours outside. The minute her husband drives up in his car he sees his wife's worried expression through the rain-streaked window. In reality, instead of seeing the wife waiting at the window, we see her at the kitchen stove attending to her "true-love's" dinner. With the pattering of the rain against the window she looks up, then she runs around the house making sure the rest of the windows are closed. So you see, concern for her husband's safely getting home can truly only find place between window-checking and trying not to burn dinner.

Ideally, on the screen, we see the wife readily at the door to greet her husband as he walks in. He, of course, is in a relaxed mood and sensitive to his wife's feelings even after a long day's work and an intense drive home through the rain. He stops and asks her if she was worried, she says, "Yes." They embrace each other. On the contrary, in real life we see things a bit differently. After the husband walks through the door, his wife comes out of the kitchen only to make sure it is him and not a burglar. Both being tired and uptight—her from a gloomy day on top of housework and him from the long drive home in the rain after a hectic day at the office—they slightly grunt a "hello." Then, after he turns on the evening news, he flings his wet overcoat onto the sofa and plops into his favorite chair, with his attention geared toward the tv screen he hollers for his wife, she by now has wandered back to the kitchen. "What's for dinner?" he asks, not even listening for her response. Reality of a husband's returning home from work turns out a bit differently than what this commercial portrays.

Back in story-book-land, we see our couple sharing a romantic evening free of interruptions. After they embrace, she helps him off with his wet overcoat and hands him a warm towel, he gazes around the room and is overtaken by the serene mood set by the romantic fire in the fireplace. They mosey on over to the sofa where they snuggle up in the warmth. There, in front of the soft, glowing flame with no TV, telephone, or trace of visitors, they relax, they enjoy the soothing, rich flavor of Taster's Choice. Now let us take a closer-to-life look at what really happens. There really may be a romantic fire crackling in the fireplace when the husband walks in, however, his first thought is that he refuses to go out and get more wood to last the rest of the night. And, even though his wife may be satisfied collapsing in front of the fireplace with a fresh cup of coffee, this certainly isn't allowable until after the ritual of eating a "good, hearty meal." Once dinner finishes cooking and the TV's evening news comes to its end, the couple sits down for a quiet dinner for two, it is quiet because they haven't much to say to each other through the entire meal. When they are both full, our faithful, little wife stays to clean up the kitchen while our "loving" husband glues himself back to the TV screen. Finally, with the last dish placed in the dishwasher, the wife joins her husband in the cozy family room. The two, as in the commercial, can be found in front of the fireplace, however, this being real life, he is in his chair and she in hers. Unlike the uninterrupted romance potrayed on the screen, this real life evening is set with the TV blaring, the husband answering the phone, and the wife running to the door to meet great-aunt Emily who, "Surprise," is visiting for two whole weeks. . . .

This commercial works well as a sales pitch because it makes what many couples dream about come to life on screen, it makes married life look appealing, once again, by setting up this romantic, uninterrupted evening shared and enjoyed by both the husband and wife. The special quality about this idealistic scenario is that it isn't entirely far-fetched. An evening like this can be shared by the typical American couple, it just isn't very often that it happens. The reason this commercial, then, has been classified as idealistic is because, contrary to the commercial's implications, this type of evening certainly isn't shared every time Taster's Choice is around nor is Taster's Choice even around every time an evening like this is shared.

—*Annette A.*

Recognizing fused sentences

The fused sentence, because it contains *no* direction markers, typically confuses readers even more than the comma splice. In a fused sentence, two independent clauses are joined with no punctuation and no connecting words:

Bill drove Mary Beth arrived later on her bike.

What? How many girls are we reading about? Does this writer mean that "Bill drove Mary" and "Beth rode her bike" or that "Bill drove himself" and "Mary Beth rode her bike." Because the two independent clauses are fused without punctuation, readers cannot decipher this sentence.

As you edit for sentence punctuation errors, remember how to join independent clauses appropriately:

Independent clause, *coord word* independent clause.
Independent clause; independent clause.
Independent clause; connecting word, independent clause.

coordinating conjunctions: *and, but, or, nor, for, yet, so*

With semicolons, use such words as *then, moreover, however, thus, nonetheless,* and so on.

REVISING TO IMPROVE COHERENCE AND TO ELIMINATE SENTENCE PUNCTUATION ERRORS

Help Julie revise this paragraph by first identifying and correcting sentence punctuation errors and then considering appropriate detail to add:

There are many steps to take when registering for school classes at the university. Begin by choosing classes you would like to take, read about them and ask friends if they are good courses. Also be sure that your classes include requirements for your major. After you have decided which courses to take. The next step is to meet with your adviser to discuss the classes chosen. You and your adviser will determine whether the credit load is reasonable you will then be able to sign up for your classes. After you have signed up for your courses, attend registration the assigned day, if not all classes were available, add substitutes to your schedule. Your schedule will then be approved a final time by someone at a registration table. After taking these steps; you are now ready to attend classes when they begin.

—*Julie B.*

1. Could you rearrange any steps here to make a more logical order in

the process? _____

_____

2. What words and phrases does she use to indicate the sequence of

steps? _____

_____

3. Could you add other, clearer transitions? _____

_____

_____

Now revise this paragraph that also needs work on sentence punctuation:

The procedure for earning an "A" on a test in calculus is simple for anyone. The materials you will need are the calculus textbook, the supplementary answer book, a pencil, paper, and a large eraser. The first step is to go into class with the right attitude, if you do not think you can get an "A," you cannot. Next you must go to every class and remain attentive; asking every question you can think of. After class comes the homework, the most important step. Although homework is seldom collected; it is vital that you complete it, this tests your knowledge and enables you to find your weaknesses, this leads you to the following step—seeing the instructor about these problems. One-on-one work with your teacher is like having your own private tutor he helps unselfishly, dealing with your specific problems. Plus in borderline cases, he gives you the higher grade if he thinks you are trying. The final step, actually studying for the tests, is easiest if you study with a friend, explaining a problem to someone not

only helps him but it reestablishes the
method in your own mind. Go back over
every homework problem and quiz until you
understand how the correct answer was
calculated then you must review by yourself.
These simple steps, if carried out to the
letter, will assure you an "A" on any calculus
test.

—Dan R.

REVISING FOR ADEQUATE DETAIL AND SENTENCE COMPLETENESS

As a review before revising your own paragraphs, you might revise Anita's paper for adequate development and clear sentences. Don't try to revise the paragraph in one quick pass through it. First, think about how you might add specific details by drawing on your own experiences in supermarkets. Then, after you add or rearrange relevant details, consider the sentences to find fragments and comma splices.

> Whenever I encounter obnoxious people at the King Soopers. I show malicious anger that I ordinarily would not express to friends. Take, for example, a time when I came back from a great day at the swimming pool. And strolled into King Soopers for a hot, chili-cheese dog. I walked over to the delicatessen in the back of the store, picked a numbered ticket to wait for service, and patiently stood in front of the ham and turkey cold cuts waiting for my turn. Not bothering to take a number, a woman rolled up beside me with her heavy cart and ordered lunch meats and cheeses. If I had known her, I would have done nothing, instead, I became bothered by her abrupt behavior and mentioned that I, and other people, had been waiting in line. I ripped a pink slip of paper from the vending machine and pushed it in her sweaty palm. The next Wednesday, I walked into King Soopers. Searching for some Top Ramen noodles. I found them behind two middle-aged women talking to each other. Determined to get my noodles; I sneaked my way up to the shelf and exclaimed, "Excuse me," in a blunt tone. The talkative ladies paid no attention and continued their conversation. Frustrated by their insensitivity, I told them that I am always more considerate to fellow shoppers than they were being. On another occasion, while heading towards a busy check-out line to buy a half-gallon of milk. I was run over by a loaded cart. Furiously, I told the man who clenched the dangerous vehicle that I only had one small carton of milk and asked if I could check out my item first. The big man turned around, he glanced at me with vicious eyes, then he haughtily ignored my plea. I became upset and told the huge man what a jerk he was, I threw my carton of milk in his overweight cart and stormed out of the store. Ordinarily, had I been shop-

ping with a friend, I would have ignored the rudeness, with this obnoxious man, however, like other rude shoppers, I lost control of my emotions and expressed my anger.

—*Anita H.*

Now edit two more paragraphs for sentence punctuation:

Drinking in excess can cause close friends to fight. For example, just the other night after having four beers and three potent gin and tonics. I became enraged with my girl friend for no apparent reason. We were at her apartment and I started lashing out at her with short answers and angry words. Then when she politely offered to take me home. I snapped at her saying that she was a bitch and I would walk home. So I proceeded to walk home, leaving her in dismay, I deeply regretted it the next morning when I was sober. Another incident where drinking caused two close friends to fight last year was in the dorm. Tex and his friend Kevin were drinking heavily from a keg; for about six hours one night when Tex thought Kevin pushed him intentionally. Tex then threw a drunken but powerful punch at Kevin, knocking him onto the ground. The two then began to wrestle furiously; striking blows to each other's head and chest. After the fight was over both of them couldn't believe they had fought, and both were ashamed of themselves and their actions. Lastly, a more recent example of the bad effects of drinking occurred last weekend. When two fraternity brothers who are good friends became drunk and started throwing punches. It started after Derek had become plastered and started calling Arron names. Arron didn't want to fight, but Derek persisted with harsh language and aggressive gestures. Finally, Derek reeled a punch to Arron's face and followed with an intoxicated jab to the ribs. Arron, not being able to control himself, swung wildly at Derek's head; causing Derek's face to turn fiery red and bloody. Eventually the fight was broken up and the following day neither Arron or Derek could believe what they had done. They both were deeply sorry about their actions the night before. Although to this day Arron and Derek are not good friends anymore. All these incidents show that alcohol can cause friends to fight irrationally.

—*Eric O.*

I could receive a trophy at least six feet tall for being "the world's worst raft passenger." Because I never seemed to be able to stay in the raft. As the time when my friends and I decided to take a rafting trip down the mighty Arkansas river during the summer of 83. Monday being the only day we all had off from work, the Fawnbrook Inn, we carpooled down there as fast as possible. Full of nervous anticipation like when you are about to ask for a raise from work we arrived just before 9:30 A.M. By 10 o'clock my luck shifted from good to bad. As I stepped into the raft I lost my balance before I knew it I was floating down the river like a piece of driftwood. Which brings me to another time when I was reaching for a piece of driftwood on the green river in Arizona. I fell head first into fast moving rapids, luckily

I was wearing a "Bell Rafting Helmet." If only I had worn my helmet last spring I would have probably stayed in the raft; I was hit in the forehead with a fast moving cork causing me to fall backwards into the Snake river. For all the times I have fallen in; I at least deserve to be in the "Guiness Book of World Records" for being the worst raft passenger.

—*Scott R.*

Editing your own work

1. Look again at one of your papers a teacher has commented on. If you see any errors in sentence punctuation, correct them.
2. Take out a paper you're working on now (preferably a draft ready for proofreading). Look carefully for errors in sentence punctuation. Correct any you find.
3. If you know you have problems proofreading for sentence punctuation, try this procedure:

   a. Starting at the end of your paper, work backward one sentence at a time.

   b. Identify all subjects and verbs. Is there only one main idea in the sentence?

   c. Identify *sub*ordinating conjunctions. If you have only a dependent clause, attach it to an adjacent independent clause or write an independent clause for it.

   d. If you have more than one subject and verb (that is, more than one independent clause), look for a *co*ordinating conjunction and a comma or a semicolon.

chapter 16

Editing for subject-verb agreement errors

As you know by now, writing skills include getting ideas, developing them fully, and expressing them clearly. Clear expression can't be ignored because mistakes detract from readers' appreciation of ideas. Mistakes sometimes happen when writers in English forget that readers expect redundancy or repetition in the language. We often give two or more signals for the same message. What we refer to as subject-verb agreement falls under the umbrella of repetitive signals to readers.

In written English sentences we expect to see a subject—the person or thing about which the writer asserts something in the sentence—and a verb that states the assertion. Furthermore, readers expect that similar information will be conveyed by both the subject and verb. Look at these sentences:

I run at least four miles every day.

John drinks coffee until he gets so nervous that he can't work efficiently.

You bring the best news whenever you visit my office.

Joe and Adele, even in the short time they work, paint houses better than professionals.

Do you notice anything about the verbs in these sentences? All verbs are present tense verbs—that is, the action is happening now—but only one form has an -*s* ending. Only the verbs following "John" and "he" change. Why? In modern English, we have lost a good many of the repeated clues that linked subjects and verbs in earlier forms of the language. But we still have one clue: the -*s* ending still appears on present-tense verbs when the subject can be replaced with "he," "she," or "it." Subjects like "I," "Joe and Adele," and "you" do not take the -*s* ending in the present tense.

Unless the sentence has a verb containing "may," "might," "can," "could," "will," "would," "shall," "should," or "ought," all sentences with present-tense verbs and subjects like "John," "the dog," "a person," or any other subject that can be replaced with "he," "she," or "it" take an -*s* ending on the verb.

Why do we need the -*s* ending? Think about long, complex sentences that have several words between the subject and verb. The sentence in the preceding box and the sentence you are now reading serve as good examples of sentences with words between the subject and verb. Readers can forget just what the subject of the sentence is when they have to remember other information before they see the verb. If the verb repeats some information about the subject, then readers have a better chance of remembering the subject without having to reread the sentence. Readers quickly learn what the -*s* ending means and use it as a clue to the subject of the sentence when verbs do not directly follow subjects.

Finding the subject of a sentence

When you check subject-verb agreement, be sure to check for the true subject of the sentence. Often, readers and writers can be confused by words in phrases. If a phrase begins with a word like "on," "of," "in," or "at," then the noun in the phrase is not the subject of the sentence. In the following sentence, "clocks," not "numbers" or "face," is the subject of the sentence:

Clocks without numbers on the face are harder for children to read.

Also look for combined subjects as in the preceding sentence about Joe and Adele. Together Joe and Adele do the action—paint—so that if we were to replace their names in the sentence, we would use "they." Only subjects representing one person take the -*s* ending.

Finally, check for pronouns like "everyone," "each," and "nobody." These words stand for one person and take the -*s* ending in sentences with present-tense verbs.

Now consider a paragraph with errors in subject-verb agreement. As you correct errors, think, too, about ways to improve the focus and development of the paragraph.

When I go to midnight movies, I change from a mellow, shy, unconfident person to an outspoken and wild person. Because I only see people I meet there for two hours, I don't care what happen. For example, my friend and I goes to *Rocky Horror Picture Show* whenever we can. We get rice, candles, squirt guns and water balloons. When the movie start, my friend throw rice at people. Then I starts squirting people. My big mistake always come when I throw my first waterballoon because it never fail that I hit a great big man and he be drenched with water. He stands up, looking like a mountain, walk to where I am sitting, and he growl as he say, "You boys better knock it off." Another favorite midnight movie is *Heavy Metal* because good-looking girls come to that show. I always look for the best looking girl. As I walk towards her, I begins to sweat and gets a lump in my throat. I begin to speak. It seem like everyone are listening to what I says. But girls at the midnight movie is nice, and I can always arranges to go out the next day. I like going to the midnight movies because I like the person I turns into better than my old, boring self.

—*Brent G.*

Finally, edit two more paragraphs for subject-verb agreement errors:

My grandma fits the typical mold for little-old-lady drivers; on a good day she reaches a maximum height of five feet and at 70 years young still drive, but after that the mold is broken. When thinking of typical little-old-lady drivers I picture a person who drive at speeds matched by the slowest of snails, who change lanes without warning, and listen to Lawrence Welk tapes. Every time I come up on a social-security-collecting female driver on the road I have to slow below the speed limit or I pass wondering if the car will rust away before she drives another mile. I never see my grandma on the road, because she reaches speeds of 75 to 80 miles per hour while traveling. My jeep couldn't keep up with her, let alone pass. Richard Petty would be proud, the way that grandma move on the road, signaling to the left and right as she passes slower cars. Signal! Remember that lever by the steering wheel? When pulled down it makes a light blink on the left side of the car and when pulled up it makes a light blink on the right? In the typical grey-haired-old-lady's car this lever doesn't exist, proven by the lack of signals used in lane changes by these ladies. Not only by watching grandma race down the road can one see she use signals, but the paint on her levers are worn to the metal. While the typical over–60-female driver is listening to Lawrence Welk on the tape deck, my grandma jumps on the C.B. radio and talk with truckers to keep informed on road conditions and the location of speed traps. Grandma may look like the typical little-old-lady driver when in fact she drives like an Indy 500 racer.

—*Jim T.*

An ideal roommate is one who routinely keep her personal items such as food, hygiene and mail in a neat, orderly fashion throughout the house whereas my present roommate leaves a messy, disruptive, "telltale" trail of her personal belongings in every room. For instance, while making lunch an ideal roommate will put her unused portions of food back in the refrigerator, places dirty dishes in the dishwasher, and disposes of her uneaten food. My present roommate will leave a distinct and detailed path of her process of making lunch with open containers left on the counter, dirty lunch dishes in the living room, and banana peels strewn on the kitchen table. Another example of an ideal roommate is one who would keep her personal mail in her bedroom whereas my roommate target and encompass every open space in the entry hall, living room and kitchen, leaving no surface untouched with her cumulative junk mail, monthly bills and magazines, and outdated newspapers. And finally, after a morning shower an ideal roommate places towels on their racks and clear the sinks and counter of her cosmetics. On the other hand, my roommate leaves the bathroom in such disarray one would think a troupe of Barnum and Bailey's circus clowns had just used our bathroom as a dressing room. Red lipstick is smeared on the white porcelain sink basin, multi-colored eyeshadow glisten on the smooth surface of the counter and walls, and her robe, towels and pajamas abounds on the floor.

—*Jackie H.*

Editing your own work

1. Look again at one of your papers a teacher has commented on. If you see any errors in subject-verb agreement, correct them.
2. Take out a paper you're working on now (preferably a draft ready for proofreading). Look carefully for errors in subject-verb agreement. Correct any you find.
3. If you know you have problems proofreading for subject-verb agreement punctuation, try this procedure:

   a. Starting at the end of your paper, work backward one sentence at a time.

   b. Identify all subjects and verbs.

   c. Do you see *may, might, can, could, will, would, shall, should,* or *ought?* If so, go on to the next sentence.

   d. Is the verb in present tense? If yes, go to step e.

   e. Can you replace the subject with *he, she,* or *it?* If yes, check for an *s* on the verb.

chapter 17
Editing for pronoun use

Because we use them so commonly to replace nouns in our speech and writing, most pronouns don't give us much difficulty. Instead of using our names to identify ourselves, we use "I" or "me"; we clearly identify the people we talk to not by calling them by name but by using "you." When we point out something, we might simply say, "Look at *that*." In short, pronouns come naturally to us.

Yet certain pronoun uses confuse writers—and speakers sometimes—because they may not know the appropriate guidelines to apply when choosing certain pronouns. For instance, many speakers are especially uncomfortable with "myself," thinking that it sounds more polite than "me." They question whether to use "myself" or "me" in "The judge asked my lawyer and me to approach the bench." Because most speakers haven't reviewed the use of "me" and "myself," they think the two words are interchangeable, but they aren't. "Myself" refers only to those actions I do to my own person or of my own will. So I can invite *myself* to the bench, but the judge can't invite *myself;* he can invite only *himself* or *me.* I can do things "by myself," meaning alone, but I can't do them by *me* unless I have a split personality.

What pronouns do

What you have probably guessed is that if most pronouns don't give us trouble, the ones that do, give us tricky problems. Let's look at some sample sentences to see what we need to know about pronouns.

John gave candy to <u>himself</u> and <u>his</u> friends.
John gave candy to <u>himself</u> and <u>her</u> friends.
John gave candy to <u>himself</u> and <u>their</u> friends.

The first sentence here seems the most straightforward. Why? It tells us who is acting and then replaces John's name with pronouns that clearly substitute for John. In other words, the pronouns repeat information that we know about John so that we know the pronouns replace "John" in the sentence. What information do they repeat? They repeat the ideas that John is one person and that he is masculine. Our pronouns tell us how many (singular or plural) and what gender (masculine, feminine, or neuter).

The second sentence introduces new information. Who is *she* referred to by "her friends? This sentence brings up an important point about clear use of pronouns. We understand pronouns because we know who or what they replace in the sentence. Now if in the preceding sentence we had read about Janet's schoolmates, we would understand that "her" refers to Janet. Pronouns, then, should appear close to the nouns they replace so that the relationship between the noun and pronoun is clear. One big problem with pronouns is faulty reference when we don't know what name the pronoun replaces. But with just this sentence we know only that "her" refers to one person of feminine gender.

What about the third sentence? Now we see the same problems with faulty reference we discussed about the preceding sentence. But what about the number of people? Now we see that "their" refers to more than one. Do we know gender? Unless we know more about the group of people represented by "their," we can't say anything about their real status, but the pronoun is the one we use in English to indicate groups, masculine or feminine or mixed. Because "they," "them," and "their" don't indicate gender, these pronouns are convenient nonsexist substitutes. We'll come back to this point in a moment.

So far, we've reviewed several important concepts about pronouns:

They substitute for nouns.

They repeat information from the noun.

They show either one person or more than one (singular or plural).

They show masculine, feminine, or neuter gender.

They should appear close enough to the noun they replace so that they clearly point to that noun.

If we think of the pronouns that refer to just one person at a time, we come up with lists like these

I	my, mine	me	myself
you	your, yours	you	yourself
he	his	him	himself
she	her, hers	her	herself
it	its	it	itself

You'll notice that the columns show pronouns that serve different functions in sentences. The first column shows words that can serve as subjects of sentences; the second shows possessive forms; the third shows forms that follow most verbs or prepositions; and the last column shows the forms for actions directed to the self.

Can you devise the same columns for the forms showing more than one person at a time? I'll set up the first column:

we

you

they

Reading across the lines also tells us something about pronouns. As you read across, you'll notice that all the words in the first line substitute for "I" as "I" serves different functions in sentences. The second row shows variations for "you." "He," "she," "it," and "they" all form a group with their variations. These groups are what we call first person, second person, and third person. You needn't remember the term, but be aware that when you write, you should consistently use just a single grouping in your paper. Readers find the shift from the "I" group to the "you" group to the "they" group confusing.

Practice—Labeling pronouns

Circle the pronouns in this essay. If you have some question about why one pronoun rather than another form is used, discuss it. Also decide what uses pronouns serve in writing—besides reducing repetition of names.

Acting as a juvenile criminal at a young age can be detrimental. Around our neighborhood and others across the country, general rules prevail in every household including "no stealing." Yet rambunctious kids between 8–12 years usually find some way of testing the rules of the household, end up getting caught and punished, but learn from the consequences of punishment never to break those rules again.

Around the age of ten or so, youngsters might try to get a taste of crime, of federal and household law, by shoplifting at the local "five and dime" or grocery store. At that age, Don lived in sunny Long Beach, California, with his family. His strict but fair parents always demanded honesty and respect at all times. One day at Dandy's Drugstore at the corner of 111th Avenue and Douglas Street, Don carefully eyed a forty-five cent red toy truck, with silver wheels and a dumpster behind. As if an act of magic, the attention-getting little truck jumped up, landed in Don's pocket, and out the door Don ran. He played with his new truck in his bedroom, vrooming it across the carpet. His father noticed the unfamiliar truck immediately. He questioned Don about where it came from and like good 'ole George Washington, Don could not tell a lie; he told his father he had taken it from Dandy's. Mr. Shay made Don march right back down to Dandy's, truck in hand, and instructed him to give back the truck and apologize for his actions. With his father's stern hand on his shoulder, Don did apologize and promised never to do it again, his stomach taut with tension and his cheeks red with shame and embarrassment. The store owner and busy customers assumed the roles of judge and jury in his shoplifting crime. The fear was intense, and Don knew he never wanted to face those consequences again; the fear and the chore of doing dishes alone for 2 months steered Don away from ever shoplifting again.

Crime with a partner is another practice of youngsters as shown by Jeff and Clint, best buddies of the Seventh Street neighborhood. On a fine summer day at the beginning of vacation, the two boys became 11-year-old shoplifters. As they made their way through the bumpy streets on their skateboards, they had the sudden impulse to do something sneaky so they scooted over to the dilapidated AG Market in the lazy town of Berthoud. First they wandered around the store trying to look inconspicuous; they looked at the various prizes in different cereal boxes, watched the old ladies squeeze the tomatoes, and waited for the perfect moment to lift a Baby-Ruth candy bar. With the crime soon accomplished, they made their way out the door when suddenly the towering store owner boomed, "Get back here or I'll call the police!" They retreated, scared stiff, and then hustled off to the police department three blocks away with the fuming owner on their heels. There the chief of police took down their names, phone numbers, and parent's names before he showed them the cold, dark jail cell. He then asked them if they'd like to spend the night. After their response of "*no way,*" the chief then gave them their one phone call to their mothers to ask them to pick them up from city hall. They were both grounded for three weeks and couldn't have dessert for a month. As this story of the visit to the jail and the modes of punishment got around the neighborhood, we all decided we never wanted to go to jail just for a Baby-Ruth.

Authority of parents, once questioned, shows itself to be strong and worthwhile in the long run. Punishment teaches a lesson, and once learned by one person it's passed on through precedence to others and that form of punishment usually never needs use again.

—Lisa K.

Problems with pronouns

I've already mentioned two problems readers have with ambiguous use of pronouns—faulty reference and shift from "I" to "you" to "he." Now let me return to the idea of nonsexist pronouns.

As you know, when we refer to John, we use *he*; when we refer to Janet, we use *she*. But what do we do when we refer to "student" or "person" or "mail carrier"? Because we usually mean "any student" or "any person" or any "mail carrier," we don't want to have to say that the student, person, or mail carrier is either male or female. Yet our language forces us to do that or else to refer to the student, person, or mail carrier as "it," clearly not a good alternative. Rather than refer to the student as "he" or "she" and thus limit the sense of who "the student" is, some writers have adopted the practice of referring to these faceless persons with "he/she," "he or she," or "s/he." While you may use any of these alternatives, consider the following sentence:

The average student last year changed his or her mind about his or her major three times and then dropped courses from his or her schedule.

Using "his/her" doesn't help the sentence much. Because of this problem with "he" and "she," "his" and "her," many writers instead switch to plural forms so that they can use "they," "their," and "them":

Average students last year changed their minds about their majors three times and then dropped courses from their schedules.

Consider the clarity and simplicity of plural forms when you are editing your own papers for nonsexist pronoun use.

A particularly vexing instance of this problem occurs with words like "everyone" or "someone." Because these words refer to one person at a time, even though logically they seem to apply to all persons, we must use singular forms of pronouns when we replace these words. For instance, in current usage,

Everyone in the room had a drink in his hand.

is correct, though it sounds odd to us. Using "their" in this sentence is not correct for formal writing. You will hear people replace "everyone" with "their" in speech, and eventually the same practice may be accepted in writing, but not yet. So when you see the words in this list, be sure to use singular pronouns or change the sentence entirely:

everyone	someone
everybody	somebody
anyone	any of
anybody	each, each of
nobody	no one

Now look again at Rick's paragraph on spanking vs. grounding. Edit specifically for faulty pronoun use.

> During my childhood, I preferred to be grounded rather than spanked as a method of being punished. Being spanked teaches a child aggressive behavioral patterns out of a form of punishment whereas grounding molds a child into a non-aggressive behavioral pattern. Another aspect of the grounding vs. spanking subject is that a spanking lasts a short period of time whereas grounding lasts anywhere from a week to a month, depending on the reasons for which the child is being grounded. A third point to be discussed is the relationship with the child and the parent. If the child is spanked everytime they do something wrong, they will definitely not be on great terms with that parent whereas with grounding a child they know that they won't be able to do certain things for a certain amount of time. During the punishment in terms of spanking, the child has no time to discuss matters with that parent because of the spontaneity of the punishment whereas with grounding the child and the parent have time to talk matters out diplomatically. No matter which of these two methods of punishment is chosen, there are both pros and cons for both grounding and spanking that must be considered.
>
> —*Rick C.*

Consider this paragraph also for its use of pronouns. Explain which pronouns are appropriate and which ones need to be revised:

> Although I have experienced physical punishment within my household, I feel that verbal punishment was more effective and beneficial for me. At the age of eleven I recall the worst beating of my life. My little sister had ratted on me for shooting rocks with my sling-shot at the neighbor's dog. I felt the spanking was unjust, for I had only hit him twice, and I felt that I was only being punished because my parents hated me. Several hours later I received my second worst beating; it was a result of me protesting my first

spanking. During and after dinner I decided not to talk to anyone and ignore anything they told me to do. This naturally angered my parents and once again I found me grounded to my room after a severe spanking. That following morning my parents came into my room to talk to me. We talked about my actions and attitude problems among other things. This made me feel so good, knowing my parents cared enough to talk things out with me and see my side. Since then my parents have realized it's better to talk out my punishment so I am able to understand what I did wrong and why I'm being punished. Physical punishment never satisfied my need for knowing why I was being punished; it just built an iron curtain between my parents and I. Talking it out seems to bring my parents and I closer together instead of further apart. I'm definitely going to discipline my children the way my parents have disciplined me because it's the system that seems to work the best.

—*Randi M.*

Look at Julie's paragraph to revise it for accurate pronoun use and clear modifiers:

Because college freshmen at CSU misread newspaper articles, they receive poor grades when using them in classes. For example, two weeks ago a freshman student in my composition class who had carelessly taken a quote out of context from a newspaper article he had read received a "C" on his paper for failure to use the quote directly and keep it in the correct context. In another class, Speech 100, a freshman stood before the entire class last Wednesday and proclaimed that, according to a newspaper article he read in *The Denver Post,* President Reagan had cut the spending budget for defense when in fact Reagan had previously spoken the night before stating the exact opposite. Needless to say, the student was quite embarrassed and received a "D" on his badly-prepared speech. Finally, after thinking that misread newspaper articles couldn't actually be a trend in the freshman class, I was surprised to find that a girl in my macroeconomics class had written an essay concerning the six month's economic forecast and had turned around every statistic which in effect resulted in conclusions totally the opposite from what the article had implied. She had carelessly misread the article and received an "D" for the little effort she put forth to get the facts straight. Because of these instances of personal experience, it is quite common to find that freshmen misread newspaper articles and unfortunately receive poor grades because of it.

—*Julie R.*

Finally, consider the pronouns in this paragraph. Be sure to revise any that aren't clear or accurate:

It really annoys me when people eat during class because it can really be distracting while trying to do your work. For example, there is this guy in my literature class that brings his lunch every day and eats it in front of the class. I remember one time he brought in a whopper from Burger King. I could smell the sweet aroma all the way from my seat, and I could taste that juicy hot burger smothered with tomatoes, cheese, and lettuce. I wanted to run out to Burger King that minute. I was so distracted that when the teacher called on me, I had no idea what they were talking about. Another time that I got distracted was when a girl that sat behind me was eating potato chips. We were all reading novels, but I couldn't concentrate on my reading with them munching their chips. I could never get any further than three or four sentences because all I could think about was the pulverized sound she was making grinding the chips with her teeth until they were reduced to powder. Needless to say, I do not get any work done during class when people are eating their lunch in front of me.

—Geraldine R.

One of my worst pet peeves is some solicitor trying to sell me their product over the phone, because they almost always catch me in a bad moment. On my family's telephone there is a device that beeps in on you while you are talking on the phone. It only does this when someone else is trying to call in. One day I was talking to one of my best friends long distance. Brad, my friend from Minnesota, and I had only been talking a few minutes, when suddenly I had a call beep in. It turned out to be a solicitor trying to sell me some cosmetics for my face. When I tried to tell the salesperson that I was on the other line talking long distance, she acted as if she didn't even hear me and kept on talking. I am not usually a rude person, but in this case I had to make an exception, and hung up on her. Another time when I got a call from a solicitor, I had been making pizza for my brother and I. The phone rang and I went to answer it, and it happened to be Fred trying to sell me solar energy for my house. By the time I had explained to Fred that I didn't even own a house, almost ten minutes had passed. As I hung up the phone, I suddenly realized that there was a pizza in the oven. It was burned to a cinder. My brother came downstairs and yelled at me for two hours about not having any pizza for him to eat. Solicitors have a place in society, but I don't believe that their place is in the privacy of my own home.

—Scott H.

Editing your own work

1. Look again at one of your papers a teacher has commented on. If you see any errors in pronoun use, correct them.
2. Take out a paper you're working on now (preferably a draft ready for proofreading). Look carefully for errors in pronoun use. Correct any you find.

chapter 18
Editing for precise language

Although most readers are confused by sentences with faulty punctuation or other errors we have practiced eliminating thus far, readers generally are not confused but are irritated by wordy and imprecise language. Even in the most enjoyable article you might read just for fun, you wouldn't want to read more words in each sentence just because the writer did not bother to edit for precision. You would expect writers whose work you read to use the most specific language possible—clear and direct language you could understand easily. Similarly, you should not subject your readers to extra words or vague words just because you haven't taken the time to look for flabby sentences and paragraphs.

We can divide precise language into several categories, four of which I'd like to take up here.

Clichés

We've all heard expressions that were once precise and evocative but have been so overused that they have lost almost all meaning. We call such expressions clichés. Some of the more familiar ones are:

busy as a bee	pretty as a picture
straight and narrow	desperate (or dire) straits
between a rock and a hard place	

Although some of these expressions are more worn than others, common expressions that seem to leap from your pen automatically are probably clichés from your speech. For instance, the familiar "I had to get my act together" and "my dreams went down the tubes" are both expressions so common that their precise meaning is lost in a vague sense of shared experience. Though such expressions communicate well enough when we talk to friends, they do not substitute for carefully chosen descriptions and details in your writing. When you find yourself drifting into automatic phrases, underline them in your draft and come back to reconsider more precise language later.

Wordiness

Perhaps the most frustrating experience any reader can have is to read thirty words when ten or fifteen could have conveyed the same message. Many wordy expressions are almost automatic in the same way that clichés are. We find ourselves trying to sound more formal and simply lapse into overworked, wordy phrases. For instance, have you ever written "due to the fact that" rather than "because"? The latter sounds so plain compared with the five-word phrase that many writers choose the former instead of the more direct "because." But readers appreciate the writer who can condense by cutting out unnecessary words.

Certain words add so little to sentences that they can almost always be deleted. Rather than using "quite," "very," and "really," see if you can't add details. If not, at least delete the words that add so little meaning as to be worthless in sentences.

Other phrases have built-in redundancy. For example, "over a short period of time" repeats the same notion in both "period" and "time." Like many other "of" phrases, "period of" can be deleted. Look also for these phrases that usually pad sentences:

sort of	type of
kind of	use of
in the field of	on the level of
by means of	total of
in the area of	month of

That last item "month of" might surprise you. Be sure whenever you find any of these phrases that you can delete them without changing your meaning. But consider this sentence: "He moved from the city in the month of May." As long as we name the month, we don't need to include "month of."

Here are some other wordy expressions. Can you see what to reduce in each expression?

small in size	plan out
of an indefinite nature	in order to
at that point in time	in connection with
in this day and age	personally I think
3 A.M. in the morning	five different kinds
final conclusion	in this modern world of today
take into consideration	

As you find other similar wordy expressions you use, keep track of them in a personal log and review that list when you edit for concise language in your own work. As you read other articles and papers, you might also notice expressions other writers use that you want to avoid. Keep those in your log as well.

Fillers

Because English requires a subject and verb, we must use extra words in sentences like "it is raining." Usually, though, "it is," "there is," and "there are" are empty fillers that simply hold a slot in the sentence without adding meaning. While these phrases are indispensable in some cases, overusing sentences beginning with them can make your writing less forceful and direct. Reduce your dependence on them if you notice several sentences in a paper beginning with these phrases.

You can also eliminate unnecessary words by checking "who is," "who are," "which is," and "which are." Most often you can simply delete these words. Or you might find that you can rearrange the sentence for smoother flow by reordering words. For example,

The boy, who is aging ten years for each year he lives, has a rare disease.

becomes

The boy, aging ten years for each year he lives, has a rare disease.

And

The chocolates, which are luscious, cream-filled delights, are more expensive than I can afford.

becomes

> The luscious, cream-filled, delightful chocolates are more expensive than I can afford.

Empty words

Although empty words are not necessarily wordy, because they contribute so little to prose, they are fillers or padding of the most pernicious sort. Words like "interesting," "fun," "nice," "problem," "situation," "entertaining," and so on, simply tell readers nothing about your attitude or about the event you are writing about. Always be as specific as possible in choosing words, especially avoiding words that mean different ideas to each person hearing or reading them.

Practice—Editing for precise language

In Chapter 10 we looked at a comparison/contrast paragraph that could benefit from more editing, especially for precise language. Practice editing for clichés or overused expressions, wordiness, fillers, and empty words.

> During my childhood, I preferred to be grounded rather than spanked, as a method of being punished. Being spanked teaches a child aggressive behavioral patterns out of a form of punishment, whereas grounding molds a child into a non-aggressive behavioral pattern. Another aspect of the grounding vs. spanking subject is that a spanking lasts a short period of time, whereas grounding lasts anywhere from a week, to a month, depending on the reasons for which the child is being grounded. A third point to be discussed is the relationship with the child and the parent. If the child is spanked everytime they do something wrong, they will definitely not be on great terms with that parent, whereas with grounding a child, they know that they won't be able to do certain things for a certain amount of time. During the punishment in terms of spanking, the child has no time to discuss matters with that parent because of the spontaneity of the punishment, whereas with grounding, the child and the parent have time to talk matters out diplomatically. No matter which of these two methods of punishment is chosen, there are both pros and cons for both grounding and spanking that must be considered.
>
> —Rick C.

Now do the same for these paragraphs:

> The present situation of America's decline in education can be traced back to the present quality of English teachers now being hired due to the

fact that they are underpaid and overworked by holding down two jobs. For example, my high school English teacher very often misspelled words on assignments due to her writing up assignments quickly before going to her second job. This caused me to learn the spelling of certain words incorrectly and additionally caused problems in the area of Physics when papers were written. Back in my junior high school, my teacher showed no real concern about the class learning and talked mainly of her very interesting experiences as a grocery checker for a local neighborhood Safeway food store. I had this teacher for a whole year of time and gained no knowledge in the field of English from her, causing me to do poorly in my other classes that involved writing. The most significant example I have seen was when my senior English teacher would fail to show up for class because he said he was really tired from working till two in the morning the night before at our local 7-11. This caused me to fall behind my other friends in the writing of essays and eventually caused me to fail the College English Exam when I took it this fall. America's decline in education is due to the fact that English teachers are underpaid and overworked by trying to hold more than one job, causing them to devote less attention to the student.

—*Jackie H.*

When I was younger I assumed that in order to become successful a person had to have a body like Cheryl Tiegs, eyes like Paul Newman, as much money as Howard Hughes, and be as smart as Albert Einstein. But, now that I am older I have my own idea of what success is; it is setting a goal for yourself and achieving that goal. However, I do think there is one main ingredient that a person must have in order to reach his goal and that is determination. For example, the only way that my father achieved his goal was because of determination. He set his goal when he was very young; he wanted to become a carpenter. He had to work for six years in the steel mills to get enough money together to build a house. He saved every penny he earned; though a cup of coffee was only five cents he never splurged. He finally saved enough money to build his first house, then his second, and now twenty years later his determination has paid off. He is now a self-employed carpenter and he loves every minute of it. Two years ago, out of desperation my brother joined the navy; he needed to do something with his life. He dropped out of high school when he was a sophomore and for five years he never had a steady job; he just wandered from one job to another never really happy and never content. He had a few conflicts with the law and he could never seem to win. Well, this month he will return home from a nine-month world tour on the U. S. Naval Coral Sea aircraft carrier. For the past nine months he has worked anywhere from ten to fourteen hours a day helping to launch airplanes from the ship's deck. He enjoys doing something that is useful and at this point he is very content. Now he has set a goal for himself; he wants to become an airplane pilot for the navy. Four years ago, I never would have thought he would succeed but now he has the determination to do it. Over the past few years, watching members of my family has made me realize that any goal can be achieved if there is the determination to succeed.

—*Jody B.*

Finally, consider Scott's paragraphs, the first underdeveloped and the second more logically and fully developed. Keep in mind the revisions you would suggest as you edit for precise language.

Original

When students show up for class unwillingly, they should show respect by not talking so that the students who want to be there can learn something. I go to class to learn but I can't learn anything if other people are talking all the time. To be put another way, if the students didn't want to learn anything, then why are they in school in the first place? Moreover, instead of listening to the professor, the students, with a lack of respect and interest for the class, tend to entertain themselves by talking to their buddies. As a result, the talking persists, which provokes me to get upset because I lose my concentration.

Look at what Scott revised and suggest still other improvements.

Revised

When students show up for class and do nothing but talk, it annoys me because I lose my concentration in taking notes over the lecture. In physiology, for example, it's difficult to concentrate on what the professor is saying when students are talking louder than the professor who's using a microphone. This situation irritates me because when I lose my concentration in class I miss some of the notes, which in my case always end up to be the important questions that I miss on the test. For instance, one day when discussing all of the parts of the inner ear, which requires a lot of concentration because it's so detailed, I was distracted by the students sitting behind me, who were talking about their weekends at home. For me, it's hard to take notes when the only voices that are heard are everyone's except the professor's. Well, in the process of listening to the professor, as well as the irrelevant chanting of the students, I missed some of the notes during the lecture. The following day was the test and I was psyched and confident going into it but a little shaky about the parts of the inner ear. Afterwards, I received a score of "C" on the test. Later, when I was going over the test, I found out that most of the questions missed were related to the inner ear. This wasn't pleasing to the eye because the only reason why I missed them was because on the day of the lecture about the inner ear, I missed some of the notes due to the fact that students were talking all around me. In other words, I wouldn't have missed those questions if the students weren't talking.

—*Scott W.*

Now consider this paragraph that overuses "big" words incorrectly. Can you use more precise words that will make Jennifer's point clear?

Cognitive development in daily interaction attributes successful qualities when making out problems in pressure situations, having dealt with stress so frequently in my life. Through my senior year in High School, I was strained to perform problem solving. For instance, Calculus required the computation of Mathematics and Logic, in addition to pressure in the time sequence given. Here, the pressure in working out problems was acquired for me in elementary school through similar experiences. Another example might be my participation in Varsity Volleyball and Tennis with coaches yelling constantly when I missed a serve during a match. But yelling tends to be a pet peeve for me, so under pressure I'd perform well and physical skills developed. From eighth grade on, working on skills in Volleyball and Tennis obtained in pressure situations. Therefore, learning became successful for me after adolescent pressure in working out problems formed. In my lifetime I will always continue to depend on this cognitive device.

—Jennifer K.

Editing your own work

1. Look again at one of your papers a teacher has commented on. If you see any imprecise language, revise for precision and clarity.
2. Take out a paper you're working on now (preferably a draft ready for proofreading). Look carefully for imprecise language. Revise for precision and clarity.

chapter 19
Editing for proofreading errors

Because errors distract readers from the writer's main point—and detract from readers' evaluation of the writer as trustworthy and knowledgeable—writers should eliminate errors from their papers. This component of the writing process can be tedious, but with practice it can become less frustrating. In this chapter, we will review proofreading techniques and some trouble spots to check for.

Comma usage

Commas give writers more trouble than they are probably worth, but most writers discover that if they classify common usages, commas are less confusing. We'll review the six most common ways we use commas:

1. Use a comma to separate items in a list or series.

This comma rule is easy to remember. No matter what elements appear in a list in a sentence, show each element by setting it apart with a comma. You might use single words, phrases, or even sentences in a list, and the words can be any part of speech. Moreover, the list can occur at the beginning, middle, or end of the sentence. (Do you see the two "lists" in my last two sentences?)

> John brought Mary, Rick, and Jean to the party.
>
> After they drank two kegs of beer, danced for hours, and consumed seven take-out pizzas, everyone felt a little queasy.

2. Use a comma to separate two independent clauses connected with a coordinating conjunction.

This rule sounds more imposing, but it means that if you have two sentences and connect them with *and, but, or, nor, for, yet,* or *so* you need a comma before the connecting word.

> After the party, we cleaned the apartment, but it was never again spotless.
>
> We discovered—even months later—cigarette butts in flower pots, and we scrubbed fingerprints off walls and lampshades for two years.

Do not simply use a comma before every instance of *and.* If you use three or more items, use a comma; if you have two complete sentences, use a comma with *and.* But if you have simply two subjects or two verbs, don't use a comma with *and.*

> Peter came to repaint the walls and stayed to wax the floors.

3. When a sentence begins with a dependent clause, separate the dependent clause from the independent clause with a comma.

In other words, if you begin a sentence with a clause headed by words like "although," "because," "when," and others we discussed in chapter 15, use a comma to let the reader know that the dependent idea has ended and the main sentence is beginning.

> When he came to help, Peter was dressed in ragged overalls.

But if the dependent clause follows the main clause, don't use a comma:

> Peter was dressed in ragged overalls when he came to help.

Practice—Editing

Before we look at the remaining comma rules, let's practice some proofreading. The first technique is not to look for every error at the same time. Instead, read first for the first comma rule; then read the paper again for each subsequent rule. After you get more used to proofreading, you can probably check commas all at once and then use separate readings for other problems you know you have. But for now, go slowly through this sample paragraph. Put commas in where they belong according to these three rules.

> Although we could classify them as beginners advanced or experts down-hill skiers are really lazy mellow or aggressive. The lazy skiers start their day about 11 A.M. have an hour lunch break at noon and quit skiing by 3 to get the good spots in the bar. Mellow skiers start skiing within an hour of opening take a half-hour lunch break at 11:30 a fifteen-minute snack break at 2 and finish skiing in time for an early dinner. Aggressive skiers walk up the mountain for their first ski run and then they ski all day while eating lunch on the lift. For their last run, aggressive skiers take the longest way down the mountain. Lazy mellow and aggressive are the new classifications for the skiers of the 1980s.
>
> *—Sue C.*

More comma usage guidelines

Let's consider three other common uses of commas.

4. Short transitional elements at the beginning of sentences may be set off with commas. Long phrases at the beginning of the sentence, though, should usually be followed by a comma:

   However, John was unhappy about the environmentalists' position.

   After having studied the white paper for hours, John couldn't determine just how many species would be endangered.

Similarly, words called interjections are set off by commas. Unlike the transitional elements, which may be set off for emphasis as the writer wishes, these words, like "yes," "no," "well," "hallelujah," and so on, require commas:

   Well, he grumped noisily all day long about the work he had to do.

5. The next rule covers the use of transitional elements in the middle

of sentences. When the writer interrupts a thought, then she must use a comma to set apart the interrupting word or phrase:

> He had given, of course, no thought to how his actions would affect the election.

> Frankly, I wish he had considered, moreover, how his family would react to the news.

6. Finally, three sets of other interrupting words and phrases get set off from sentences by commas. First, whenever we address someone directly by name or title, we set the name or title off by commas:

> Joan, you should remember your parents' anniversary next year.

> I hope you agree, Mr. President, that we need a new policy.

Similarly, clauses with nonessential information introduced by *who, which, whom* are set off by commas:

> The popular TV show, which now airs on Thursday nights, is a critical success as well.

> The man on the left, who is holding the bouquet of flowers, just became a father.

Be sure the clause contains nonessential information, though, because the commas indicate that readers could remove the clause without misunderstanding the sentence. In the preceding sentences, readers don't need to know which night the TV show airs or that the new father is the man holding a bouquet. The details help readers, no doubt, but the information could be deleted without changing the sense of the sentence. Compare those sentences with this one:

> Women drivers who are reckless should be denied licences.

Were we to include commas so that the "who" clause were marked nonessential, the sense of the sentence changes to "women drivers should be denied licenses," a meaning few writers would care to defend.

As the writer, you determine by your use of commas whether the information is essential or nonessential, so use commas with care.

Finally, remember that nonessential information need not appear only in full clauses; it can also appear in phrases set off with commas just as the clauses are:

> The popular TV show, now airing on Thursday nights, is a critical success as well.

The man on the left, holding the bouquet of flowers, just became a father.

When you can, reduce clauses to phrases to eliminate unnecessary words. But remember that commas set off only the nonessential information.

Practice—Editing

Again, read first for the first comma rule; then read the paper again for each subsequent rule. Put commas in where they belong according to all six rules.

What's in a piece of chocolate? It depends on who made it. Some chocolates have more than 300 ingredients in their secret formulas—leaving little room for chocolate. Usually only 12 to 15 percent of an assembly-line milk chocolate bar is "raw" chocolate, according to the Chocolate Manufacturers Association. The rest unfortunately is sugar (45 to 55 percent) powdered whole milk (15 to 17 percent) extra cocoa butter (a vegetable fat found in pure chocolate) lecithin (which keeps ingredients from separating) artificial flavorings such as vanilla and often preservatives.

Expensive, exotic chocolates generally include more chocolate, depending on the type used. A sweet (or dark) chocolate typically contains 20 to 25 percent pure chocolate. Bittersweet (semisweet) chocolate contains at least 35 percent chocolate and baking (bitter) chocolate is 100 percent chocolate which accounts for its bitterness.

Expensive gourmet milk chocolates found in speciality shops are made with cocoa beans sugar fresh cream real butter cocoa butter and natural flavorings (no preservatives). Whereas run-of-the-mill chocolates are usually refined for only eight hours or so gourmet chocolates are blended for up to three days.

—"Inside Info," *Health,* February 1984, p. 52.

Try another student classification essay. Some of the commas here are correctly placed; others are not. Justify each comma.

Having grown up watching TV with my family and taking several broadcasting classes I would be willing to speculate that there exist several distinct types of TV viewers. Almost everyone watches TV at some time during the course of a week, but each individual watches for different reasons.

For example there are those "viewers" such as housewives, who have the TV on practically all day, but actually watch their sets only a few hours. The tube is on simply to provide background while doing something else, like washing dishes. This class of viewers also includes individuals who turn the TV on to take away the emptiness in a room. Children also have a habit of turning the TV on and then becoming interested in something else.

Another class of TV viewers only turns on the TV for specific programs, and then turns it off when the program finishes. For example, some college students have their favorite soap opera they watch faithfully every day at one o'clock. These viewers go so far as to work their class schedules, around this program. Many adults are not particularly interested in watching the sit-coms and night time dramas, but become irate if they miss the five or ten o'clock news. Children who hate to get up early to go to school willingly get up at the crack of dawn to catch the early morning cartoons on Saturday.

Then there are those viewers, who are indifferent to TV. These individuals tend to watch only occasionally because they can't seem to find any programs worth watching. Or else these individuals lead such busy lives that they can rarely grab a moment to sit down and watch a whole program. To these people, the world does not revolve around TV. Perhaps other media such as radio or newspapers fill their needs and desires better.

A final class of TV viewers are those individuals who are "glued" to their sets every chance they get. These viewers know what programs come on, which channels what time of day. They tend to watch the same programs every week. Many children start this routine at an early age because they get bored easily or have no one but the TV to entertain them all day. Older, retired people also tend to be addicted to TV. With so much time on their hands, TV makes the days go faster.

There probably exist several more categories of TV viewers but I have discussed some of the common ones. Those included viewers who like the noise of the TV, those who watch only certain programs or at certain times of the day, those who are indifferent toward TV and those who are "glued" to their sets. The people who fit into these classes tend to share some similar characteristics and life styles.

—Wendee N.

Apostrophes

The apostrophe may be an easy piece of punctuation to overlook, but writers should proofread carefully to be sure to use apostrophes correctly. In current usage, apostrophes show possession and contractions. The contractions give few writers problems because the apostrophe replaces letters omitted as two words are joined into one.

John's going to work early this morning so he can take a long weekend.

In this sentence, the apostrophe shows that "John is going" has been reduced to "John's going."

The contractions that confuse people are the ones created from personal pronouns and forms of to be:

I am	= I'm	we are	= we're
you are	= you're	they are	= they're
it is	= it's	who is	= who's
he is	= he's		
she is	= she's		

Just remember that when these pronouns have apostrophes, the apostrophe shows the contraction of two words into one. The possessive pronouns are unique words that show possession for the pronoun form:

my, mine	= belonging to me	our, ours	= belonging to us
your, yours	= belonging to you	their	= belonging to them
his, hers	= belonging to him, her	whose	= belonging to whom
its	= belonging to it		

Possessives of other nouns are not so difficult to punctuate correctly either. First, determine if the word is singular or plural as you want to use it. If it is plural, add the appropriate plural ending. Now treat all words the same way: if the word ends in any letter other than *s*, add an apostrophe and *s* to show possession. If the word already ends in *s*, you may add simply an apostrophe or an apostrophe and *s*.

> one boy has a hat = boy's hat
> two boys have hats = boys' hats
> one glass has a lens = glass' lens, glass's lens
> Mark has a book = Mark's book
> the Jones family has a car = the Jones' car, the Jones's car

But remember that even though the logic of the phrase does not seem to imply possession as such, certain phrases use an apostrophe to show possession:

a week's vacation	a month's rest
two weeks' vacation	two years' sabbatical
money's worth	heaven's sake

Since apostrophe errors seem to be among the hardest for writers to spot when proofreading, be sure to check carefully for apostrophe errors.

Commonly confused words

As you proofread for spelling errors, be aware of commonly confused words. Words like "affect" and "effect," "accept" and "except" sound similar enough that we cannot always hear the difference even if we proofread aloud. Thus, you need to know which of these word groups give you trouble. I've listed several groups below, but you might want to keep list of your problem groups as you run across those you check in your dictionary.

there their they're	to too two
affect effect	then than
accept except	rise raise
proof prove	principal principle
chose choose	leave let
advice advise	imply infer
already all ready	fewer less
altogether all together	farther further
among between	everyone every one
amount number	awhile a while
anyone any one	

Practice—Proofreading

Proofread the following paragraphs for errors in sentence punctuation, comma usage, apostrophes, pronouns, and spelling. Be sure to suggest possible revisions as well.

"Pumbled" is a commonly used word by many surfers in California that means to be overtaken by a wave. It is used when somebody loses control of their board in the waves. It can also be used when someone loses thier balance because of an opposing force. A good example of "pumbled" is when a surfer falls off his surf board into the waves and is carried towards the shore. When he recovers again his fellow surfers might say, "you've been pumbled." The term comes from the word rumble. The rumble of the wave signifys power and when the power overturns you you have been "pumbled." Like most slang terms "pumbled" is only used in certain areas but if your a California surfer it is a term that is commonly used.

—*Charles V.*

REVISING TO IMPROVE FOCUS AND DEVELOPMENT; EDITING FOR PROOFREADING ERRORS

Now look at this early version of Pam's definition paragraph. What revisions can you suggest?

To unfamiliar listeners the term "wah" sounds like made-up jibberish or baby talk but to the residents of 2nd floor Westfall it has special meanings. The most unique feature of the word "wah" is that it does not have one specific meaning, but many varied meanings. For instance if you are upset with someone you may call them a "wah brain," indicating that you think they are stupid. Or when you are excited about an upcoming party or whatever else you may express yourself with? "wah." Still another use for this word would be if you do not want to show any feeling at all. Then you would simple reply "wah," also using a disinterested tone of voice. The word "wah" as I have said, is a generic type word. When used in combination with other words, and voice tone it can mean absolutely anything. You can use it to answer any question, or express any feeling. Therefore, I suggest that this word is one of the best to come around in a long time, and that you should use it to.
— *Pam D.*

Pam needs to revise her focus in this paragraph, as well as the examples and details she uses to define the term. In this draft, the meanings of "wah" are not clear to readers. Moreover, Pam has errors of all sorts, including several imprecise words. Go through her paragraph again looking for proofreading problems you would direct her attention to.

Now consider Pam's revision. What would you still suggest she work on? She has improved the conclusion but can still work on examples. She has also still overlooked several proofreading errors.

To unfamiliar listeners the term "wah" sounds like made-up jibberish, but to the residents of 2nd floor Westfall it has special meanings. The most unique feature of the word "wah" is that it does not have one specific meaning, but many varied meanings. For instance if you happen to be upset with a friend you may call her a "wah brain," indicating that you think that person is stupid. Or when you are excited about an upcoming party or trip, you may express yourself with "wah." Using any word that fits the situation, usually a profane one. Still another use for this word would be if you do not want to show any feeling at all. Then you would simply reply "wah," also using a disinterested tone. The word "wah," as I have said, is a generic word. When used in combination with other words and tone, it can mean absolutely anything. The word can be used to answer any question or express any feeling. Therefore, I suggest that the word "wah" may be babble to those individuals who are not familiar with how it is used, but to me and the other residents on my floor it is an important part of our vocabulary.

—*Pam D.*

A few more proofreading tips

When proofreading, look first for those problems you know you have. For instance, if you know you make errors with sentence punctuation, check all sentences for completeness first. Then read the paper again for each problem teachers have suggested you work on.

Even after you go through this sequence of steps, don't forget to proofread once more for typos and spelling errors. The final product you share should not distract readers with any errors. A good way to proofread for spelling is to read from right to left, from the bottom to the top of the page. If you read only from the beginning to the end of the paper, you may overlook typos. Also, as you discover spelling errors, keep track of those. You can keep a list of common misspellings taped to the front inside cover of your dictionary so that you don't have to look up the same words over and over. Or you can tape short lists of words to several books you carry with you during the day. Just by glancing at the list from time to time, you can learn to spell the words correctly.

Practice—Editing

The following paragraphs have errors of several sorts. First look for sentence punctuation errors (fragments, comma splices). You might also consider combining some sentences to reduce repetition and wordiness. Then check subject-verb agreement and pronoun reference. Finally, check all commas and proofread one last time for spelling.

Most people visualize sorority girls as snobby and very "house" oriented, my friend Lisa is much more friendly and barely involves herself in house activities or conforms to their regulations. Snobbery is an aspect of the sorority girl image, they accomplish this task by interacting with a selective crowd which consist of girls from the house, fraternity boys, and possibly family. The frat boys serve as potential dates; seeing as frats and sororities exclusively party together. A sorority girl would never think of picking up a man off the street. On the other hand, theres Lisa who is no snob, as a matter of fact shes in no way judgemental of who she talks to, if they are friendly to her she will be the same. Its obvious that shes friendly to just about everyone because thats how she met her boyfriend by just saying "hi" one day. Another aspect of the sorority girl stereotype is strict conformity to house rules which prohibit drinking and men in the room, making the girls seem so disciplined and innocent. But then there is Lisa who loves to party, and theres nothing she likes more than to stay out late at a good party completely blowing off curfews. Also, if she wants to bring a guy home she won't hesitate to sneak him in the back way and up to her room. Another way the sorority girls seem so house oriented is shown in the constant dances, parties, and dinners they attend. All the girls goes as a house and are expected to act like she's having a good time even when its a terrible party and they're bored. Lisa refuses to go to these boring parties. And pretend she's having fun. She'd rather forget the party the house goes to and go out with other friends, even if she knows she'll be in trouble. Threfore, as you can see by my description of Lisa's personality she doesn't fit the normal stereotype of a sorority girl.

—*Mary W.*

To enhance my ego, I tell little white lies to my friends. "I am the best football player in town"; is an example of a little white lie I tell. I tell this lie to my friends so they will think I play football well. It does not matter that the last time I played football, I fumbled the ball six times, threw three interceptions, and scored a touchdown for the opposing team. If a little white lie is available, and my friends will believe it, I will use a little white lie to avoid embarrasment, and to inflate my ego. When a friend ask me how my date with Marcia was; I certainly will not tell him the truth: that she dropped me flat for some football player. I will tell a little white lie, to inflate my ego, and say: "Marcia and I had a great time together," or "I broke up with Marcia, she's too ugly, I have a better looking girlfriend now." I will not tell the truth and damage my ego when a little white lie can mask the truth and magnify my ego. To avoid embarrasment and to protect my ego; I tell little white lies to my freinds.

—*Scott G.*

Thinking about how I can improve my grade usually help me deal with the stress I feel after I have done poorly on an exam. Because I realize that I can do better the next time. My first college exam I took was in Psychology and I felt a tremendous amount of stress after I had taken them. This was because I knew I had not done well, and I thought that all my exams were going to turn out that way. I began to think, though, of how I could improve my grade in that class, I knew that the next time I would have to complete the assigned reading. I also would have to try to understand the concepts in the book, not just the facts, since the test material seemed to cover it. I decided to also go over my lecture notes and not just review them, thinking that I knew the material. Going over these ideas in my head really relieved the stress I felt because I started to convince myself that I could do better on the next Psychology test. I also realized that just because I did badly on my first college exam it did not mean that all my exams were going to turn out that way. This stress relieving technique still come in handy a year later in my history class. After my latest exam, I decided I would get my reading done two days before the next test and during those two days most of my studying would be for the history exam. I told myself that I would also use the study guide that coincides with the text. This would enable me to get practice answering questions. Just thinking of how I could do better next time made the stress I felt after the history exam disappear because I was able to think of the future possibilities and not my past mistakes.

—*Cathy K.*

As a final reminder of the importance of proofreading, read this humorous essay written by a history teacher:

It Was 'Gorilla Warfare' to Some Students

Lillian Stewart Carl, *Smithsonian*

I've served my time—three years trying to teach American History 101 at a community college—and now I'm quitting to stay home and write fiction. What forced my hand was the fiction some of my students tried to pass off as the answers to my essay questions.

Not all the kids (there are still a lot of literate ones around) but enough of them. Their exams were full of misspellings, misapprehensions, malapropisms and sheer ignorance, no matter how many times I had outlined the relevant points.

And yet the process of grading tests often would bring me a smile: at times the student's mistakes had a certain delightfully weird logic to them. One student assured me, for example, that the Whiskey Rebellion took place when Carrie Nation attacked the local saloons with her tomahawk. Another said that Uncle Tom's cabin was about the first slave to have his own place on the plantation.

"Tripes" of Indians—25 million of them—walked over from North Central Asia, someone else wrote, but this number declined because of the long trek. Another said that when the Europeans gave guns to the Indians, they proceeded to kill each other off and thus saved the Europeans the trouble. After all, the English colonist's attitude toward the Indians was "move or die"—at least that's what I had told my class. One student, however, wrote that the Indian's were expected to "get with it or die."

And the Europeans brought Christianity to the Americas; they set up missions, I was told, to "Christize" the Indians. I also learned that the missionaries believed in the Trinity, and that the Indians converted because they thought they were getting a "three for one deal."

Then there are the students who panic in the face of an exam. One wrote that the Proclamation of 1763 prohibited the colonists from settling west of the Himalayas; another said that the colonists were angered by the proclamation because they couldn't get to all the oil discovered west of the Appalachians (John D. Rockefeller, where were you when we needed you?).

The students were especially intent on simplification. One assured me that the English sent convicts to the American colonies; if you could not afford the trip yourself, you could go steal a loaf of bread and get to the new world free, along with other "petite criminals such as thiefes and prostitutes and tax invaders."

Some students became disoriented whenever they had to express themselves in writing. One thought the Monroe Doctrine "was the way that we kept the forgein countrys from colonying the western hemonsfere; that Manifest Destiny concerned "the Atalca to the Pacific; that the Missouri Compromise concerned "the 36/30 parrell; and that in the South "the plaintions had ecomic problems." Spelling does seem to be a lost art.

The Indians, I learned, had "premature" (read primitive) war methods before the Europeans came. I grew to expect students to say that Pennsylvania was founded by the "Quackers"; I always had a vision of Donald or Daffy Duck waddling the narrow streets of Philadelphia.

And when someone wrote "gorilla" for "guerilla" during our study of the Revolution, I wondered just what that person thought I had been talking about. King Kong swinging from the Liberty Tree?

One student said that the Revolution inspired such works as Thomas Paine's *Common Science*. Another wrote that the Americans were divided into patriots and "tourists," not Tories.

One of my favorite misspellings was of "militia"; someone once misspelled it as "malicia," and went on to describe how the American mali-cia "squirmished" with British regulars at Lexington and Concord. And after telling my students that New Jersey was the "cockpit" of the American Revolution, one of them volunteered that New Jersey was the "crackpot" of the war.

The Wilmot Proviso came out "Wilmont" so frequently on exams that I'm starting to think of it that way myself. And I wonder what the person was thinking who changed Santa Anna, the President of Mexico, into "De Santa" (I was tempted to ask where "de elves" were).

While such misspellings and misinterpretations are often humorous, I do wonder how a teacher can hope to instill some knowledge of American History and the English language into students who evidently couldn't care less. Do you suppose a five minute song-and-dance version of the constitution could be inserted between "Dukes of Hazzard" and "Dallas"? Or maybe a spelling bee?

Editing your own work

1. Look again at one of your papers a teacher has commented on. If you see any errors in proofreading, correct them.
2. Take out a paper you're working on now (preferably a draft ready for proofreading). Look carefully for errors in proofreading. Correct any you find.
3. If you know you have problems proofreading, try this procedure:
   a. Edit your paper for one problem at a time. Read the paper aloud and listen for errors.
   b. Do I need to combine sentences for clarity, precision, variation?
   c. Do I need to change sentence punctuation?
   d. Do I need to choose more precise, active words?
   e. Do I see any errors in subject-verb agreement?
   f. Do I see any errors in pronoun usage?
   g. Do I see any wordy, clichéd, or empty sentences I should rewrite?
   h. Do I see any proofreading errors?
      — Comma usage
      — Apostrophes
      — Commonly confused words
      — Spelling
      — Other errors I know I make

Index

Copyright Acknowledgments *(continued from page iv)*

(continued on p. 418)